Selected **Bed** and **Breakfast** in

FRANCE 2000

Selected **Bed** and **Breakfast** in **FRANCE 2000**

Featuring the unique 'sun' rating system

Every B&B included in this book has been visited and allocated between 1 and 4 'suns' by our experienced team of examiners.

✸✸✸✸

See page 5 for more details

Welcome Guides

Selected **Bed** and **Breakfast** in

FRANCE 2000

Your guide to a great welcome in France

Published by Thomas Cook Publishing
The Thomas Cook Group Ltd

PO Box 227
Thorpe Wood
Peterborough PE3 6PU
United Kingdom

Telephone: 01733 503571
email: books@thomascook.com

ISBN 1 841570 25 7

Publisher: Stephen York

Manager, Special Projects:
Bernard Horton

Text design, imagesetting and layout by
PDQ Reprographics, Bungay

Printed and bound by Stamford Press Pte
Ltd, Singapore

Why Bed & Breakfast in France?

It is fashionable to have a "Mission Statement" these days, but nevertheless it is important for a guide to clearly identify and mark out its position in the market.

There are thousands of B&B's in France, and it is clear to us that the quality varies enormously, and that there is a need for a good guide at a sensible price which sorts out the wheat from the chaff. The coverage of the country needs to be good, but a vast database-style directory giving no guidance on quality or style is confusing and little help in making a choice on grounds of quality, atmosphere and welcome. On the other hand, an exclusive selection of a few homes inevitably means that there is never one near to where you want to stop and if there is, it is usually full.

Thomas Cook Publishing, in cooperation with Bed & Breakfast, France, have therefore decided not to concentrate only on those at the top of the market, where the price is also pitched accordingly. This guide aims to bring you a wide selection, from simple farm-houses right up to the grandest châteaux, where all offer comfortable, clean accommodation and where above all, you are really made to feel at home by an outstanding welcome. Our classification by 1, 2, 3 or 4 '***suns***' reflects the warmth of the welcome that radiates from our hosts, just as much as the quality of the property. In some quarters the French have a reputation for being abrupt and unfriendly, but with our hosts you will be received like a friend of the family and feel completely at ease.

We love France. Our team is mainly French, essential to build up a really good rapport with our hosts, but sprinkled with British and other nationalities so that the views of overseas visitors are reflected in the guide. This keeps us tuned into the demands of clients outside France, and also keeps the French on their toes. All hosts are members of the French Bed & Breakfast Association (Bed & Breakfast France) to which they pay a small membership fee. We work with our hosts as partners to improve their welcome for the benefit of both clients and hosts alike. However, low standards or a poor welcome are not tolerated, and each year our inspections mean applicants are rejected, and your comments may also result in some being weeded out if standards fall. "Would I be happy to stay there?" is our inspector's ultimate test, not a check-list of standard facilities that guarantee an official rating.

"Le B&B" is an internationally recognised term for guest rooms in private homes, and brings this uniquely French style of accommodation to a wider audience. We urge you to try it. Any language barriers will melt away and you will make many new friends and our mission will be accomplished.

CONTENTS

NORTH SEA
UNITED KINGDOM
NETHERLANDS
NORD PAS-DE-CALAIS
BELGIUM
GERMANY
ENGLISH CHANNEL
LUX.
HAUTE NORMANDIE
PICARDIE
PARIS
BASSE NORMANDIE
LORRAINE
ILE DE FRANCE
CHAMPAGNE-ARDENNE
ALSACE
BRETAGNE
PAYS DE LA LOIRE
CENTRE
FRANCHE-COMTÉ
LIEC.
BOURGOGNE
SWITZERLAND
POITOU CHARENTES
ATLANTIC OCEAN
LIMOUSIN
AUVERGNE
RHÔNE-ALPES
ITALY
AQUITAINE
MIDI-PYRÉNÉES
PROVENCE-ALPES-CÔTE D'AZUR
LANGUEDOC-ROUSSILLON
ANDORRA
CORSICA
SPAIN
MEDITERRANEAN SEA
SARDINIA
MENORCA
MALLORCA

HOW TO BOOK

There are two options, choose whichever suits you best.

Book direct with your host

Telephone or mail the 'book direct' letter at the back of this guide. If hosts also have faxes and E-mail, this is indicated. Your host will reply, advising you on their procedure for confirming a booking. Some hosts may ask you to send them a deposit in French francs or Euros to hold rooms for you. If you book direct, we advise you to confirm in writing to your host, and to give them a phone call about 24 hrs before you arrive.

TO PHONE HOSTS IN FRANCE
From Outside France:
Dial +33 then the number of your host. Remove any zero before the first number.
(e.g.: from U.K. 00 33 1 34 68 83 15)
From Within France:
Dial the number of your host
(e.g.: 01 34 68 83 15)
It is cheaper to phone after 6pm. Do not forget to take account of time differences.

Use the Bed & Breakfast (France) Central Reservations Office

Bed & Breakfast (France) can make your bookings for you and save you time, language problems and the complications of sending payment to France. This is essential for Paris hosts. There is a booking fee for this service.

I) Decide on the dates of your stay and the number of persons in your party and complete the Reservation Form on page 573.
II) Select your hosts.
Give a first and second choice and quote the host numbers. In the unlikely event that all your choices are full, we will always come up with the nearest available to your requirements. There may also be hosts that have joined us since this guide went to press, but with this number of hosts, you will never be far from your first choice. Your trip will be more enjoyable and less tiring if you stay more than one night at each host, which will also give you the opportunity to get to know them better.
III) Send the Reservation Form and the deposit to Bed & Breakfast (France).
The Reservation Form indicates the various ways to pay.

Each host is located in a 'Région', in relation to the nearest main town. The map of each 'Région' shows the 'Départements' (counties) with their number, the main towns and the main roads. Use this in conjunction with a detailed road map. Each host has a Code Number which is made up of two parts. The first part is the number of the 'Département' and the second part is the number of that host in its 'Département'. There is a description of each host giving general facilities for each bedroom. You can see the facilities contained in each room immediately, thereby avoiding any unpleasant surprises. This enables you to request a specific room when you book, often by name.

IV) You will be sent a Provisional Booking
As soon as your Reservation Form and the deposit are received, a Provisional booking

will be made. This will give brief details of the hosts that have been booked, the balance to pay and the latest date by which payment should be received.

V) You confirm your booking.

In order to confirm your booking, you should pay the balance to Bed & Breakfast (France) no later than the date indicated. Alterations can be made to your Provisional Booking until you are happy with it and confirm it. However, an administrative charge of £25 will be made for the following alterations, once the Provisional Booking has been issued: changes to dates, reduction in number of persons in your party or reduction in total number of nights booked.

VI) Bed & Breakfast (France) send you a Confirmation Voucher.

Once the full balance of your payment has been received, you will be sent a Confirmation Voucher, which will give the full details of your hosts and directions on how to find them. If you are leaving home several weeks before your arrival in France, your Confirmation Voucher can be sent to another address if you request it.

It is not possible to make changes once the Confirmation Voucher has been issued.

After this point, a booking has to be cancelled and rebooked again and cancellation fees apply. Booking fees are non refundable. A booking is only confirmed and guaranteed when the final balance has been received before the payment-date given. Last minute reservations cannot be guaranted if the final payment arrives too late.

You can also book by telephone or fax using a credit card.

› If calling from Britain :

Tel : 01491 578803 - Fax : 01491 410806

› If calling from outside Britain :

Tel: + 44 1491 578803 - Fax : +44 1491 410806

E-mail: bookings@bedbreak.demon.co.uk

The service is quick and efficient and the total cost can be charged to a Visa or Mastercard.

The Reservations Office is open Mondays to Fridays from 9.30am to 6pm UK time. Outside of these hours, you may leave your reservation request on the voice-mail service or send a fax or E-mail.

At certain times of the year, if you need an answer in less than 48 hours, you will have to use the EXPRESS SERVICE, for which there is a surcharge of £25. You will be advised if this surcharge is applicable when you book.

Book via the Internet

This service is also available on the Bed & Breakfast (France) website: www.bedbreak.com

– Conditions of Reservation of Bed & Breakfast (France)

1. Role of Bed & Breakfast (France)

Bed & Breakfast (France) acts only as a booking agent. It makes the reservations as agent for the person(s) providing the accommodation and does not accept liability in connection with the reservations.

2. Booking Fee

a) A booking fee is charged by Bed & Breakfast (France). It is non refundable.

b) If you state that only certain specified hosts are acceptable to you, and we are unable to find you accommodation with any of these hosts, your deposit will be refunded.

3. Payment

All reservations must be pre-paid and a reservation is not confirmed until full payment is received by Bed & Breakfast (France). We cannot take any responsibility for problems arising due to reservations being confirmed at the last minute or payment not reaching us in time. If hosts have to collect payment of the balance from you (except for additional services, dinner etc…) a £25 admin. fee will be charged.

4. Alterations

Alterations can be made to your Provisional Booking until you are happy with it and confirm it. However, an administrative charge of £25 will be made for the following alterations, once the Provisional Booking has been issued: changes to dates, reduction in number of persons in your party or reduction in total number of nights booked.

5. Cancellations

If you cancel a booking before it is confirmed, only your deposit is lost, unless condition no. 2b applies. If you cancel a confirmed booking, notice must be received by Bed & Breakfast (France) in writing, by fax or by E-mail. The booking fee is non refundable and the following Cancellation Conditions apply:

› if received 15 days or more before the first night :
FULL REFUND (less booking fee + £25 administrative charges)

› if received 14 to 4 days before the first night booked: REFUND of 5% (less booking fee + £25 administrative charges)

› if received less than 4 days before the first night booked: NO REFUND.

N.B. The 'first night booked' is the earliest date on your Confirmation Voucher, and applies to the whole itinerary, and not individual stops.

PRICES

After the description of each room, the two prices shown are the costs of THE ROOM in French francs per night including breakfast.

The first price is for two people sharing the room, the second price is based on the maximum capacity of the room.

You will find places as low as 60FF per person per night, right up to a maximum of 500FF per person per night.

NB: Not all hosts had their year 2000 prices available as we went to press, so please check room rates carefully when you make a reservation, prices are liable to alteration.

OTHER REDUCTIONS/DISCOUNTS

– Reductions for a long stay :

Many hosts offer good discounts for stays of several nights. This is indicated on their entry.

– Reductions for children :

Many hosts accept babies free of charge or offer reductions for children.

– Off-Peak Discounts:

Some hosts offer good discounts for stays out of the main season. This is indicated on their entry.

– Family Rooms: These are much cheaper where available.

6. Circumstances beyond our control.

Bed & Breakfast (France) cannot be held liable for problems and delays resulting from circumstances beyond their control (force majeure) e.g. strikes, postal delays, transport delays, serious and unforeseen problems in the host families, etc.

7. Extra Services

Bed & Breakfast (France) cannot be held liable for payment of additional charges for extra services and facilities not included in the basic prices paid to Bed & Breakfast (France). It is the client's responsibility to settle these charges before departing from the host.

8. Quality of Hosts

Bed & Breakfast (France) has taken all reasonable care to ensure the quality of the hosts and accommodation reserved for clients, and cannot be held liable for any dissatisfaction the clients may have with the hosts or accommodation. Any complaints must be registered with your hosts before departure, so that they have the opportunity to put matters right.

9. Telephone Bookings

Bookings made by telephone are accepted on the clear understanding that Bed & Breakfast (France) cannot accept liability for errors or misunderstandings that may occur. We advise you to leave sufficient time for written documents to reach you.

10. Responsibility

Bed & Breakfast (France) or the person(s) providing accommodation shall be governed by English Law and subject to the exclusive jurisdiction of English Courts. These only apply to confirmed bookings made via the Central Reservations Office of Bed & Breakfast (France).

Cancellation Insurance

Bed & Breakfast hosts are small, private homes, and if you cancel a confirmed reservation they may not be able to re-let the room and will expect to be paid. For your protection, Bed & Breakfast (France) have arranged a special insurance scheme with travel insurance specialists PJ Hayman & Company Limited to cover all clients booking with us. The small premium is mandatory, and will be added to your balance to pay when you confirm your reservation, unless you provide written proof that you already hold valid cancellation insurance. You must be covered, either by your own policy or this one. Full details will be supplied with your reservation.

HELPLINE

When in France our HELPLINE is available to you if you have a problem with a reservation.

Tel: 01 34 68 83 15 (office hours only).

If you require a reservation, at least 48 hours notice must be given.

CENTRAL PARIS

All Central Paris hosts have to be booked via our reservations office and cannot be booked direct.

Tel: 01491 578803
Fax: 01491 410806
E-mail: bab@bedbreak.com
http//www.bedbreak.com

Full addresses and directions will be notified on booking.

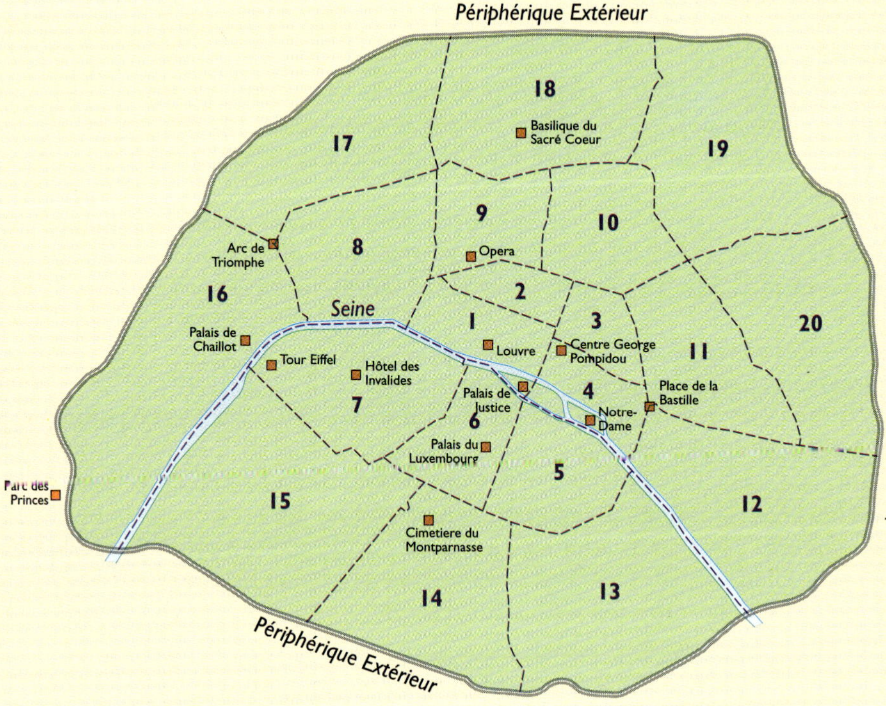

Périphérique Extérieur

18
Basilique du Sacré Coeur
17
19
9
10
Arc de Triomphe
8
Opera
16
2
Seine
1
3
20
Palais de Chaillot
Louvre
Centre George Pompidou
11
Tour Eiffel
Hôtel des Invalides
Palais de Justice
4
Place de la Bastille
7
6
Notre-Dame
Palais du Luxembourg
5
Parc des Princes
15
12
Cimetiere du Montparnasse
14
13

Périphérique Extérieur

Abbeville
80
AMIENS
St. Quentin
02
Laon
76
PICARDIE
ROUEN
Beauvais
Compiègne
Soissons
60
Reims
HAUTE NORMANDIE
27
95
Senlis
Pontoise
Evreux
Mantes
Meaux
93
51
PARIS
78
92
75
Versailles
ILE DE FRANCE
CHAMPAGNE-ARDENNE
Dreux
94
Evry
77
28
Melun
91
Chartres
Fontainebleau
10
Troyes
Sens
Châteaudun
Montargis
ORLÉANS
45
89
Vendôme
41
Auxerre
Blois
BOURGOGNE
18
37
Vierzon
58
CENTRE
Bourges
Nevers

Mona

tel: +33 1 34 68 83 15/
+44 1491 578803
fax: +33 1 34 72 29 31/
+44 1491 410806

Flat

75.38 PARIS

Mona's place is warm and lively. A charming and pretty bedroom is furnished so as to give you maximum privacy. In a very quiet street in the centre of Paris. An excellent address. Advance booking only

Châtelet- Hotel de Ville- Marais- 1e - PARIS
nearest metro: Châtelet-Les Halles
airport: 20 km

PROPERTY

hosts have pets, pets not accepted, closed: 1/12-2/01 & 8/07-7/09

Fluent English spoken

PRICE STRUCTURE

1 Bedroom along corridor bathroom with wc, 2 single beds: FF420

Capacity: 2 people

Brigitte

tel: +33 1 34 68 83 15/
+44 1491 578803
fax: +33 1 34 72 29 31/
+44 1491 410806

Flat

Opéra - 1e PARIS
nearest metro: Pyramides
airport: 20 km

75.46 PARIS

In the centre of Paris, this apartment offers comfort, space, and peace and quiet. You can walk to the Louvre, to the Opéra and to Châtelet. If you are music lovers, so is your hostess. The kitchen is available, where you can prepare your own breakfast. Advance booking only

PROPERTY

✱✱✱

lounge, pets not accepted, kitchen, 10 years old minimum age, no smoking, 2 nights minimum stay

Fluent English spoken

PRICE STRUCTURE

2 Bedroom

First room: television, telephone, along corridor shower room with wc, 2 single beds: FF400

Second room: telephone, double bed: FF400

Capacity: 4 people

Jean-Charles

tel: +33 1 34 68 83 15/
+44 1491 578803
fax: +33 1 34 72 29
31/+44 1491 410806

Flat

Marais - 4e - PARIS
nearest metro: StPaul
airport: 20 km

75.44 PARIS

A flat with a slightly Bohemian atmosphere in the heart of the very central and charming Marais district. There is a pleasant dining room for breakfast, but you will have to go down and fetch your fresh baguette from the boulangerie. Advance booking only.

PROPERTY

✱✱✱

pets not accepted, telephone, 10 years old minimum age, 2 nights minimum stay

Fluent English spoken

PRICE STRUCTURE

1 Apartment

lounge, television, telephone, kitchen, bathroom with wc, double bed, single bed (childrens size): FF500 (2 people)
FF600 (3 people)

Capacity: 3 people

75.35 PARIS

Brigitte will give you a warm welcome to her charming appartment in this 18th century building, a short walk from Notre Dame. The bedroom is independant on a mezzanine floor, and is quiet and pleasant. There are also two extra beds for children. A great base from which to wander through the Latin Quarter. Advance booking only.

Brigitte

tel: +33 1 34 68 83 15/ +44 1491 578803
fax: +33 1 34 72 29 31/+44 1491 410806

Flat

PROPERTY

✸✸✸

pets not accepted, 2 nights minimum stay

Fluent English spoken

PRICE STRUCTURE

1 Bedroom television, along corridor bathroom with wc, double bed, 2 single beds (childrens size): FF360 (2 people) FF560 (4 people)

Extra bed: 100FF

Capacity: 4 people

Quartier Latin - Notre Dame - 5e - PARIS
nearest metro: Maubert-Mutualité & St Michel
airport: 20 km

Lélia

tel: +33 1 34 68 83 15/
+44 1491 578803
fax: +33 1 34 72 29 31/
+44 1491 410806
E-mail:
bab@bedbreak.com
http://www.bedbreak.
com

Flat

Quartier Latin-
Jardin des Plantes-
5e- PARIS
nearest metro:
Austerlitz
airport: 20 km

75.31 PARIS

A small, cosy apartment, quietly situated with an extensive view from the lounge. The nearby 'Jardin des Plantes' is ideal for walking from the Grande Bibliothèque and Bercy. You can continue to the Rue Mouffetard via the typical small streets of the Latin Quarter. Advance booking only.

PRICE STRUCTURE

2 Bedroom

First room: television, shower room with wc, double bed, single bed: FF390 (2 people) FF534 (3 people)

Second room: double bed: FF334

Capacity: 5 people

PROPERTY

✸✸✸

pets not accepted, telephone, 2 nights minimum stay

Fluent English spoken

75.45 PARIS

Karen

tel: +33 1 34 68 83 15/
+44 1491 578803
fax: +33 1 34 72 29 31/
+44 1491 410806

Flat

Karen is a sculptress, and you may be able to watch her at work in her studio and admire some of her creations. Her apartment, which is very close to the Jardin des Plantes, is particularly quiet and relaxing and the atmosphere is easy-going and friendly. Advance booking only.

PROPERTY

hosts have pets, 4 years old minimum age, 3 nights minimum stay

Fluent English spoken

PRICE STRUCTURE

1 Bedroom twin beds: FF330

Capacity: 2 people

Quartier Latin-Jardin des Plantes- 5e- PARIS
nearest metro: Austerlitz
airport: 20 km

75.02 PARIS

tel: +33 1 34 68 83 15/
+44 1491 578803
fax: +33 1 34 72 29 31/
+44 1491 410806

Hotel

This 2 star hotel is pleasant and comfortable. It has 36 rooms and is situated on a corner of the Champs Elysées. The rooms are of a good standard and very charming, all with private bathrooms, mini-bar, television, telephone and security box. Advance booking only.

PROPERTY

tv lounge, telephone

PRICE STRUCTURE

36 Bedroom

Single: television, telephone, bathroom with wc, single beds: FF478

Double: television, telephone, bathroom with wc, double bed: FF567

Twin: television, telephone, bathroom with wc, twin beds: FF567

Triple: television, telephone, bathroom with wc, double bed, single beds: FF667

Champs-Elysées - 8e - PARIS
nearest metro: Franklin-Roosevelt
airport: 20 km

Marie-Carmen

tel: +33 1 34 68 83 15/ +44 1491 578803
fax: +33 1 34 72 29 31/ +44 1491 410806

Flat

75.03 PARIS

An ideal place in a quiet cul-de-sac in the theatre district between the Place Clichy and the large department stores. Chez Marie-Carmen rooms are basic and clean. Warm Spanish hospitality. Advance booking only

PROPERTY

✸

television, hosts have pets, dinner available, closed: 25/12-02/01

PRICE STRUCTURE

3 Bedroom

double bed: FF245

twin beds, single bed: FF245 (2 people) FF365 (3 people)

Capacity: 5 people

Grands Magasins - 9e - PARIS
nearest metro: Liège
airport: 20 km

---

tel: +33 1 34 68 83 15/ +44 1491 578803
fax: +33 1 34 72 29 31/+44 1491 410806

Hotel

75.16 PARIS

A recently renovated hotel, conveniently situated opposite the Gare du Nord (Eurostar) and several métro and RER lines (direct to Charles de Gaulle airport). Good rooms with private facilities and TV. Take your breakfast in the room. Advance booking only

PROPERTY

✸✸

telephone

PRICE STRUCTURE

Single: television, bathroom with wc, single bed: FF420

Double: television, bathroom with wc, double bed: FF460

Twin: television, bathroom with wc, twin beds: FF460

Triple: television, bathroom with wc, double bed, single bed: FF620 (3 people)

Gare du Nord - 10e - PARIS
nearest metro: Gare du Nord
airport: 20 km

75.40 PARIS

Very charming welcome. Maryse is a teacher. Her small apartment is warm and cosy. You are in the heart of Paris. Ideal for a young student. Advance booking only.

Maryse

tel: +33 1 34 68 83 15/ +44 1491 578803
fax: +33 1 34 72 29 31/ +44 1491 410806

Flat

PROPERTY

lounge

Adequate English spoken

PRICE STRUCTURE

1 Bedroom single bed: FF145

Capacity: 1 person

République - 11e - PARIS
nearest metro: République
airport: 20 km

75.32 PARIS

This hotel is very well placed in a quiet street, in the pleasant area near the Place d'Italie. It is between the Chinese Quarter and the Latin Quarter, 10 minutes walk from the Rue Mouffetard. They have 37 basic, comfortable rooms with TV. There is a special lounge for smokers. Advance booking only

tel: +33 1 34 68 83 15/ +44 1491 578803
fax: +33 1 34 72 29 31/ +44 1491 410806

Hotel

PROPERTY

telephone

Fluent English spoken

PRICE STRUCTURE

37 Bedroom

television, bathroom with wc, single bed: FF378

television, bathroom with wc, double bed: FF411

television, bathroom with wc, double bed, single beds: FF467 (2 people) FF511 (3 people)

Place d'Italie - 13e - PARIS
nearest metro: Place d'Italie
airport: 20 km

75.12 PARIS

tel: +33 1 34 68 83 15/ +44 1491 578803
fax: +33 1 34 72 29 31/ +44 1491 410806

Hotel

René and Jacqueline welcome you warmly to their comfortable 32 rooms family run hotel. In a convenient location with garage, private facilities, TV, telephones, bar. Practically in Montmartre. Advance booking only

PROPERTY

private parking, telephone

Montmartre - Clichy - 17e - PARIS
nearest metro: Rome
airport: 20 km

PRICE STRUCTURE

32 Bedroom

Single: television, telephone, bathroom with wc, single bed: FF445

Double: television, telephone, bathroom with wc, double bed: FF445

Twin: television, telephone, bathroom with wc, twin beds: FF445

Triple: television, telephone, bathroom with wc, double bed, single beds: FF600 (3 people)

75.14 PARIS

Danièle

tel: +33 1 34 68 83 15/ +44 1491 578803
fax: +33 1 34 72 29 31/ +44 1491 410806

Flat

Danièle and Franck welcome you to their flat in this well-to-do building, typical of Paris, opposite the métro. Montmartre is nearby. Be sure to visit the famous cemetery where many famous artists and writers rest. Advance booking only

PROPERTY

private parking, tv lounge

English spoken

Montmartre-Marché aux Puces- 17e - PARIS
nearest metro: GuyMoquet
airport: 20 km

PRICE STRUCTURE

1 Bedroom double bed: FF245

Capacity: 2 people

75.17 PARIS

A warm smile welcoms you to this modern hotel, conveniently situated behind the Gare du Nord (Eurostar), served by several métro lines and the RER (direct to Charles de Gaulle airport). Spotless rooms with private facilities. Pleasant lounge in the basement. Advance booking only

PROPERTY

*

lounge, telephone

PRICE STRUCTURE

34 Bedroom

Single: bathroom with wc, single bed: FF410

Double: bathroom with wc, double bed: FF460

Twin: bathroom with wc, twin beds: FF460

Triple: bathroom with wc, double bed, single bed: FF575 (3 people)

Quadruple: bathroom with wc, double bed, 2 single beds: FF700 (4 people)

tel: +33 1 34 68 83 15/ +44 1491 578803
fax: +33 1 34 72 29 31/ +44 1491 410806

Hotel

Gare du Nord - 18e - PARIS
nearest metro: La Chapelle & Gare du Nord
airport: 20 km

Geneviève

tel: +33 1 34 68 83 15/
+44 1491 578803
fax: +33 1 34 72 29 31/
+44 1491 410806

Flat

Place du Tertre-
Sacré Coeur- 18e -
PARIS
nearest metro:
Abesses
airport: 20 km

75.18 PARIS

You may have dreamt of the Place du Tertre, of a clear view over Paris and an open fire. Voilà! Geneviève's place offers all this. She is relaxed, loves art and culture, museums and animals. The flat reflects her character and has a soul. Advance booking only

PRICE STRUCTURE

1 Bedroom double bed:
FF330

Capacity: 2 people

PROPERTY

Tv lounge, hosts have pets, dinner available

Fluent English spoken

Bernard

tel: +33 1 34 68 83 15/
+44 1491 578803
fax: +33 1 34 72 29 31/
+44 1491 410806
Flat

75.47 PARIS

Advance booking only

PROPERTY

tv lounge, pets not accepted

Basic English spoken

Buttes Chaumont -
Belleville - 19e PARIS
nearest metro: Belleville
airport: 20 km

PRICE STRUCTURE

1 Bedroom shower room with wc, double bed: FF330

Capacity: 2 people

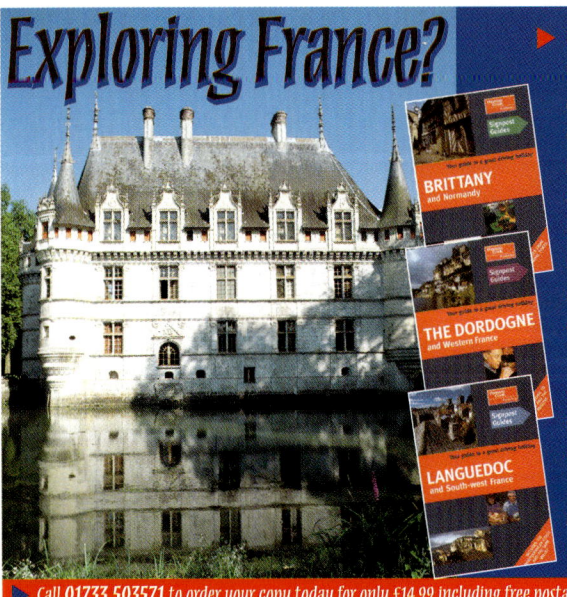

Florence & Bruno

tel: +33 1 34 68 83 15/
+44 1491 578803
fax: +33 1 34 72 29
31/+44 1491 410806

Flat

Père Lachaise -
Nation - 20e - PARIS
nearest metro:
Porte de Montreuil
airport: 20 km

75.43 PARIS

Florence and Bruno have 3 small children, a dog and a cat. Their very pleasant apartment is organised so that guests are quite independent with their own private garden...a dream come true for Parisians! The welcoming smile of Florence and little Nicolas will make you feel at home. The room is bright, with direct access to the garden and is comfortable and tastefully decorated. Advance booking only

PRICE STRUCTURE

1 Bedroom bathroom with wc, double bed: FF330

Extra bed: 100FF

Reduction: 01/11-30/11 & 01/02-28/02 & 7 nights & children

Capacity: 2 people

PROPERTY

✹✹✹

garden, tv lounge, hosts have pets, pets not accepted, babies welcome, cot supplied, 2 nights minimum stay

Adequate English spoken

75.13 PARIS

Soufiane

tel: +33 1 34 68 83 15/
+44 1491 578803
fax: +33 1 34 72 29 31/
+44 1491 410806

Flat

Advance booking only. An extra bed is available in the lounge

PROPERTY

tv lounge, no smoking, cycling,
Fluent English spoken

PRICE STRUCTURE

1 Bedroom bathroom with wc, double bed: FF290

Extra bed: 145FF

Capacity: 4 people

Ménilmontant - Père Lachaise - 20e PARIS
nearest metro: Ménilmontant
airport: 20 km

92.01 PARIS

Cécilia

tel: +33 1 34 68 83 15/
+44 1491 578803
fax: +33 1 34 72 29 31/
+44 1491 410806

Private Home

Cecilia will welcome you with great warmth and kindness and is full of smiles. Her house is quiet and next to the station (from where you can reach the Place de l'Opéra in 10 minutes). She loves Italian culture, and also speaks Hebrew. You will appreciate the relaxing garden after a tiring day's sightseeing! Advance booking only

PROPERTY

garden, television, hosts have pets, pets not accepted, wheelchair access, no smoking
Fluent English spoken

PRICE STRUCTURE

2 Bedrooms and 1 Suite and 2 Apartments

along corridor shower room with wc, double bed: FF330 (2 people)

double bed, single bed: FF478 (3 people)

both rooms: FF811 (5 people)

kitchen, single bed: FF255

kitchen, shower room with wc, double bed: FF390

Extra bed: 165FF
Reduction: 01.10–31.01

Capacity: 8 people

La Défense - Asnières (N W) - PARIS
ASNIERES:will collect from station,
airport: 20 km

Leila

tel: +33 1 34 68 83 15/
+44 1491 578803
fax: +33 1 34 72 29 31/
+44 1491 410806

Flat

Montmartre - Clichy (N W) - PARIS
CLICHY: nearest metro: Mairie de Clichy
airport: 20 km

92.02 PARIS

Leila is learning English, all the better to communicate her 'joie de vivre'. You will enjoy chatting to her husband, and they both have that warmth of welcome, so typical of people from the South. The street is quiet and pleasant and near the métro. The room is self-contained, and very comfortable. Advance booking only

PROPERTY

✸✸✸

tv lounge, hosts have pets

PRICE STRUCTURE

1 Apartment television, kitchen, shower room with wc, double bed: FF330

Capacity: 2 people

Ruth

tel: +33 1 34 68 83 15/
+44 1491 578803
fax: +33 1 34 72 29 31/
+44 1491 410806

Flat

Neuilly sur Seine - (N W) - PARIS
NEUILLY SUR SEINE:nearest metro: Pont de Levallois
airport: 20 km

92.04 PARIS

Ruth is a painter, sculptor and tourist guide. Some of her works are in her apartment, which is bright and very quiet, in the chic, residential area of Neuilly. This is ideal for a student. Advance booking only

PROPERTY

lounge

Fluent English spoken

PRICE STRUCTURE

1 Bedroom along corridor, shower, single bed: FF250

Capacity: 1 person

94.01 PARIS

This young couple and their 2 small daughters will welcome you with an aperitif. The rooms are in a separate house in the garden. Do not miss the rose garden at l'Hay. Within easy reach of Paris. On sale: Honey, marmalade.

PROPERTY

off street parking, garden, tv lounge, hosts have pets, dinner available, babies welcome, cot supplied, interesting flora

Fluent English spoken

PRICE STRUCTURE

3 Bedroom

Jaune: television, shower room with wc, double bed: FF280

Rose: television, shower room with wc, double bed: FF280

Verte: television, shower room with wc, 2 double beds: FF280 (2 people) FF400 (4 people)

Extra bed: 80FF
Reduction: children

Capacity: 8 people

Aline MATHIEU

69, Av du Général
de Gaulle
94240 L'Hay les Roses

tel: (0) 1 45 46 16 50

Private Home

5 km - S - PARIS
L'HAY LES ROSES:
airport: 7 km
car essential
— At the Porte d'Italie, follow the signs to A6 (Lyon) but do not take the autoroute. Instead , head for Arcueil-l'Hay les Roses for 5km. At l'Hay turn left, towards the Continent hypermarket.

Jocelyne FRAYSSINES

«La Frênaie»
27 rue des Merlettes
78360 LE VESINET
MONTESSON

tel: (0) 1 30 71 92 12
fax: (0) 1 47 51 15 83

Private Home

10 km - W - PARIS
LE VESINET:
nearest metro:
LeVésinet-LePecq
airport: 40 km

78.05 PARIS

PRICE STRUCTURE

2 Bedroom

La Pacifique: television, shower room with wc, twin beds: FF400

L'Orientale: television, shower room with wc, twin beds: FF450

Extra bed: 100FF

Reduction: 7 nights

Capacity: 4 people

Jocelyne will give you a warm welcome. Her bedrooms on the first floor are pleasantly decorated, impeccably furnished and offer a high level of comfort. After visiting Paris and the surroundings (be sure to ask her for advice), it is very pleasant to relax in the garden.

PROPERTY

✷✷✷

private parking, garden, lounge, pets not accepted, telephone, dinner available, packed lunch, babies welcome, cot supplied, cycling, sea or lake watersports 1km, gliding 1km, interesting flora 2km, golf course 2km, hiking 2km, mushroom picking 2km

Fluent English spoken

— Take Exit rue Alexandre Dumas from the station and take this street as far as the steps. Straight on rue Watteau and right in to the Bd de Belgique. After 100m turn left in to the 1st street for 50m. The Rue des Merlettes is on the right.

Hubert & Françine CHARPENTIER

«Manoir de Beaumarchais»
77610 LES CHAPELLES BOURBON

tel: (0) 1 64 07 11 08
fax:(0) 1 64 07 14 48
E-mail: hubert.charpentier@wanadoo.fr

Manor House

77.10 PARIS

This manor house was built in 1927. It is an outstanding example of the style of Norman architecture at the end of 16th century, and is listed as an historic monument. Superb grounds of 12 hectares are ideal for quiet walks. You are 30 mins. from Paris and 10 mins. from Disneyland. An outstanding place.

43 km - E - PARIS
LES CHAPELLES BOURBON: railway station: 8 km
airport: 50 km
car essential

PROPERTY

✱✱✱✱

private parking, extensive grounds, tv lounge, pets not accepted, telephone, fishing, hiking, cycling, river watersports, golf course 15km

Fluent English spoken

PRICE STRUCTURE

1 Bedroom lounge, television, shower room with wc, bathroom, twin beds: FF750

Capacity: 2 people

— On the A4, Exit 13 Provins. Then take the D231 towards Provins. When you reach Villeneuve-le-Comte, take the D96 towards Tournan. At the first crossroads, 250 m after Neufmoutiers, take a small road on the left. The manor is on the left, after a bridge (with white bars).

Patrick & Isabelle
GALPIN

«Bellevue»
77610
NEUFMOUTIERS
EN BRIE

tel: (0) 1 64 07 11 05
fax: (0) 1 64 07 19 27

Residence of character

77.11 PARIS

40 km - E - PARIS
NEUFMOUTIERS
EN BRIE: will collect from station,
railway station: 7 km
airport: 30 km
car essential

You will be warmly welcomed by Isabelle and Patrick in their beautiful 19th century house, typical of the Brie region. It is a quiet, little village overlooking the plain with beautiful walks in the nearby forest. You are only 30 minutes from Paris and 10 minutes from Disneyland.

PRICE STRUCTURE

6 Bedroom

television, shower room with wc, wash basin, double bed, 3 single beds: FF290 (2 people) FF560 (5 people)

(3 rooms) television, shower room with wc, wash basin, double bed, 2 single beds: FF270 (2 people) FF470 (4 people)

television, shower room with wc, wash basin, 3 single beds: FF270 (2 people) FF350 (3 people)

wheelchair access, television, shower room with wc, wash basin, double bed, 2 single beds: FF390 (2 people) FF580 (4 people)

Extra bed: 90FF
Reduction: 7 nights

Capacity: 2 people

PROPERTY

off street parking, garden, lounge, hosts have pets, telephone, dinner available, wheelchair access, fishing, hiking, cycling, golf course 10km, river watersports 10km

Adequate English spoken

— From the A4 Exit Villeneuve-le-Comte. In Villeneuve, head in the direction of Neufmoutiers. At Neufmoutiers, follow signs to "Chambres d'hotes" and "Bellevue".

77.09 FONTAINEBLEAU

Jeannine and her husband, a warm and courteous couple, invite you into their beautiful home dating from the beginning of the century, situated on the edge of the Fontainebleau forest, near to the main road. Walk in the majestic forests, and be sure to visit the châteaux of Fontainebleau and Vaux le Vicomte.

Jeannine PERRIN

«La Tourelle»
65, avenue de la forêt
77590 BOIS LE ROI

tel: (0) 1 60 69 52 73
fax: (0) 1 60 69 52 73
E-mail:
jeanineperrin@minitel.net

Flat/Apartment

PROPERTY

✱✱

private parking, garden, tv lounge, hosts have pets, telephone, babies welcome, cot supplied, hunting 10km, fishing 2km, mushroom picking, interesting flora 5km, golf course 2km, hiking, cycling, gliding

Fluent English spoken

10 km - N E - FONTAINEBLEAU
BOIS LE ROI:
airport: 30 km
car essential
— At the Croix de Vitry crossroads, on the N6 between the A6 and Fontainebleau, take the D138 towards Champagne sur Seine. In the centre of Bois le Roi turn left. The house is on the corner on the right.

PRICE STRUCTURE

3 Bedroom

Rose: double bed: FF240

Bleue: double bed: FF220

Enfants: 3 single beds, Childrens size: FF180 (2 people) FF180(3 people)

Extra bed: 90FF
Reduction: 5 nights

Capacity: 7 people

Philippe et Jeanne MAUBAN

«Ferme de Vert St Père»
77390 CRISENOY

tel: (0) 1 64 38 83 51
fax: (0) 1 64 38 83 52
E-mail: mauban.vert@wanadoo.fr

Residence of character

10 km - N E - MELUN
CRISENOY:
airport: 40 km
car essential

77.02 MELUN

A farmhouse, restored with great taste, with beautiful old furniture and a large, pleasant garden. Ideal location for Disneyland and the forest of Fontainebleau. Paris is less than 1 hour away (Autoroute A5 and RER nearby). On sale: Competition horses.

PRICE STRUCTURE

1 Bedroom and 1 Apartment

First room: along corridor shower, wc, double bed, single bed: FF250 (2 people) FF350 (3 people)

Second room: kitchen, shower room with wc, double bed, 2 single beds: FF350 (2 people) FF450 (4 people)

Extra bed: 100FF
Reduction: 4 nights

Capacity: 7 people

PROPERTY

***

private parking, garden, tv lounge, hosts have pets, pets not accepted, telephone, kitchen, babies welcome, cot supplied, closed: 24/12-01/01 riding, birdwatching, golf course 10km, hiking 18km, cycling 18km, hunting 18km, mushroom picking 18km

Fluent English spoken

— In Melun, N36 towards Meaux. From Paris, A4 Metz-Nancy, Exit N104 towards Troyes then take the A5. First Exit after the 'péage' (tollbooths). On the N36, after the St Germain-Laxis roundabout (Exit of the A5), turn right on to the 2nd road towards Crisenoy. Cross Crisenoy and head towards the 'Tennis' and the 'Stade'. The farm is just after the village.

Patrick & Marie-Josephe VANDEWEGHE

«Ferme de Forest»
Forest
77390 CHAUMES
EN BRIE

tel: (0) 1 64 06 27 35
fax: (0) 1 64 06 25 33

Residence of character

77.04 MELUN

A friendly couple of Belgian origin, welcome you to their cereal growing farm, built of chestnut wood in the Vietnamese style. Pleasant, quiet rooms and beautiful bathrooms. Ideal for Paris, Disneyland and the châteaux.

20 km - N E - MELUN
CHAUMES EN BRIE:
airport: 40 km
car essential

PROPERTY

private parking, garden, television, hosts have pets, pets not accepted, kitchen, babies welcome, cot supplied, wheelchair access, hiking, cycling, mushroom picking, fishing 1km, golf course 15km, river watersports 20km

Adequate English spoken

PRICE STRUCTURE

6 Bedroom

(2 rooms) television, bathroom with wc, double bed: FF270

(1 room) television, bathroom with wc, double bed, single beds: FF240 (2 people) FF370 (3 people)

(1 room) wheelchair accesss, television, shower room with wc, double bed: FF255

(2 rooms) television, bathroom with wc, double bed, 2 single beds: FF240 (2 people) FF470 (4 people)

Extra bed: 100FF
Reduction: 5 nights

Capacity: 17 people

— Leave the A4 at the Exit «Melun/Nancy par RN» (A104). After 8km follow the signs to Nancy (N4). Exit in the direction of Melun Fontenay Trésigny (N36). After 6km turn left towards Chaumes en Brie then right towards Forest. Follow signs 'chambres d'hotes'

77.06 MELUN

Pierre & Dominique LAURENT

«Le Portail Bleu»
2, Route de Fontenay
77610 CHÂTRES

tel: (0) 1 64 25 84 94
fax: (0) 1 64 25 84 94

Residence of character

A warm welcome in this old farmhouse which has been prettily furnished. It is at the heart of a small country village but only 15 minutes from Disneyland. You will like the quiet garden and the friendly atmosphere. Ideal for families. The apartment is also available to rent on a weekly basis.

PROPERTY

✱✱✱

private parking, garden, tv lounge, hosts have pets, pets not accepted, telephone, dinner available, packed lunch, babies welcome, cot supplied, hiking, interesting flora, birdwatching, cycling, golf course 10km

English spoken

25 km - N E - MELUN
CHATRES: will collect from station,
railway station: 7 km
airport: 30 km
car essential
— On the A5 Exit St Germain Laxis and take the N36 towards Fontenay-Trésigny. After Forest turn left towards Châtres.

PRICE STRUCTURE

1 Bedroom and 1 Suite and 1 Apartment

Rez de chaussée: television, shower room with wc, double bed, single bed: FF270 (2 people) FF370 (3 people)

Suite: television, shower room with wc, double bed, 3 single beds: FF270 (2 people) FF570 (5 people)

Apartment: lounge, television, kitchen, along corridor bathroom with wc, double bed, 3 single beds: FF670 (2 people) FF970 (5 people)

Capacity: 15 people

78.04 MANTES LA JOLIE

Patricia & Jean RODRIGUEZ

«Chez Pati & Jean»
31, rue Emile Zola
78270 BENNECOURT

tel: (0) 1 30 42 26 18
fax: (0) 1 30 42 26 18

Private Home

This bed and breakfast is in a village nestling in a loop of the Seine, 30 minutes from Paris, 20 minutes from Versailles and 5 minutes from Giverny. Pati is an artist and you will sleep near her sculpture studio where she casts her work. Carriage rides, picnics on the banks on the Seine...the «good life» so dear to the Impressionists.

PROPERTY

private parking, lounge, hosts have pets, kitchen, babies welcome, cot supplied, sea or lake watersports, cycling, fishing, mushroom picking, hunting 3km, golf course 7km, gliding 15km

Fluent English spoken

15 km - N W - MANTES LA JOLIE
BENNECOURT:
railway station: 2 km
airport: 80 km
car essential
— Head towards Rouen on the A13. Exit 14 in the direction of Giverny. Go over the bridge (le Pont de Bonnières) and take the first right, following the river bank. You are in the rue Emile Zola.

PRICE STRUCTURE

1 Bedroom

television, kitchen, bathroom with wc, double bed, 2 single beds: FF300 (2 people) FF300 (4 people)

television, kitchen, bathroom with wc, double bed, cot: FF300

Extra bed: 100FF

Capacity: 6 people

François le BRET

«Le Château de Poigny»
2, rue de l'Eglise
78125 POIGNY LA
FORET

tel: (0) 1 34 84 77 63
fax: (0) 1 34 84 74 38

Château

8 km - N W -
RAMBOUILLET
POIGNY LA
FORET: will collect
from station,
railway station: 8 km
airport: 40 km
car essential

PRICE STRUCTURE

5 Bedrooms and 1 Suite

Louis XIII: Bridal room, along corridor shower room with wc, double bed: FF395

Asiatique: shower room with wc, double bed: FF395

Marocaine: shower room with wc, double bed: FF395

Coca-cola: Bridal suite, shower room with wc, double bed: FF395

Collection: shower room with wc, double bed: FF395

Suite: Rustique/Empire: shower room with wc, wash basin, double bed, 3 single beds: FF395 (2 people) FF720 (5 people)

Extra bed: 90FF

Capacity: 15 people

78.03 RAMBOUILLET

Here, everything is spot on and of good quality. The very unusual interior decor is made up of momentos of travels. The welcome is really friendly and the bedrooms are charming and amusing (eg. Coca-Cola). You are welcome to use the barbecue. An excellent address.

PROPERTY

✸✸✸✸

off street parking, extensive grounds, tv lounge, hosts have pets, pets not accepted, telephone, babies welcome, cot supplied, mushroom picking, hiking, interesting flora, birdwatching 4km, fishing 4km, cycling 7km, golf course 8km

English spoken

— At Rambouillet take the D936 towards Montfort l'Amaury and the D107 as far as Poigny. Follow the 'chambre d'hotes' signs. The house adjoins the church.

95.01 AUVERS SUR OISE

Here, you can feel the presence of Van Gogh, so close to the landscapes that he immortalised and the inn where he lived. On your return, you will certainly appreciate Monique's wonderful meals. The swimming pool is "friendly", as Charles Henri has done his best to ensure this. Paris is only 30 mins. away.

PROPERTY

off street parking, garden, tv lounge, hosts have pets, dinner available, babies welcome, cot supplied, no smoking, swimming pool, mushroom picking, hiking, cycling, interesting flora 1km, river watersports 4km, fishing 8km, gliding 10km, golf course 10km

PRICE STRUCTURE

3 Bedroom

(2 rooms) double bed: FF240

twin beds: FF260

Extra bed: 50FF

Capacity: 6 people

Monique & Charles Henri GUEGUEN

23, rue des Fichets
95300 HÉROUVILLE

tel: (0) 1 34 66 22 84
fax: (0) 1 34 66 22 84

Private Home

4 km - N W - AUVERS SUR OISE
HEROUVILLE:
railway station: 10 km
airport: 40 km
car essential
— At Auvers, take the D928 towards Beauvais, as far as Hérouville. Look for the B&B France sign.

BELGIUM
LUXEMBOURG
GERMANY
SWITZERLAND
ITALY
LORRAINE
ALSACE
CHAMPAGNE-ARDENNE
BOURGOGNE
FRANCHE-COMTE
RHÔNE-ALPES
02
08
51
10
89
21
58
71
03
69
42
01
74
39
25
70
90
68
67
88
52
54
55
57
Sedan
Laon
Rethel
Reims
CHÂLONS
Vitry
St. Dizier
Troyes
Auxerre
DIJON
Beaune
Autun
Chalon-sur-Saône
Macon
Bourg
Vichy
Roanne
Thiers
LYON
Aix-les-Bains
Annecy
Albertville
Chamonix
Lons
Dole
Pontarlier
BESANÇON
Vesoul
Belfort
Mulhouse
Colmar
Èpinal
St. Die
Lunéville
Nancy
STRASBOURG
Haguenau
Sarreguemines
METZ
Thionville
Verdun
Bar-le-Duc
Neufchâteau
Chaumont
Langres

Tilly & Gérard HAZE-MANN

«Tilly's & Café d'Alsace»
28, rue Principale
67140 LE HOHWALD

tel: (0) 3 88 08 33 34/ 30 17
fax: (0) 3 88 08 30 17

Private House

15 km - W - BARR
LE HOHWALD:
railway station: 14km
airport: 35 km
car essential

PRICE STRUCTURE

3 Bedroom

First room: television, kitchen, bathroom with wc, wash basin, double bed: FF456F

Second room: television, kitchen, bathroom with wc, wash basin, twin beds: FF426F

Third room: television, along corridor bathroom with wc, twin beds: FF420

Reduction: 01.09–30.06 and 3 nights and groups

Capacity: 6 people

67.02 BARR

Quite an experience. Of course this area is magnificent but you will also breathe deeply and go for unforgettable walks. Here, in the heart of Alsace, the area is steeped in European culture. The bedrooms are spacious with beautiful bathrooms. 2 self-catering apartments, rented weekly.

PROPERTY

✱✱

private parking, pets not accepted, dinner available, kitchen, packed lunch, babies welcome, cot supplied, hunting, fishing, mushroom picking, interesting flora, birdwatching, hiking, cycling, winter sports,

Fluent English spoken

— On the A36 from Strasbourg towards Colmar take the Barr Exit. Follow Andiau. Le Hohwald is on the D425

68.04 COLMAR

This house is in a typical Alsacien village on the wine route. Buy nothing and plan nothing until you have stopped at Guy's place. After a warm welcome, Guy will give you all the addresses you need, as he knows this area like the back of his hand.

PROPERTY

private parking, garden, lounge, telephone, kitchen, babies welcome, cot supplied, hiking 1km, cycling 1km, golf course 1km, gliding 10km, interesting flora 16km, river watersports 15km, winter sports 15km

Basic English spoken

PRICE STRUCTURE

4 Bedroom

Damien & Noëlle: television, kitchen, shower room with wc, double bed: FF265F

Marguerite: television, kitchen, bathroom with wc, double bed: FF265F

Sabrina: television, kitchen, shower room with wc, twin beds, 2 single beds: FF265 (2 people) FF325 (4 people)

Guy: television, kitchen, shower room with wc, 2 double beds: FF265 (2 people) FF510 (4 people)

Capacity: 14 people

Guy THOMAS

«Maison Thomas»
41, Grand'Rue
68770
AMMERSCHWIHR

tel: (0) 3 89 78 23 90
fax: (0) 3 89 47 18 90

Private House

10 km - N W - COLMAR
AMMERSCHWIHR:
railway station: 10 km
airport: 10 km
car essential
— On the A35, take exit 24. At Colmar, take the N83, then the N415 towards St Dié via the Col du Bonhomme. At Ammerschwihr, turn left at the traffic-lights, and go up the 'Grand'rue' as far as the high gate.

Jean Louis & Monique PROBST

2, route de Ferrette
68480 WERENTZHOUSE

tel: (0) 3 89 40 43 60
fax: (0) 3 89 08 22 18

Farm

35 km - S - MULHOUSE WERENTZHOUSE: will collect from station, railway station: 18km airport: 20km

68.03 MULHOUSE

A really warm welcome awaits you in this typical old farmhouse near the Swiss border, in the heart of the Sundgau region, between the Rhine and the Vosges. Horses, goats and above all... their delicious Pinot Gris wine from Alsace and the speciality: 'la Carpe frite' On sale: Wine from Alsace.

PROPERTY

✷

private parking, garden, lounge, hosts have pets, pets not accepted, telephone, dinner available, babies welcome, cot supplied, no smoking, closed: 01/01-31/01 fishing 5km, hiking, mushroom picking, birdwatching 5km, cycling, interesting flora, golf course 10km, river watersports 20km, winter sports 40km, sea or lake watersports 10km

PRICE STRUCTURE

3 Bedrooms and 1 Apartment

(2 rooms) shower room with wc, double bed, 2 single beds: FF220 (2 people) FF340 (4 people)

(1 room) shower room with wc, double bed: FF220F

(1 room) shower room with wc, 2 double bed, 2 single beds: FF220 (2 people)FF680 (6 people)

Extra bed: 60FF

Reduction: 01.09–30.06 and 3 nights and groups

Capacity: 2 people

— In Mulhouse, take the D432 towards Altkirch. In Hirsingue turn left on to the D9B towards Waldighofen, Werentzhouse. The farm is near the church.

Jacques DURIN

37, rue François Richard
54300 LUNÉVILLE

tel: (0) 3 83 73 75 26

Private House

30 km - S E - NANCY
LUNEVILLE: will collect from station, railway station: 3 km
airport: 50 km

54.01 NANCY

Just the place for garden lovers. Jacques is a landscape gardener so flowers, bridges, streams, ponds...are all part of the decor. Immaculate bathrooms, lovely bed linen, and a warm welcome from Jacques. Mediterranean style swimming pool. 2 self-catering apartments, rented weekly.

PROPERTY

✱✱

private parking, garden, tv lounge, hosts have pets, telephone, dinner available, kitchen, packed lunch, babies welcome, cot supplied, swimming pool, cycling, fishing, hiking 1km, river watersports 3km, gliding 3km, mushroom picking 5km, golf course 30km, birdwatching 40km, sea or lake watersports 40km, interesting flora 40km

— Exit Lunéville-Château from A33 and the N4 for 10km. In Lunéville straight on to roundabout. Head towards Château Salins (on left a square with trees). 70m after square take small street on left. 500m on left.

PRICE STRUCTURE

3 Bedroom

First room: lounge, television, shower room with wc, wash basin, double bed: FF260F

Second room: shower room with wc, wash basin, double bed: FF260

Third room: shower wc, wash basin, single bed: FF190

Extra bed: 100FF
Reduction: 01.10–31.05

Capacity: 5 people

88.02 EPINAL

A well-known spa town in the Vosges Mountains (Alt. 550m). An old farmhouse, typical of the Vosges, with country views. Farm activities: mixed livestock, sheep, poultry, donkeys, horses, dairy cattle, pigs. Other activities: hiking, mountain biking, riding, fishing, excursions and visits to the spa. On sale: poultry, eggs and terrines. 3 rooms for 2 and 4 people. Private facilities. Farmhouse dinners.

Annie& Claude CORNU

Route de Ruaux
88370 PLOMBIERES LES BAINS

tel: (0) 3 29 66 08 13

Farm

PROPERTY

off road parking, garden, hosts have pets, dinner available, hiking, cycling, fishing 4km

35km - S EPINAL
PLOMBIERES LES BAINS:
hosts can collect from station,
rail station: 10km
car essential
— From Epinal, take the N57 towards Remiremont then Plombières where you take the direction of Ruaux.

PRICE STRUCTURE

3 Bedrooms

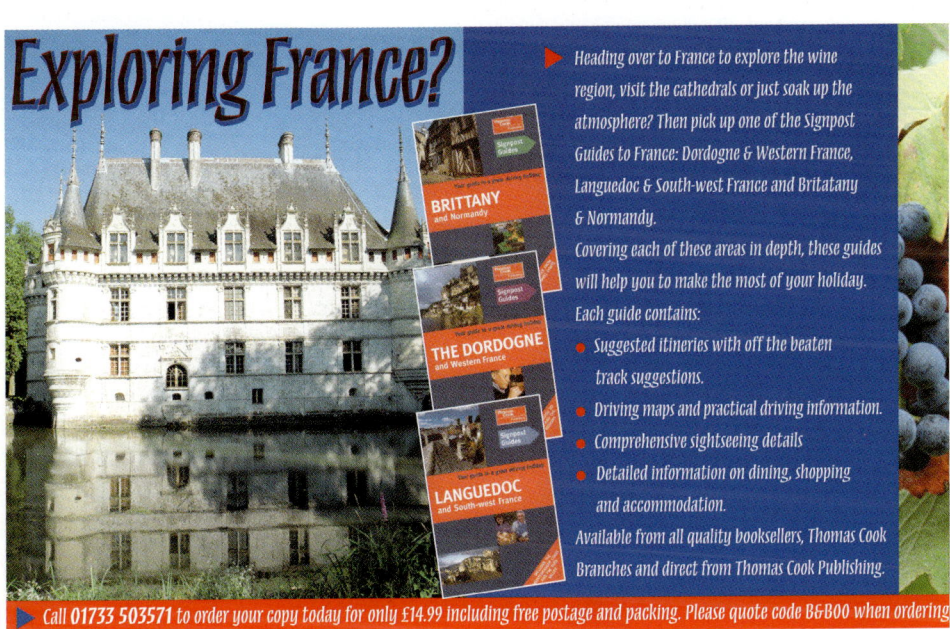

(3) shower room, wc, double bed.
Half board: 350FF per 2 people.
Reduction: 3 nights & children.
Capacity: 6 people

Guy HOYET

«La Maison Royale»
70140 PESMES

tel: (0) 3 84 31 23 23
fax: (0) 3 84 31 23 23

Château or
Manor House

24 km - N - DOLE
PESMES: will collect from station,
railway station: 25km
airport: 48km

70.01 DOLE

This superb listed building from the 13th century offers comfort, perfect taste, exceptional furniture, a warm welcome and great class. The medieval village of Pesmes is one of the hundred most beautiful villages in France, situated on the border between Franche Comté and Bourgogne.

PRICE STRUCTURE

9 Bedroom

(7 rooms) bathroom with wc, double bed: FF450

(1 room) bathroom with wc, twin beds: FF450

(1 room) bathroom with wc, 3 single beds: FF450 (2 people) FF500 (3 people)

Extra bed: 100FF
Reduction: 2 nights

Capacity: 19 people

PROPERTY

✹✹✹✹

off street parking, garden, lounge, pets not accepted, dinner available, packed lunch, 5 years minimum age, closed: 1/10-31/03 hiking, cycling, fishing, mushroom picking, interesting flora, birdwatching, river watersports, hunting, gliding 18km, golf course 50km

Fluent English spoken

— From the A36, take the Exit for Dole. Join the D475 and turn right towards Gray. (If you are coming from the Auxonne Exit on the A39, head for Auxonne then take the D20, D112 and D475 towards Gray.).

Cholet
PAYS DE LA LOIRE
CENTRE
Châtellerault
Châtsauroux
La Roche
85
POITIERS
79
86
Niort
POITOU CHARENTE
La Rochelle
Rochefort
87
16
LIMOGES
LIMOU
Saintes
Cognac
Royan
17
Angoulême
Périgueux
ATLANTIC OCEAN
Brive
24
33
Libourne
BORDEAUX
Bergerac
Arcachon
AQUITAINE
46
Cahors
Villeneuve
47
Agen
82
40
Montauba
Mont-de-Marsan
MIDI-PYRÉNÉES
Auch
32
TOULOUSE
Bayonne
Biarritz
31
64
Pau
Tarbes
65
St.Gaudens
09
SPAIN

24.02 BERGERAC

In the heart of a secret valley, you will discover this Périgord house, surrounded by its own beautiful grounds. There is a terrace with barbecue, and a conservatory full of flowers. This is a relaxing place, near many châteaux. Fluent Flemish spoken.

Joséphine MORAL

«Les Mazeaux»
24520 LAMONZIE MONTASTRUC

tel: (0) 5 53 23 41 83

Residence of character

PROPERTY

off street parking, extensive grounds, tv lounge, hosts have pets, closed: 01/01-28/02 fishing 2km, sea or lake watersports 10km

Adequate English spoken

PRICE STRUCTURE

6 Bedroom

First, second and third rooms: bathroom with wc, double bed: FF250

6th room: 2 single beds: FF170

4th room: bathroom with wc, double bed, single bed: FF250 (2 people) FF330 (3 people)

5th room: double bed: FF230

Extra bed: 80FF
Reduction: 01.03–01.06 and 01.11–31.12 and 3 nights

Capacity: 13 people

10 km - N E - BERGERAC LAMONZIE MONTASTRUC: will collect from station, railway station: 10 km airport: 13 km
— In Bergerac, take the N21 towards Périgueux. After 6km turn right on to the D21E. Follow the signs.

Serge & Véronique
PARDOUX

«Château de Régagnac»
Montferrand du Périgord
24440 BEAUMONT

tel: (0) 5 53 63 27 02
fax: (0) 5 53 73 39 08

Château

24.25 BERGERAC

40 km - S E -
BERGERAC
MONTFERRAND
DU PERIGORD:
railway station: 12km
airport: 145km
car essential

Be sure not to miss your hosts' candle-lit dinners, when you will enjoy superb local produce. We love the "vieille France" atmosphere that Véronique and Serge have created, watched over by their ancestral suits of armour. The setting, the ambiance and your host's warm welcome easily deserve 4 suns.

PRICE STRUCTURE

5 Bedroom

Château bleue: bathroom with wc, shower, double bed, single bed: FF650 (2 people) FF650 (3 people)

Château jaune & Aile premier: Duchesse & Lino: shower room with wc, double bed: FF650F

Aile Rez de Chaussée-Espagnole: bathroom with wc, twin beds: FF650

Capacity:7 people

PROPERTY

✹✹✹✹

off street parking, extensive grounds, tv lounge, hosts have pets, telephone, dinner available, 13 years minimum age, tennis, 2 nights minimum stay, hiking, fishing 1km, cycling 14km, river watersports 20km

Fluent English spoken

— At Bergerac, take the D703 then the D29 towards Sarlat. Turn right on to the D28 towards Le Cadouin, then the D2 towards Montferrand. Régagnac is on the D12, on the left before Montferrand.

Françoise & Christian GAUBUSSEAU

«La Rouquette»
24240 MONBAZILLAC

tel: (0) 5 53 58 30 60
fax: (0) 5 53 73 20 36

Château or Manor House

7 km - S - BERGERAC MONBAZILLAC: will collect from station, railway station: 7 km airport: 4 km car essential

24.26 BERGERAC

Situated in a sought-after spot near to the Château of Montbazillac, this elegant residence has been beautifully restored on the outside. Inside, the emphasis is on practicality and comfort. A stay here will considerably add to your enjoyment of this region.

PROPERTY

✵✵✵✵

off street parking, garden, tv lounge, hosts have pets, telephone, kitchen, babies welcome, cot supplied, hunting, hiking, mushroom picking, river watersports 4km, fishing 6km, golf course 15km

English spoken

PRICE STRUCTURE

5 Bedroom

Roxane: Bridal room, bathroom with wc, twin beds, single bed: FF650 (2 people) FF730 (3 people)

Muscadelle: bathroom with wc, double bed: FF400F

Belvédère: bathroom with wc, double bed, single bed: FF550 (2 people) FF630 (3 people)

La Treille: bathroom with wc, double bed: F350

Rez de Jardin-Le Baldaquin: bathroom with wc, double bed, twin beds: FF500 (2 people) FF660 (4 people)

Extra bed: 80FF

Capacity: 14 people

— At Bergerac take the N21 towards Agen for 7km and then turn right towards Monbazillac. Go through Monbazillac towards the D933. The property is on the right after 500m.

Nicole VANHEMELRYCK

«Les Rocailles»
RN 21
24520 LAMONZIE MON-
TASTRUC

tel: (0) 5 53 58 20 16
fax: (0) 5 53 58 20 16

Residence of chararcter

10 km - N E - BERGERAC LAMONZIE MONTASTRUC: will collect from station, railway station: 10km airport: 14km

24.38 BERGERAC

You will be charmed by this authentic 18th century Périgourdine farm, which has been completely restored. Nicole, who is Belgian, will welcome you with a smile, and help you plan your trips. The pool is ideal for «swimming off» the vast amounts of foie-gras you are bound to consume! A wonderful address. Gite for 6 persons, rented out for 3 days or a week.

PRICE STRUCTURE

2 Bedrooms and 1 Suite

Caractère: Bridal room, lounge, television, telephone, along corridor bathroom with wc, double bed, twin beds: FF310 (2 people) FF480 (4 people)

Rez de Chaussée: television, bathroom with wc, double bed: FF260F

Suite: lounge, television, bathroom with wc, twin beds, single bed: FF295 (2 people) FF380 (3 people)

Extra bed: 85FF
Reduction: 01.09–30.06

Capacity: 9 people

PROPERTY

✱✱✱

off street parking, extensive grounds, tv lounge, hosts have pets, kitchen, wheelchair access, swimming pool, closed: 15/02-15/03 & 20/11-20/12 fishing, mushroom picking, interesting flora, hiking, river watersports 40km, golf course 8km, cycling 10km

Adequate English spoken

— From Bergerac, take the N21 towards Périgueux. After Lembras, continue for 5km towards Campsegret. Follow the signs on the main road. From there go up to the hill for 250m

Germaine PETIT

«Le Repos»
24240 ROUFFIGNAC DE SIGOULÈS

tel: (0) 5 53 24 96 91

Residence of character

6 km - S - BERGERAC
ROUFFIGNAC DE SIGOULÈS: will collect from station,
railway station: 7 km
airport: 7 km
car essential

24.39 BERGERAC

Discover the informal courtesy of Germaine and her son, who invite you to their old wine-growing estate, dating from the 19th century, nestling in the heart of the famous Monbazillac vineyards. This elegant residence, with large, tree-filled grounds, deserves its name.

PROPERTY

✱✱✱

private parking, extensive grounds, lounge, hosts have pets, telephone, babies welcome, cot supplied, hiking, cycling 3km, sea or lake watersports 3km, golf course 10km

Basic English spoken

PRICE STRUCTURE

3 Bedrooms

(3 rooms) bathroom with wc, double bed: FF290

Extra bed: 80FF
Reduction: 4 nights

Capacity: 6 people

— From Bergerac, head towards Mont de Marsan on the D933. Continue for 7km along the winding road. Go past «La Grappe d'Or» restaurant. The house is 200m on the right.

Jennifer LYON

«Château Les Merles»
24520 MOULEYDIER

tel: (0) 5 53 63 13 42
fax: (0) 5 53 63 13 45

Château

10 km - E -
BERGERAC
MOULEYDIER:
railway station: 15km
airport: 15km
car essential

PRICE STRUCTURE

6 Bedroom and 1 Suite

Rose & Pivoine: telephone, bathroom with wc, double bed: FF400

Iris: telephone, bathroom with wc, double bed: FF350

Marguerite: telephone, bathroom with wc, shower, twin beds: FF500

Coquelicot: telephone, shower room with wc, twin beds: FF400

Lys: telephone, shower room with wc, double bed: FF400

Suite: telephone, shower room with wc, double bed, single bed: FF600 (2 people) FF700 (3 people)

Extra bed: 100FF

Capacity: 15 people

24.43 BERGERAC

This château dating, from 1677, is situated in magnificent surroundings. It has been renovated and modernised and provides an elegant setting for the numerous activities available on site such as golf, tennis and swimming. Do not miss out on Bergerac, the ancient city of Périgord, and its festival. An excellent place to relax.

PROPERTY

✸✸✸✸

off street parking, extensive grounds, tv lounge, hosts have pets, telephone, kitchen, babies welcome, cot supplied, wheelchair access, swimming pool, tennis, mushroom picking, birdwatching, interesting flora, golf course, hiking, fishing 1km, cycling 2km, hunting 10km, gliding 12km

English spoken

— From Bergerac, take the D660 towards Sarlat. Go through Mouleydier then at Tuilières, turn left on to the D36 towards Clause de Clérans. The château is 200 metres further on.

Henri & Françoise
PEYRE

«Château de Pechalbet»
47800 AGNAC

tel: (0) 5 53 83 04 70
fax: (0) 5 53 83 04 70

Château or
Manor House

25 km - S -
BERGERAC
AGNAC: will collect from station,
railway station: 30km
airport: 30km

47.16 BERGERAC

Here in the Périgord Pourpre you will be welcomed to this magnificent 17th century gentilhommière, typical of this region. It is surrounded by 40 hectares of woods and fields. Be sure to try the local dishes as you are in foie gras country.

PROPERTY

✱✱✱✱

private parking, garden, tv lounge, hosts have pets, dinner available, babies welcome, cot supplied, wheelchair access, swimming pool, closed: 05/01-25/03 hunting, mushroom picking, interesting flora, hiking, cycling, fishing 2km, river watersports 2km, sea or lake watersports 15km, golf course 18km

Fluent English spoken

PRICE STRUCTURE

4 Bedrooms and 1 suite

First room: bathroom with wc, double bed: FF550

Second & Third room: shower room with wc, double bed: FF490

Suite: shower room with wc, double bed, 2 single beds, childrens size: FF550 (2 people) FF700 (4 people)

Fifth room: shower room with wc, twin beds: FF550

Extra bed: 100FF
Reduction: 01.10–01.05 and 3 nights and groups

Capacity: 12 people

— At Bergerac take the D933 towards Marmande. When you are 1km south of Eymet follow the signs.

Michel & Sheila
BRASSEUR

«Le Petit Cousset»
24360 VARAIGNES

tel: (0) 5 53 56 52 58

Private Home

15 km - N W - NONTRON
VARAIGNES: will collect from station, railway station: 32km
car essential

24.24 NONTRON

Situated between the Dordogne and Charente, near the Angoulème-Périgueux road, Michel and Sheila's place offers a great place to stay in a self-contained apartment with every comfort. Ideal for a family or two couples. There are also 2 rooms on the first floor of the house. Sheila is English.

PRICE STRUCTURE

2 Bedroom and 1 Apartment

First room: double bed, cot: FF210

Second room: double bed: FF180

Apartment: lounge, television, kitchen, shower room with wc, 2 double beds: FF250 (2 people) FF400 (4 people)

Extra bed: 70FF
Reduction: children

Capacity: 8 people

PROPERTY

private parking, extensive grounds, tv lounge, hosts have pets, telephone, dinner available, packed lunch, babies welcome, cot supplied, hunting, mushroom picking, cycling 1km, fishing 1km, hiking 1km, sea or lake watersports 10km, golf course 20km, river watersports 30km, interesting flora 30km

Fluent English spoken

— At Nontron, take the D75 towards Angoulème. "Le Petit Cousset" is sign-posted 2km after Javerlhac. Coming from Angoulème, take the D939 towards Périgueux. 4.5km after Soyaux, take the D4 then the D75 towards Marthon-Nontron. On this road, 2km after the Route Varaignes, turn left to "Le Petit Cousset" (signposted 500 metres on the left).

Michel & Claude
DUSEAU

«Château de La Borie»
24530 CHAMPAGNAC
DE BELAIR

tel: (0) 5 53 54 22 99
fax: (0) 5 53 08 53 78

Château

30 km - N -
PERIGUEUX
CHAMPAGNAC DE
BELAIR: will collect
from station,
railway station: 50km
airport: 30km

24.07 PERIGUEUX

A totally authentic ancient 13th century fortress, restored and furnished with period furniture. Spend your day visiting the caves and the Abbey of Brantome and, on summer evenings, dine under the stars in the inner courtyard of the château.

PROPERTY

✱✱✱✱

private parking, extensive grounds, tv lounge, hosts have pets, telephone, dinner available, swimming pool, tennis, closed: 01/01-01/02, cycling, river watersports, fishing, golf course 30km

Basic English spoken

— In Périgueux, take the D939 towards Angoulême. In Brantome, go in the direction of Angoulême, Montron. Before the Total petrol station, take the road "chez Ravailles" (VC3) for 3.5km.

PRICE STRUCTURE

4 Bedrooms and 1 Suite

Jaune: bathroom with wc, double bed, single bed: FF480 (2 people) FF590 (3 people)

Verte: bathroom with wc, double bed: FF490

Turquoise: bathroom with wc, twin beds, single bed: FF450

Bleu/Rose: shower room with wc, 2 double beds, single bed: FF450 (2 people) FF690 (5 people)

Grise: bathroom with wc, twin beds: FF390

Extra bed: 130FF
Reduction: 6 nights and children

Capacity: 2 people

24.27 PERIGUEUX

Yvette MERILLOU

Avenue André Maurois
24310 BRANTOME

tel: (0) 5 53 05 74 04

Private Home

22 km - N - PERIGUEUX
BRANTOME:
railway station: 25 km
airport: 30 km
car essential
— At Périgueux, take the D939 towards Angoulème. Cross Brantome, heading towards Angoulème. As you leave the town, after the bridge, turn right towards Thiviers, and then take the first country lane on the left.

Very basic (be sure to ask for the room with private bathroom), but the warm kindness of Yvette and the photosque village of Brantome, (the little Venice of the Périgord), more than compensates.

PROPERTY

off street parking, garden, hosts have pets, hiking, mushroom picking, fishing, river watersports, hunting, cycling, golf course 20km, gliding 32km

PRICE STRUCTURE

1 Bedroom classified television, shower room with wc, 2 single beds: FF203

Extra bed: 51,50FF

Capacity: 2 people

24.30 PERIGUEUX

Jacobs & Jacqueline GEROLF

«La Ferme de Laubicherie»
Laubicherie
24270 SARLANDE

tel: (0) 5 53 52 69 90
fax: (0) 5 53 52 69 90
E-mail:
Gerolf@wanadoo.fr

Farm

50 km - N E - PERIGUEUX
SARLANDE: will collect from station,
railway station: 8 km
airport: 50 km
car essential
— At Limoges, take the D704 as far as St Yriex la Perche, which you should cross, heading towards Périgueux. After 6km, you are in the Dordogne, and you should take the first on the left and follow the daisy signs 'Bienvenue à la Ferme'. (At Périgueux, N21 towards Limoges. At Sarliac, D705 on the right then D704 towards Limoges).

On the main Limoges-Sarlat road, you will find this friendly Belgian couple. In their restored farmhouse, they make bread, foie-gras and Belgian beer! You will have the opportunity to taste their own produce at dinner. Jacqueline will no doubt tell you of her love of cats. On sale: Summer fruit, poultry, rabbits, foie gras, lambs. 2 self-catering apartments, rented weekly.

PROPERTY

private parking, garden, tv lounge, hosts have pets, pets not accepted, dinner available, hiking, cycling, mushroom picking, fishing, interesting flora, sea or lake watersports 7km, golf course 40km, river watersports 45km

Fluent English spoken

PRICE STRUCTURE

5 Bedroom

Amanda: bathroom with wc, wash basin, double bed, 2 single beds (1=childrens size): FF235 FF310

Bleuet: shower room with wc, wash basin, double bed, single bed (childrens size): FF220

Vanille: shower room with wc, wash basin, 2 double beds: FF220 (2 people) FF320 (4 people)

Faïence: shower, wc, double bed: FF220

Melon: shower room with wc, twin beds: FF220

Extra bed: 75FF
Reduction: groups

Capacity: 15 people

Jean-Claude SALIVES

«Peyssut»
24330 LADOUZE

tel: (0) 5 53 06 72 92

Farm

18 km - S E - PERIGUEUX
LADOUZE: will collect from station,
railway station: 18km
airport: 14km
car essential

PRICE STRUCTURE

6 Bedroom

(5 rooms) shower room with wc, wash basin, double bed, single bed: FF240 (2 people) FF315 (3 people)

(1 room) shower room with wc, wash basin, double bed: FF260

Extra bed: 75FF

Capacity: 17 people

24.31 PERIGUEUX

Claude and Claudine will give you a hearty welcome to their livestock farm surrounded by fields and woods. There are caves and medieval towns to visit, and after a hard day's sight-seeing, you will enjoy unwinding beside the swimming pool. On sale: Wine, Pineau, Cognac, honey.

PROPERTY

off street parking, garden, tv lounge, hosts have pets, pets not accepted, telephone, babies welcome, cot supplied, wheelchair access, swimming pool, river watersports 20km, mushroom picking, interesting flora, hiking, cycling, golf course 10km, fishing 12km

— At Périgueux head towards Cahors (N89) then turn right to Le Bugue, Sarlat (D710). Peyssut is on the D710.

Guy & Marie URVOY

Les Granges
24260 MAUZENS-MIREMONT

tel:(0) 5 53 03 25 71

Private Home

30 km - S E - PERIGUEUX MAUZENS-MIREMONT: will collect from station, railway station: 15km airport: 40km car essential

24.32 PERIGUEUX

You will be staying in a beautiful house in the middle of the countryside amongst the vines and the woods. Breakfast is served on the flower-filled terrace with a panoramic view. Peace and quiet is guaranteed.

PROPERTY

off street parking, garden, tv lounge, hosts have pets, pets not accepted, telephone, dinner available, kitchen, swimming pool, tennis, closed: 15/11-30/03, hunting, mushroom picking, golf course 3km, river watersports 13km, fishing 13km, hiking 13km, river watersports 13km, sea or lake watersports 20km, gliding. 40km

PRICE STRUCTURE

4 Bedrooms

First room & Third room: shower room with wc, wash basin, double bed: FF260

Second room: shower room with wc, wash basin, double bed, single bed: FF260 (2 people) FF350 (3 people)

Fourth room: shower room with wc, wash basin, double bed, 2 single beds,Childrens size: FF260 (2 people)FF440 (4 people)

Extra bed: 90FF

Capacity: 11 people

— At Périgueux take the N89 towards Cahors then turn right on to the D710 towards Le Bugue. Continue 18km towards Sarlat and the turn left on to the D32 for Mauzens-Miremont.

Stuart&Robert
SHIPPEY & CHAPPELL

«Le Moulin Neuf»
Paunat
24510 STE ALVERE

tel: (0) 5 53 63 30 18
fax: (0) 5 53 73 33 91

Residence of character

30 km - S -
PERIGUEUX
PAUNAT:
railway station: 6km
airport: 40km
car essential

24.33 PERIGUEUX

Guests are accommodated in an old house which is separate from the mill. Robert and Stuart have given a touch of English charm to this place, and the garden is delightfully designed with flowers, a lake, weeping willow and a stream. Really cosy, very pleasant and near to Sarlat. Small pets accepted by arrangement.

PROPERTY

✱✱✱

Off street parking, extensive grounds, TV lounge, hosts have pets, telephone, hiking, cycling, fishing, interesting flora, mushroom picking, birdwatching, river watersports 5km, sea or lake watersports 6km, golf 20km

Fluent English spoken

PRICE STRUCTURE

6 Bedroom

First room & second room: bathroom with wc, double bed: FF394

Third room & sixth room: shower room with wc, twin beds: FF394

Fourth room: bathroom with wc, double bed, single bed: FF394 (2 people) FF541 (3 people)

Fifth room: shower room with wc, double bed: FF394

Extra bed: 147FF

Capacity: 13 people

— At Périgueux, N89 towards Cahors. Right on to the D710 as far as Le Bugue. Then D31 towards Limeuil. After the “cingle”, go downhill. At the cross-roads straight on towards St Alvère. After 100m turn left. It is 2km further on, on the left.

Michèle & Georges PEROL

Le Bourg
24600 ALLEMANS

tel: (0) 5 53 90 08 19
fax: (0) 5 53 90 08 19

Private Home

40 km - W - PERIGUEUX
ALLEMANS:
railway station: 40km
airport: 40km
car essential

PRICE STRUCTURE

4 Suites

3 Suites: shower room with wc, double bed, 2 single beds: FF240 (2 people) FF420 (4 people)

Suite: shower room with wc, bathroom, double bed, 2 single bed: FF240 (2 people) FF420 (4 people)

Capacity: 16 people

24.46 PERIGUEUX

This place is in a quiet Roman village in the Pays de l'Homme and is an 18th century house, full of character, with a pleasant garden. The bedrooms are comfortable and there is a lounge, TV and reading room available to you. Within 6km there is riding, tennis, a swimming pool and good hiking country. Canoeing, fishing, the Roman Ribéracois route, castles, caves and Perigueux, with its cathedral and museums, are all within easy reach. Fleur de Soleil member

PROPERTY

***

Off street parking, garden, TV lounge, pets not accepted, dinner available, hiking, fishing 2km, river watersports 6km

On the D709, in the centre of the village of Allemans, it is opposite the church. From Paris, take the TGV to Angoulême, and then the bus to Riberac.

24.13 SARLAT

A "farmhouse-inn" on the edge of the "beaches" of the Dordogne river. Here you can swim, canoe, fish or visit Sarlat and its surroundings. Your hosts make their own foie-gras and "confits". An opportunity not to be missed.

Alain LASSIGNARDIE

«Ferme Auberge d'Enveaux»
Port d'Enveaux
24220 ST VINCENT DE COSSE

tel: (0) 5 53 29 52 15

Farm

PROPERTY

Off street parking, garden, hosts have pets, pets not accepted, dinner available, fishing, sea or lake watersports, river watersports, golf 15km

Basic English spoken

PRICE STRUCTURE

6 Bedroom

A: shower room with wc, double bed: FF249

B: shower room with wc, twin beds: FF249

C: shower room with wc, double bed, single bed: FF309 (2 people) FF331 (3 people)

D & E: shower room with wc, double bed: F229

F: shower room with wc, 2 double bed: FF349 (2 people) FF393 (4 people)

Extra bed: 52FF

Capacity: 15 people

12 km - S-W - SARLAT
PORT D'ENVEAUX:
car essential
— In Sarlat, take the D57 towards Vézac. After this village, turn right on to the D703 towards Beynac. 4km after Beynac, turn left and continue for 1km (follow the signs).

24.15 SARLAT

A house in the Périgord style, hidden away in its own grounds amongst superb trees. From here, you can see all the valley of Sarlat. There is the whole of the Dordogne to visit, full of wonderful châteaux and medieval villages

Françoise
HERPIN FORGET

«Le Verseau»
49, route des Pechs24200
SARLAT LA CANEDA

tel: (0) 5 53 31 02 63

Private Home

PROPERTY

✱✱

private parking, extensive grounds, hosts have pets, pets not accepted, telephone, babies welcome, free cot, sea or lake watersports 6km, cycling 10km, golf 10km, river watersports 10km

Basic English spoken

PRICE STRUCTURE

6 Bedroom

1: shower room with wc, double bed, twin beds: FF210 (2 people) FF320 (4 people)

2: double bed, single bed: FF180 (2 people) FF235 (3 people)

3: single bed: FF125

4: shower room with wc, double bed, single bed: FF210 (2 people) FF265 (3 people)

4b: television, shower room with wc, double bed: FF220

5: television, bathroom with wc, double bed: FF250

Extra bed: 55FF

Capacity: 15 people

SARLAT
railway station: 1km
airport: 50km
— From the centre of Sarlat, go to the railway station. Turn left towards 'Les Pechs' and continue for 1.2km. The house is on the right.

24.18 SARLAT

A quiet and pleasant place in the country, ideal for families. Children will get on well with those of Brigitte and will be able to get to know the many animals on this farm, while you enjoy the farm produce. On sale: Farm produce, foie-gras, confits, patés.

Brigitte
GUILLE OMARINI

«La Ferme du Combal»
24620 TAMNIES

tel: (0) 5 53 29 64 17

Farm

PROPERTY

✱✱

Off street parking, garden, hosts have pets, dinner available, babies welcome, free cot, closed: 22/12-02/01 hiking, fishing 4km, sea or lake watersports 5km, river watersports 8km, cycling 15km, golf 25km

Basic English spoken

PRICE STRUCTURE

4 Bedroom

First room: bathroom with wc, double bed, single bed: FF242 (2 people) FF318 (3 people)

Second room: bathroom with wc, 2 double bed: FF242 (2 people) FF394 (4 people)

Third room: bathroom with wc, double bed, 2 single bed: FF242 (2 people) FF394 (4 people)

Fourth room: bathroom with wc, double bed: FF242

Extra bed: 75FF

Capacity: 13 people

15 km - N W - SARLAT
LE COMBAL:
airport: 45 km
car essential
— In Sarlat, take the D704 towards Brive for 5km. Turn left towards 'Etang de Tamniès'. From there it is 10km. Follow the signs.

24.23 SARLAT

Danielle is charming, as is her pleasant house in verdant surroundings. The small individual loggias allow you to relax in complete peace, calm and privacy, yet you are only 15 minutes on foot from the centre of the beautiful bown of Sarlat.

Danielle BARILLEAU

La Gendonie - Vignera
24200 SARLAT LA CANEDA

tel: (0) 5 53 59 30 65

Private home

PROPERTY

✱✱

private parking, extensive grounds, hosts have pets, closed: 01/10-01/05, 3 nights minimum stay 1/05-1/07, hiking, cycling, mushroom picking, sea or lake watersports 6km, fishing 8km, golf 10km

Basic English spoken

PRICE STRUCTURE

4 Bedrooms

Marron: bathroom with wc, twin beds: FF240

Verte: bathroom with wc, double bed: FF240

Jaune: along corridor bathroom with wc, double bed: FF240

Lambris-Indépendante: shower room with wc, double bed: FF210

Extra bed: 65FF

Capacity: 8 people

SARLAT
will collect from station,
railway station: 1km
airport: 50km
— In Sarlat, go in the direction of Bergerac, then Domme. Opposite the Casino supermarket, turn right towards Le Bugue. After 100m, turn left into the first small road towards Vignera. The house is the second on your left.

William & Michèle
VIDAL d'HONDT

«Château du Pas du Raysse»
Le Raysse
24370 CAZOULES

tel: (0) 5 53 29 84 41
fax: (0) 5 53 59 62 16
http://www.bedbreak.com

Château

24 km - E - SARLAT
LE RAYSSE: will collect from station,
railway station: 3km
airport: 35km
car essential

24.28 SARLAT

This is a real discovery. Peace and quiet pervades William and Michèle's château which melts into the soft landscapes of the Dordogne. You will be enchanted as you taste William's fine cooking and his wines chosen with skill. We fell in love with this place and gave it an extra sun. On sale: Foie-gras, wine.

PROPERTY

✱✱✱✱

private parking, extensive grounds, TV lounge, dinner available, babies welcome, free cot, wheelchair access, swimming pool, closed: 15/09-15/10&20/12-15/01, 3 nights minimum stay, 01/07-31/08, hiking, fishing, cycling 3km, river watersports 3km, mushroom picking 4km, golf 5km

Fluent English spoken

PRICE STRUCTURE

3 Bedrooms and 2 Suites

First room: shower room with wc, double bed, single bed: FF490 (2 people) FF590 (3 people)

Second room: shower room with wc, double bed: FF490

Suite first floor: shower room with wc, double bed, twin beds: FF490 (2 people) FF690 (4 people)

Suite second floor: shower room with wc, double bed, twin beds: FF690 (2 people) FF690 (4 people)

Annex second floor: shower room with wc, single bed: FF350

Extra bed: 100FF
Reduction: 01.10–30.06 and groups

Capacity: 14 people

— In Sarlat take the D704A and then the D703 towards Souillac. As you enter Cazoulès turn left by the sign on the left to "chambres d'hotes". Then climb up the little road at right angles and, when facing the gate, take the unmade road.

Konrad & Elisabeth HOLLEIS

«Le Jaonnet»
Liabou Bas
24250 NABIRAT

tel: (0) 5 53 29 59 29
fax: (0) 5 53 29 59 29

Residence of character

16 km - S E - SARLAT
LIABOU BAS:
airport: 150km
car essential

24.29 SARLAT

A charming couple from Guernsey. Konrad is a professional chef (his "zabaglione" is fantastic). Their old farmhouse has been restored with great charm, and the dining room, with its solid oak gallery, is very attractive.

PRICE STRUCTURE

5 Bedrooms

Fermain: shower room with wc, wash basin, double bed, single bed: FF320 (2 people) FF405 (3 people)

Icart: bathroom with wc, double bed, single bed: FF280 (2 people) FF365 (3 people)

Portelet: lounge, bathroom with wc, twin beds: FF300

Saints: shower room with wc, double bed: FF300

Moulin Huet: shower room with wc, double bed: FF300

Extra bed: 85FF

Capacity: 12 people

PROPERTY

***

Off street parking, garden, lounge, pets not accepted, dinner available, babies welcome, free cot, wheelchair access, non smoking, closed: 01/11-1/03, 3 nights minimum, 01/06-30/09, hiking, interesting flora, sea or lake watersports 2km, cycling 5km, river watersports 5km, golf 8km, gliding 12km

Fluent English spoken

— In Sarlat take the D704 towards Gourdon-Cahors. 2km after the Dordogne river, turn right (D50), continue towards Domme for 50m. At La Poste, turn left towards Nabirat. 2nd turning on left (signposted).

Françoise & Alain TILLY

Chemin du Plantier
24200 SARLAT LA
CANEDA

tel: (0) 5 53 59 39 89
fax: (0) 5 53 59 39 89
E-mail: tillya@minitel.
net

Private Home

24.37 SARLAT

A new house overlooking the medieval town of Sarlat. An ideal location for discovering the most famous prehistoric sites in Europe. Francoise and Alain, both keen walkers know how to guide you to the best places to visit off the beaten track in this green and pleasant region. On sale: honey.

SARLAT
will collect from station,
railway station: 2km
airport: 50km

PROPERTY

✱✱

Off street parking, garden, lounge, hosts have pets, pets not accepted, babies welcome, free cot, non smoking, hiking, cycling, mushroom picking, golf 8km, fishing 8km, river water-sports 8km, gliding 13km

Basic English spoken

PRICE STRUCTURE

2 Bedrooms

First room & second room: shower, wash basin, double bed, single bed: FF230 (2 people) FF280 (3 people)

Extra bed: 30FF Reduction: 6 nights

Capacity: 2 people

— From Sarlat station, go up the 'Route des Pechs' (F. Mistral) for 1500 metres. The house is situated on the corner of the 'Chemin du Plantier'. There is a "B&B France" sign outside.

Chantal GAYRARD

«Domaine Les Tourelles»
Le Poujol
24590 ST CREPIN ET CARLUCET

tel: (0) 5 53 31 09 38
fax: (0) 5 53 31 09 38

Château or Manor house

13 km - N - SARLAT
LE POUJOL:
railway station: 11km
airport: 38km
car essential

24.40 PERIGUEUX

In this 18th century former winery, which combines classic skills with regional flavours, the visitor can enjoy the swimming pool and tennis court. Then finish the evening with a glass of Armagnac in good company with good music.

PRICE STRUCTURE

2 Bedrooms

Bleu: bathroom with wc, shower, double bed: FF535

Fleurs: along corridor bathroom with wc, along corridor shower, double bed: FF535

Extra bed: 130FF

Capacity: 4 people

PROPERTY

✱✱✱✱

private parking, extensive grounds, TV lounge, 14 years minimum age, babies welcome, free cot, swimming pool, tennis, hiking, cycling, interesting flora 7km, golf 9km, fishing 10km, hunting 10km, river watersports 15km

Adequate English spoken

— From Sarlat, take the D704 towards Montignc. After 9km, turn left on to the D60 in the direction of Salignac. Continue for 4km as far as 'Le Poujol' then follow the signs for 'Domaine des Tourelles'.

Monique SALZMANN

«Lassagne»
24200 ST ANDRE
D'ALLAS

tel: (0) 5 53 31 06 28

Residence of character

5 km - W - SARLAT
ST ANDRE
D'ALLAS:
railway station: 25km
car essential

24.41 SARLAT

Very close to Sarlat in the heart of Périgord countryside, the home of caves and châteaux, you will be impressed by this authentic stone house. Monique is a charming hostess, generous and kind. There is a lovely view from the terrace garden and a sun-drenched swimming pool.

PROPERTY

✱✱✱

Off street parking, extensive grounds, TV lounge, hosts have pets, pets not accepted, babies welcome, free cot, non smoking, swimming pool, hiking, mushroom picking, cycling 6km, river watersports 10km, golf 15km

Fluent English spoken

— From Sarlat, head in the direction of Bergerac on the D57. 500 metres after the viaduct, turn right towards St André - Le Bugue (D25). After 6km, turn left towards St André CI. Lassagne is 700 metres further on, on the left, just before the church

PRICE STRUCTURE

1 Bedroom Rose: bathroom with wc, double bed, cot: FF260

Reduction: children

Capacity: 2 people

Nicole & Jean QUERRE

«Les Granges Hautes»
St Crépin
24590 ST CREPIN ET CARLUCET

tel: (0) 5 53 29 35 60
fax: (0) 5 53 28 81 17
E-mail: jquerre@aol.com

Residence of character

13 km - N - SARLAT
ST CREPIN ET CARLUCET:
railway station: 10km
airport: 35km
car essential

24.44 SARLAT

This beautiful Perigourd house is at the centre of superb grounds. Each room is different, and has its own individual style which will transport you to Italy, the Orient... A delicious breakfast, an excellent swimming pool and the warm welcome of your hosts all add up to an enchanting place. Credit cards accepted.

PROPERTY

✱✱✱✱

Off street parking, extensive grounds, TV lounge, pets not accepted, telephone, packed lunch, babies welcome, free cot swimming pool, closed: 01/10-1/04, hiking, cycling, interesting flora 10km, golf 15km, fishing 15km

Basic English spoken

PRICE STRUCTURE

5 Bedrooms

Toscane: bathroom with wc, double bed, single bed: FF480 (2 people) FF625 (3 people)

Virginie: bathroom with wc, twin beds: FF480

Irina: shower room with wc, double bed, single bed: FF480 (2 people) FF625 (3 people)

Oiseaux: shower room with wc, double bed, twin beds: FF480 (2 people) FF770 (4 people)

Pamela: shower room with wc, twin beds: FF480

Reduction: 10 nights

Capacity: 14 people

— At Sarlat, take the D704 towards Montignac. After 9km, turn right and take the D60 towards St. Crépin and Carlucet. In the village, follow the signs to “Les Granges Hautes”.

Olivier Le ROUX

«Manoir de la Moissie»
La Moissie
24170 BELVES

tel: (0) 5 53 30 31 97
fax: (0) 5 53 29 15 34
E-mail:sunset.creation
@wanadoo.fr

Residence of character

30 km - S W - SARLAT
BELVES: will collect from station,
railway station: 2km
airport: 75km
car essential

24.45 SARLAT

Here, you will get a really warm, genuine welcome in the centre of Belvès, a listed medieval village. This former 16th century hunting lodge is surrounded by extensive, and very attractive, wooded grounds. Your rooms are in a comfortably restored little house in the grounds, and the bedrooms are in the tower of the "pigeonnier".

PROPERTY

✱✱✱

Off street parking, extensive grounds, TV lounge, pets not accepted, dinner available, kitchen, babies welcome, free cot, hiking 2km, cycling 2km, mushroom picking 2km, golf 3km, fishing 5km, river watersports 10km

Fluent English spoken

PRICE STRUCTURE

1 Bedroom and 1 Apartment

Studio: kitchen, shower, twin beds, double bed: FF280 (2 people) FF400 (4 people)

Extra bed: 60FF
Reduction: 5 nights

Capacity: 4 people

— At Sarlat, take the D57 and then the D703 for Bergerac. At Siorac, take the D770 on the left as far as Belvès. Head towards Monpazier. Turn right immediately after the municipal swimming pool, and it is the first lane on the left in front of a small wall. Go up this lane (following signs to "La Moissie").

Peter KERKHOFF

«Les Maurelles»
Le Bourg
46300 MILHAC

tel: (0) 5 65 41 48 59
fax: (0) 5 65 41 66 21
E-mail:maurelles
@wanadoo.fr

Private Home

46.13 SARLAT

This young couple have faithfully restored the old solicitor's house in this little stone hamlet parts dating from the 17th century. The welcome is warm and hearty and together with the Dordogne this green, peaceful location will conspire to make you extend your stay. On sale: Walnuts, local produce.

PROPERTY

✱✱✱

Off street parking, garden, TV lounge, hosts have pets, telephone, dinner available, packed lunch, babies welcome, free cot, swimming pool, hiking, cycling, fishing, mushroom picking, sea or lake watersports 5km, river watersports 7km, golf 17km

Fluent English spoken

19 km - S E - SARLAT
MILHAC: will collect from station, railway station: 7km
airport: 150km
car essential
— In Sarlat, take the D704 towards Gourdon. In Groléjac, turn left towards Milhac. As you enter the village, the house is on the left.

PRICE STRUCTURE

5 Bedrooms

First room: & Fifth room: shower room with wc, double bed: FF300

Second room: shower room with wc, double bed, 2 single beds: FF300 (2 people) FF350 (4 people)

Third room: & Fourth room: double bed: FF250

Extra bed: 50FF
Reduction: 01.10 –31.05 and 7 nights and children

Capacity: 12 people

Jane Elisabeth BARKER

«La Pinière»
Sous la Plaine
46350 MASCLAT

tel: (0) 5 65 32 29 80
fax: (0) 5 65 32 29 80
E-mail: piniere@hotmail.com

Private Home

Aquitaine

SARLAT

46.26 SARLAT

This is a really peaceful house, full of character in the woods. The rooms are homely and comfortable, with their own terrace and separate access. Jane Elisabeth is English and an ex-chef, and will prepare delicious local dishes for you.

20 km - S E - SARLAT
MASCLAT: will collect from station, railway station: 10km
airport: 150km

PROPERTY

***

Off street parking, extensive grounds, TV lounge, pets not accepted, telephone, dinner available, non smoking, swimming pool, hiking, mushroom picking, fishing 1km, river watersports 5km, cycling 10km, golf 10km

Fluent English spoken

PRICE STRUCTURE

2 Bedrooms

First room: ground floor, lounge, bathroom with wc, double bed: FF350

Second room: ground floor, shower room with wc, double bed: FF350

Extra bed: 100FF

Capacity: 4 people

— From Sarlat, take the D704 towards Souillac. In Roufillac, cross the Dordogne towards St Julien de Lampon, then Masclat. In Masclat, follow the signs to "La Pinière".

Michèle TARDAT

«Cantemerle»
9, Rue des Châtaigniers-BOURDIN
33180 VERTHEUIL-MEDOC

tel: (0) 5 56 41 96 24
fax: (0) 5 56 41 96 24

Residence of Character

55 km - N W - BORDEAUX VERTHEUIL:
airport: 60km
car essential

33.06 BORDEAUX

A beautiful house in the Spanish Moorish style, in the heart of the Médoc vineyards. Here you will find peace and quiet and an outstanding decor, which reflects your hosts' love of travelling. Nearby are the famous Médoc wine-châteaux, beaches and the wine-museum. On sale: Wine.

PRICE STRUCTURE

2 Bedrooms

Tour: along corridor shower room with wc, twin beds: FF320

Bleue: along corridor bathroom with wc, double bed: FF300

Extra bed: 100FF

Reduction: 01.11 – 28.02 and children

Capacity: 4 people

PROPERTY

***

private parking, extensive grounds, TV lounge, hosts have pets, pets not accepted, dinner available, babies welcome, free cot, non smoking, cycling, fishing 1km, sea or lake watersports 35km

Fluent English spoken

— In Bordeaux, take Exit 7 on the A630 then the D1 towards Le Verdon/Soulac. In Castelnau, take the N215 in the same direction, for 25km. Turn right on to the D205 towards Cissac and take the D104 towards Vertheuil where you turn left by the church, towards Bourdin. The property is on your left as you leave the hamlet.

Yolande BONNET

«Gravelande»
7, Chemin du Bergey
33850 LEOGNAN

tel: (0) 5 56 64 72 04
E-mail:
alexbonnet@aol.com

Residence of Character

33.07 PERIGUEUX

Only 20 min. from the centre of Bordeaux, this house is surrounded by impressive grounds in the heart of the famous Pessac-Léognan vineyards. You will find it very difficult to tear yourself away from Yolande's wonderful, warm hospitality, so allow plenty of time.

14 km - S -
BORDEAUX
LEOGNAN: will collect from station,
railway station: 15km
airport: 20km
car essential

PROPERTY

***

private parking, extensive grounds, TV lounge, hosts have pets, pets not accepted, dinner available, babies welcome, free cot, swimming pool, closed: 15/10-15/05, 2 nights minimum stay, golf 10km, sea or lake watersports 50km

Fluent English spoken

PRICE STRUCTURE

2 Bedrooms

First room: bridal room, television, bathroom with wc, shower, twin beds: FF350

Second room: kitchen, shower, bathroom, wc, double bed: FF350

Extra bed: 100FF
Reduction: 4 nights

Capacity: 4 people

— In Bordeaux, take Exit 18 on the A630 towards Léognan. There, on the square, take the D214 towards Cestas. Take the fourth lane on the right, and the first gate on the left.

Alain GENESTINE

«Domaine Les Sapins»
Bouqueyran
33480 MOULIS EN
MEDOC

tel: (0) 5 56 58 18 26
fax: (0) 5 56 58 28 45

Residence of Character

25 km - N W -
BORDEAUX
MOULIS EN
MEDOC:
railway station: 4km
airport: 24km
car essential

33.08 BORDEAUX

Here the atmosphere is cosy and you feel like one of the family. The large house dates from the beginning of the 19th century and is set amongst vines, surrounded by beautiful grounds. Nathalie who is a Cordon Bleu cook will serve you her specialities and Alain will share his expertise in wine with you. You will love this place. On sale: Wine. Dinner must be booked in advance.

PRICE STRUCTURE

5 Bedrooms and 1 Suite

Hortensia/Albarose: bathroom with wc, 2 double bed, single bed: FF300 (2 people) FF600 (3 people)

Marguerite: shower room with wc, double bed: FF300

Menuet: shower room with wc, twin beds: FF300

Country Rose: shower room with wc, double bed, single bed: FF300 (2 people) FF450 (3 people)

Charleston: shower room with wc, double bed, 2 single bed: FF300(2 people) FF450 (4 people)

Chinatown: shower, wash basin, 2 single bed: FF300

Extra bed: 150FF
Reduction: 01.11–30.11 and 01.01–15.03 and 5 nights
Capacity: 18 people

PROPERTY

❋❋❋

Off street parking, extensive grounds, TV lounge, telephone, dinner available, babies welcome, free cot, hiking, cycling 1km, hunting 1km, mushroom picking 1km, golf 12km, fishing 20km, interesting flora 25km, sea or lake watersports 25km, birdwatching 60km

Fluent English spoken

— At Bordeaux, on the A630 take Exit 7 and the D1 towards Le Verdon sur Soulac. In Castelnau, take the N215 in the same direction, for 3km. In Bouqueyran, you turn left (large sign).

33.12 BORDEAUX

This château, which has recently been restored, has large, comfortable rooms and king-size beds. Its vineyard produces Premières Cotes de Bordeaux. Enjoy the 5 hectares of peaceful grounds and try to fit in a few châteaux visits between the wine tasting! On sale: Wine 'Premières Cotes de Bordeaux'.

PROPERTY

***

Off street parking, extensive grounds, TV lounge, pets not accepted, telephone, dinner available, kitchen, packed lunch, hiking, cycling, hunting, mushroom picking, fishing 8km, golf 30km

Basic English spoken

PRICE STRUCTURE

4 Bedrooms and 1 Suite

Rose: lounge, bathroom with wc, double bed: FF345

Bleuet: shower room with wc, twin beds: FF295

Pivoine & Jonquille: shower room with wc, double bed: FF345

Iris: lounge, shower room with wc, 2 double bed: FF345 (2 people) FF505 (4 people)

Extra bed: 80FF

Capacity: 12 people

Blanche MAINVIELLE

«Château de Grand Branet»
859, Branet Sud
33350 CAPIAN

tel: (0) 5 56 72 17 30
fax: (0) 5 56 72 36 59

Château

30 km - S E - BORDEAUX
CAPIAN: railway station: 25km
airport 30km
car essential
— Take Exit La Brède from the A62, and then the N113 towards Agen, and then the D115 towards Langoiran as far as the D10. Then turn right towards Cadillac. At Pied du Château, turn left towards Capian. At the top of the hill, turn right and then take the 5th made-up road on the right. Continue 200m to the château.

Jean-P. & Marie-Ange
FROMENT

18, Route de Soulac
33930 VENDAYS-
MONTALIVET

tel: (0) 5 56 41 73 52

Private Home

70 km - N W - BORDEAUX VENDAYS MONTALIVET: will collect from station, railway station: 6km airport: 75km

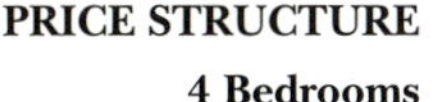

33.13 BORDEAUX

Marie-Ange and Jean-Pierre, "young" senior citizens, will give you a warm welcome in their beautiful villa, with its beautiful gardens in the heart of the Médoc, famed for its 'grands crus'. They are only 10km from beautiful, sandy beaches. (Please note, that the bedroom 'Verte' has a shower in the room.)

PRICE STRUCTURE

4 Bedrooms

Rez de Jardin: along corridor shower room with wc, double bed, single bed: FF340 (2 people) FF400 (3 people)

First floor Blanche-Baldaquin: shower, double bed: FF300

First floor Bleue: bathroom with wc, double bed, single bed: FF320 (2 people) FF380 (3 people)

First floor Verte: shower, wash basin, double bed: FF290

Extra bed: 90FF

Capacity: 10 people

PROPERTY

✱✱

private parking, extensive grounds, lounge, hosts have pets, babies welcome, free cot, sea or lake watersports 7km

Basic English spoken

— At Bordeaux, on the motorway take Exit 7 and follow the D1 towards Le Verdon. At Castelnau, take the N215 towards Soulac-Le Verdon. Turn left on to the D102 towards Vendays. At La Mairie, towards Soulac, the house is on the left, 300m after the traffic lights.

Jeannette SENELAR

«Domaine de Fauquey»
33670 LA SAUVE

tel: (0) 5 56 23 01 41
fax: (0) 5 56 23 01 41

Château or
Manor House

20 km - S E - BORDEAUX
LA SAUVE: railway station: 15km
airport: 30km
car essential

Aquitaine

BORDEAUX

33.17 BORDEAUX

Chez Jeanette, you are in a quiet and pleasant spot, and you will find a very warm welcome. The bedrooms are spacious, comfortable and pleasantly furnished. Stabling for horses is also available.

PROPERTY

***

Off street parking, extensive grounds, TV lounge, hosts have pets, pets not accepted, dinner available, packed lunch, babies welcome, free cot, swimming pool, riding, cycling, interesting flora, hiking 1km, mushroom picking 2km, golf 5km, fishing 5km, birdwatching 20km, sea or lake watersports 50km

Adequate English spoken

PRICE STRUCTURE

3 Bedrooms

Verlaine: telephone, bathroom with wc, twin beds: FF350

Claudel: telephone, shower room with wc, double bed, single bed: FF350 (2 people) FF420 (3 people)

Ronsard: telephone, shower room with wc, 2 double bed: FF350 (2 people) FF520 (4 people)

Reduction: 01.10 – 31.05 and 3 nights

Capacity: 9 people

— From Bordeaux, go towards Bergerac. Take the D671 towards Créon. Follow the D671 towards La Sauve-Sauveterre. When you are 2 km from Créon and 1 km from La Sauve-Sauveterre, turn left. The house is the first on the right, 800 m further on.

Monique & Yves
CORNAZ

12, allée des Ramiers
33970 CAP FERRET-
OCEAN

tel: (0) 5 56 60 61 45
fax: (0) 5 56 03 76 29
E-mail: monique.
cornaz@wanadoo.fr

Private Home

65 km - S W -
BORDEAUX
CAP FERRET
OCEAN: railway
station: 60km
airport: 45 km
car essential

33.18 BORDEAUX

Excellent welcome in this modern house, situated in a quiet district of 'Le Ferret'. Enjoy the swimming pool and the lovely garden with lots of trees. You are only 10 minutes walk from the ocean beaches and those of the Arcachon lake. Be sure not to miss this highly rated area.

PRICE STRUCTURE

3 Bedrooms

First room: bridal room, television, kitchen, shower room with wc, double bed: FF500

Second room: kitchen, bathroom with wc, twin beds: FF450

Third room: kitchen, shower room with wc, twin beds: FF400

Reduction: 7 nights

Capacity: 6 people

PROPERTY

****

Off street parking, garden, pets not accepted, telephone, dinner available, 18 years minimum age, non smoking, swimming pool, 3 nights minimum stay, hiking, sea or lake watersports, fishing 1km, cycling 2km, birdwatching 50km

Adequate English spoken

— From Bordeaux, take the D106 as far as Cap Ferret. From there, stay on the D106 and head in the direction of Le Mirador for 1.6 km. In front of the Shell-Peugeot garage, turn left. The house is 150 metres along on the right.

Liliane & Michel KORBER

«Petit Hotel Labottière»
14, rue Francis Martin
33000 BORDEAUX

tel: (0) 5 56 48 44 10
fax: (0) 5 56 48 44 14

Château or
Manor House

BORDEAUX
airport: 11km

33.25 BORDEAUX

Do not miss this place in the centre of the elegant city of Bordeaux. It is a long story, but this magnificent "hotel particulier" originally belonged to an 18th century batchelor gentleman of good taste. The building is listed, and combines refined comfort with an authentic heritage. Your host will be delighted to show you around the house. Extra bed supplied free of charge - Secure private parking: 50FF per day.

PRICE STRUCTURE

2 Bedrooms

(2 rooms) television, telephone, shower room with wc, bathroom, double bed: FF1000

Capacity: 4 people

PROPERTY

****

private parking, garden, lounge, telephone, 8 years minimum age, golf 15km, sea or lake watersports 60km

Fluent English spoken

— From the Place de Tourny, take the Rue de Fondaudège. At the 4th set of traffic lights, turn right into the Rue St. Laurent and at the end, turn immediately left into the Rue Francis-Martin.

Béatrice & Pierre
LABUZAN

«Château de Monbazan»
Place de l'Eglise
33720 LANDIRAS

tel: (0) 5 56 62 42 82
fax: (0) 5 56 62 54 47

Château or
Manor House

15 km - W - LANGON
LANDIRAS:
railway station: 15km
airport: 45km
car essential
— From the A62, Exit 2, take the D11 towards Landiras for 6km. In Landiras, the house is opposite the church, next to the petrol station. The entrance to the car park is from the Cabanac road.

33.21 LANGON

This is a wine growerís house, in the heart of the Graves vineyards, 6km from Sauternes. Pierre and Béatrice are into organic farming, and will be delighted to show you round their property. The redecorated bedroom is excellent value and an ideal place for spending several days. On sale: Organically produced wine, grape juice.

PROPERTY

**

private parking, garden, TV lounge, hosts have pets, pets not accepted, babies welcome, free cot, non smoking, hiking, cycling, mushroom picking, birdwatching, fishing 6km, hunting 6km, river watersports 6km, golf 15km, sea or lake watersports 25km

Fluent English spoken

PRICE STRUCTURE

1 Bedroom shower room with wc, wash basin, double bed, cot: FF220

Capacity: 2 people

33.16 LA REOLE

You will be welcomed into the family atmosphere in this old farmhouse which has been recently restored. It nestles in the countryside, surrounded by woods and fields. Here you can unwind and relax. On sale: Local wine.

PROPERTY

***

Off street parking, extensive grounds, TV lounge, hosts have pets, telephone, dinner available, packed lunch, babies welcome, free cot, wheelchair access, closed: 20/10-05/11, hiking, cycling, fishing, hunting, river watersports 12km, golf 20km, sea or lake watersports 30km

Fluent English spoken

PRICE STRUCTURE

5 Bedrooms

Handicapé: wheelchair access, shower room with wc, wash basin, 2 single bed: FF300

Bleu & Rouge 2: bathroom with wc, wash basin, double bed: FF300

Rose & Rouge 1: shower room with wc, wash basin, double bed: FF300

Extra bed: 100FF Reduction:

Capacity: 10 people

Claire & Antoine
LABORDE

«La Tuilerie»
33190 NOAILLAC

tel: (0) 5 56 71 05 51
fax: (0) 5 56 71 05 51
http://www.bedbreak.com

Private Home

8 km - S - LA REOLE
NOAILLAC: will collect from station,
railway station: 12km
airport: 60km
car essential
— Take Exit 4 La Réole from the A62. After the "péage" (toll booths) on the D9 turn left towards Bazas and take the first on the left after the autoroute bridge. Follow the signs "chambres d'hotes" for 3km.

Margreet&Erik NETTO-VAN DER MEER

«La Bonne Maison»
Lieu Dit La Bonne
33580 ROQUEBRUNE

tel: (0) 5 56 71 34 17
fax: (0) 5 56 71 35 11

Manor House

5 km - N E - LA REOLE ROQUEBRUNE: will collect from station, railway station: 9km airport: 60km car essential

33.20 LA REOLE

You will be warmly welcomed to this manor house in the heart of the country, beside a river. Eric is a translator, and Margreet loves horse-riding. Between them, they will be able to organise your stay and excursions if you wish. This is an area known for its "bastides" and vineyards.

PRICE STRUCTURE

2 Bedrooms and 1 Suite

Rooms 1 & 2: shower room with wc, double bed: FF260

Suite: shower room with wc, 2 double bed: FF260 (2 people) FF460 (4 people)

Extra bed: 80FF

Reduction: 5 nights

Capacity: 8 people

PROPERTY

✱✱✱

Off street parking, garden, TV lounge, hosts have pets, pets not accepted, dinner available, packed lunch, riding, hiking, cycling, fishing, hunting, mushroom picking, river watersports 5km, sea or lake watersports 20km

Fluent English spoken

— From La Réole, follow signs to Sauveterre on D670. 4 km after Le Réole, turn off this road on the right towards Bagas and Loubens (D126). Go through these two villages, and then continue straight on towards La Violette. The house is 3 km further on, on the left.

Christine & Neil MORRIS

«Les Ormeaux»
1, Chassereau
33420 NAUJAN ET POSTIAC

tel: (0) 5 57 84 69 08
fax: (0) 5 57 84 69 08

Private Home

33.23 ST EMILION

This charming old stone house has been prettily restored, and the garden is full of aromatic and culinary herbs. It is just at the exit of a village surrounded by vineyards. You will appreciate Neil's kindness and his specialist knowledge of rare plants. On sale: aromatic and culinary plants.

15 km - S - ST EMILION
NAUJAN & POSTIAC: railway station: 18km
airport: 45km
car essential

PROPERTY

**

Off street parking, garden, television, dinner available, babies welcome, free cot, closed: 15/12-15/01, hiking, cycling 3km, fishing 5km, river watersports 5km, sea or lake watersports 6km, golf 20km

Fluent English spoken

PRICE STRUCTURE

3 Bedrooms

First room: shower room with wc, twin beds, single bed, cot: FF280 (2 people) FF360 (3 people)

Second room: shower room with wc, twin beds: FF280

Third room: shower room with wc, double bed: FF280

Reduction: 5 nights

Capacity: 7 people

— At Bordeaux, take the D936 towards Bergerac for 22km. Then take the D128 on the right towards "Naujan et Rauzan". In this village, after the post office, turn right and then left behind the sports stadium.

Jacqueline & Wilfrid

FRANC de FERRIERE
«Château de
Carbonneau»
33890 PESSAC SUR
DORDOGNE

tel: (0) 5 57 47 46 46
fax: (0) 5 57 47 46 46
E-mail:
carbonneau@wanadoo.fr

Château

Aquitaine

ST EMILION

20 km - S E - ST EMILION PESSAC SUR DORDOGNE: will collect from station, railway station: 12km airport: 60km car essential

33.24 ST EMILION

Vineyard vacations! In this 19th century château on a family estate of 50 hectares, you will savour the peace and quiet of this place. Wilfred and Jacquie, a New Zealand couple, will be delighted to tell you about their wine growing business. On sale: wine

PRICE STRUCTURE

3 Bedrooms

Téléphone: bathroom with wc, twin beds: FF300

Master bedroom: bathroom with wc, double bed: FF300

Pigeonnier: shower room with wc, twin beds, single bed: FF300 (2 people) FF400 (3 people)

Extra bed: 100FF

Capacity: 7 people

PROPERTY

***

Off street parking, extensive grounds, TV lounge, hosts have pets, telephone, babies welcome, free cot, wheelchair access, swimming pool, closed: 15/11-1/03, hiking, fishing, interesting flora, birdwatching, cycling 2km, river watersports 2km, sea or lake watersports 10km, golf 18km

Adequate English spoken

— At St Emilion, go towards Bergerac (D936). At La Tête Noire, turn right on to the D9 towards Gensac, Pessac. In the village, follow the signs.

Ass HOUNTANS
EN TE BIBE

«Château d'Aon»
Centre d'Hébergement
Collectif
40190 HONTANX

tel: (0) 5 58 03 83 22 /
58 03 80 18
fax: (0) 5 58 03 83 22

Residence of Character

40.08 MONT DE MARSAN

This place is ideal for a group or a large family, and is in a beautiful setting. It is run by an association who will give you a warm welcome, and explain that their objective is to complete the restoration of the château. The dormitory accommodation is cleverly furnished and the cooking is good family fare.

20 km - S E - MONT DE MARSAN
HONTANX: will collect from station, railway station: 22km
airport: 60km
car essential

PROPERTY

✸

Off street parking, extensive grounds, television, telephone, dinner available, kitchen, packed lunch, wheelchair facilities, hiking, cycling, fishing, hunting, interesting flora, mushroom picking, golf 6km, river watersports 20km, gliding 20km

English spoken

PRICE STRUCTURE

3 Bedrooms

First room: 10 single beds: FF166 (2 people) FF830 (10 people)

Second room: 9 single beds: FF166 (2 people) FF747 (9 people)

Third room: 6 single beds: FF166 (2 people) FF498 (6 people)

Extra bed: 83FF
Reduction: 2 nights

Capacity: 25 people

— At Mont de Marsan, take the D30 towards Le Houga, Nogaro. Cross the D934 and turn left on to the D104 towards Hontanx.

40.09 PERIGUEUX

Liliane JEHL

«Moulin Vieux»
40420 GAREIN

tel: (0) 5 58 51 61 43

Residence of Character

This house is at the heart of an oak forest, in grounds with a lazy river and lakes. Liliane is a yoga teacher, and will take you to springs claimed to have healing powers. Everything; flowers, wildlife and the quiet of this place combine to make this a perfect spot to recharge your batteries. On sale: Honey.

PROPERTY

✱✱

Off street parking, extensive grounds, TV lounge, hosts have pets, telephone, dinner available, babies welcome, free cot, wheelchair access, hiking, fishing, hunting, mushroom picking, cycling 15km, birdwatching 15km, sea or lake watersports 20km, interesting flora 40km, golf 50km

Fluent English spoken

15 km - N - MONT DE MARSAN
GAREIN: will collect from station, railway station: 15km airport: 100km car essential
— At Mont de Marsan, take the N134 towards Bordeaux as far as Garein. Then take the D57 towards Ygos for 1km. Take the lane on the left and follow the signs for 1.2km.

PRICE STRUCTURE

3 Bedrooms and 1 Suite

Oiseaux: shower room with wc, twin beds: FF250

Rose: shower, wc, wash basin, double bed, single bed: FF220 (2 people) FF310 (3 people)

Bleue: shower, wc, wash basin, double bed: FF220

Suite: bathroom with wc, 10 single beds: FF180 (2 people) FF900 (10 people)

Extra bed: 50FF

Capacity: 17 people

Christiane DOUBESKY

«Domaine de Pouzergues»
47310 MONCAULT

tel: (0) 5 53 97 53 97
fax: (0) 5 53 97 15 25

Residence of Character

10 km - S W - AGEN
MONCAUT:
airport: 130km
car essential

47.02 AGEN

An 18th century manor house in a beautiful flower garden. Here the rooms have great style and the whole atmosphere is refined and discreet. You can either laze the days away by the heated swimming-pool or visit nearby châteaux

PROPERTY

✱✱✱✱

Off street parking, extensive grounds, TV lounge, hosts have pets, pets not accepted, kitchen, babies welcome, free cot, swimming pool, hiking, sea or lake watersports 3km, fishing 8km, golf 20km

Basic English spoken

PRICE STRUCTURE

4 Bedrooms and 1 Suite

Les Oiseaux & Baldaquin & Pigeonnier: telephone, bathroom with wc, double bed: FF432

Primevère: telephone, bathroom with wc, double bed, 2 single beds: FF432 (2 people) FF630 (4 people)

Jaune: telephone, shower room with wc, double bed: FF432

Extra bed: 100FF
Reduction: 10 nights

Capacity: 12 people

— In Agen, go towards 'Le Passage' and take the D656 towards Nérac. The property is on the right, after Pléchac, at the corner of the road to Ste Colombe.

Maria VAN STRAATEN

«Le Marchon»
47130 BAZENS

tel: (0) 5 53 87 22 26
fax: (0) 5 53 87 22 26

Private Home

47.06 AGEN

Maria & Henri welcome you, around the fire. They try to cater for everybody's individual tastes. Organic and vegetarian dishes and excellent wine, some home made, can be provided. This region is rich in caves and châteaux. Henri is a sculptor.

PROPERTY

✱✱

Off street parking, extensive grounds, TV lounge, hosts have pets, dinner available, non smoking, swimming pool, closed: 01/11-01/04, hiking, cycling

Fluent English spoken

22 km - W - AGEN
BAZENS: will collect from station, railway station: 4km airport: 22km
— In Agen take the RN113 towards Bordeaux, for 20Km. Turn right towards Bazens (D118) and D231 towards Galapian until you reach to the sign.

PRICE STRUCTURE

5 Bedrooms

First room: shower room with wc, twin beds: FF275

Second room: bathroom with wc, double bed, 2 single bed: FF275 (2 people) FF400 (4 people)

Third room: bathroom with wc, double bed: FF275

Fourth room: wash basin, twin beds: FF230

Sixth room: wash basin, double bed, single bed: FF230 (2 people) FF285 (3 people)

Extra bed: 65FF
Reduction: 01.09 – 30.06 and 2 nights

Capacity: 13 people

Pierre & Bernadette
MENDIONDO

«Villa Arrosen-Artean»
Chemin d'Ithulrraldia
64210 AHETZE

tel: (0) 5 59 41 93 03
fax: (0) 5 59 41 93 03

Private Home

64.13 BIARRITZ

The welcome is very warm and the view over the valley and the village is uninterrupted! A very relaxing spot near the beach. The shower is in the room in the Jaune, Bleue and Green bedrooms. In the little neighbouring restaurants you can try 'piperade' or 'poulet basquaise'. Basque pelota, traditional dances and surfing are worth seeing. On sale: Eggs, vegetables.

6 km - S - BIARRITZ
AHETZE: railway
station: 5km
airport: 8km
car essential

PROPERTY

❋❋❋

Off street parking, garden, TV lounge, pets not accepted, 2 nights minimum stay, cycling, fishing, hunting, mushroom picking 2km, hiking 3km, sea or lake watersports 4km, birdwatching 5km, golf 7km, river watersports 30km

PRICE STRUCTURE

5 Bedrooms

Rose: double bed, single bed: FF265 (2 people) FF350 (3 people)

Saumon baldaquin: double bed, single bed: FF265 (2 people) FF350 (3 people)

Jaune & Bleue & Verte: shower, wash basin, double bed: FF265

Extra bed: 50FF
Reduction: 01.09 – 30.06 and 2 nights

Capacity: 12 people

— On the A63 take the Biarritz Exit. Take the N10 towards Bidart for 3km. At the set of traffic lights by 'Monsieur Bricolage', turn left towards Ahetze for 4km. At the church, go towards St Peel sur Nivelle for 300m. Turn right on to the 'chemin d'Ithurraldia' then take the 2nd lane on the left. The house is at the end.

Eliane CHARDIET

«Villa Erresinolettean»
4, rue de la Tour
64500 CIBOURE

tel: (0) 5 59 47 87 88
fax: (0) 5 59 47 27 41

Private Home

15 km - S W - BIARRITZ
CIBOURE: railway station: 2km
airport: 15km
car essential

Aquitaine

BIARRITZ

PRICE STRUCTURE

3 Bedrooms

Hortensia: lounge, television, shower room with wc, double bed: FF450

Louis XIII: lounge, television, shower room with wc, bathroom, double bed: FF450

Romantique: bridal room, television, bathroom with wc, double bed: FF450

Extra bed: 160FF/2 people

Capacity: 6 people

64.17 BIARRITZ

You have a choice of views from this beautiful modern house: either the Bay of St Jean de Luz or the Pyrenees. A warm welcome with embroided sheets on your bed, quality furniture and decor, real silver, porcelain from Paris and spacious bedrooms. Well worth a detour! Fleur de Soleil member.

PROPERTY

✱✱✱

private parking, garden, hosts have pets, pets not accepted, babies welcome, free cot, swimming pool, hiking, cycling, sea or lake watersports, fishing 1km, golf 2km, interesting flora 2km, mushroom picking 2km, hunting 10km, river watersports 15km, gliding 20km

Adequate English spoken

— On the A63 towards Spain Exit number 2, St Jean de Luz-Sud and follow the signs towards Ciboure. 200m after the traffic-lights, follow signs to Tour de Bordagain. 100m before the tower, look for the blue gate with the weeping willow.

64.19 BIARRITZ

Annette ROCAFORT

20 bis, rue de Tartillon
64600 ANGLET

tel: (0) 5 59 03 55 68

Private Home

Annette will give you a warm welcome to her home, situated in a residential area. This is a very quiet place, and you will love relaxing in her pleasant little garden after visiting the Basque country. Biarritz is 3km away, and the beach 2km away.

PROPERTY

✱✱

private parking, garden, hosts have pets, pets not accepted, dinner available, packed lunch, babies welcome, free cot, cycling 2km, fishing 3km, sea or lake watersports 3km, interesting flora 5km, mushroom picking 10km, birdwatching 10km, river watersports 15km, gliding 15km, winter sports 80km

Fluent English spoken

PRICE STRUCTURE

2 Bedrooms

First room: double bed, single bed (Childrens size): FF240 (2 people) FF240 (3 people)

Second room: twin beds: FF240

Extra bed: 90FF

Capacity: 5 people

BIARRITZ
ANGLET: will collect from station,
railway station: 5km
airport: 4km
— From the A63, take the Biarritz La Négresse Exit. Head towards Anglet, Cinq Cantons, Plage de la Chambre d'Amour.

64.16 PAU

Michèle DUFOUR

«La Benjamine»
Quartier Candeloup
64360 MONEIN

tel: (0) 5 59 21 37 09
fax: (0) 5 59 21 32 90

Residence of Character

This old farmhouse has just been modernised, and is as good as new. It is particularly geared for receiving groups. Here, there is lots of space and a beautiful view over the Pyrenees. This is also the Jurançon wine country, and an ideal place for excursions, walking and ... singing!

PROPERTY

✱

Off street parking, garden, TV lounge, hosts have pets, pets not accepted, telephone, dinner available, kitchen, babies welcome, free cot, closed: 02/01-31/01, hiking, cycling, fishing 5km, hunting 5km, mushroom picking 5km, sea or lake watersports 5km, birdwatching 10km, river watersports 20km, winter sports 45km, gliding 45km

Basic English spoken

PRICE STRUCTURE

9 Bedrooms

First room: wash basin, double bed, single bed: FF170 (2 people) FF240 (3 people)

Second room & seventh room: double bed, single bed: FF170 (2 people) FF240 (3 people)

Third room: 3 single beds: FF170 (2 people) FF240 (3 people)

Fourth room, eighth room & ninth room: 2 single beds: FF170

Fifth room: 4 single beds: FF170 (2 people) FF320 (4 people)

Sixth room: 6 single beds: FF170 (2 people) FF450 (6 people)

Reduction: groups

Capacity: 28 people

25 km - S W - PAU
MONEIN: will collect from station,
railway station: 25km
airport: 25km
car essential
— At Pau, head for Bayonne via Lescar. There, turn left towards Mourenx(D2). After Tarsacq turn left (D2) towards Abos-Monein. The house is on the D9 towards Oloron, 5km after Monein.

Marie-Jeanne BACHOC

«Maison Etchemendigaraya»
64780 SUHESCUN

tel: (0) 5 59 37 60 83
E-mail: bruno.bachoc@wanadoo.fr

Farm

12 km - N - ST JEAN PIED DE PORT
SUHESCUN: railway station: 12km
airport: 45km
car essential

64.10 ST JEAN PIED DE PORT

This beautiful farm, with lots of character, dates from the 17th century and is in the heart of the Basque country. A warm farmhouse welcome awaits you. Be sure to go to St Jean Pied de Port (with numerous restaurants) and try "pelote Basque". On sale: Farm produce.

PROPERTY

✱✱

Off street parking, TV lounge, hosts have pets, telephone, dinner available, kitchen, packed lunch, babies welcome, free cot, hiking, cycling, river watersports 10km, winter sports 30km

PRICE STRUCTURE

2 Bedrooms and 1 Suite

First room & second room: shower room with wc, double bed: FF220

Suite: along corridor bathroom with wc, double bed, 2 single beds: FF220 (2 people) FF440 (4 people)

Extra bed: 50FF

Capacity: 8 people

— In St Jean Pied de Port go towards St Palais and turn left on to the D22 towards Lopeinea and Suhescun. In the village, go in the direction of the 'Camping'.

Sens
10
Châteaudun
45
Montargis
ORLÉANS
Auxerre
89
Blois
41
BOURGOGNE
21
DIJON
Vierzon
37
58
Bourges
Beaune
Nevers
Autun
CENTRE
18
Châtellerault
Châtsauroux
36
Chalon-sur-Saône
71
POITIERS
Moulins
86
Montluçon
03
POITOU
CHARENTE
Macon
Vichy
Guéret
23
Roanne
87
69
16
CLERMONT-FERRAND
LIMOGES
Thiers
RHÔNE-ALPES
LIMOUSIN
LYON
63
42
Angoulême
Vienne
AUVERGNE
St.-Etienne
19
Tulle
Périgueux
15
43
Brive
le Puy
24
Valence
AQUITAINE
Aurillac
07
Bergerac
Privas
46
Mende
48
Villeneuve
Cahors
Rodez
47
Agen
12
Alès
84
Millau
82
30
Avignon
Montauban
Albi
LANGUEDOC-ROUSSILLON
MIDI-PYRÉNÉES
81
Nimes
13
Arles
32
Auch
TOULOUSE
Castres
Béziers
MONTPELLIER
31
34

Nicole & Jacques
BEAUREGARD

«Château de Longeville»
03240 DEUX-CHAISES

tel: (0) 4 70 47 32 91
fax: (0) 4 70 47 33 84

Château

10 km - N E - MONTMARAULT
DEUX-CHAISES: will collect from station,
railway station: 35km
airport: 80km

PRICE STRUCTURE

3 Bedrooms and 1 Suite

Buckingham, Louis XV & Frédéric Chopin: bathroom with wc, double bed: FF450

George Sand: bathroom with wc, double bed, 2 single beds: FF450 (2 people) FF650 (4 people)

Capacity: 10 people

03.01 MONTMARAULT

A 19th century château in the heart of the Bourbonnais, where the Roman influence is always present. Nicole and Jacques have just restored this place and recreate unforgettable evenings in the beautiful period surroundings of their home. ... Fantastic!

PROPERTY

✱✱✱✱

private parking, extensive grounds, TV lounge, hosts have pets, pets not accepted, dinner available, non smoking, hiking, cycling, mushroom picking, river watersports 20km, golf 35km

— On the A71, take the Exit 'Montmarault' and the N145 towards Moulins. Exit Deux-Chaises and follow the signs 'Chambres d'hotes'.

Francis & Gillian DEGNAN

«La Charvière»
St Priest en Murat
03390 MONTMARAULT

tel: (0) 4 70 07 38 24
fax: (0) 4 70 02 91 27

Farm

5 km - N W - MONTMARAULT
ST PRIEST EN MURAT: will collect from station,
railway station: 30km
airport: 70km

03.03 MONTMARAULT

Gillian and Francis, an English couple, will welcome you with great warmth and kindness, and you will be introduced to their pedigree pets. Their attention to detail and your well-being, gives a really cosy feeling to their farmhouse. Excellent walks nearby.

PROPERTY

✱✱✱

Off street parking, garden, TV lounge, hosts have pets, telephone, dinner available, babies welcome, free cot, swimming pool, hiking, cycling, fishing 5km, hunting 5km, mushroom picking 10km, sea or lake watersports 20km

Fluent English spoken

— On the A71, take the Exit 'Montmarault' and the D68 towards Chappes for 5km. Follow the signs on your right.

PRICE STRUCTURE

2 Bedrooms and 2 Apartments

First room: bathroom with wc, 2 double beds: FF240 (2 people) FF340 (4 people)

Second room: shower room with wc, double bed, single bed: FF240 (2 people) FF300 (3 people)

Gite 1: lounge, television, kitchen, shower room with wc, 3 double beds, single bed: FF240 (2 people) FF560 (7 people)

Gite 2: lounge, television, kitchen, shower room with wc, double bed, twin beds: FF240 (2 people) FF340 (4 people)

Extra bed: 40FF
Reduction: 01.09 – 30.06 and 7 nights and groups

Capacity: 18 people

Chantal CHATEAU

«Les Gîtes de Bord»
03170 DOYET

tel: (0) 4 70 07 74 83
fax: (0) 4 70 07 36 07

Private Home

18 km - W - MONTMARAULT
BORD: will collect from station, railway station: 15km
airport: 95km
car essential

03.09 MONTMARAULT

Here, you will be staying in a tastefully restored old farmhouse. The three separate cottages are fully-equipped and extremely comfortable. The grounds are magnificent. Your hosts, who are now retired, have travelled widely and continue to keep themselves busy.

PRICE STRUCTURE

3 Apartments

La Grange: lounge, television, telephone, kitchen, shower room with wc, bathroom, double bed: FF290

La Réserve: lounge, television, telephone, kitchen, shower room with wc, bathroom, wc, double bed, 2 single beds, childrens size: FF290 (2 people) FF580 (4 people)

Le Verger: lounge, television, telephone, kitchen, bathroom with wc, double bed, 2 single beds: FF290 (2 people) FF580 (4 people)

Reduction: 7 nights

Capacity: 10 people

PROPERTY

***

Off street parking, extensive grounds, TV lounge, hosts have pets, telephone, dinner available, kitchen, babies welcome, free cot, wheelchair access, hiking, cycling, hunting, mushroom picking 2km, fishing 3km, golf 12km, sea or lake watersports 18km, river watersports 40km, interesting flora 45km

Fluent English spoken

— From the A71, take the N145 towards Montluçon. At Le Copt, turn right 150m after the hotel "Est-Ouest". Pass through the hamlet of Bord (signposted).

Michèle & Alain LAFON

Le Bourg
15130 GIOU DE
MAMOU

tel: (0) 4 71 64 51 55

Residence of Character

7 km - E -
AURILLAC
GIOU DE MAMOU:
will collect from
station,
railway station: 8km
airport: 8km
car essential

15.06 MONTMARAULT

This charming 19th century house with lots of character is near to the Cantal Mountains. There is a nice contrast between the rugged exterior stone walls and the bright pastel shades inside. The charm of the interior decor, the warm welcome and the mass of tourist information available, give you all you need for an excellent stay. Fleur de Soleil member.

PROPERTY

✱✱✱

Off street parking, garden, pets not accepted, non smoking, hiking, cycling, fishing, hunting, interesting flora, golf 4km, sea or lake watersports 20km, winter sports 25km

Basic English spoken

PRICE STRUCTURE

4 Bedrooms

Campagne: bathroom with wc, double bed: FF270

Tilleul: shower room with wc, twin beds: FF290

Gentiane & Croix des Champs: shower room with wc, double bed, single bed: FF290 (2 people) FF370 (3 people)

Extra bed: 80FF
Reduction: 01.09 – 30.06 and 5 nights and groups

Capacity: 10 people

— At Aurillac, take the N122 towards Murat. After 7 km, turn left towards Giou de Mamou. The house in the centre of the village (look for the B&B France sign).

Jean-Louis WELSCH

«Château de Courbelimagne»
15800 RAULHAC

tel: (0) 4 71 49 58 25
fax: (0) 4 71 49 58 25

Château

29 km - E - AURILLAC
RAULHAC: will collect from station,
railway station: 25km
airport: 70km
car essential

15.07 AURILLAC

A 16th century château, 700 metres up amongst the trees. Jean-Louis and his wife will welcome you to their home with its cosy ambience and candle-lit dinners. You will be charmed by the helpfulness of your hosts, their beautiful house and all its facilities. Weddings can be held in the château's chapel.

PRICE STRUCTURE

3 Bedrooms and 2 Suites

First room, second room & Alsacienne: shower room with wc, double bed: FF450

Suite Henry II: shower room with wc, double bed, single bed: FF500 (2 people) FF650 (3 people)

Suite Royale: bathroom with wc, double bed, single bed: FF500 (2 people) FF650 (3 people)

Extra bed: 100FF
Reduction: 4 nights and children

Capacity: 12 people

PROPERTY

****

private parking, extensive grounds, TV lounge, hosts have pets, telephone, dinner available, packed lunch, babies welcome, free cot, closed: 30/09-15/04, hiking, cycling, hunting, mushroom picking, fishing 2km, sea or lake watersports 10km, river watersports 10km, gliding 15km, interesting flora 20km

Adequate English spoken

— From Aurillac, take the D990 towards Mur de Barrez. Go through Raulhac (still heading towards Mur de Barrez) on the D660. The château is situated 4km further on, on the left.

Claude BRUEL

Aubespeyre de Junhac
15120 MONTSALVY

tel: (0) 4 71 49 22 70/
29 43

Private Home

30 km - S -
AURILLAC
AUBESPEYRE:
railway station: 40km
airport: 40km
car essential

15.09 AURILLAC

750m up in the heart of the country between Auvergne and Rouergue, Claude will welcome you as a friend. He will be delighted to guide and advise you on your trips throughout this region, which he knows particularly well. The house is simple and very well designed. Do not miss Conques.

PROPERTY

✱✱

Off street parking, extensive grounds, TV lounge, pets not accepted, telephone, closed: 30/11-01/03, hiking, fishing, hunting, interesting flora, mushroom picking, cycling 4km, sea or lake watersports 4km, golf 40km

PRICE STRUCTURE

6 Bedrooms

First room: bathroom, wc, double bed, single bed: FF240 (2 people) FF270 (3 people)

Second, third and fifth rooms: shower room with wc, wash basin, double bed: FF240

Fourth room: wash basin, 2 double beds: FF220 (2 people) FF300 (4 people)

Sixth room: wash basin, double bed, single bed: FF220 (2 people) FF240 (3 people)

Reduction: 01.09 – 30.06 and groups

Capacity: 16 people

— At Aurillac, take the D920 as far as Montsalvy, and then the D41 on the right towards Aubespeyre. In Aubesperre, follow the signs.

Jacqueline & Laurent LENA

«Le Cambon»
15130 ARPAJON SUR CERE

tel: (0) 4 71 63 52 49

Private Home

4 km - S - AURILLAC
ARPAJON SUR CERE: will collect from station,
railway station: 4km
airport: 4km
car essential

Auvergne

AURILLAC

15.10 AURILLAC

10 minutes from Aurillac, this old farmhouse in the heart of the countryside is the ideal spot for nature and plant lovers. Be sure to take Jacqueline's advice on what to do, but a must is a flight over Le Cantal in a private aircraft or a hot air balloon; an unforgettable experience. Do not miss their dinners, using their own produce from the garden.

PRICE STRUCTURE

3 Bedrooms

First room & second room: television, shower, double bed: FF260

Third room: television, shower, double bed, twin beds: FF280 (2 people) FF380 (4 people)

Reduction: 4 nights

Capacity: 8 people

PROPERTY

✱✱

private parking, garden, TV lounge, telephone, dinner available, packed lunch, babies welcome, free cot, hiking, fishing, hunting, mushroom picking, cycling 2km, golf 6km, sea or lake watersports 10km, winter sports 30km, birdwatching 50km

— At Aurillac, take the D920 towards Rodez and Arpajon. Cross Arpajon, and after 2km, just before the timber yard, turn right and follow signs to Le Cambon. When you reach this hamlet, it is the first house on the left.

Marie-Claude LOUIS-FERT

La Malétie
15310 TOURNEMIRE

tel: (0) 4 71 47 63 49
fax: (0) 4 71 47 65 81

Private Home

20 km - N -
AURILLAC
TOURNEMIRE:
railway station: 20km
airport: 20km
car essential

15.11 AURILLAC

The village of Tournemire has been selected as one of the "most beautiful villages in France", and is at 900m altitude. Your hostess will be delighted to share her knowledge and tips with you on what to see in the area. Fleur de Soleil member.

PRICE STRUCTURE

1 Suite bathroom with wc, 4 single beds: FF200 (2 people) FF400 (4 people)

Capacity: 4 people

PROPERTY

✱✱✱

Off street parking, pets not accepted, closed: 01/11-15/04

English spoken

— At Aurillac, take the D992 direct to St. Cernin. From there, take the D160 as far as Tournemire, then the D60 towards St. Projet, for 1km.

Auvergne

MAURIAC

Jean-Michel & Annie BESSON

«Château de Bassignac»
15240 BASSIGNAC

tel: (0) 4 71 40 82 82
fax: (0) 4 71 40 82 82

Flat/Apartment

20 km - N E - MAURIAC BASSIGNAC: airport: 75km car essential

PRICE STRUCTURE

3 Bedrooms and 1 Suite

Verte(Tour arrière): bathroom with wc, double bed: FF520

Jaune/Rouge: lounge, bathroom with wc, double bed, single bed: FF520 (2 people) FF750 (3 people)

Rose: bridal room, lounge, bathroom with wc, twin beds: FF620

Pêche: shower room with wc, double bed: FF340

Extra bed: 130FF
Reduction: 3 nights

Capacity: 9 people

15.03 MAURIAC

Jean-Michel is an artist, Annie a wonderful cook. Together they will introduce you to "La vie de château" in an elegant, family atmosphere. On the edge of the national park "Les Volcans", this is a verdant, wooded area, where the meadows are full of wild flowers.

PROPERTY

****

Off street parking, extensive grounds, lounge, hosts have pets, telephone, dinner available, hiking, fishing, interesting flora, mushroom picking, cycling 10km, sea or lake watersports 10km

Adequate English spoken

— In Mauriac, take the D922 towards Bort les Orgues. 4km before Ydes, turn right on to the D422 and follow the signs "Bassignac Eglise".

Bernadette & Jean-Pierre
LA GANE

«Maison de la Ronade»

15140 SALERS

tel: (0) 4 71 40 72 91
fax: (0) 4 71 40 77 39

Private Home

SALERS: Railway station: 42 km, airport: 45 km, car essential

15.12 AURILLAC

This hotel familial, dating from the 14th–18th centuries is in the heart of the medieval town. The family have lived here for 400 years, and descend from the magistrate, Andre de la Ronade. There is a nice, welcoming family atmosphere and a charming walled garden. Guided tours arranged. Suggested excursions: the Upper Auvergne, chateaux and Roman churches. The area is also well known for its fishing and gastronomy

PROPERTY

✱✱✱

safe off street parking garden, pets not accepted, no smoking, hiking, fishing

English spoken

— At Aurillac, take the D992 direct to St. Cernin. From there, take the D160 as far as Tournemire, then the D60 towards St. Projet, for 1km.

PRICE STRUCTURE

1 Suite

Frédéric: telephone, bathroom with wc, double bed: FF230 (2 people)

Valentine: telephone, twin beds: FF280 (2 people)

Extra bed: 50FF
Capacity: 4 people

19.08 MAURIAC

This 17th century manor house had been abandoned for 50 years until Annie-Claude and Noël started enthusiastically restoring it.. The fireplace is very impressive. Try the long carriage rides through the beautiful Corrèze countryside. On sale: Farm and garden produce, jam, dried flowers.

PROPERTY

✱✱✱

Off street parking, extensive grounds, TV lounge, hosts have pets, telephone, dinner available, 2 years minimum age, hiking, cycling, fishing, hunting, mushroom picking, river watersports, sea or lake watersports 10km, winter sports 30km, gliding 30km

English spoken

PRICE STRUCTURE

2 Bedrooms

Emeraude: television, shower room with wc, double bed: FF250

Rose: shower room with wc, double bed: FF200

Reduction: 01.10 – 01.05

Capacity: 4 people

Annie Claude & Noël CLERGOT

«Manoir des Ribières»
Attelage de Xaintrie
19220 ST JULIEN AUX BOIS

tel: (0) 5 55 28 74 96
fax: (0) 5 55 28 74 96

Residence of Character

20 km - S W - MAURIAC
ST JULIEN AUX BOIS:
will collect from station,
railway station: 50km
airport: 50km
car essential
— At Mauriac take the D680 for 13km. Then at Pléaux take the D980 towards St Privas for 6km. At St Julien aux Bois take the D111 and follow the signs "Attelage de Xaintrie".

Eric & Isabelle BON-NEVIALLE

«Centre Equestre de Jax»
Chastenuel
43230 JAX

Tel: (0) 4 71 74 25 57/ 27 69
fax: (0) 4 71 74 21 41

Private Home

30 km - N W - PUY EN VELAY CHASTENUEL: airport: 10km car essential — In Le Puy, take the N102 for 30km towards Clermont-Ferrand. 2km after Fix-St Geneys, turn right and follow the signs for 2km through the woods.

43.02 PUY EN VELAY

This friendly young couple welcome you in the heart of the Auvergne. At the foot of the extinct volcanoes, between the wooded mountain sides and the green valleys, you will savour the warmth of this restored old farmhouse, where life goes on at its own pace.

PROPERTY

✱✱

Off street parking, garden, TV lounge, hosts have pets, dinner available, packed lunch, riding, hiking, mushroom picking, winter sports, cycling 10km, fishing 15km, river watersports 15km

Adequate English spoken

PRICE STRUCTURE

3 Bedrooms

Rose: shower room with wc, double bed, single bed: FF230 (2 people) FF260 (3 people)

Verte: shower room with wc, double bed, twin beds: FF230

Capacity: 7 people

Daniel & Chantal CLAVEL

«La Paravent»
43700 CHASPINHAC

tel: (0) 4 71 03 54 75

Private Home

11 km - N - PUY EN VELAY CHASPINHAC: car essential — At Le Puy, take the N88 towards St Etienne for 5km. Turn left on to the D156 towards Chaspinhac.

43.04 PUY EN VELAY

Daniel and Chantal are very friendly. Their large old farm-house is very comfortable, quiet and with a beautiful view. The rooms are spacious, bright and pleasant and there is a shower and wash-hand basin in the rooms. Breakfast is served by the fireplace.

PROPERTY

✱✱✱

Off street parking, garden, pets not accepted, dinner available, hiking, mushroom picking, fishing 3km

PRICE STRUCTURE

6 Bedroom

First & sixth room: shower room with wc, wash basin, twin beds: FF250

Second, third, fourth & fifth room: shower room with wc, wash basin, double bed: FF250

Capacity: 12 people

Jacqueline CHAILLY

«La Jacquerolle»
Rue Maréchal
43160 LA CHAISE DIEU

tel: (0) 4 71 00 07 52

Private Home

35 km - N W - PUY EN VELAY
LA CHAISE DIEU:
railway station: 40km
airport: 40km
car essential

43.05 PUY EN VELAY

La Chaise Dieu is well-known for the wonderful atmosphere of its abbey and its famous sacred music festival at the end of August. Now we would add Jacqueline's hospitality, her delicious meals and her comfortable home as another good reason to return here regularly. On sale: Local produce, honey.

PROPERTY

✱✱✱

off street parking, garden, lounge, pets not accepted, dinner available, hiking, cycling, interesting flora, mushroom picking, winter sports, sea or lake watersports 2km, fishing 5km

English spoken

PRICE STRUCTURE

5 Bedrooms

Bleue: along corridor shower room with wc, along corridor bathroom, double bed: FF300

Rose: shower room with wc, double bed, 2 single bed: FF300 (2 people) FF440 (4 people)

Fleur rose: shower room with wc, double bed, single bed: FF300 (2 people) FF380 (3 people)

Fleur jaune: shower room with wc, double bed, single bed: FF300 (2 people) FF380 (3 people)

Blanche: along corridor shower room with wc, twin beds: FF300

Extra bed: 100FF
Reduction: 01.09 – 01.06 and 7 nights

Capacity: 14 people

— At Le Puy take the N102 for 8km. At Borne take the D906 for 27km. The house is situated below the abbey, below the square with the memorial.

Henriette MARCHAND

«Château de Pasredon»
63500 ST REMY DE
CHARGNAT

tel: (0) 4 73 71 00 67
fax: (0) 4 73 71 08 72

Château

63.01 ISSOIRE

Henriette will give you a warm welcome. She knows this area like the back of her hand and will help you organise your visits so that you do not miss the volcanoes, Roman churches and châteaux unique to this region. Nearby there is a gastronomic restaurant that should not be missed.

PROPERTY

✱✱✱✱

off street parking, extensive grounds, tv lounge, hosts have pets, pets not accepted, babies welcome, free cot, non smoking, tennis, closed: 1/11-1/04, hiking, cycling, fishing 5km, sea or lake watersports 5km, river watersports 6km, gliding 6km, interesting flora 35km, birdwatching 35km, golf course 40km

Adequate English spoken

6 km - S E - ISSOIRE ST REMY DE CHARGNAT: hosts will collect from station
railway station: 8km
airport: 40km
car essential
— On the A75, take Exit N°13 for Issoire then the D999 towards St Germain l'Herm. The house is on the right, as you leave St Rémy

PRICE STRUCTURE

6 Bedrooms

Reine Margot: bridal room, bathroom with wc, shower, double bed: FF470

Jaune: bathroom with wc, 2 single beds: FF425

Bleue: bathroom with wc, double bed: FF385

Domes: lounge, bathroom with wc, shower, 2 single beds: FF555

Comtesse: shower room with wc, double bed: FF385

Polonaise: bathroom with wc, shower, double bed: FF470

Extra bed: 115FF
Reduction: 4 nights

Capacity: 12 people

Marie-Louise BERTHUY

«Auberge de Vazerat»
15500 MASSIAC

tel: (0) 4 71 23 03 05
fax: (0) 4 71 23 03 05

Farm

30 km - S - ISSOIRE
MASSIAC: hosts will collect from station
railway station: 2km
airport: 70km

15.05 ISSOIRE

On the main north-south route via the pleasant A75, this is a good place to stop overnight in green countryside, off the beaten track. Marie-Louise is not far from the autoroute, and her magnificent ferme-auberge serves local specialities in a superb dining room. Supplement for pets: 22FF per day. OVERNIGHT STOPS (341-365FF for two persons).

PROPERTY

✱✱

off street parking, hosts have pets, telephone, dinner available, swimming pool, 3 nights minimum stay, 01/08-20/08, hiking, cycling, fishing, hunting, interesting flora, mushroom picking, river watersports 25km, birdwatching 40km, sea or lake watersports 40km, winter sports 40km

PRICE STRUCTURE

4 Bedrooms and 1 Suite

First room: shower room with wc, washbasin, double bed, single bed: FF260 (2 people) FF340 (3 people)

Second room: shower room with wc, washbasin, twin beds: FF260

Third room & fourth room: shower room with wc, washbasin, double bed, single bed: FF240 (2 people) FF290 (3 people)

Fifth/sixth rooms: shower room with wc, washbasin, double bed, 2 single beds: FF280 (2 people) FF400 (4 people)

Reduction: 15.09 – 15.06 and 4 nights and groups

Capacity: 15 people

— On the A75 Exit number 23 or 24 towards Massiac. After the church, follow the signs.

Brigitte LAROYE

7, rue du 8 Mai
63590 CUNLHAT

tel: (0) 4 73 72 20 87

Residence of Character

63.03 THIERS

This large, impressive house is very comfortable, and here you will enjoy the atmosphere of grandmother's era. It is in the village and all the rooms overlook the wooded garden.

PROPERTY

✸✸✸

off street parking, garden, lounge, hosts have pets, pets not accepted, dinner available, babies welcome, free cot, riding, hiking, cycling, fishing, interesting flora, mushroom picking, sea or lake watersports, birdwatching 40km, golf course 50km, winter sports 50km

English spoken

40 km - S - THIERS
CUNLHAT:
airport: 53km
car essential
— From the A72, Exit Thiers-Ouest, take the D906 towards Ambert. 11km after Courpière, turn right on to the D225 towards Cunlhat. The house is behind the church (signposted).

PRICE STRUCTURE

4 Bedrooms

Rez de Chaussée-Louis XVI: shower room with wc, double bed, 2 single beds: FF330 (2 people) FF400 (4 people)

1930 & Fleurie: shower room with wc, double bed: FF280

Glycine: bathroom with wc, double bed, FF300

Extra bed: 100FF

Capacity: 10 people

Bernard COSTE

«La Croix Blanche»
42440 LES SALLES

tel: (0) 4 77 24 93 86
fax: (0) 4 77 24 93 86
E-mail:mcbedu@
club-internet.fr

Private Home

25 km - E - THIERS
LES SALLES: hosts will collect from station
railway station: 4km
airport: 45km

42.13 THIERS

You will find a cool spring rising just by the conservatory... The ambience is friendly in this old farm-house which has been completely restored. Although only 2km from the A72, it is situated in a totally unspoilt piece of countryside.

PROPERTY

✱✱

private parking, garden, tv lounge, hosts have pets, pets not accepted, dinner available, babies welcome, free cot, tennis, riding, cycling, fishing, hunting, interesting flora, mushroom picking, golf course 40km

English spoken

PRICE STRUCTURE

3 Bedrooms

First room: double bed: FF290

Bleu: double bed: FF290

Third room: double bed, single bed: FF330 (2 people) FF330 (3 people)

Capacity: 7 people

— On the A72 take Exit 4 to Noiretable. Turn right 100m after the autoroute «péage» (tollbooths). Then go to the top of the village of Salles towards Cervières. After 150m stay on the right-hand side of the road and it is the first farm on the

15.02 BORT LES ORGUES

Jean GÉRARD

Mérigot
15270 CHAMPS / TARENTAINE

tel: (0) 4 71 78 71 36

Farm

12 km - E - BORT LES ORGUES MERIGOT: hosts will collect from station railway station: 12km airport: 80km:car essential — In Bort les Orgues, take the D679 towards Champs sur Tarentaise where you turn left on to the D22 for 5km towards Marchal Besse then follow the signs to "Camping de l'Etang"

A large farm in the heart of the country, completely peaceful with a superb view of the Puy de Sancy. Family atmosphere and delicious regional cooking washed down with the local wine. An interesting architectural heritage and themed walks.

PROPERTY

✸✸

private parking, garden, pets not accepted, dinner available, packed lunch, babies welcome, free cot, non smoking, hiking, cycling, fishing, hunting, mushroom picking, sea or lake watersports 4km, winter sports 20/30km

Basic English spoken

PRICE STRUCTURE

5 Bedrooms

Digitale, Bruyère & Gentiane: shower room with wc, double bed, single bed: FF250 (2 people) FF330 (3 people)

Oeillet: shower, washbasin, double bed: FF210

Campanule: shower, double bed, single bed: FF210 (2 people) FF280 (3 people)

Extra bed: 85FF
Reduction: 01.10 – 31.05 and 3 nights and groups

Capacity: 14 people

19.07 BRIVE LA GAILLARDE

Jacqueline VERLHAC

Belveyre
19600 NESPOULS

tel: (0) 5 55 85 82 58

Farm

This is an unusual village, in white stone. If Jacqueline is not in the house, you will probably find her on her tractor...She is restoring her farmhouse, and the bedrooms are very comfortable. Sit in the shade of the vine, and soak up the peace and quiet of this place.

PROPERTY

✸

private parking, garden, television, pets not accepted, dinner available, babies welcome, free cot, hiking, birdwatching, sea or lake watersports 6km, golf course 10km, fishing 10km, river watersports 20km

PRICE STRUCTURE

5 Bedroom

Bleu: shower room with wc, washbasin, double bed: FF200

Rose & Beige: shower room with wc, washbasin, double bed, single bed: FF200 (2 people) FF250 (3 people)

Sous les combles-Rouge: bathroom with wc, washbasin, double bed, single bed: FF200 (2 people) FF250 (3 people)

Sous les combles-Verte: bathroom with wc, washbasin, double bed, 2 single beds: FF200 (2 people) FF300 (4 people)

Capacity: 15 people

15 km - S - BRIVE LA GAILLARDE BELVEYRE NESPOULS: railway station: 15km airport: 15km car essential — From the A20, take Exit 53, 10km from Brive. Turn right on to the D19 towards Larche and right towards Belveyre. Follow the signs "gîte de la ferme" and then look for the B&B France (France) sign.

19.05 TULLE

Sylvie & André RICHARD
SOUDANT

«Ferme Equestre de Leix»
Leix
19320 CLERGOUX

tel: (0) 5 55 27 75 49
fax: (0) 5 55 27 75 49

Farm

Wonderful food. You are also in the middle of 20 hectares of fields and woods and, whether you are a beginner or an expert, your hosts will be pleased to accompany you to explore this area on horseback. Well worth a stop, even if only overnight.

21 km - E - TULLE
CLERGOUX: railway station: 21km
car essential
— At Tulle take the D978 towards Mauriac for 21km. At the hamlet of Les Cambuzes turn right and follow the signs to "chambres d'hotes-ferme équestre" for 3km on the C5 road.

PROPERTY

✸✸

off street parking, extensive grounds, hosts have pets, dinner available, packed lunch, babies welcome, free cot, riding, hiking, cycling, fishing, hunting, interesting flora, mushroom picking, birdwatching, sea or lake watersports 8km, river watersports 20km

Fluent English spoken

PRICE STRUCTURE

5 Bedrooms

Jaune: shower room with wc, washbasin, double bed: FF260

Vanille - Mezzanine: shower room with wc, washbasin, double bed, twin beds: FF260 (2 people) FF420 (4 people)

Saumon-Mezzanine: shower room with wc, washbasin, double bed, 2 single bedS: FF260 (2 people) FF420 (4 people)

Extra bed: 80FF
Reduction: 5 nights and groups

Capacity: 10 people

23.02 GUERET

Michel & Martine
LIMOUSIN

«Ferme de Montenon»
Montenon
23240 LE GRAND
BOURG

tel: (0) 5 55 81 30 00

Farm

This farm is perched on top of a hill. You will love the peace and quiet and lack of pollution. There is a rich variety of flora and fauna, with birds, deer and fish in abundance. The area is known for its music festivals and an Impressionist school of painting. On sale: Regional produce

PROPERTY

✸✸✸

off street parking, garden, lounge, pets not accepted, dinner available, swimming pool, closed: 3/01-31/01, hiking, cycling, fishing, mushroom picking, sea or lake watersports 15km, river watersports 15km, golf course 25km

Fluent English spoken

PRICE STRUCTURE

5 Bedrooms

Anzème & Crozant: shower room with wc, double bed, 3 single beds: FF250 (2 people) FF490 (5 people)

Aubusson: shower room with wc, twin beds, FF250

Boussac & St Pardoux: shower room with wc, double bed, single bed: FF250 (2 people) FF335 (3 people)

Extra bed: 85FF
Reduction: 4 nights

Capacity: 18 people

20 km - W - GUERET
MONTENON: hosts will collect from station
railway station: 30km
airport: 45km
car essential
— In Guéret, take the D914 towards Le Grand Bourg-Benevent, then the D4 towards Le Grand Bourg-La Brionne. Near the bridge over the river 'La Gartempe', turn left on to the D96 for 2.5km. The farm is on a hill.

Michel DAURIAC

«Domaine du Loubier»
Le Loubier
87420 ST VICTURNIEN

tel: (0) 5 55 03 29 22

Château or
Manor House

4 km - N -
ORADOUR sur
GLANE
LE LOUBIER: hosts
will collect from
station
railway station: 3km
airport: 12km

PRICE STRUCTURE

3 Bedrooms and 1 Suite

Verte: bathroom with wc, double bed, cot: FF270

Jaune: shower room with wc, double bed, single bed: FF270 (2 people) FF320 (3 people)

Bleue: shower room with wc, twin beds, single bed, cot: FF270 (2 people) FF360 (3 people)

Rouge: shower room with wc, washbasin, double bed, 3 single bed: FF270 (2 people) FF500 (5 people)

Extra bed: 100FF
Reduction: 5 nights

Capacity: 13 people

87.08 ORADOUR SUR GLANE

Michel's two grown-up daughters will welcome you to his home in two hectares of ground, surrounded by magnificent trees. Be sure to visit the Gallo-Roman ruins nearby, the Limoges Porcelain Museum and Oradour sur Glane.

PROPERTY

✱✱✱

private parking, extensive grounds, tv lounge, hosts have pets, dinner available, kitchen, packed lunch, babies welcome, free cot, wheelchair facilities, hiking, cycling, mushroom picking, birdwatching, fishing 2km, river watersports 3km, golf course 10km, interesting flora 20km, sea or lake watersports 25km

Fluent English spoken

— At Oradour, head for Limoges then turn right on to the D3. At the crossroads with the N141, there is a stop, you turn right into dead-end road. Continue for 200m

Soissons
Reims
Verdun
METZ
55
LORRAINE
CHÂLONS
51
Bar-le-Duc
Vitry
Evry
ILE DE FRANCE
St. Dizier
77
CHAMPAGNE-
ARDENNE
91
Melun
Fontainebleau
Neufchâteau
Troyes
Sens
52
10
Chaumont
Montargis
Langres
45
Auxerre
89
FRANCHE-
COMTE
21
DIJON
CENTRE
BESANÇON
BOURGOGNE
58
Bourges
Dole
Beaune
Nevers
Autun
18
Chalon-sur-
Saône
39
71
Lons
Moulins
Montluçon
03
Macon
AUVERGNE
Bourg
Vichy
01
Roanne
69
CLERMONT-
FERRAND
Thiers
RHÔNE-
ALPES
LYON
Aix-les-
Bains
63
42

Patrick & Françoise ROCHET

«Château d'Ecutigny»
21360 ECUTIGNY

tel: (0) 3 80 20 19 14
fax: (0) 3 80 20 19 15

Château

20 km - N W - BEAUNE
ECUTIGNY: hosts will collect from station
railway station 25km
airport 60km

21.04 BEAUNE

This château, dating from the 12th and 17th centuries, is a listed historic monument situated close to the wine slopes. The owners have restored the place beautifully and with very good taste. You will be offered a welcoming drink in a unique venue. Carriage rides and stabling for horses. On sale: Wine, home-baked bread.

PROPERTY

****

private parking, extensive grounds, tv lounge, hosts have pets, telephone, dinner available, packed lunch, babies welcome, free cot, tennis, riding, hiking, fishing, golf course 25km

Fluent English spoken

— In Beaune, take the D970 towards Bligny sur Ouche then turn left on to the D33 towards Ecutigny.

PRICE STRUCTURE

5 Bedrooms and 1 Suite

au Parquet: television, bathroom with wc, double bed, single bed: FF650 (2 people) FF750 (3 people)

Jaune: television, along corridor bathroom with wc, double bed, single bed: FF500 (2 people) FF600 (3 people)

au Baldaquin: television, shower room with wc, double bed: FF700

Suite: television, shower room with wc, 2 double beds, single bed: FF600 (2 people) FF1100 (5 people)

du Four à Pain: television, bathroom with wc, double bed, single bed: FF650 (2 people) FF750 (3 people)

de la Tour: television, bathroom with wc, double bed: FF500

Extra bed: 100FF

Capacity: 18 people

Christiane de LOISY

«Domaine Comtesse M. de Loisy»
21700 NUITS ST GEORGES

tel: (0) 3 80 61 02 72
fax: (0) 3 80 61 36 14

Residence of Character

Bourgogne

BEAUNE

13 km - N E - BEAUNE
NUITS ST GEORGES: railway station 1km
airport 20km

21.05 BEAUNE

The Countess de Loisy, Master of Wine and a registered guide, welcomes you to her wonderful home with comfortable rooms, furnished with antiques. The splendid salon and the dining room on the ground floor open on to indoor gardens. Please book ahead and do not arrive before 5 p.m.

PRICE STRUCTURE

3 Bedrooms and 2 Suites

Madame: bathroom with wc, double bed: FF800

Monsieur: along corridor bathroom with wc, double bed: FF600

Boudoir: bathroom with wc, twin beds: FF650

Suite Enfants bleus: bathroom with wc, double bed, 4 single beds: FF750 (2 people) FF950 (6 people)

Suite Mademoiselle: shower room with wc, double bed, 4 single beds: FF700 (2 people) FF900 (6 people)

Extra bed: 100FF

Capacity: 18 people

PROPERTY

****

private parking, extensive grounds, lounge, hosts have pets, dinner available, non smoking, closed: 1/11 31/03, 2 nights minimum stay, golf course 16km

Fluent English spoken

— In Beaune, take the A31 towards Dijon. Take Exit Nuits St Georges. Follow the signs to Beaune. The street starts at the 2nd set of traffic lights.

21.19 BEAUNE

This delightful house amongst the vines, welcomes you through its doors to a world of colour and charm. Dominique will give you invaluable tips on how to get the most out of your stay in this wonderful region, whose name is synonymous with gastronomy. This is a very special place, near to the N74 and close to Nuits St Georges.

Dominique PETIN

«La Closerie des Ormes»
21 rue de la Grand'Velle-
Vosne-Romanée 21700
NUITS ST GEORGES

tel: (0) 3 80 62 35 19
fax: (0) 3 80 62 17 59

Residence of character

PROPERTY

✱✱✱✱

private parking, extensive grounds, tv lounge, hosts have pets, telephone, dinner available, packed lunch, babies welcome, free cot, tennis, riding, hiking, fishing, golf course 25km

Fluent English spoken

PRICE STRUCTURE

5 Bedrooms

Les Chats: telephone, along corridor shower room with wc, double bed, single bed: FF500 (2 people) FF700 (3 people)

Les Roses: telephone, along corridor shower room with wc, double bed: FF500

Chapeaux: telephone, bathroom with wc, twin beds: FF550

Provence: television, telephone, along corridor shower room with wc, double bed, single bed: FF450 (2 people) FF650 (3 people)

Bécassine: television, telephone, along corridor shower room with wc, double bed: FF450

Capacity: 12 people

19 km - N - BEAUNE
VOSNE-ROMANEE:
railway station 2km
airport 30km
car essential
— From the A31 towards Beune, Exit Nuits St Georges. Then take the N74 towards Dijon, as far as Vosné-Romanée. At the entrance of the village, take the fourth street on the left. The house is 50 m on the right.

Bourgogne

DIJON

Bertrand BERGEROT

«Château de Rosières»
St Seine sur Vingeanne
21610 FONTAINE FRANÇAISE

tel: (0) 3 80 75 82 53
fax: (0) 3 80 75 82 53

Château

40 km - N E - DIJON
ST SEINE / VINGEANNE:
railway station 40km
airport 40km
car essential

PRICE STRUCTURE

2 Bedrooms and 1 Apartment

Chambre du Puits: along corridor shower room with wc, twin beds: FF250
Etage: bathroom with wc, double bed: FF400
Appartement: lounge, television, kitchen, bathroom with wc, 2 double beds: FF600 (2 people) FF740 (4 people)
Extra Bed: 50 FF
Reduction: 4 nights

Capacity: 8 people

21.07 DIJON

This fortress situated on the edge of Bourgogne, Champagne and Franche-Comté is tastefully furnished. We did not hesitate in giving this place 4 suns as it has so much character, and dominates the Vingeanne valley in the heart of an area steeped in history. Excellent for walking, cycling and horse-riding.

PROPERTY

✱✱✱✱

private parking, extensive grounds, hosts have pets, babies welcome, free cot, riding, hiking, cycling, fishing

Basic English spoken

— On the A31 Dijon-Chaumont autoroute, take the Til-Chatel Exit. Go toward Lux. After Lux, turn left towards Bourberain and Fontaine Française. Continue towards Gray for 5km. St Seine sur Vigeanne is on your right. Follow the signs 'Château de Rosières' for 4km

Patrick BERGER

«Le Vieux Moulin»
21610 FONTAINE
FRANÇAISE

tel: (0) 3 80 75 82 16
fax: (0) 3 80 75 82 16

Residence of character

40 km - N E - DIJON
FONTAINE
FRANCAISE: hosts will collect from station
railway station 37km
airport 40km

21.08 DIJON

Patrick's passions are art, history and archaeology. His home is a beautiful 17th century watermill, completely restored right down to the waterwheel and its associated machinery. You will have some great evenings here. Hikers are welcome. On sale: Home-made jam.

PROPERTY

✱✱✱

off street parking, extensive grounds, hosts have pets, telephone, dinner available, packed lunch, babies welcome, free cot, wheelchair access, swimming pool, riding, hiking, cycling, fishing,

Basic English spoken

— On the A31 Dijon to Chaumont autoroute, Exit number 5 at Til-Chatel. Head towards Fontaine Française via Orville and Chazeuil (15km). Follow the signs in the village.

PRICE STRUCTURE

4 Bedrooms and 2 Apartments

Jardin & Nénuphar: television, kitchen, shower room with wc, double bed, 2 single beds: FF330 (2 people) FF470 (4 people)

Château: shower room with wc, double bed, 3 single beds: FF290 (2 people) FF570 (5 people)

Etang: along corridor bathroom with wc, double bed, single bed: FF290 (2 people) FF430 (3 people)

Piscine: shower room with wc, 2 twin beds: FF290 (2 people) FF430 (4 people)

Terrasse: shower room with wc, double bed: FF290

Extra Bed: 70FF
Reduction: 4 nights & groups

Capacity: 22 people

Peter & Véréna
ZIMMERMANN

9 Grand Chemin
21310 RENÈVE

tel: (0) 3 80 47 78 40
fax: (0) 3 80 47 78 40

Private home

30 km - E - DIJON
RENEVE: airport 30km
car essential
— On the A31, take the Exit Dijon-Arc sur Til. Then take the D70 towards Gray - Vesoul for 20km. At Renève, turn left immediately after the bridge and continue for 1km. The house is on the left at the crossroads.

21.11 DIJON

A lovely Swiss-German couple, Peter and Verena have transformed this old post office into a charming little haven of tranquillity. There is a salon with a fireplace, an unobstructed and relaxing view over the valley, a pleasant swimming pool and flowers everywhere. All this near to the A31 Autoroute.

PROPERTY

**

private parking, extensive grounds, tv lounge, hosts have pets, pets not accepted, dinner available, swimming pool, closed: 01/11-31/03, hiking, cycling, fishing 1km

Fluent English spoken

PRICE STRUCTURE

2 Bedrooms

Rez de Chaussée: shower, wc, twin beds: FF270

First room: Etage shower room with wc, twin beds: FF270

Extra bed: 80FF

Capacity: 4 people

Jeanne ESMONIN

Paquis de Rolanges
21700 ST BERNARD

tel: (0) 3 80 62 81 60
fax: (0) 3 80 62 89 14

Private home

20 km - S - DIJON
ST BERNARD:
railway station 8km
airport 23km
car essential

21.15 DIJON

A warm welcome from this couple in their spotlessly clean home. You are very close to the autoroute but this spot is completely quiet in the middle of the Nuits St Georges vineyards (only 5km from Clos Vougeot). A magical place for lovers of vintage Burgundy. On sale: Honey.

PROPERTY

✱✱✱

private parking, garden, tv lounge, hosts have pets, telephone, wheelchair facilities, non smoking, fishing 1km, hiking 5km

PRICE STRUCTURE

5 Bedrooms

First room: shower room with wc, double bed: FF280

Second room: along corridor bathroom with wc, twin beds: FF320

Third room & fourth room: shower room with wc, double bed: FF320

Fifth room: shower room with wc, double bed: FF300

Reduction: 01/11–31/03 and 7 nights and groups and children

Capacity: 10 people

— From the A31 Exit Nuits St Georges and then take the D8 as far as Boncourt le Bois. In this village take the first on the left which is the D116b towards St Bernard. Follow the signs

François ISTACE

21700 VILLEBICHOT

tel: (0) 3 80 61 22 07
fax: (0) 3 80 61 22 07

Private home

20 km - S - DIJON
VILLEBICHOT:
hosts will collect from station
railway station 9km
car essential

21.17 DIJON

A large house in a small, quiet village near the famous vineyards. You will be captivated by the living room, with a mezzanine that leads to the bedrooms with exposed beams. François has a wonderful collection of African artefacts that he has picked up during his travels there. Bedroom 2 will surprise you with its enormous elephant's tusks!

PRICE STRUCTURE

2 Bedrooms

First room: bathroom with wc, shower, double bed: FF270

Second room: telephone, bathroom with wc, twin beds: FF270

Extra bed: 70FF
Reduction: 01/10–28/02 and 7 nights

Capacity: 4 people

PROPERTY

***

off street parking, garden, tv lounge, hosts have pets, telephone, dinner available, packed lunch, cycling, hiking 1km, fishing 1km, hunting 1km, mushroom picking 1km, golf course 26km

Basic English spoken

— Take the Nuits-St-Georges Exit from the A31, and head towards Agencourt, Boncourt and Villebichot on the D8. With the town hall (mairie) in front of you, head towards St Bernard for 100 metres. The house is on the right.

Monique ANOUILH-PETITHUGUENIN

19, rue Dom Edmond Martène
21000 DIJON

tel: (0) 3 80 63 84 63

Private home

DIJON
airport 5km
car essential

21.22 DIJON

This town house is quiet and has a beautiful walled garden, yet it is only 15 minutes walk from the town centre (there are also buses). This is the capital of Les Ducs de Bourgogne and the famous Burgundy wine region, and Monique will be delighted to advise you on its rich cultural and architectural heritage. Fleur de Soleil member.

PRICE STRUCTURE

1 Suite

First room: bathroom with wc, double bed, single bed: FF200 (2 people) FF360 (3 people)

Capacity: 3 people

PROPERTY

✱✱✱

off street parking, garden, dinner available.

English spoken

— In the centre of Dijon, head for the CHRU (Bocage) area. Then phone your host for detailed directions.

Anne & François
BRUGERE

7 rue Jean Jaurès
21160 COUCHEY

tel: (0) 3 80 52 13 05
fax: (0) 3 80 52 93 20

Private home

21.23 DIJON

You are in the heart of the wine-growing country in deepest Burgundy. This old house, full of character, is on the "Grand Crus" wine route that links Dijon and Nuits St. George via Gevrey Chambertin (4km away). Should you not be interested in wine, there are museums, châteaux and churches nearby and this is a good area for hiking and cycling. On sale: Burgundy wine from their own cellar (wine tastings). Fleur de Soleil member.

PROPERTY

✹✹✹

off street parking, hiking, cycling,

English spoken

8 km - S - DIJON
COUCHEY: railway station 8km
airport 150km
car essential
— Contact your host for detailed directions.

PRICE STRUCTURE

4 Bedrooms

Nuptiale: shower room with wc, bathroom, double bed, single bed: FF320 (2 people) FF400 (3 people)

Verte: shower room with wc, double bed, single bed: FF290 (2 people) FF370 (3 people)

Jaune: shower room with wc, double bed, single bed: FF270 (2 people) FF350 (3 people)

Rose: shower room with wc, double bed: FF270

Capacity: 11 people

Michel & Chantal
RANCE

«La Rente d'Eguilly»
Eguilly
21320 POUILLY EN
AUXOIS

tel: (0) 3 80 90 83 48

Farm

8 km - N W -
POUILLY EN
AUXOIS
EGUILLY: hosts will
collect from station
airport 12km
car essential

21.12 POUILLY EN AUXOIS

Here you will find absolute peace and quiet, not far from the Exit from the A6 autoroute. A beautiful farmhouse in the middle of the countryside and pleasant surroundings. Chantal and Michel offer a warm welcome and, having stopped here once, theirs is an address you will hang on to.

PROPERTY

✱✱

off street parking, garden, hosts have pets, pets not accepted, dinner available, packed lunch, non smoking, closed: 01/10-15/10&01/12-15/01, hiking, cycling, hunting, interesting flora, mushroom picking, fishing 2km, golf course 4km, bird-watching 10km, sea or lake watersports 10km, gliding,12km

— A6, Exit Pouilly en Auxois. Back to Pouilly and cross the village on the D970. After 4.5km, turn left towards Eguilly. Cross the A6 and turn left, then right towards Blancey. The farm is on the left.

PRICE STRUCTURE

4 Bedrooms and 1 Suite

Four: bridal room, shower room with wc, twin beds: FF240

Rez de Chaussée: along corridor bathroom with wc, washbasin, twin beds: FF240

Second room: bathroom with wc, double bed, twin beds: FF300 (2 people) FF400 (4 people)

additional room: washbasin, double bed: FF200

Third room: along corridor shower room with wc, twin beds, single bed (childrens size): FF230

Fourth room: double bed, single bed (childrens size): FF240 (2 people) FF450 (3 people)

Extra bed: 60FF
Reduction: 4 nights

Capacity: 16 people

Judith LEMOINE

«Couvent des Castafours»
21150 FLAVIGNY sur
OZERAIN

tel: (0) 3 80 96 24 92

Private home

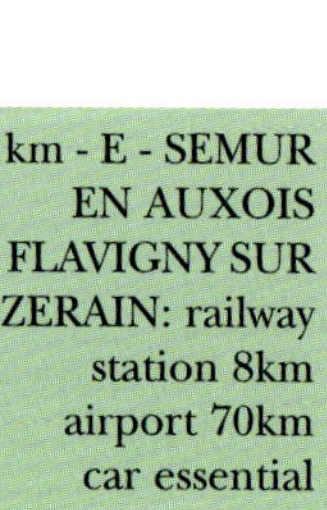

17 km - E - SEMUR
EN AUXOIS
FLAVIGNY SUR
OZERAIN: railway
station 8km
airport 70km
car essential

21.03 SEMUR EN AUXOIS

A superb location. Judith is English and a great cook. You will be surprised to find yourself going downstairs to the bedrooms. They are in a 17th century convent in the centre of what is considered to be one of the most beautiful medieval villages in France. The view of L'Auxois and the Valley of Alésia is also superb.

PRICE STRUCTURE

2 Bedrooms

Beige: along corridor shower room with wc, double bed: FF260

Rose: shower room with wc, twin beds: FF260

Extra bed: 60FF
Capacity: 4 people

PROPERTY

✱✱✱

off street parking, garden, tv lounge, hosts have pets, pets not accepted, dinner available, babies welcome, free cot, hiking, cycling, fishing,

Fluent English spoken

— On the A6, take the Exit "Bierre les Semur" towards Semur. Take the D9 towards Pouillenay and Flavigny. Go to the church and you can see the house below in the courtyard.

Elisabeth & Yves
DONOIS

«La Passerose»
Route d'Aisy
21500 ROUGEMONT

tel: (0) 3 80 92 46 18
fax: (0) 3 80 92 40 75
E-mail:
lapasserose@infonie.fr

Residence of character

28 km - N W -
SEMUR EN
AUXOIS
ROUGEMONT:
hosts will collect
from station
railway station 10km
airport 90km
car essential

21.16 SEMUR EN AUXOIS

Are you looking for a place where you can unwind, with a relaxed and friendly atmosphere and charming hosts? Elisabeth and Yves will welcome you to their 14th century home (which explains the steep staircase and low doorways!). You are close to one of the most beautiful villages in France.

PROPERTY

✱✱

private parking, garden, lounge, dinner available, babies welcome, free cot, non smoking, hiking, fishing, sea or lake watersports 10km, golf course 24km

Fluent English spoken

— On the A6, take the Bierre les Semur Exit, and then head towards Semur en Auxois. Take the D980 to Montbard, then the D905 towards Tonnerre. Rougemont is situated 10km after Montbard. The house is in the centre of the town, 300 metres from the church towards Aisy. (If coming from Paris, take the Nitry Exit.).

PRICE STRUCTURE

4 Bedrooms

Dauphin: shower room with wc, 3 single beds: FF220 (2 people) FF290 (3 people)

Grenouille: along corridor shower room with wc, twin beds: FF220

Pinson: telephone, twin beds: FF220

Oie: telephone, 4 single beds: FF200 (2 people) FF300 (4 people)

Extra bed: 70FF
Reduction: 5 nights and groups

Capacity: 11 people

Pierre BAEHLER

«L'Oasis»
Porte de Chatillon
21400 POTHIERES

tel: (0) 3 80 81 94 44
fax: (0) 3 80 81 94 44

Private home

30 km - E -
TONNERRE
POTHIERES:
railway station 28km
airport 85km
car essential

21.20 TONNERRE

Pierre is Swiss, and his place near the main Troyes-Dijon road is a paradise for nature lovers. Particularly well-known for shooting and fishing (this is an excellent area for fly-fishing). The wildlife in the forest is exceptional: stags, hinds, birds.... Ideal for eco-tourists. On sale: Handmade wooden crafts.

PRICE STRUCTURE

3 Bedrooms

Coccinelle & Papillon: television, double bed, single bed: FF248 (2 people) FF298 (3 people)

Orchidée: television, shower room with wc, double bed, single bed: FF290 (2 people) FF350 (3 people)

Extra bed: 50FF

Reduction: 01/11–28/02 and 7 nights and groups

Capacity: 9 people

PROPERTY

✱✱✱

private parking, extensive grounds, hosts have pets, telephone, dinner available, packed lunch, closed: 15/12-15/01, hiking, fishing, birdwatching, hunting 1km, mushroom picking 2km, cycling 6km, sea or lake watersports 6km

— At Tonnere, head for Châtillon-sur-Seine on the D965 and the N71 towards Troyes. Cross Montliot, and turn left towards Vix, then head towards Pothières. It is the first house on the right in the village.

Jean&Dominique MEL-LET-MANDARD

«Le Bois Dieu»
58400 RAVEAU

tel: (0) 3 86 69 60 02
fax: (0) 3 86 70 23 91
leboisdieu@wanadoo.fr

Farm

6 km - E - LA CHARITE SUR LOIRE
RAVEAU:
railway station 6km
airport 25km
car essential

58.04 LA CHARITE SUR LOIRE

This friendly couple live on the pilgrims' route to Compostella, near to a beautiful village. For fishermen, this is paradise. The house is quiet, comfortable and, when the weather is good, your meals, prepared using organic farm produce, will be served beneath the majestic cedar. On sale: Honey. 01/11–31/03 : advance booking only

PROPERTY

✸✸✸

off street parking, garden, lounge, hosts have pets, pets not accepted, dinner available, babies welcome, free cot, non smoking, hiking, fishing, hunting, interesting flora, mushroom picking, cycling 6km, river watersports 6km, sea or lake watersports 15km, gliding 20km, golf course 30km

Fluent English spoken

PRICE STRUCTURE

4 Bedrooms

Philibert: bathroom with wc, twin beds: FF310

Lucie & Colette: shower room with wc, double bed: FF310

Irma: shower room with wc, twin beds: FF310

Extra bed: 90FF

Capacity: 8 people

— On the A7 at la Charité sur Loire, take the turning to Clamecy-Auxerre (N151). Cross the bridge and immediately on the right, take the D179 towards Raveau. At Raveau, take the D138 for 3km. Le Bois Dieu is 250m past Peteloup.

«Château de Chanteloup»

58420 BRINON SUR BEUVRON

tel: (0) 3 86 29 02 08/61 17
fax: (0) 3 86 29 67 71

Château

22 km - S - CLAMECY
BRINON SUR BEUVRON: hosts will collect from station
railway station 9km
airport 50km
car essential

PRICE STRUCTURE

2 Bedrooms and 1 Suite and 2 Apartments

Suite: bridal room, television, kitchen, shower room with wc, double bed, single bed: FF330 (2 people) FF400 (3 people)

First room: television, bathroom with wc, double bed, single bed: FF330 (2 people) FF360 (3 people)

Baldaquin: television, bathroom with wc, double bed: FF330

Extra bed: 60FF

Capacity: 8 people

58.01 CLAMECY

In this very beautiful 16th-17th century château, enjoy the peaceful grounds and take your meals under the pergola or organise a barbecue. Sailing, riding, mountain-biking or walking are possible on over 60km of trails enabling you visit the famous places of interest in this area.

2 Apartments : self-catering

PROPERTY

✱✱✱

off street parking, extensive grounds, tv lounge, hosts have pets, telephone, kitchen, babies welcome, free cot, closed: 01/11-01/03, riding, hiking, cycling, mushroom picking, birdwatching, fishing 5km, hunting 8km, sea or lake watersports 12km, golf course 50km

Adequate English spoken

— On the D951 Clamecy–Vezelay, turn on to the D985 to Corbigny where you go towards Guipy. Follow the signs to the château. (8km from Corbigny). Your host requests that you ring in advance for directions.

58.03 NEVERS

Marie-France is a writer. She opens her spacious country house to you, overlooking woodland gardens. She spares no effort to ensure you feel good and relax. Only 40km from the Magny-Cours motor-racing circuit. Well worth the detour. On sale: Books and CD's.

Marie-France POIRIER O'LEARY

«Les Beauvais»
58330 ST SAULGE

tel: (0) 3 86 58 29 98
fax: (0) 3 86 58 29 97

Private home

PROPERTY

✱✱✱

off street parking, extensive grounds, lounge, pets not accepted, dinner available, packed lunch, babies welcome, free cot, wheelchair access, closed: 01/01-31/01, hiking, cycling, sea or lake watersports 5km, fishing 12km

Fluent English spoken

PRICE STRUCTURE

4 Bedrooms

Verte: telephone, shower room with wc, double bed: FF600

Bleue: lounge, telephone, bathroom, wc, double bed: FF600

Pêche: along corridor shower room with wc, washbasin, 2 single beds: FF300

Jaune: wheelchair facilities, television, telephone, shower, wc, double bed: FF600

Reduction: 2 nights

Capacity: 8 people

25 km - N E - NEVERS
ST SAULGE: airport 35km
car essential
— In Nevers, take the D978 towards Autun-Dijon, for 10km. Turn left on to the D958 towards St Saulge where you follow the signs.

Georges & Claire
RAUCAZ

«Manoir Le Plaix»
Route de Le Veudre-
POUZY MESANGY
03320 LURCY-LEVIS

tel: (0) 4 70 66 24 06
fax: (0) 4 70 66 25 82

Residence of character

35 km - S W - NEVERS
POUZY MESANGY: hosts will collect from station
railway station 35km
airport 100km
car essential

PRICE STRUCTURE

5 Bedrooms

Ground floor - First room: shower room with wc, double bed, single bed: FF200 (2 people) FF300 (3 people)

First floor - Second room: shower room with wc, double bed: FF220

First floor - Third room: shower room with wc, double bed, single bed: FF250 (2 people) FF350 (3 people)

Second floor - Fourth room: bathroom with wc, twin beds: FF250

Second floor - Fifth room: bathroom with wc, double bed, single bed: FF250 (2 people) FF350 (3 people)

Extra bed: 100FF

Reduction: 1/09–30/06 and 4 nights and groups and children

Capacity: 13 people

03.06 NEVERS

Claire's welcome and cooking are well known. This area, with its rich cultural past, stays close to the land, and is not yet too busy with tourists. Near to Lurcy Levis, this fortified farmhouse from the 16th century, breathes peace and quiet, yet it is only 25km from the Magny-Cours motor-racing circuit.

PROPERTY

✱✱✱

off street parking, garden, lounge, hosts have pets, dinner available, babies welcome, free cot, hiking, cycling, fishing, hunting, mushroom picking, interesting flora 20km, golf course 25km, birdwatching 25km

Basic English spoken

— At Nevers, take the N7 towards Moulins. At St Pierre le Moutier, turn right on to the D978A as far as Le Veudre where you take the D13 then the D234 to Pouzy Mésangy. (From Moulins, cross the river. Just after the bridge, turn right on to the D13 towards Montilly, Couzon, Pouzy-Mésangy where you go towards Le Veudre).

71.06 MACON

This house, with its typical balcony and stone staircase, is on a winegrowers estate. It is situated between the famous 'Roches Maconnaises', Vergisson and Solutré, in the heart of the Pouilly Fuissé wine region. For literary buffs, Lamartine Trail nearby. On sale: Their own wine

Daniel & Colette GUYOT

«Domaine d'Entre les Roches»
71960 VERGISSON

tel: (0) 3 85 35 84 55
fax: (0) 3 85 35 87 15

Farm

PROPERTY

✵✵✵

private parking, garden, hosts have pets, kitchen, hiking, fishing 5km, sea or lake watersports 10km, gliding 10km

Basic English spoken

10 km - W - MACON
VERGISSON: railway station 5km
car essential
— On the A6, take the Exit 'Macon-Sud'. Turn left towards Crèches sur Saone then turn right towards TGV - Prissé. By the restaurant 'La Patte d'Oie' turn left and continue towards Davayé, then Vergisson where you follow the signs.

PRICE STRUCTURE

2 Bedrooms and 2 Apartments

Studio 1: lounge, television, kitchen, shower room with wc, double bed: FF270

Studio 2: television, kitchen, shower room with wc, double bed, 2 single beds: FF270 (2 people) FF430 (4 people)

Saumon: shower room with wc, double bed: FF250

Grande Chambre: shower room with wc, double bed, single bed: FF250 (2 people) FF330 (3 people)

Extra bed: 80FF

Capacity: 11 people

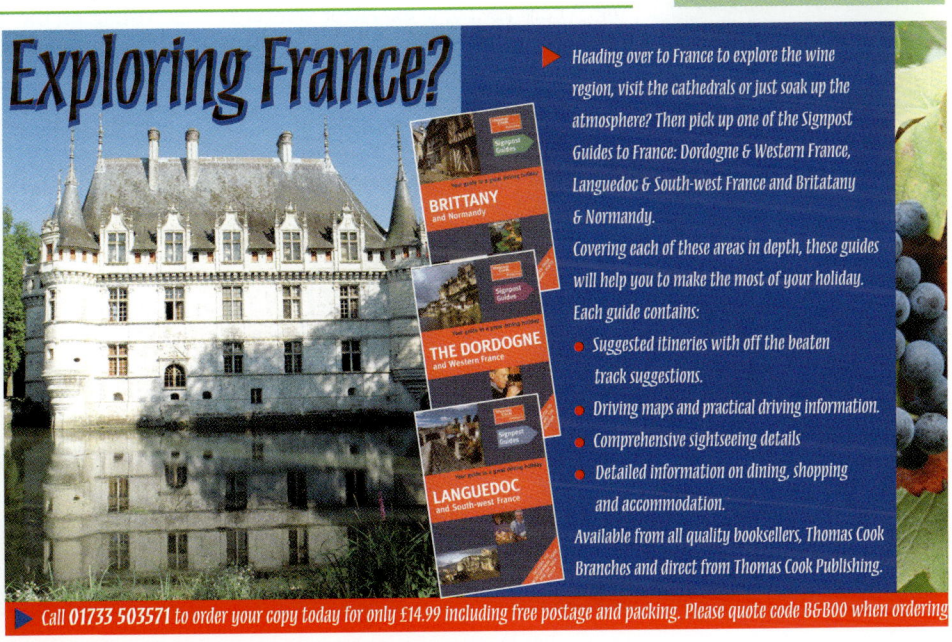

Christopher BLACK

«La Tour de Bassy»
Bassy
71260 St GENGOUX DE SCISSE

tel: (0) 3 85 33 28 77
fax: (0) 3 85 33 24 69

Château or manor house

25 km - N - MACON
ST GENGOUX DE SCISSE: hosts will collect from station
railway station 20km
airport 90km
car essential

Bourgogne

MACON

PRICE STRUCTURE

2 Bedrooms

(2 rooms) bathroom with wc, double bed: FF500

Capacity: 4 people

71.11 MACON

This is the old priory of La Tour de Bassy, and still bears witness to a time when the monks from the abbey of Cluny worked this land. The setting is attractive, quiet and charming. There are some excellent vineyards to be visited on the picturesque 'Route des Vins'. On sale: Wine.

PROPERTY

****

off street parking, garden, tv lounge, pets not accepted, telephone, 10 years minimum age, hiking, hunting, mushroom picking 2km, golf course 5km, fishing 7km, sea or lake watersports 20km

Fluent English spoken

— At Macon, head towards Cluny. At La Roche Vineuse, take the D85 on the right towards Verzé, Igé then Bassy. La Tour de Bassy is situated in the hamlet of Bassy.

Jean-François MON-
CORGER

Le Bourg
71120 OZOLLES

tel: (0) 3 85 88 35 00

Private home

25 km - S E - PARAY LE MONIAL OZOLLES: car essential

71.02 PARAY LE MONIAL

Choose between Lamartine, La Roche de Solutré, Roman churches, Cluny, the countryside, Burgundy... and Jean-François, whose sense of humour even rivals that of his English guests. You will love this comfortable 19th century house, as well as his cooking and wine.

PROPERTY

✱✱✱

off street parking, garden, lounge, pets not accepted, dinner available, babies welcome, free cot, riding, hiking, fishing, sea or lake watersports, interesting flora 15km

Fluent English spoken

PRICE STRUCTURE

3 Bedrooms

(2 rooms) shower room with wc, double bed: FF220

(1 room) shower room with wc, twin beds: FF220

Extra bed: 50FF

Capacity: 6 people

— At Paray le Monial take the N79 towards Macon. At Charolles, take the D25 then the D168 for Vaudebarrier and Ozolles. In the village, the house is the first on the right, after the bridge.

Michèle et Pierre
WILLOCQ

«les Tourterelles»
8, Allée du Bois -
Chazelles
89240 LINDRY

tel: (0) 3 86 47 12 82

Private home

13 km - W - AUXERRE
CHAZELLES: hosts will collect from station
railway station 13km
airport 150km
car essential

Bourgogne

AUXERRE

PRICE STRUCTURE

4 Bedrooms

First room: bathroom with wc, double bed: FF230

Second & third rooms: bathroom with wc, twin beds: FF230

Fourth room: bathroom with wc, double bed, 2 single beds: FF230 (2 people) FF370 (4 people)

Extra bed: 60FF

Reduction: 3 nights

Capacity: 10 people

89.02 AUXERRE

A quiet place to relax in la Puisaye. This old farmhouse has been beautifully restored, showing off to good effect its old beams and stonework. Michèle will always have something delicious cooking when you return from your visit to Auxerre, St Fargeau, Escollves and the vallée de la Cure, and the potteries.

PROPERTY

✱✱

off street parking, garden, tv lounge, hosts have pets, dinner available, kitchen, packed lunch, babies welcome, free cot, cycling, hiking 2km, mushroom picking 3km, fishing 6km, golf course 20km, sea or lake watersports 35km

Adequate English spoken

— On the A6, take the Exit 'Auxerre-Sud', then go towards Auxerre, to take the D965 towards St Fargeau. In Pourrain, go towards Lindry. In Chazelles, take the small lane on the right.

Daniel & Jeannette
CHAUMET

«La Posterle»
2, Place Aristide Briand
89110 ST AUBIN
CHATEAU NEUF

tel: (0) 3 86 73 64 09
fax: (0) 3 86 73 64 09

Private home

20 km - W -
AUXERRE
ST AUBIN CHAT.
NEUF: hosts will collect from station
railway station 20km
airport 20km

89.05 AUXERRE

This house was originally a café at the turn of the century, in this village with many beautiful houses. Daniel and Jeannette have made this place extremely welcoming, decorated with impeccable taste, which make it excellent value for money. It is next to the bell tower ... but the bells sleep at night too!

PROPERTY

✸✸

private parking, garden, tv lounge, pets not accepted, telephone, dinner available, packed lunch, babies welcome, free cot, non smoking, hiking, cycling, hunting, interesting flora, mushroom picking 2km, golf course 3km, fishing 3km, sea or lake watersports 30km

PRICE STRUCTURE

4 Bedrooms

Bouton d'Or & Bleuet: bathroom with wc, double bed: FF370

Eglantine: bathroom with wc, 2 double beds: FF370 (2 people) FF570 (4 people)

Violette: television, bathroom with wc, double bed: FF420

Extra bed: 80FF
Reduction: 15/10–15/12 and 15/01–15/03 and 3 nights and children

Capacity: 10 people

— A6, Exit Joigny. Then D943 towards Montargis, and turn left on to the D3 towards Toucy. Turn left on to the D955 towards Les Placeaux and right to St Aubin C.N. The house is in the upper part of the village on the square next to the church.

Monique JOULLIÉ

«Le Petit Manoir des Bruyères»
5, Allée de Charbuy-Les Bruyères
89240 AUXERRE-VILLEFARGEAU

tel: (0) 3 86 41 32 82
fax: (0) 3 86 41 28 57

Manor house

6 km - W - AUXERRE VILLEFARGEAU: hosts will collect from station
railway station 7km
airport 16km
car essential

89.10 AUXERRE

Situated in La Puisaye, in the heart of the forest, this superb 18th century manor house is distinguished by its typical Burgundy roof. Monique is very welcoming and so is Pierre who will show you his wine cellar. Charmingly decorated, perfect rooms, and luxury bathrooms. On sale: Wine, honey and home-made jam.

PRICE STRUCTURE

4 Bedrooms

Maintenon: television, telephone, shower room with wc, double bed: FF600

La Vallière: television, telephone, bathroom with wc, double bed: FF700

Sévigné: television, telephone, bathroom with wc, double bed: FF900

Montespan: lounge, television, telephone, bathroom with wc, double bed: FF900

Capacity: 8 people

PROPERTY

✱✱✱✱

private parking, extensive grounds, tv lounge, hosts have pets, pets not accepted, dinner available, babies welcome, free cot, hiking, mushroom picking, fishing 6km, interesting flora 6km, golf course 15km

Fluent English spoken

— On the A6 Exit Auxerre-Nord, then N6 towards Auxerre, and right on to the D31 towards Perrigny. At the roundabout at St Georges take the right turn towards Lindry. Continue for 4km.

Martine COSTAILLE

«Château Jaquot»
RN6
89420 STE MAGNANCE

tel: (0) 3 86 33 00 22

Château

13 km - E -
AVALLON
STE MAGNANCE:
car essential

89.04 AVALLON

If you had any doubts that Burgundy was a region famed for its gastronomy and wine, a stay at this 12th century château, restored with loving care and great attention to originality, will leave you in no doubt. Well worth the price and a detour ... Their dinners use mostly organic produce.

PROPERTY

✱✱✱✱

off street parking, extensive grounds, tv lounge, telephone, dinner available, 8 years minimum age, hiking 2km, interesting flora 2km, mushroom picking 2km, fishing 10km, hunting 10km, river watersports 10km, cycling 15km, sea or lake watersports 20km

Basic English spoken

— From the A6, take the exit to Avallon. Then join the N6 and turn left towards Saulieu. You can see the château as you arrive at Ste Magnance.

PRICE STRUCTURE

1 Bedroom

shower room with wc, bathroom, double bed, twin beds: FF500 (2 people) FF900 (4 people)

Capacity: 4 people

Marie-France
DESVIGNES

«Domaine de La Cour Alexandre»
89120 MARCHAIS-BETON

tel: (0) 3 86 41 32 82
fax: (0) 3 86 41 28 57

Château or manor house

28 km - S W - JOIGNY
MARCHAIS-BERN: airport 28km
car essential

89.06 JOIGNY

In the Puisaye country, you will enjoy Marie-France's welcome in her restored old farmhouse, in a calm, picturesque setting. The stylish furniture is a family treasure, and the rustic dining room is decorated with old farm utensils.

PROPERTY

✱✱✱

off street parking, extensive grounds, tv lounge, hosts have pets, dinner available, babies welcome, free cot, swimming pool, riding, hiking, cycling, fishing, hunting, mushroom picking, golf course 20km

English spoken

PRICE STRUCTURE

6 Bedrooms

First room: television, bathroom with wc, double bed, single bed: FF400 (2 people) FF650 (3 people)

Second room: television, bathroom with wc, twin beds, 2 single beds: FF500 (2 people) FF500 (4 people)

Nuptiale: bridal room, television, bathroom with wc, double bed: FF500

Baldaquin: television, bathroom with wc, double bed: FF500

Fifth room: shower room with wc, double bed: FF450

Sixth room: television, shower room with wc, double bed, 2 single beds: FF450 (2 people) FF750 (4 people)

Extra bed: 120FF

Capacity: 17 people

— A6, Exit to Courtenay. There, left towards Joigny and D34 towards Douchy. In Douchy follow Charny (D943), then right on to D950. In Charny, right towards Chambeugle, then left towards Marchais-Béton. 800m on D64 towards Le Charme.

89.07 JOIGNY

Alain and Chantal are a friendly and dynamic couple. They live just 10 minutes from the exit from the motorway. The rooms are in a separate building, which has been restored and is very pleasant. You are only 25km from the famous vineyards of Chablis.

PROPERTY

✱✱

private parking, garden, tv lounge, hosts have pets, kitchen, babies welcome, free cot, fishing 2km, hiking 5km, cycling 5km, mushroom picking 5km, golf course 7km, hunting 7km

Basic English spoken

Alain & Chantal
CHEVALLIER

5, Route de St Aubin -
Bleury
89110 POILLY sur
THOLON

tel: (0) 3 86 63 51 64
fax: (0) 3 86 91 53 37

Private home

PRICE STRUCTURE

3 Bedrooms

First room: television, shower room with wc, double bed: FF240

Second room: television, shower room with wc, twin beds: FF260

Third room: television, shower room with wc, double bed, single bed: FF240 (2 people) FF300 (3 people)

Extra bed: 80/100FF
Reduction: 5 nights

Capacity: 7 people

20 km - S - JOIGNY
BLEURY: car essential
— From the A6, take the Exit to Joigny. Then head towards Joigny for 1km and then turn right on to the D89 towards Auxerre. In Bleury, the street is in the centre of the village, opposite two restaurants.

Dominique & Daniel ACKERMANN

«Ferme de Plénoise»
Plénoise
89120 CHARNY

tel: (0) 3 86 63 63 53

Farm

30 km - S W - JOIGNY
PLENOISE: railway station 30km
car essential

Bourgogne

JOIGNY

89.11 JOIGNY

This is a working beef and dairy farm in the Puisaye, and this lovely couple and their two young children will be delighted to show you around. It is in a super setting, right out in the country beside a river. You can learn everything you ever wanted to know about dairy farming, thanks to the workshop "Traite des Vaches"! On sale: Milk, cider, and top quality homemade patisserie.

PRICE STRUCTURE

4 Bedrooms

Saumon: bathroom with wc, double bed: FF280

Rose: bathroom with wc, twin beds, cot: FF280

Verte: bathroom with wc, double bed, single bed: FF280 (2 people) FF350 (3 people)

Bleu: bathroom with wc, twin beds, 2 single beds: FF280 (2 people) FF420 (4 people)

Extra bed: 70FF
Reduction: 2 nights

Capacity: 11 people

PROPERTY

✹✹✹

off street parking, garden, tv lounge, hosts have pets, pets not accepted, telephone, dinner available, babies welcome, free cot, hiking, cycling, fishing, mushroom picking, golf course 20km, sea or lake watersports 30km, gliding 30km

Basic English spoken

— From the A6, Exit Joigny. Take the D943 towards Montargis, then left on to the D16 towards Charny. Head towards the covered market and continue on the D16, towards Chatillon Coligny. Go over the bridge and up the hill as you leave the village. At the top, turn right, signposted "Plénoise-Chambres d'hotes". Follow signs to Plénoise (about 5km from Charny).

Catherine BALOURDET

«Clos Mélusine»
16, Place de la Liberté
89140 LIXY

tel: (0) 3 86 66 11 39

Residence of character

10 km - W - SENS
LIXY:
airport 100km
car essential

89.12 SENS

This charming Bourgogne farmhouse is in the centre of an attractive village, under the watchful eye of the church which it adjoins. This is the place to fill your lungs with fresh air, to play golf or go riding. For the more adventurous, you can also try microlight flying or 4x4 driving. However, if you prefer to follow the cider trail, ask Cathy! She is an expert on this, as well as medieval towns.

PROPERTY

✱✱✱

private parking, garden, lounge, hosts have pets, pets not accepted, dinner available, packed lunch, hiking, golf course, hunting, mushroom picking, cycling 5km, fishing 10km, interesting flora 15km, river watersports 15km, sea or lake watersports 20km

Basic English spoken

—— On the N6 between Sens and Fontainbleau, at Pont sur Yonne, take the D82 towards Sérotin, then Branay and then right towards Lixy. The house is in the centre of the village.

PRICE STRUCTURE

3 Bedrooms

(2 rooms) shower room with wc, double bed: FF250

Third room: shower room with wc, twin beds: FF250

Extra bed: 60FF
Capacity: 6 people

ENGLISH CHANNEL
Guernsey
(to UK)
Jersey
(to UK)
Cherbourg
50
St. Lô
BASSE
NORMANDIE
Lannion
St. Malo
Avranches
Morlaix
Guingamp
Brest
St. Brieuc
Dinan
29
22
BRETAGNE
Fougères
Châteaulin
53
RENNES
Quimper
Pontivy
35
56
Lorient
Vannes
Redon
Châteaubriant
PAYS
DE LA LOIRE
44
Belle Ile
St. Nazaire
ATLANTIC
OCEAN
NANTES
Cholet
PAYS DE
LA LOIRE
La Roche
85
les Sables-d'Olonne

Sylvie RONSSERAY

«Le Logis de Jerzual»
25-27, rue du Petit Fort
22100 DINAN

tel: (0) 2 96 85 46 54
fax: (0) 2 96 39 46 94

Flat/Apartment

DINAN
railway station 1km
airport 12km

22.02 DINAN

A real gem! An interesting and very welcoming couple who work for the Ministry of Historic Monuments. The house is near the yacht harbour, in the centre of the old fortified town. There is a large (5000 square metres), interesting terraced garden with a fantastic view of the old harbour. Credit cards accepted.

PROPERTY

***

garden, tv lounge, hosts have pets, telephone, kitchen, golf course 15km, sea or lake watersports 15km

Fluent English spoken

— From the port of Dinan, the street is opposite the old bridge. The car park is 150m higher up on the right

PRICE STRUCTURE

5 Bedrooms and 1 Apartment

Baldaquin: television, shower room with wc, double bed: FF432

Husbeck: shower room with wc, double bed, twin beds: FF392 (2 people) FF574 (4 people)

Perse: shower room with wc, 2 double beds: FF342 (2 people) FF474 (4 people)

Pastorale: shower room with wc, double bed: FF312

La Halte: kitchen, shower room with wc, double bed: FF442

Jardin: shower, wc, single bed: FF206

Extra bed: 80/100FF
Reduction: 01.11 – 31.03 and 3 nights

Capacity: 15 people

Pierre & Yvonne JOUFFE

«Le Chesnay-Chel»
22980 LA LANDEC

tel: (0) 2 96 27 65 89

Farm

10 km - W - DINAN
LA LANDEC:
airport 20km
car essential
— In Dinan take the N176 towards St Brieuc. At the crossroads, do not follow the sign 'La Landec', but take the opposite direction. After 1km you will see a sign to the farm.

22.05 DINAN

On the way from Dinan to St Brieuc, this is an old stone farm with lots of character, near a lake. Quiet and rural but handy for Dinan. Beautifully decorated with hanging flower baskets. There is a riding centre nearby. A great place to relax, and less than half an hour from the Mont St Michel and St Malo.

PROPERTY

off street parking, garden, lounge, hosts have pets, dinner available, kitchen, non smoking, hiking, cycling, golf course 5km, sea or lake watersports 15km

English spoken

PRICE STRUCTURE

3 Bedrooms

First room: shower room with wc, double bed, single bed: FF200 (2 people) FF250 (3 people)

Second room: shower room with wc, double bed: FF200

Third room: bathroom with wc, double bed, single bed: FF200 (2 people) FF250 (3 people)

Extra bed: 50FF

Capacity: 8 people

Jean POMMERET

«La Gravelle»
22690 PLEUDIHEN-SUR-RANCE

tel: (0) 2 96 83 20 82

Farm

10 km - N E - DINAN
PLEUDIHEN SUR RANCE: hosts will collect from station
railway station 10km
airport 10km

22.09 DINAN

A stone farmhouse in a pretty hamlet in pleasant surroundings with lots of flowers. Friendly Madame Pommeret will give you an excellent, warm welcome and ensure you are well looked after in her clean rooms. Ideal for an overnight stop or a longer stay to explore this part of Brittany.

PROPERTY

✱✱

off street parking, garden, tv lounge, pets not accepted, dinner available, golf course 5km, sea or lake watersports 15km

PRICE STRUCTURE

4 Bedrooms

First room: washbasin, double bed: FF200

Second room: wc, washbasin, double bed: FF220

Third room: shower room with wc, double bed, 2 single beds: FF220 (2 people) FF300 (4 people)

Fourth room: shower room with wc, double bed: FF220

Extra bed: 50FF

Capacity: 10 people

— Go throught the centre of Dinan following the signs Rennes-Caen. Continue for 6km then turn left on to the D29 towards Pleudihen. Go past the church and the cemetery. Turn right at the crossroads and follow the signs for “Camping La Vilger.”

Bernard & Déborah
KERKHOF

«La Tarais»
Calorguen
22100 DINAN

tel: (0) 2 96 83 50 59
fax: (0) 2 96 83 50 59

Private House

7 km - S - DINAN
CALORGUEN:
railway station 7km
airport 20km
car essential
— In Dinan, take the D12 towards Léhon then Calorguen. Just before Calorguen, turn left and follow the signs "La Tarais".

Bretagne

DINAN

22.27 DINAN

In this quiet little hamlet close to Dinan, you are ideally placed for excursions to Les Cotes d'Armor. All year round there is a warm welcome from this Anglo-Dutch couple in their gaily decorated old farmhouse.

PRICE STRUCTURE

4 Bedrooms and 1 Suite

Rez-de-chaussée: shower room with wc, double bed, single bed: FF275 (2 people) FF350 (3 people)

Second, third & fourth rooms: shower room with wc, double bed: FF275

Suite 3 star: shower room with wc, 2 twin beds, single bed: FF275 (2 people) FF550 (5 people)

Extra bed: 75FF
Reduction: 3 nights

Capacity: 14 people

PROPERTY

***

off street parking, garden, tv lounge, hosts have pets, pets not accepted, dinner available, 4 years minimum age, wheelchair access, non smoking, closed: 01/11-01/04, 3 nights minimum stay 10/07-10/09, hiking, fishing, hunting, river watersports 7km, golf course 20km, sea or lake watersports 20km

Fluent English spoken

— In Dinan, take the D12 towards Léhon then Calorguen. Just before Calorguen, turn left and follow the signs "La Tarais".

Claudine GUERIN

«Les Colverts»
22490 TREMEREUC

tel: (0) 2 96 27 17 65

Private Home

10 km - N - DINAN
TREMEREUC:
airport 5km
car essential

22.34 DINAN

Claudine welcomes you to her restored old stone farmhouse in the centre of Trémereuc. You are only 15 minutes from St Malo and Dinard. The breakfast room and the salon are spacious, the latter having a particularly attractive fireplace.

PROPERTY

✸✸

off street parking, garden, tv lounge, hosts have pets, golf course 15km, sea or lake watersports 15km

— At Dinan, take the D766 towards Dinard. The house is in the centre of Trémereuc.

PRICE STRUCTURE

4 Bedrooms

First room: shower, bathroom, wc, double bed, twin beds: FF250 (2 people) FF430 (4 people)

Second room: along corridor shower room with wc, double bed: FF230

Third room: along corridor shower room with wc, twin beds: FF230

Fourth room: bathroom with wc, double bed, single bed: FF230 (2 people) FF280 (3 people)

Extra bed: 65FF

Capacity: 11 people

Helen & Joe
GOODMAN

«La Ville Gout»
22130 CORSEUL

tel: (0) 2 96 27 99 33
fax: (0) 2 96 82 77 56

Private Home

22.39 DINAN

Helen and Joe, of English origin, gave up their restaurant in Australia to settle in this little, old Breton farmhouse, between Dinan and the sea. It is quaint and charming, just like an English doll's house! They even have a "barby".

PROPERTY

✱✱✱

private parking, garden, tv lounge, hosts have pets, telephone, dinner available, packed lunch, babies welcome, free cot, cycling, mushroom picking, hiking 1km, interesting flora 6km, fishing 10km, sea or lake watersports 10km, golf course 15km, river watersports 15km

English spoken

PRICE STRUCTURE

3 Bedrooms

First room: telephone, shower room with wc, double bed, 2 single beds: FF270 (2 people) FF470 (4 people)

Second room: telephone, shower room with wc, double bed, single bed: FF270 (2 people) FF370 (3 people)

Third room: telephone, twin beds: FF220

Extra bed: 75FF
Reduction: 01.10 – 31.05 and 3 nights

Capacity: 9 people

10 km - N W - DINAN
CORSEUL:
railway station 8km
car essential
— From Dinan, take the D794 towards Plancoët. After 12 km, enter Corseul and take the first road on the right towards Ville Gout (B & B signs).

35.02 DINAN

Modern house in its own grounds, great for picnics. A pleasant spot not far from the main St Malo/Rennes road. Tennis, golf and riding are available nearby. Marie-Paule is very keen on ancestor-tracing.

Marie Paule
LEAUSTIC

«Les Ajoncs d'Or»
11b, rue des Ajoncs d'Or
35540 MINIAC-MORVAN

tel: (0) 2 99 58 55 08

Residence of Character

PROPERTY

✱✱✱

off street parking, extensive grounds, tv lounge, hosts have pets, pets not accepted, kitchen, babies welcome, free cot, golf course 3km, sea or lake watersports 15km

Basic English spoken

PRICE STRUCTURE

3 Bedrooms

Ti Koad: shower room with wc, washbasin, twin beds: FF210

Amzerz'o: along corridor shower room with wc, washbasin, double bed: FF160

Karantez ar mor: along corridor shower room with wc, washbasin, double bed: FF210

Extra bed: 70FF

Capacity: 6 people

10 km - N E - DINAN
MINIAC MORVAN: hosts will collect from station
railway station 2km
airport 25km
— Go in to the centre of Dinan, go through the centre and follow the signs to Rennes-Caen. On the viaduct go straight on towards Caen. After 13km, turn left on to the D73 towards Miniac-Morvan. Near to the church, go towards Pleudihen for 300m then turn right and follow the signs for 300m. The house is on the left (private lane).

Anne COLLINET

«La Chênevière»
35270 MEILLAC

tel: (0) 2 99 73 04 25

Manor House

17 km - S E - DINAN
MEILLAC: hosts will collect from station
railway station 8km
airport 50km
car essential

PRICE STRUCTURE

1 Bedroom and 1 Suite

Suite: shower room with wc, double bed, 2 single beds: FF320 (2 people) FF570 (4 people)

long corridor shower room with wc, double bed: FF320

Extra bed: 100FF

Capacity: 6 people

35.37 DINAN

Anne is a charming lady, and will give you a courteous welcome to her 350 year old manor house (which explains the rather steep staircase). The place exudes an ambience of the good life, French style. She has also accumulated souvenirs of her travels, particularly from the Polynesian Islands, and these are part of the decor throughout the house. The grounds are very romantic.

PROPERTY

✹✹✹

private parking, extensive grounds, lounge, hosts have pets, pets not accepted, telephone, dinner available, hiking, cycling 5km, golf course 15km, river watersports 20km, sea or lake watersports 30km

Adequate English spoken

— From Dinan take the D794 towards Rennes. Meillac is then 5km further on. Before the church, heading towards Bonnemain, take the second lane on the left, and there is a sign to "La Chenevière . Go along this lane for 500m, and you will come to a large house with three white gates. Ring the bell on the large gate.

Yannick & Annick
LE TENO

14, rue Notre Dame
22400 LAMBALLE

tel: (0) 2 96 31 00 41
fax: (0) 2 96 31 00 41

Residence of Character

LAMBALLE
railway station 500m
airport 30km

22.11 LAMBALLE

The setting and your welcoming hosts will together create the mood for an unforgettable stay. The painter Méheut was born in this attractive 18th century town-house, which is furnished with genuine antiques and is just 10 minutes from the beach. Outstanding value for money and well worth a detour.

PROPERTY

***

garden, tv lounge, telephone, kitchen, babies welcome, free cot, wheelchair access, closed: 15/12-31/01, hiking, golf course 15km, sea or lake watersports 15km

English spoken

PRICE STRUCTURE

5 Bedrooms

Armelle: bridal room, shower, double bed: FF195

Nicolas & Isabelle: shower room with wc, double bed, single bed: FF240 (2 people) FF300 (3 people)

Bleu: along corridor bathroom, double bed: FF195

Rouge: bathroom with wc, twin beds: FF225

Extra bed: 60FF

Capacity: 12 people

— Go in to the centre of Lamballe. The street is close to the Place du Marché.

Michel HAQUIN

«Les Quatre Vents»
22640 PLESTAN

tel: (0) 2 96 34 10 97

Private Home

6 km - S E -
LAMBALLE
PLESTAN: railway
station 8km
airport 30km
car essential

PRICE STRUCTURE

1 Suite

Chambre: 2 double beds: FF200 (2 people) FF400 (4 people)

Capacity: 4 people

22.40 LAMBALLE

This relatively modern house is in the heart of the country, 8km from Lamballe, 30km from Dinan and 25km from the sea. It is a little oasis of calm, far from the busy beaches and tourist attractions.

PROPERTY

✱✱

off street parking, garden, tv lounge, pets not accepted, telephone, kitchen, babies welcome, free cot, non smoking, cycling, fishing 2km, golf course 10km, sea or lake watersports 25km

— From Lamballe, take the dual carriageway N12 towards Rennes. Exit Plestan. At Plestan, go towards Plénée Jugon on the D59. "Les Quatre Vents" are 2km further on, on the right.

Marie-Louise & Jacques
KERAMOAL

D786-Hameau de
Crec'h Choupot
22220 TRÉDARZEC

tel: (0) 2 96 92 40 49
jacques.keramoal@
wanadoo.fr

Private Home

18 km - E - PERROS GUIREC
TREDARZEC: hosts will collect from station
railway station 30km
airport 20km
car essential

22.19 PERROS GUIREC

Comfortable Breton house in an elevated position, conveniently situated on the Perros-Guirec to Paimpol road. 2 km from the sea, in a pretty garden. An ideal base for visiting the Pink Granite Coast, the Ile du Bréhat and the famous "House between the two rocks" at Plougrescant. Spacious rooms.

PROPERTY

private parking, garden, tv lounge, telephone, babies welcome, free cot, closed: 15/09-30/04, sea or lake watersports 2km

Adequate English spoken

PRICE STRUCTURE

3 Bedrooms

Bretonne: lounge, television, shower room with wc, double bed: FF250

Retro: along corridor shower room with wc, washbasin, double bed: FF250

Le Lys: along corridor shower room with wc, double bed: FF250

Extra bed: 70FF

Capacity: 6 people

— South of Perros-Guirec take the D6 then the D786 towards Paimpol. When you are 2km from Tréguier and before you reach the D20 look on the left for a pretty white house with a large front lawn.

22.35 ST BRIEUC

Lucien & Marie-Hélène
CHOUPAUX

11, rue du Tertre
de la Motte
22440 PLOUFRAGAN

tel: (0) 2 96 78 65 81
fax: (0) 2 96 76 60 91

Private Home

2 km - S W - ST BRIEUC
PLOUFRAGAN: hosts can collect from station, railway station 3km
airport 8km
car essential
— From the suburbs of St. Brieuc go in the direction of Loudéac. When you get to the village of Ploufragan, follow signs to Plédran and then signs to "Chambre des Métiers". Continue for 1km and then turn left about 300m after the Hotel Beaucemaine.

Marie-Hélène and Lucien are retired, and welcome you to their modern house in a large garden. They will go out of their way to ensure that you feel at home. Marie-Hélène practices yoga. You also have use of a barbecue, lounge and kitchenette.

PROPERTY

✱✱✱✱

off street parking, garden, tv lounge, pets not accepted, telephone, kitchen, non smoking, closed: 1/09-30/06, hiking, cycling, fishing 2km, sea or lake watersports 2km, river watersports 2km

Adequate English spoken

PRICE STRUCTURE

5 Bedrooms

First room: shower, washbasin, double bed: FF245

Second room: shower, washbasin, double bed: FF230

Third room: shower room with wc, washbasin, double bed: FF240

Fourth room: bathroom with wc, double bed: FF260

Fifth room: television, shower room with wc, double bed: FF60

Extra bed: 100FF
Reduction: 4 nights and groups and children

Capacity: 10 people

Michelle MORVAN

«La Chataigneraie»
Keraveloc
29490 GUIPAVAS

tel: (0) 2 98 41 52 68
fax: (0) 2 98 41 48 40

Private Home

29.02 BREST

A warm and sophisticated welcome awaits in this charming, impressive, and spacious old stone house thoughtfully renovated with good taste. Situated in wooded grounds a few minutes from Brest, you can view the harbour and marina from the terrace. There is direct access to the Botanical Gardens (34 hectares). Heated swimming pool and solarium.

4 km - N E - BREST
KERAVELOC: hosts can collect from station,
railway station 4km
airport 7km

PROPERTY

****

private parking, extensive grounds, lounge, hosts have pets, pets not accepted, kitchen, babies welcome, free cot, swimming pool, interesting flora, sea or lake watersports 2km, golf course 12km

Fluent English spoken

PRICE STRUCTURE

3 Bedrooms and 1 Suite

First room: television, bathroom with wc, double bed: FF280

Second room: television, shower room with wc, double bed: FF280

Suite: television, shower room with wc, 2 double beds, single bed: FF260 (2 people) FF440 (5 people)

Fifth room: television, bathroom with wc, washbasin, double bed: FF280

Extra bed: 60FF
Reduction: 15.09 – 15.06

Capacity: 11 people

— Coming from Rennes, take the Quimper-Nantes Exit and go in the direction of Quimper-Nantes. At the second roundabout on the N265, take the first right and continue for 200 metres on the D205, then first left towards Coataudon. Go left at the traffic lights and follow the signs. If you are coming from Quimper, after the Elorn bridge, head for Brest-Nord, come off at Guipavas and turn left towards Brest. At the first set of traffic lights, turn left and follow the signs.

Michèle LESCOAT

«La Maison d'Hippolyte»
2, quai Surcouf
29300 QUIMPERLE

tel: (0) 2 98 39 09 11

Residence of Character

28 km - E - CONCARNEAU
QUIMPERLE: hosts can collect from station,
railway station, 2km
airport, 18km

29.08 CONCARNEAU

This was the home of Hippolyte, the 'World's greatest salmon fisherman'. His charming daughter has dedicated the house to his memory and it overlooks the river with its salmon ladder. Hippolyte's fishing rods are on display. Well worth a detour. On sale: Watercolours, photos.

PRICE STRUCTURE

4 Bedrooms

First room: television, shower, double bed: FF277

Second room: bridal room, television, shower room with wc, double bed: FF277

Third room: television, shower room with wc, double bed: FF277

Fourth room: television, shower, double bed: FF277

Extra bed: 70FF

Capacity: 8 people

PROPERTY

✹✹✹

garden, tv lounge, hosts have pets, fishing, river watersports, sea or lake watersports 12km, golf course 15km

Fluent English spoken

— From Concarneau, go to Pont Aven, then Quimperlé. (In Lorient, take the N165 towards Quimper. Take the Exit Quimperlé). The house is on the bank of the river Laïta, 50m from the tourist office.

Anne OLIER

«Kérantun»
Mahalon
29790 PONT CROIX

tel: (0) 2 98 74 51 93
fax: (0) 2 98 74 51 93

Farm

10 km - S W - DOUARNENEZ
MAHALON:
airport 18km
car essential

29.12 DOUARNENEZ

A typical stone farm with all modern comforts. They have 3 spacious and comfortable rooms with separate entrances. Close to Pont-Croix, a town of great character, and La Pointe du Raz. There is an excellent, reasonably priced restaurant nearby. On sale: Eggs, vegetables.

PROPERTY

✱✱✱

off street parking, garden, lounge, hosts have pets, kitchen, babies welcome, free cot, hiking, cycling, fishing, interesting flora 8km, golf course 10km, sea or lake watersports 10km, birdwatching 15km

Basic English spoken

PRICE STRUCTURE

3 Bedrooms

shower room with wc, double bed, single bed: FF260 (2 people) FF350 (3 people)

shower room with wc, double bed: FF260

shower room with wc: FF260

Extra bed: 70FF
Reduction: 01.10 – 30.04 and 2 nights

Capacity: 7 people

— In Douarnenez, take the D765 towards Pont Croix. As you enter Confort Meilars, 200m after the Renault garage on your right, turn left on to the first road and follow the signs for 2.5km

Yves & Hervelina BERTHOU

«La Ferme de Porz Kloz»
Trédudon-le-Moine
29690 BERRIEN

tel: (0) 2 98 99 61 65
fax: (0) 2 98 99 67 36

Residence of Character

20 km - S - MORLAIX
TREDUDON LE MOINE: railway station 20km
airport 20km
car essential

PRICE STRUCTURE

7 Bedrooms

Maison1: Rez de Chaussée Andro: wheelchair access, television, telephone, bathroom with wc, shower, twin beds, single bed: FF480 (2 people) FF580 (3 people)

Maison1: 1er étage Laridée: television, telephone, bathroom with wc, twin beds: FF400

Maison1: 1er étage Gavotte: television, telephone, bathroom with wc, twin beds, single bed: FF400 (2 people) FF500 (3 people)

Maison2: Jabadao: television, telephone, bathroom with wc, twin beds, single bed: FF480 (2 people) FF580 (3 people)

Maison3: Pach-Pi: television, telephone, bathroom with wc, twin beds, single bed: FF420 (2 people) FF520 (3 people)

Maison3: Kost Ar'hoad: television, telephone, bathroom with wc, twin beds: FF400

Maison3: Piler Lann: telephone, bathroom with wc, 2 single bed: FF340

Extra bed: 60FF

Reduction: 3 nights and groups and children

Capacity: 18 people

29.30 MORLAIX

In this pretty, Breton hamlet, they have 3 charming maisonettes, with 2-4 rooms, each named after Breton dances. The garden is beautiful and the ambiance is romantic. In the evening, your host will entertain you by playing the bombarde and the bagpipes around the fire, after a delicious dinner. On sale: Honey, goat's cheese, cider

PROPERTY

✱✱✱✱

private parking, garden, lounge, hosts have pets, pets not accepted, telephone, dinner available, packed lunch, babies welcome, free cot, wheelchair access, closed: 01/12-01/03, 3 nights minimum stay 1/07-31/08, hiking, interesting flora, mushroom picking, birdwatching, fishing 1km, hunting 1km, sea or lake watersports 10km, river watersports 10km, golf course 15km, gliding 40km

Fluent English spoken

— At Morlaix, take the D769 towards Huelgoat. At Le Plessis, turn right on to the D111, and then turn left towards Trédudon.

29.11 QUIMPER

Annick QUILFEN

«Kerjaouen»
23, route de Kerouter
Clohars Fouesnant
29950 BENODET

tel: (0) 2 98 57 01 86

Private Home

Dynamic, generous, happy, pleasant, natural: this is the way in which past guests have described Annick. Two rooms in a large modern house, furnished with every comfort. This place is situated 2km from Bénodet, a charming fishing port with many restaurants. On sale: Honey, mead, cider.

PROPERTY

***

off street parking, garden, tv lounge, kitchen, babies welcome, free cot, golf course 2km, sea or lake watersports 2km

20 km - S - QUIMPER CLOHARS FOUESNANT BENODET:hosts can collect from station, railway station 13km airport 14km
— In Quimper, take the D34 towards Bénodet. Take the 2nd road on the right towards Gouesnac'h (at Bénéteau boats) then left into the 'Rue de Kerouter' and twice left.

PRICE STRUCTURE

2 Bedrooms

shower room with wc, double bed: FF300

bathroom with wc, double bed: FF300

Extra bed: 90FF

Capacity: 4 people

Bretagne

QUIMPER

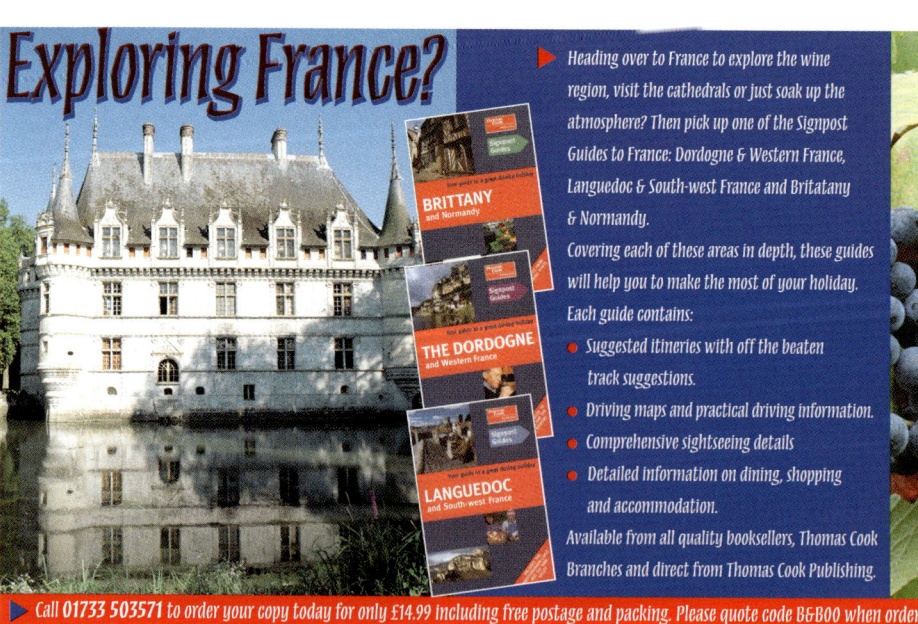

Alix de LAUBRIERE

34, rue de Kerilis
29750 LOCTUDY

tel: (0) 2 98 87 43 79
fax: (0) 2 98 87 43 79

Private Home

25 km - S - QUIMPER
LOCTUDY: hosts can collect from station,
railway station 25km
airport 70km
car essential

29.34 QUIMPER

What a delightful spot for this house, at the waters edge, opposite the little fishing port of Loctudy, which is typical of this region. From here, you can watch the amazing sunset, enjoy the fresh fish and seafood or take part in the evening festivities. Typically Breton.

PRICE STRUCTURE

2 Bedrooms

First room: twin beds, single bed: FF300 (2 people) FF350 (3 people)

Second room: twin beds: FF300

Extra bed: 50FF

Capacity: 5 people

PROPERTY

off street parking, garden, closed: 01/10-01/05, hiking, sea or lake watersports, river watersports, cycling 1km, fishing 1km, birdwatching 5km, interesting flora 8km, gliding 10km, golf course 15km

Fluent English spoken

— Quimper - Pont l'Abbé , then Loctudy (on the D2). At Loctudy, at the first roundabout turn left (take the street marked "Interdite sauf aux Riverains", as you will be staying with one of the residents). Follow the unmade road, and the house is No.34.

Philippe DAVY

«Château du Guilguiffin
29710 LANDUDEC

tel: (0) 2 98 91 52 11
fax: (0) 2 98 91 52 52
http://www.guilguiffin.com

Château

13 km - W - QUIMPER
LANDUDEC: hosts can collect from station,
railway station 16km
airport 8km
car essential

Bretagne

QUIMPER

29.35 QUIMPER

This luxurious, listed 18th century château in Finistère offers space, peace and quiet and is totally authentic. It is a family property, surrounded by vast grounds which contain areas full of wild flowers, as well as magnificent gardens planted with 350,000 daffodils and 3,800 hydrangeas. You will find your host's enthusiasm for this place irresistible.

PROPERTY

****

off street parking, extensive grounds, tv lounge, hosts have pets, telephone, babies welcome, free cot, closed: 15/11-31/03, 3 nights minimum stay, hiking, sea or lake watersports 11km, cycling 15km, fishing 15km, golf course 20km, interesting flora 25km

Fluent English spoken

PRICE STRUCTURE

4 Bedrooms and 2 Suites

Chambre Bleue & Chambre Rose: television, bathroom with wc, twin beds: FF800

Chambre Jaune: television, shower room with wc, double bed: FF800

Chambre Chapelle: television, bathroom with wc, double bed: FF800

Suite Bleue: television, bathroom with wc, 2 twin beds: FF1300

Suite Jaune: television, bathroom with wc, 2 twin beds: FF1300

Extra bed: 150FF
Reduction: 01.04 – 15.06 and 16.09 – 15.11 and 3 nights

Capacity: 16 people

— At Quimper, go towards Audierne on the D784. 13km from Quimper and 3km before Landudec, you will see the entrance to the estate on the left. Follow the signs.

Jean & Annie MARTIN

«Ty-Dreux»
29410 LOC EGUINER
ST THEGONNEC

tel: (0) 2 98 78 08 21
fax: (0) 2 98 78 01 69

Farm

8 km - S - ST THEGONNEC
LOC EGUINER ST THEGONNEC:
airport 40km
car essential

PRICE STRUCTURE

5 Bedrooms

(1 room) shower room with wc, double bed, single bed: FF260 (2 people) FF350 (3 people)

Baldaquin: shower room with wc, double bed: FF260

(2 rooms) shower room with wc, double bed: FF260

Suite: shower room with wc, double bed, single bed: FF260 (2 people) FF350 (3 people)

Extra bed: 100FF

Capacity: 12 people

29.05 ST THEGONNEC

Well worth a detour. This farm is furnished in authentic style in an old 18th century weaving village. Your hosts are proud of their Breton traditions and language and will help you discover the nearby Parish Enclosures. They have a beautiful collection of antiques and Breton costumes. On sale: Farm produce. Self-catering apartments available to rent weekly.

PROPERTY

***

off street parking, garden, tv lounge, hosts have pets, kitchen, hiking, cycling, fishing, sea or lake watersports 5km, golf course 10km

Adequate English spoken

— In St Thégonnec, go towards Loc-Eguiner-St-Thégonnec (D118 then D18). In the village, continue on to the D111 towards Plonéour-Ménez.

Pierre & Nicole HUBER

«La Margriette»
34, Av Pasteur
35260 CANCALE

tel: (0) 2 99 89 73 27
fax: (0) 2 99 89 55 41

Private Home

CANCALE
hosts can collect from station,
railway station 14km
airport 30km

35.14 CANCALE

Here you will find an attentive hostess in a very attractive, modern house, which is beautifully furnished, and in a peaceful location. The bedrooms are pretty. Close to tennis courts and several art and regional history museums. Cancale is a charming fishing port, well known for its oysters.

PROPERTY

✱✱

off street parking, garden, tv lounge, hosts have pets, pets not accepted, babies welcome, free cot, 3 nights minimum stay 11/11-28/02, hiking, cycling, sea or lake watersports 3km, birdwatching 5km, golf course 25km

Adequate English spoken

PRICE STRUCTURE

3 Bedrooms

Rez de Ch - Blanche-Bordeaux: television, bathroom with wc, shower, double bed: FF320

Baldaquin Bleu-Blanc: double bed: FF270

Verte-Rose: twin beds: FF270

Extra bed: 105FF
Reduction: 01.10 – 30.03

Capacity: 6 people

— In Cancale, the street is to the south of the town, parallel to the sea front, heading towards Rennes.

Eugène & Marie-Thérèse
Le SAULNIER

20, Avenue Pasteur
35260 CANCALE

tel: (0) 2 99 89 66 07

Private Home

CANCALE
hosts can collect from station,
railway station 15km
airport 20km

35.22 CANCALE

This beautiful, tranquil house has beautiful bathrooms, a piano, relaxing chairs in the garden and private parking ... and believe it or not, you are in the town centre, 500m from the port of Cancale, where you must taste their famous oysters. The bedrooms have mini-bars.

PRICE STRUCTURE

2 Bedrooms

La Rose: lounge, television, bathroom with wc, twin beds: FF370

Le Bleuet: lounge, television, shower room with wc, double bed, twin beds: FF350 (2 people) FF440 (3 people)

Extra bed: 90FF

Reduction: 5 nights

Capacity: 6 people

PROPERTY

✸✸✸

private parking, garden, pets not accepted, 2 years old minimum age, non smoking, closed: 1/10-01/04, hiking, cycling, sea or lake watersports, birdwatching 5km, golf course 25km

Basic English spoken

— From the port, take the main street towards the centre of the town. Then take the first on the left towards Rennes, and the first on the left again.

35.33 CANCALE

Madame Simon's place is very quiet and near the beaches. It has its own lake, so you will not be surprised to learn she also collects ornamental ducks. She also runs a restaurant nearby. Be sure to try her mother's famous jam: apple jelly from la Motte Jean. Duck is off.

Marie-France SIMON

«Auberge de la
Motte Jean»
35350 ST COULOMB

tel: (0) 2 99 89 41 99
fax: (0) 2 99 89 92 22

Private Home

PROPERTY

****

off street parking, garden, hosts have pets, pets not accepted, telephone, kitchen, packed lunch, hiking 1km, gliding 2km, cycling 3km, fishing 3km, mushroom picking 3km, sea or lake watersports 3km, birdwatching 5km, golf course 15km

Basic English spoken

PRICE STRUCTURE

5 Bedrooms and 1 Apartment

Rose Elisabeth: television, telephone, bathroom with wc, washbasin, double bed: FF560

Jonquille: television, telephone, shower room with wc, washbasin, double bed: FF560

Glycines: television, telephone, shower room with wc, washbasin, twin beds: FF560

Bleuets: television, telephone, shower room with wc, washbasin, double bed: FF530

Capucines: television, telephone, bathroom with wc, washbasin, double bed: FF530

Petite Maison: lounge, television, telephone, kitchen, shower room with wc, washbasin, double bed: FF560

Extra bed: 100FF
Reduction: 01.10 – 31.03

Capacity: 12 people

2 km - W - CANCALE
ST COULOMB: railway station 18km
airport 25km
car essential
— From Cancale, head towards St Malo on the D355. Turn left after 2km following the large sign 'Auberge de la Motte Jean'.

Yvonnick LE MIRE

«Château de la Villerobert»
22130 ST LORMEL

tel: (0) 2 96 84 12 88
fax: (0) 2 96 84 03 27

Château

20 km - S W - DINARD
ST LORMEL: airport 18km
car essential

PRICE STRUCTURE

3 Bedrooms

Bleue: shower, wc, double bed, single bed: FF420 (2 people) FF510 (3 people)

Rose: along corridor bathroom, wc, twin beds: FF420

Jaune: shower room with wc, double bed, single bed: FF420 (2 people) FF510 (3 people)

Extra bed: 60FF
Reduction: 01.05 – 30.06 and 01.10 – 31.10 and 3 nights

Capacity: 2 people

22.23 DINARD

Monsieur and Madame Le Mire will receive you like old friends in their 17th century château, quietly situated in its own grounds. It is furnished with antiques and only 5km from the sea. Ideal base for the 'Emerald Coast'. Fleur de soleil member. Charge for pets: 30 FF each.

PROPERTY

✸✸✸

private parking, extensive grounds, tv lounge, babies welcome, free cot, golf course, sea or lake watersports 8km

Adequate English spoken

— In Dinard, go towards Ploubalay, Plancoët. After Créhen, turn right towards St Lormel. Cross St Lormel then 50m after the sign as you exit the village, the château is on the left.

Jean-François STENOU

«Manoir de la Duchée»
ST BRIAC SUR MER
35800 DINARD

tel: (0) 2 99 88 00 02

Residence of Character

7 km - W - DINARD
ST BRIAC SUR MER:
railway station 13km
airport 3km
car essential

35.28 DINARD

Jean-François's house is meant to be fun. When you enter this 16th century manor house, you could quite easily shake the hand of the lady in Breton folk costume, who turns out to be a statue! You will be captivated. On sale: Paintings

PROPERTY

****

off street parking, extensive grounds, lounge, pets not accepted, telephone, hiking, cycling, fishing 1km, golf course 3km, sea or lake watersports 3km

— At Dinard take the D786 coast road, exit St Briac. Go towards the Camping Municipal and follow the signs.

PRICE STRUCTURE

4 Bedrooms and 2 Suites

Suite Rose: lounge, television, along corridor bathroom with wc, double bed, single bed: FF500 (2 people) FF600 (3 people)

Lilas: bridal room, television, shower room with wc, double bed: FF500

Bleuet: television, bathroom with wc, double bed: FF400

Coquelicot: television, bathroom with wc, single bed: FF350

Camélia: television, bathroom with wc, double bed: FF500

Pivoine - Duplex: television, bathroom with wc, double bed, twin beds: FF500 (2 people) FF700 (4 people)

Extra bed: 100FF

Capacity: 14 people

35.35 DINARD

Hugues & Marie-Christine
BARBERE

«La Sauvageais»
35730 PLEURTUIT

tel: (0) 2 99 88 82 47
fax: (0) 2 99 88 82 47

Private Home

You will be welcomed to a recently-built house with a large garden, situated in the village of Pleurtuit. It is an ideal base for visiting this part of Brittany, renowned for its tourist towns: Dinard (4km), St.Malo (8km), Cancale (20km). The blue and green rooms are self-contained. Don't miss the Breton crêpes and galettes.

PROPERTY

✸

private parking, garden, lounge, hosts have pets, dinner available, non smoking, hiking, cycling, fishing 2km, interesting flora 2km, sea or lake watersports 2km, gliding 2km, golf course 8km, river watersports 15km

Adequate English spoken

4 km - S - DINARD
PLEURTUIT: hosts can collect from station, railway station 15km
airport 6km
car essential
— From Dinard, take the D266 to Pleurtuit. Turn left just as you enter the village, towards "Les Sauvageais". Continue for 800m to the "Stop" sign, then turn right. Continue for another 50m.

PRICE STRUCTURE

4 Bedrooms

Rose: washbasin, double bed: FF225

Marron: double bed, 2 single beds: FF225 (2 people) FF335 (4 people)

Bleue: shower room with wc, twin beds, 2 single beds: FF255 (2 people) FF365 (4 people)

Verte: shower room with wc, double bed, 2 single beds, FF255 FF365

Extra bed: 55FF

Capacity: 14 people

35.36 DINARD

Jacqueline & Gérard
VIDMANN

42, rue des Ecoles
35800 DINARD

tel: (0) 2 99 46 45 92

Private Home

This is a great place for moonlight walks, being in the centre of Dinard, 80m from the beach and totally quiet. You will be sure to relax in the pleasant garden, full of flowers. Gérard is a retired hotelier, and he now keeps pigeons, whose cooing will gently send you off to sleep. There is a very practical little bedroom on the ground floor. Barbecue available.

PROPERTY

✸✸

garden, hosts have pets, riding, hiking, cycling, fishing, sea or lake watersports, golf course 3km

Fluent English spoken

PRICE STRUCTURE

2 Bedrooms and 1 Apartment

First room: shower room with wc, washbasin, double bed: FF230

Second room: shower room with wc, washbasin, double bed: FF250

Apartment: lounge, television, kitchen, along corridor shower room with wc, double bed, single bed: FF250 (2 people) FF320 (3 people)

Extra bed: 50FF
Reduction: 7 nights

Capacity: 7 people

DINARD
railway station 8km
airport 4km
— Go to the centre of Dinard. At the Notre Dame church, take the first on the left, and then left again. You are then in the Rue des Ecoles, and the house is No.42.

35.07 DOL DE BRETAGNE

Andy ANDREWS

«La Higourdais»
Parc de la Higourdais
35120 EPINIAC

tel: (0) 2 99 80 01 46
fax: (0) 2 99 80 01 46

Private Home

Andy and his small Franco-British family clearly know how to create a cosy atmosphere, a very warm welcome and friendly ambiance. In this rustic and relaxing house, in the heart of a protected nature park, you will share their family life. Vegetarian meals are a speciality.

PROPERTY

✱✱

off street parking, extensive grounds, hosts have pets, dinner available, kitchen, packed lunch, babies welcome, free cot, fishing, golf course 7km, sea or lake watersports 15km

Fluent English spoken

10 km - S - DOL DE BRETAGNE
EPINIAC: hosts can collect from station, railway station 10km airport 50km
— In Dol de Bretagne, take the D795 towards Combourg then the D4 towards Epiniac. Near the church, head in the direction of Cuguen for 4km. Turn left and follow the signs for 'La Higourdais'.

PRICE STRUCTURE

6 Bedrooms

Senteurs du jardin: wc, double bed, single bed: FF200 (2 people) FF275 (3 people)

Lake view: wc, twin beds: FF200

Petit Nid: twin beds: FF180

Blue Moon: wc, washbasin, double bed, 2 single beds: FF200 (2 people) FF325 (4 people)

Crystal room: television, wc, double bed, 2 single beds: FF200 (2 people) FF325 (4 people)

Tudor room: along corridor shower room with wc, double bed, single bed: FF200 (2 people) FF275 (3 people)

Extra bed: 75FF

Capacity: 18 people

Gaëlle & Bernard RIO

Le Petit Bois
56350 ALLAIRE

tel: (0) 2 99 71 87 63
fax: (0) 2 99 71 97 05

Residence of Character

10 km - W - REDON
ALLAIRE: railway station 10km
airport 50km
car essential

56.15 REDON

A place for those who love picturesque villages and the countryside. This is a listed building where time stands still. Gaelle will go to great lengths to welcome you to her 16th century farmhouse, which is stylish and cosy. Bernard, an archaeological enthusiast, will reveal all the secrets of the region.

PROPERTY

✱✱

off street parking, extensive grounds, hosts have pets, babies welcome, free cot, closed: 31/09-30/04, hiking, hunting, interesting flora 2km, golf course 5km, fishing 5km, cycling 8km, birdwatching 8km, river watersports 8km

Basic English spoken

PRICE STRUCTURE

1 Bedroom
lounge, television, shower room with wc, washbasin, double bed: FF240

Extra bed: 60FF
Reduction: 7 nights

Capacity: 2 people

— At Redon, take the D775 towards Allaire. Once in Allaire, head towards St Jacut Les Pins. At the 2nd roundabout, head towards St Perreux. Continue for 2km, and take the 2nd road on the left. Continue for 1km.

Odile & Alain LE CLAINCHE

«Le Logis du Bonamenec'h»
BONAMENAY
35380 PAIMPONT

tel: (0) 2 99 06 82 13
fax: (0) 2 99 06 82 13
logisbo@club-internet.fr

Residence of Character

30 km - W - RENNES
BONAMENAY: hosts can collect from station,
railway station 17km
airport 30km
car essential

Bretagne

RENNES

35.30 RENNES

If you enjoy mystery and the legends of knights and their ladies, then this is the place for you. You are right by the forest of Brocéliande and your host, who is an architect, has restored the interior of this 16th century Breton house with great taste and skill. Fleur de Soleil member.

PRICE STRUCTURE

3 Bedrooms

First room: shower room with wc, washbasin, double bed: FF300

Second room: shower room with wc, washbasin, twin beds: FF300

Third room Annex: double bed: FF300

Extra bed: 100/120FF

Capacity: 6 people

PROPERTY

✱✱✱

private parking, garden, lounge, hosts have pets, dinner available, babies welcome, free cot, hiking, cycling, fishing 5km, hunting 5km, mushroom picking 5km, birdwatching 5km, sea or lake watersports 10km

Basic English spoken

— At Rennes take the dual-carriageway towards Lorient. Take the Exit at Plelan Le Grand and then turn right off the slip road. Cross the N24 and follow the D61 for 3km. Then take the gravel road on the left, 500m after Bonamenay le Breuil.

Marie Léone de FLORIS

8, Place de l'Eglise
35380 PLELAN LE GRAND

tel: (0) 2 99 06 83 05

Private Home

30 km - W - RENNES
PLELAN LE GRAND: railway station 30km
airport 30km
car essential

35.39 RENNES

This beautiful old house, which dates from the 17th and 18th centuries, is very comfortable and only a short walk from the Brocéliande forest. Here you will find charm in a welcoming, peaceful setting. Fleur de Soleil member.

PROPERTY

✱✱✱

off street parking, garden, pets not accepted, hiking,

English spoken

PRICE STRUCTURE

1 Bedroom and 1 Suite

Rouge: shower room with wc, double bed, 2 single beds: FF300 (2 people) F450 (4 people)

Jaune: bathroom with wc, double bed: FF300

Capacity: 6 people

— Contact your host for detailed directions.

Madeleine ROUX-EVILLE

«Parc Ombragé»
rue de St Ideuc
35400 ST MALO

tel: (0) 2 99 40 09 41

Private Home

ST MALO
hosts can collect from station,
railway station 1km
airport 12km

35.20 ST MALO

Detached house in residential area of St Malo near to the main roads, furnished and decorated with great taste. Your hosts are a newly retired couple who welcome you in style. Be sure to visit St Malo and try the seafood. Fleur de soleil member. Advance booking only

PRICE STRUCTURE

3 Bedrooms

Yann, Pascal: along corridor shower room with wc, 2 double beds: FF300 (2 people) FF560 (4 people)

Frédérique: along corridor bathroom, double bed, single bed: FF480 (2 people) FF600 (3 people)

Extra bed: 120FF

Reduction: 2 nights and groups

Capacity: 7 people

PROPERTY

✱✱✱

off street parking, extensive grounds, tv lounge, pets not accepted, non smoking, hiking, cycling, fishing, sea or lake watersports, golf course 15km, birdwatching 30km

Basic English spoken

— Coming from Rennes, at St Malo take the D301 towards Cancale and "Centre-Ville". At the 4th roundabout go towards 'Stade Lemarié' At the set of traffic lights, take the road in front of you as far as the roundabout. and again in front of you, enter the courtyard of the 'beige château'. It is the last house on your left. (white gate).

35.21 ST MALO

You will be well looked after by Ginette, who is recently retired and adores meeting new friends. This small apartment block is well served by buses for the town & the beaches, which stop outside. Her daughter gives jazz-dancing classes.

Ginette ROUILLER

16, rue Duparquier
35400 ST MALO

tel: (0) 2 99 82 89 37

Flat

PROPERTY

✱✱

off street parking, garden, tv lounge, babies welcome, free cot, hiking, cycling, fishing, sea or lake watersports, golf course 15km, birdwatching 30km

ST MALO: hosts can collect from station, railway station 2km airport 7km
— In the south-west suburb of St Malo. Follow the signs 'Bellevue Centre Commercial'. At the traffic lights, turn into the 'Rue Duparquier'.

PRICE STRUCTURE

1 Bedroom television, double bed: FF200

Extra bed: 100FF

Capacity: 2 people

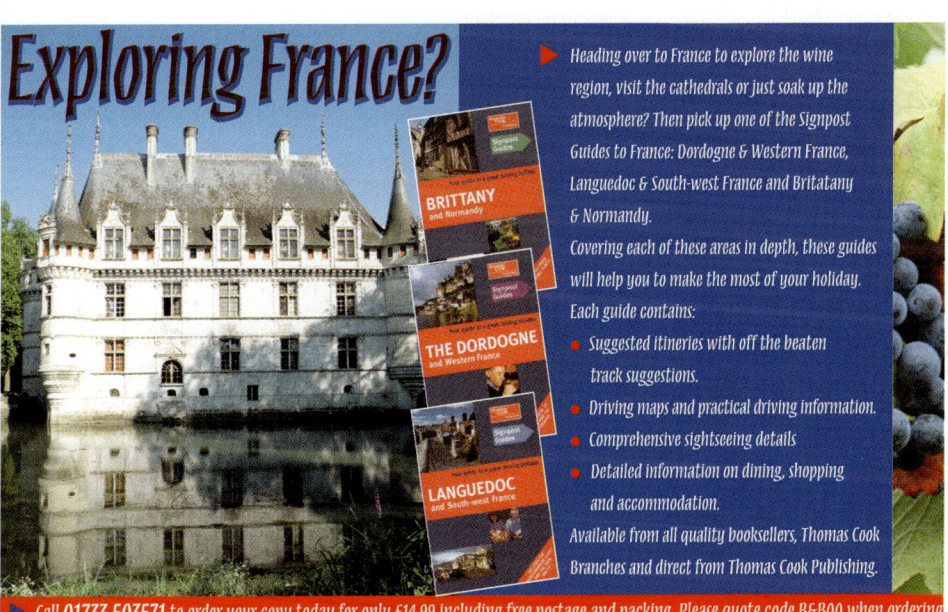

Martine MONSIMET

La Rimbaudais
35350 ST MELOIR DES ONDES

tel: (0) 2 99 89 19 75

Private Home

7 km - E - ST MALO
ST MELOIR DES ONDES:
airport 16km
car essential

PRICE STRUCTURE

2 Bedrooms

First room: shower room with wc, double bed, single bed: FF225 (2 people) FF290 (3 people)

Second room: along corridor shower room with wc, double bed: FF225

Extra bed: 50FF

Capacity: 5 people

35.24 ST MALO

Martine is a charming person. Her house is very well situated, 5km from Cancale and 7km from St Malo. The barbecue, dishwasher and fridge are available for your use. There are many restaurants and crêperies nearby, and of course you are in the land of oysters and mussels. On sale: Oysters, mussels, honey, cider, calvados...

PROPERTY

✱✱

private parking, garden, hosts have pets, babies welcome, free cot, hiking 5km, cycling 5km, fishing 5km, birdwatching 5km, sea or lake watersports 5km, river watersports 5km, golf course 10km, gliding 10km

Basic English spoken

— At St Malo, head in the direction of the Mont St Michel via the D155, and then turn right towards St Méloir. At the Mairie, take the D2 towards St Servan for 1.5km as far as La Rimbaudais.

Peter SOBEK

«La Goëlette»
2, rue Besnier
35430 ST SULIAC

tel: (0) 2 99 58 47 03
fax: (0) 2 99 58 47 03

Residence of Character

35.27 ST MALO

This Franco-German couple will welcome you to their 17th century stone house, in the heart of one of the most beautiful fishing villages in Brittany. The bedrooms have been tastefully modernised. You will love the courtyard and the garden. Large breakfast.

PROPERTY

✹✹

garden, tv lounge, pets not accepted, dinner available, babies welcome, free cot, hiking, cycling, fishing, sea or lake watersports, birdwatching 2km, golf course 15km

Adequate English spoken

10 km - S - ST MALO
ST SULIAC: hosts can collect from station,
railway station 12km

PRICE STRUCTURE

2 Bedrooms

bathroom with wc, double bed: FF290

shower room with wc, double bed, single bed: FF350 (2 people) FF510 (3 people)

Extra bed: 50FF
Reduction: 01.11 – 30.04 and 4 nights

Capacity: 5 people

— On the N137 dual carriageway (Rennes to St Malo road) turn off between the N137 and the N176 at the exit to St Suliac. 50 metres before the church on the square, in front of the post office (PTT) you will see the large white gates on your left.

Gisèle THEAULT

60, rue du Bord de Mer
35114 SAINT-BENOIT-DES-ONDES

tel: (0) 2 99 58 76 90

Private Home

10 km - S - ST MALO
ST BENOIT DES ONDES: hosts can collect from station, railway station 10km
airport 80km
car essential

35.29 ST MALO

Gisèle is a lively, retired lady, full of kindness. Her house is very well-situated and in all weathers you have an unobstructed view of the Mont St Michel, thanks to her large conservatory. A wonderful place at any time of the year to take a deep breath of fresh air.

PRICE STRUCTURE

6 Bedrooms

(4 rooms) shower room with wc, double bed: FF200

(2 rooms) shower room with wc, 2 double bed: FF200 (2 people) FF300 (4 people)

Extra bed: 80FF

Capacity: 16 people

PROPERTY

✱✱

private parking, garden, tv lounge, wheelchair access, hiking, cycling, fishing, interesting flora, mushroom picking, sea or lake watersports

— When coming from St Malo take the D155 coast road towards Mont St Michel. St Benoit des Ondes is on this road, and the house is number 60 of the road along the sea front.

Jean-Paul RAUX

«Maison de Quokelunde»
41, rue du Bord de Mer
35120 HIREL

tel: (0) 2 99 48 80 12
fax: (0) 2 99 48 80 12

Private Home

17 km - S E - ST MALO
HIREL: railway station 10km
airport 85km
car essential

35.31 ST MALO

This is a restored Breton house and the host is an expert on Canada. The rooms are spacious, well-equipped, and some have a view over the bay. An ideal and practical base for visiting this area.

PROPERTY

***

off street parking, garden, pets not accepted, kitchen, wheelchair access, 7 nights minimum stay 4/07-2/09, hiking, birdwatching, sea or lake watersports, golf course 15km, fishing 15km

Basic English spoken

— When coming from St Malo take the D155 coast road towards Mont St Michel. Hirel is situated on this road at number 41 on the sea front.

PRICE STRUCTURE

2 Bedrooms and 3 Apartments

Opale: television, kitchen, shower room with wc, washbasin, double bed: FF200

Améthyste: lounge, television, kitchen, shower room with wc, washbasin, double bed, 3 single beds: FF200 (2 people) FF400 (5 people)

Emeraude: lounge, television, kitchen, shower room with wc, washbasin, double bed, 2 single beds: FF250 (2 people) FF400 (4 people)

Saphir: lounge, television, telephone, kitchen, shower room with wc, washbasin, twin beds, 2 single beds: FF250 (2 people) FF400 (4 people)

Topaze: lounge, television, kitchen, shower room with wc, washbasin, double bed, 2 single beds: FF250 (2 people) FF400 (4 people)

Extra bed: 80FF
Reduction: 01.09 – 30.06

Capacity: 19 people

Alain & Josyane
TEMPIER NOVACK

«Villa Iduna»
7, Avenue Pasteur
35400 ST MALO

tel: (0) 2 99 56 68 69
fax: (0) 2 99 56 68 69

Residence of Character

35.38 ST MALO

Alain and Josyane have restored this beautiful 18th century residence, right in the centre of St. Malo and 20m from the sea. It is comfortably furnished, and the decor is exquisite art-déco style. After dinner (St. Malo has an excellent choice of restaurants), take a stroll along the harbour wall right next to the house.

PROPERTY

***

off street parking, garden, tv lounge, hosts have pets, babies welcome, free cot, hiking, cycling, fishing, sea or lake water-sports, river watersports

Adequate English spoken

ST MALO: hosts can collect from station, railway station 1km airport 10km — As you enter the town, follow signs to "St. Malo Centre", then "Thermes marins". Just before the entrance to the spa complex, continue along the Avenue Pasteur, as far as No.7.

PRICE STRUCTURE

5 Bedrooms

First room: double bed, 2 single beds (1 childrens size): FF300 (2 people) FF400 (4 people)

Second room: double bed, single bed (childrens size): FF300

Third room: twin beds, 2 single beds (1 childrens size): FF300 (2 people) FF400 (4 people)

(2 rooms) double bed, single bed (childrens size): FF300

Extra bed: 100FF
Reduction: 15.11 – 30.01

Capacity: 17 people

Solange GUILLOUX

«La Dame de Nage»
13, rue de Bellevue -
Loc Maria
56590 ILE DE GROIX

tel: (0) 2 97 86 55 90
fax: (0) 2 97 86 55 90

Private Home

ILE DE GROIX
LOC MARIA

56.19 ILE DE GROIX

Tie up and enjoy and the magic of of L'Ile de Groix, with its nature reserve and its beach of white sand. Solange welcomes you to her house, typical of the island. From the shade of the garden, you can see the sea only 100m away. The charm of this enchanting place is enhanced by nauticalia, old chests and wood carvings.

PROPERTY

✹✹✹

off street parking, garden, tv lounge, hosts have pets, kitchen, closed: 01/10-15/03, hiking, cycling, fishing, interesting flora, birdwatching, sea or lake watersports

Basic English spoken

PRICE STRUCTURE

3 Bedrooms

Primiture & Piwisi: shower room with wc, double bed: FF330

Thoniers: television, bathroom with wc, twin beds, 2 single beds, cot: FF330 (2 people) FF580 (4 people)

Extra bed: 75FF
Reduction: 2 nights

Capacity: 8 people

— From Lorient, head towards L'Ile de Groix. There is a free car park opposite the jetty (a car is not essential on the island). The crossing takes 45 minutes, and as you leave the boat at Port Tudy, go up to the village and follow the signs (on the ground) to "Locmaria". The house is at the top of the village. If you do not bring your car, there is a regular taxi service (15FF per person), which goes all round the island

Monique POUPEE

«La Christe Marine»
Locqueltas
56590 ILE DE GROIX

tel: (0) 2 97 86 83 04
fax: (0) 2 97 86 83 04
la-christe-marine@
wanadoo.fr

Private Home

ILE DE GROIX
LOCQUELTAS:
airport, 10km

PRICE STRUCTURE

2 Bedrooms

Pimprenelle: bathroom with wc, double bed: FF350

Grand mère: along corridor bathroom with wc, double bed: FF350

Extra bed: 125FF

Capacity: 4 people

56.20 ILE DE GROIX

You will be captivated by the L'Ile de Groix, and even more so by your stay chez Monique. This is a modern house, constructed of old building material, in a special verdant spot. From the garden, your bedroom window or the terrace, there is an uninterrupted sea view (100m away). A very special place, particularly for nature lovers.

PROPERTY

❋❋❋

off street parking, garden, tv lounge, hosts have pets, pets not accepted, babies welcome, free cot, closed: 21/12-11/01, cycling, fishing, interesting flora, birdwatching, sea or lake watersports

Basic English spoken

— From Lorient, head towards L'Ile de Groix. There is a free car park opposite the jetty (a car is not essential on the island), and the crossing takes 45 minutes. As you leave the boat at Port Tudy, go up to the village and follow the signs (on the ground) to "Lomener, Locqueltas". Otherwise there is a regular taxi service (15FF per person), which goes round the whole island.

Madeleine & Jean GRU

Evas - St Laurent
sur Oust
56140 MALESTROIT

tel: (0) 2 97 75 02 62

Flat/Apartment

56.11 PLOERMEL

Madeleine and Jean's cosy home in the centre of a small village, has a beautiful garden. The bright bedrooms have rural views, and little extras like a home-made aperitif and the Breton breakfast with home-made jam, add to the enjoyment of your stay here.

18 km - S - PLOERMEL
ST LAURENT SUR OUST: railway station 30km
airport 65km
car essential

PROPERTY

✱✱

off street parking, extensive grounds, tv lounge, hosts have pets, pets not accepted, dinner available, kitchen, babies welcome, free cot, non smoking, hiking, fishing, hunting, mushroom picking, cycling 4km, river watersports 4km, golf course 15km, interesting flora 20km, gliding 20km

PRICE STRUCTURE

3 Bedrooms

television, kitchen, shower room with wc, double bed: FF210

kitchen, shower, wc, twin beds: FF210

television, shower room with wc, double bed: FF210

Extra bed: 60FF

Capacity: 6 people

— At Ploermel, N166 towards Vannes. Take the Exit 'Malestroit'. In Malestroit head towards Ruffiac for 4km. Then turn right to St. Laurent-sur-Oust and follow the signs

Daniel & Monique le DOUARAN

Guerlan - Plougoumelen
56400 AURAY

tel: (0) 2 97 57 65 50
fax: (0) 2 97 57 65 50

Farm

15 km - W - VANNES
GUERLAN:
airport 40km
car essential

56.05 VANNES

Monique and Daniel, a friendly young farming couple, welcome you with a smile into their imposing house. Much of the typical Breton furniture has been restored by Monique as a labour of love. 10km from the Bay of Morbihan.

PRICE STRUCTURE

5 Bedrooms and 1 Suite

Chambre au balcon: shower room with wc, double bed: FF220

Chambre verte: shower room with wc, twin beds: FF220

Rez de chaussée: wheelchair access, shower room with wc, double bed: FF260

Suite: shower room with wc, 2 double beds: FF260 (2 people) FF520 (4 people)

Etage: chambre 1: shower room with wc, double bed, single bed: FF260 (2 people) FF360 (3 people)

Etage: chambre 2: shower, wc, 3 single beds: FF260 (2 people) FF360 (3 people)

Extra bed: 40FF

Capacity: 16 people

PROPERTY

**

off street parking, garden, tv lounge, hosts have pets, kitchen, babies welcome, free cot, wheelchair access, sea or lake watersports 30km

Adequate English spoken

— In Vannes, take the N165 towards Lorient. After Vannes, take the first exit 'Ploeren-Meriadec' and take the D127 towards Meriadec for 3.5km. 2nd farm on the left (after the level-crossing).

Patrick & Marie COSSÉ

«Auberge du Château de Castellan»
Castellan
56200 ST MARTIN sur OUST

tel: (0) 2 99 91 51 69
fax: (0) 2 99 91 57 41

Château

40 km - E - VANNES
CASTELLAN: hosts can collect from station,
railway station 23km
airport 65km
car essential

56.10 VANNES

This 18th century château is in superb surroundings, and one bedroom is listed as an historic monument. This is a farm-house inn, run by the family, famous for their 'paté en croute', as well as other excellent traditional Breton dishes. On sale: Jam, gingerbread, terrines, local produce.

PROPERTY

✱✱✱✱

off street parking, extensive grounds, pets not accepted, dinner available, babies welcome, free cot, hiking, cycling, fishing 2km, interesting flora 18km, sea or lake watersports 40km, birdwatching 45km

English spoken

— At Vannes, N166 towards Rennes. D776 towards Malestroit. In Malestroit, D764 towards St Congard. D149 towards St Martin. Sign 'Auberge', on the left, before you reach St Martin.

PRICE STRUCTURE

5 Bedrooms

Saumon: shower room with wc, double bed, single bed: FF450 (2 people) FF560 (3 people)

Verte: shower room with wc, twin beds: FF450

Médaillon: bathroom with wc, double bed, twin beds: FF600 (2 people) FF820 (3 people)

Roland: bathroom with wc, double bed: FF450

Dortoir: shower room with wc, double bed, twin beds: FF500 (2 people) FF720 (4 people)

Extra bed: 110FF

Capacity: 15 people

Bretagne

VANNES

Maria FLOHIC

7 rue Er
Vammenn - Kerguillé
56470 LA TRINITE
SUR MER

tel: (0) 2 97 55 76 74

Private Home

30 km - S W -
VANNES
LA TRINITE SUR
MER:
railway station 12km
airport 50km

56.14 VANNES

A world famous port, La Trinité is the rendezvous of lovers of the sea, and famous skippers. Close to the port and its restauraunts, the beaches and menhirs, a peaceful house, painted white, awaits you. Breathe in the sea air and dream of distant horizons...

PRICE STRUCTURE

3 Bedrooms

telephone, shower room with wc, double bed: FF270

shower room with wc, twin beds: FF270

along corridor shower room with wc, double bed, single bed: FF270 (2 people) FF345 (3 people)

Extra bed: 70FF

Capacity: 7 people

PROPERTY

private parking, garden, babies welcome, free cot, fishing, birdwatching 1km, hiking 2km, cycling 15km

— At Vannes, take the N165 to Auray, where you will take the D28 to to La Trinité. From the port, head towards Auray (D186). 300 metres after leaving the town, turn left towards Kerguillé. Rue Er Vammen is the first on the right.

Maria & Eric DE MAGALHAES

Kerbissac de Lesnoyal
56230 QUESTEMBERT

tel: (0) 2 97 26 65 89

Residence of Character

56.16 VANNES

Maria, who used to be an air-hostess, has brought a knowledge of many foreign languages and the art of the perfect welcome, back from her travels. Her longhouse, marvellously constructed (even if the staircase is a little steep), boasts excellent facilities and a swimming pool. Be sure to try Eric's honey. This place is a real find! On sale: embroidery, hand-painted earthenware.

27 km - E - VANNES
QUESTEMBERT:
hosts can collect from station,
railway station, 2km
airport, 100km
car essential

PROPERTY

***

private parking, garden, tv lounge, hosts have pets, telephone, packed lunch, babies welcome, free cot, swimming pool, hiking, mushroom picking 1km, cycling 5km, fishing 5km, sea or lake watersports 11km, golf course 18km, interesting flora 30km, birdwatching 30km, gliding 30km

Fluent English spoken

PRICE STRUCTURE

2 Bedrooms

Jaune: television, shower room with wc, washbasin, double bed, 2 single beds: FF280 (2 people) FF380 (4 people)

Rose: television, telephone, bathroom with wc, washbasin, double bed: FF270

Extra bed: 50FF Reduction: 01.10 – 01.04 and groups

Capacity: 6 people

— At Vannes, take the N166 towards Ploermel, then the D775 towards Redon. At the Bel Air roundabout, head towards the race-course. After the stands, take the 3rd left, and then the 1st left. The house is at the end of the small lane.

Laurence & Luc PADIL-LA

4, impasse Lausseul - Langle
56860 SENE

tel: (0) 2 97 66 02 01
fax: (0) 2 97 66 02 01

Private Home

6 km - S - VANNES
SENE: railway station 10km
airport 20km
car essential

56.21 VANNES

This recently built house is set on a peninsula in the centre of a really typical fishing village. It is the ideal place from which to explore the nature reserve of Séné, which is one of the most outstanding in Europe. Laurence and Luc, who are young teachers, will give you invaluable advice for trips through the marshlands and the Golfe du Morbihan.

PRICE STRUCTURE

4 Bedrooms

First room: shower room with wc, double bed: FF200

Second room: shower, dou  ble bed: FF200

Third & fourth rooms: twin beds: FF200

Reduction: 7 nights

Capacity: 8 people

PROPERTY

✱✱

off street parking, garden, tv lounge, pets not accepted, hiking, fishing, river watersports 4km, birdwatching 5km, cycling 10km

Basic English spoken

— From the Vannes - Nantes dual carriageway, head towards Séné-Bourg. When you reach the "Donegal" roundabout (distinguished by a fishing boat), head towards Bellevue-Porana. After 4km, at Langle, head towards the school (l'ecole) and follow the green and blue signs.

Jeanne CHEILLETZ-MAIGNAN

«Chaumière de Kérisac»
56390 LOCQUELTAS

tel: (0) 2 97 66 60 13
fax: (0) 2 97 66 67 57
chaumierekerisac@
minitel.net

Residence of Character

12 km - N - VANNES
LOCQUELTAS:
railway station 12km
airport 100km
car essential

56.22 VANNES

Jeanne has finished travelling, and now she loves welcoming and making a fuss of her guests in this thatched cottage dating from 1750, which is full of life and warmth. She serves you a hearty breakfast in a dining room decorated with souvenirs from the colonies. There is also the peaceful garden in which to relax.

PROPERTY

✹✹✹

off street parking, garden, tv lounge, hosts have pets, pets not accepted, babies welcome, free cot, closed: 05/01-05/02, hiking, fishing 1km, mushroom picking 6km, birdwatching 15km, sea or lake watersports 15km, golf course 25km

Fluent English spoken

PRICE STRUCTURE

3 Bedrooms

Blé-noir: shower room with wc, double bed: FF350

Chanvre: bathroom, wc, double bed, single bed: FF350 (2 people) FF450 (3 people)

Seigle: bathroom with wc, twin beds: FF380

Capacity: 7 people

— From Vannes, head in the direction of Pontivy-St. Brieuc on the D767 as far as the dual carriageway. Take the third Exit - Locqueltas. Go through the village, and as you exit the village, after 500m turn left at the first crossroads. This is the "Chemin de Kerisac". Then follow the signs.

Marie Madeleine
BOCANDÉ

32, rue Châteaubriand
56450 THEIX

tel: (0) 2 97 43 12 37

Private Home

8 km - S E - VANNES
THEIX: railway station 10km
car essential

PRICE STRUCTURE

3 Bedrooms

(2 rooms) shower room with wc, double bed, single bed: FF210 (2 people) FF260 (3 people)

Third room: along corridor bathroom with wc, double bed: FF210

Extra bed: 50FF

Capacity: 8 people

56.23 VANNES

This detached house is on the edge of the village and the countryside, 6km from Vannes. It is easy to find, and very convenient for the sea, only 3km away. Do not worry about the fox on the lounge table, he is stuffed. On the other hand, Marie-Madeleine is full of life and joie de vivre.

PROPERTY

✱✱

off street parking, garden, tv lounge, fishing 2km, birdwatching 3km, sea or lake watersports 3km, golf course 12km

— From the Vannes - Nantes dual carriageway, take Exit Theix. Theix, by the post office, head towards Noyalo. At the second roundabout, turn right towards the "ZA du Landy". Continue straight on, and then take the last street on the left before leaving the village (Rue Lesage), which leads to the Rue de Châteaubriand on the right.

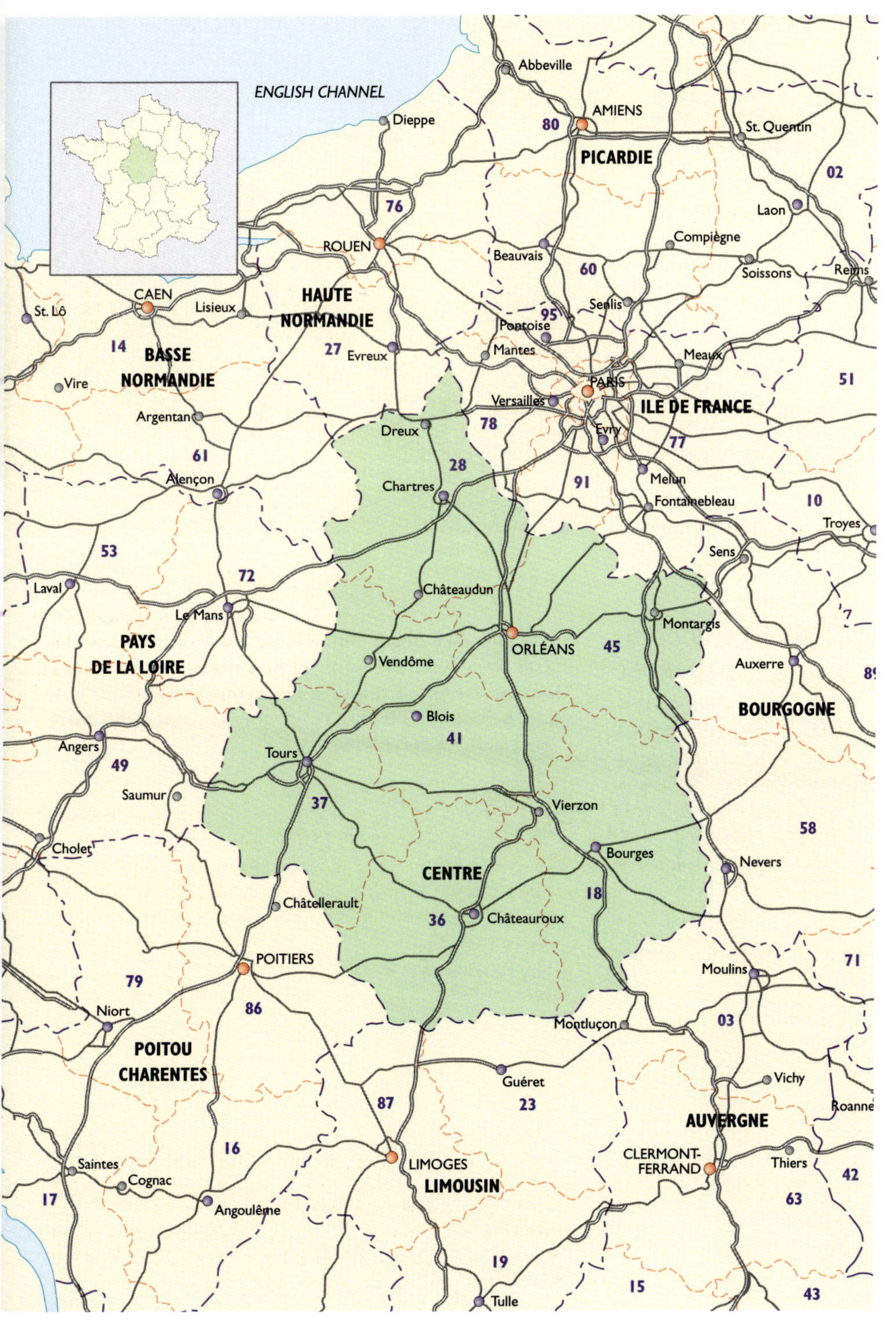

ENGLISH CHANNEL
Abbeville
AMIENS
80
PICARDIE
St. Quentin
02
Dieppe
76
ROUEN
Laon
Compiègne
Soissons
Reims
Beauvais
60
CAEN
St. Lô
Lisieux
HAUTE NORMANDIE
Senlis
95
Pontoise
14
BASSE NORMANDIE
27
Evreux
Mantes
Meaux
Vire
PARIS
51
Versailles
ILE DE FRANCE
Argentan
Dreux
78
Evry
77
61
28
Alençon
Chartres
91
Melun
Fontainebleau
10
Troyes
53
Sens
72
Laval
Châteaudun
Le Mans
Montargis
PAYS DE LA LOIRE
ORLÉANS
45
Vendôme
Auxerre
Blois
BOURGOGNE
41
Angers
Tours
49
Saumur
37
Vierzon
58
Cholet
Bourges
Nevers
CENTRE
18
Châtellerault
36
Châteauroux
POITIERS
71
Moulins
79
86
Niort
Montluçon
03
POITOU CHARENTES
Guéret
Vichy
87
23
Roanne
AUVERGNE
16
CLERMONT-FERRAND
Thiers
Saintes
LIMOGES
42
Cognac
LIMOUSIN
63
17
Angoulême
19
15
43
Tulle

Yves & Odile PROFFIT

«La Chaume»
Rians
18220 LES AIX
D'ANGILLON

tel: (0) 2 48 64 41 58
fax: (0) 2 48 64 29 71

Farm

17 km - N E - BOURGES RIANS:
airport 20km
car essential

Centre

BOURGES

18.03 BOURGES

Small detached house with a living room, kitchen and barbecue at the side of the farm. The care and attention that Madame has lavished on the bedrooms also extends to her warm welcome. This area produces excellent milk, goats cheese and Sancerre wine.

PRICE STRUCTURE

3 Bedrooms

Bas 1: shower room with wc, twin beds: FF240

Bas 2: along corridor shower room with wc, double bed, single bed: FF220 (2 people) FF310 (3 people)

Haut 3: shower room with wc, twin beds: FF240

Extra bed: 90FF

Capacity: 7 people

PROPERTY

✸✸✸

off street parking, garden, tv lounge, hosts have pets, telephone, dinner available, kitchen, babies welcome, free cot, hiking, cycling, fishing 5km, golf course 17km, sea or lake watersports 20km

Adequate English spoken

— Exit "Bourges" on the A71. In Bourges, take the N151 towards Auxerre. Turn left on to the D955 towards Les Aix d'Angillon where you take the D46 towards Ste Solange for 4km. Follow the signs.

Robert ROY

«Relais des Gaillards»
Route de
Neuvy/Barangeon
18110 ALLOGNY

tel: (0) 2 48 64 00 84
fax: (0) 2 48 70 52 50

Private home

18 km - N W -
BOURGES
ALLOGNY: railway
station 20km
airport 20km
car essential

18.04 BOURGES

Formerly an old working farm, this place is on a 110 hectare estate in the "Sologne du Cher", on the "Route Jacques Cœur". There are wild animals on the estate (nothing dangerous), as well as golf, riding and five lakes.

English breakfast : 15 FF supplement.

PROPERTY

✱✱✱

off street parking, extensive grounds, tv lounge, hosts have pets, kitchen, babies welcome, free cot, wheelchair access, hiking, cycling, fishing, hunting, golf course 10km

— In Bourges, take the D944 towards Orléans. The house is 3km on the right, after Allogny. From the A71, take the Salbris exit. In Salbris, take the D944 towards Bourges. 7km on the left after Neuvy sur Barangeon.

PRICE STRUCTURE

8 Bedrooms

First, second, third, fifth & sixth rooms: television, shower room with wc, double bed: FF300

Fourth room: television, shower room with wc, double bed: FF275

Seventh room: television, shower room with wc, 3 single beds: FF300 (2 people) FF375 (3 people)

Eighth room: television, shower room with wc, 2 double beds, FF375 (2 people) FF430 (4 people)

Extra bed: 50FF

Capacity: 19 people

Dany BAUCHEZ

«Le Bien Dormir»
12, Av de Paris
18700 AUBIGNY SUR NÈRE

tel: (0) 2 48 81 04 04
fax: (0) 2 48 81 04 04

Private home

18.14 BOURGES

A large house on the main Bourges to Paris road in Stuart country. You will find a warm welcome from Dany and her two small boys. The rooms are spacious and comfortable. You will particularly enjoy the delicious, generous breakfast and their cute little pony. On sale: Sancerre and Menetou wine, dairy and goat's cheese and 'sablé' biscuits.

PROPERTY

✱✱

private parking, garden, tv lounge, hosts have pets, telephone, kitchen, packed lunch, babies welcome, free cot, 4 nights minimum stay, hiking 2km, fishing 2km, hunting 3km, gliding 4km, cycling 10km, mushroom picking 10km, golf course 25km

Fluent English spoken

46 km - N - BOURGES
AUBIGNY SUR NERE: railway station 30km
car essential
— At Bourges, take the D940 towards Paris. The house is in Aubigny, 150m from the Intermarché supermarket.

PRICE STRUCTURE

5 Bedrooms

Triple bas: telephone, shower room with wc, double bed, single bed: FF300 (2 people) FF380 (3 people)

Feuillage & Printanière: bathroom with wc, double bed: FF300

Triple: bathroom with wc, double bed, single bed: FF300 (2 people) FF380 (3 people)

Bow window: shower, washbasin, double bed: FF250

Reduction: 15/10–15/03 and 3 nights and groups and children

Capacity: 12 people

18.15 BOURGES

Véra KIRCHHOFF

«Les Aulnains»
Route de Presly
18380 LA CHAPELLE D'ANGILLON

tel: (0) 2 48 73 40 09
fax: (0) 2 48 73 44 56

Residence of character

This adorable couple live in an 18th century manor house on a 150 hectare estate, with a lake and lots of wildlife. Ideal for keen fisherman (Black Bass), hunting, and the peace and quiet of La Sologne. Excellent dinner.

PROPERTY

✱✱✱✱

off street parking, extensive grounds, tv lounge, hosts have pets, telephone, dinner available, closed: 1/03-31/03, hiking, cycling, fishing, hunting, mushroom picking, golf course 20km, sea or lake watersports 25km

Fluent English spoken

30 km - N - BOURGES
LA CHAPELLE D'ANGILLON: railway station 35km
airport 35km
car essential
— Exit Bourges on the A71. At Bourges take the D940 towards Gien. At La Chapelle d'Angillon turn left on to the D12 towards Presly and follow the signs "Chambres d'Hotes".

PRICE STRUCTURE

1 Bedroom and 1 Suite

First room: television, bathroom with wc, double bed: FF325

Second room: television, bathroom with wc, double bed: FF325 (2 people)

Third room: double bed: FF325

Capacity: 6 people

Marie Dominique &
Jacques GREAU

Villemenard
18500 VIGNOUX sur
BARANGEON

tel: (0) 2 48 51 53 40
fax: (0) 2 48 51 58 77

hâteau or manor house

15 km - N W - BOURGES
VIGNOUX SUR BARANGEON:
railway station 6km
airport 20km
car essential

18.17 BOURGES

You will remember this beautiful place for its china and pottery. The walls inside the house are covered with blue pottery from Portugal, and the dining room is decorated with porcelain. They have a professional snooker table in the large lounge. Excellent value for money. 1 apartment also available to rent weekly.

PRICE STRUCTURE

6 Bedrooms

(2 rooms) television, bathroom with wc, double bed, single bed: FF260 (2 people) FF340 (3 people)

(2 rooms) television, bathroom with wc, twin beds: FF260

(2 rooms) television, bathroom with wc, double bed: FF260

Extra bed: 90FF

Capacity: 14 people

PROPERTY

****

off street parking, extensive grounds, tv lounge, hosts have pets, pets not accepted, riding, hiking, fishing, hunting, interesting flora, mushroom picking, river watersports 6km, golf course 10km, sea or lake watersports 25km

Basic English spoken

— At Bourges, take the N76 towards Vierzon as far as Mehun. Then turn right on to the D79 towards Vouzeron. Then turn left after 5.5km.

Wilfrid de POMMEREA

«Château de Beaujeu»
18300 SENS-BEAUJEU

tel: (0) 2 48 79 07 95
fax: (0) 2 48 79 05 07

Château

10 km - W -
SANCERRE
SENS BEAUJEU:
hosts can collect from station,
railway station 20km
airport 200km
car essential

Centre

SANCERRE

18.13 SANCERRE

You will enjoy the relaxed atmosphere and the warm welcome in this 16th century family château, situated in large grounds through which a river flows. For wine lovers, you are in the heart of the Sancerre vineyards.

PROPERTY

****

off street parking, extensive grounds, hosts have pets, dinner available, babies welcome, free cot, closed: 15/11-1/03, fishing, hiking 3km, cycling 10km, birdwatching 10km, sea or lake watersports 12km, gliding 12km, golf course 15km, river watersports 15km

Adequate English spoken

PRICE STRUCTURE

3 Bedrooms

La Tour: bathroom with wc, double bed, single bed: FF700 (2 people) FF900 (3 people)

Louis XVI: bathroom with wc, double bed: FF650

Bleue: bathroom with wc, twin beds: FF650

Capacity: 7 people

— At Sancerre take the D7 towards Sens-Beaujeu. In this village then take the D74 towards Neuilly.

Pierre & Colette PARENT

«Les Caillotières»
54, Chemin Blanc
18120 MEREAU

tel: (0) 2 48 71 11 56

Private home

2 km - S - VIERZON MEREAU: hosts can collect from station, railway station 2km airport 55km — On the A20, Exit 7 to Vierzon heading towards Mereau/Issoudun via the D320. On this road, look out on the right for the signs "Chambres d'hotes" (do not go as far as Mereau, as the house is nearer to the autoroute Exit at Vierzon).

18.16 VIERZON

Pierre is a pastry cook, and you will enjoy the delicious results of his skills at breakfast. Each bedroom has its own personality: one with soft pastel colours, a rustic room with a piano and another with a gaming table. The family welcome is warm and relaxing. On sale: Honey, wine.

PROPERTY

✱✱

private parking, garden, tv lounge, hosts have pets, telephone, dinner available, kitchen, packed lunch, babies welcome, free cot, fishing 2km, river watersports 2km, hiking 4km, cycling 4km, golf course 5km, mushroom picking 5km, sea or lake watersports 10km, interesting flora 20km, hunting 30km

Basic English spoken

PRICE STRUCTURE

4 Bedrooms

Serin & Rouge-Gorge: television, single bed: FF160

Mésange: double bed, 2 single bed childrens size: FF190 (2 people) FF300 (4 people)

Pivert: double bed, single bed childrens size: FF190 (2 people) FF300 (3 people)

Extra bed: 60FF

Capacity: 9 people

Roger PARMENTIER

2, rue des Champarts - Blévy
28170 BLEVY

tel: (0) 2 37 48 01 21
fax: (0) 2 37 48 01 80
E-mail: parti@club-internet.fr

Private home

35 km - N W - CHARTRES
BLEVY: hosts can collect from station, railway station 20 km

28.03 CHARTRES

Dagmar and Roger, an adorable couple whom our clients always praise the most, offer a warm welcome. Dagmar is German and Roger is a retired chef, so, make sure you try his cooking. The bedrooms are very pretty, and the breakfast plentiful. Well worth a detour.

PROPERTY

✱✱✱

private parking, garden, tv lounge, dinner available, packed lunch, closed: 1/02-28/02, hiking, cycling, golf course 8km

Fluent English spoken

PRICE STRUCTURE

1 Bedroom and 1 Suite

Blévy: television, along corridor bathroom with wc, double bed: FF270

Paris: lounge, television, shower room with wc, double bed: FF320

Extra bed: 150/180FF

Capacity: 4 people

— Exit Chartres on the A11. In Chartres, take the D939 towards Verneuil sur Avre. In Maillebois, turn right on to the D20 towards Blévy and Dreux. In Blévy go towards Laons and as you leave the village, the house is the first on the right.

Claire & Etienne BROSSOLLET

49, rue des Fontaines
28300 ST PREST

tel: (0) 2 37 22 25 31
fax: (0) 2 37 22 26 07
E-mail:
claire.etienne.brossollet@libertysurf.fr

Private home

8 km - N - CHARTRES
ST PREST: railway station 2km
airport 80km
car essential

PRICE STRUCTURE

1 Suite

bathroom with wc, double bed, 2 single beds: FF250 (2 people) FF450 (4 people)

Capacity: 4 people

28.07 CHARTRES

The ambience is warm in this old farmhouse with a thatched roof and, in the winter, the smoke from the wood fire makes the welcome even warmer. They serve dinner in the garden in summer. It is 8km from Chartres and its famous cathedral and old town. There is an airfield nearby, and you are only 10km from the château at Maintenon. Golf, riding, hang-gliding and cycling are available in the area, as well as lots of excellent walks and hiking. Fleur de Soleil member.

PROPERTY

❋❋❋

off street parking, garden, lounge, pets not accepted, dinner available, hiking, cycling, golf course, gliding,

English spoken

— On the Chartres Road, head for Maintenon via the Eure Valley and Les Moulins Neufs de Saint Prest.

Wilhem&Renée
SCHAFFNER ORVOEN

«La Musardière»
28270 LA MANCELIÈR

tel: (0) 2 37 48 39 09
fax: (0) 2 37 48 42 63
E-mail:
lamuse.cdh@wanadoo.f

Residence of character

12 km - S -
VERNEUIL sur
AVRE
LA MANCELIERE:
railway station 12km
airport 120km
car essential

28.05 VERNEUIL SUR AVRE

Wilhelm is of German origin and with his lovely wife, Renée, gave up a computer business for this beautiful region of Le Perche. The rustic-style bedrooms are in separate little farmhouses full of character, and overlook extensive grounds. There is an indoor heated pool. Flour dc soleil member.

PROPERTY

***

private parking, extensive grounds, tv lounge, hosts have pets, kitchen, babies welcome, free cot, swimming pool, closed: 11/11-31/03, 2 nights minimum stay 01/06-15/09, golf course 3km, mushroom picking 3km, fishing 4km, hunting 5km, hiking 6km, cycling 8km, interesting flora 8km, sea or lake watersports 15km

Fluent English spoken

PRICE STRUCTURE

3 Bedrooms and 1 Suite and 1 Apartment

Passerose: television, bathroom with wc, double bed: FF390

Chevrefeuille: shower room with wc, double bed: FF390

Marguerite: lounge, television, kitchen, bathroom with wc, twin beds, 2 single beds: FF550 (2 people) FF800 (4 people)

Capucine: shower room with wc, double bed: FF390

Valériane: lounge, television, kitchen, bathroom with wc, twin beds: FF490

Extra bed: 90FF
Reduction: 2 nights

Capacity: 12 people

— From the N12 at Verneuil, take the D25 towards Senonches. In La Mancelière, the house is situated on the D4 (the road between La Ferté-Vidame and Brézolles).

Danièle SCHOLL

«Moulin Foulon»
36200 TENDU

tel: (0) 2 54 24 31 66

Private home

36.04 CHATEAUROUX

A warm welcome from this couple in their little country house beside the river. The house has a conservatory and a view over the river, and the one bedroom is in the main house. If you stay for a week, you will have use of the kitchen, but otherwise there is a good restaurant nearby.

PROPERTY

*

off street parking, garden, hosts have pets, dinner available, English spoken, fishing, sea or lake watersports 15km, interesting flora 25km, birdwatching 35km, river watersports 40km, golf course 45km

English spoken

23 km - S - CHATEAUROUX TENDU: airport 100km car essential — At Châteauroux, take the A20 (Exit 16 : Tendu) towards Limoges. At Tendu, go behind the church and follow the signs "Vallée de la Bouzanne". The house, which is 3.5km from the village, adjoins the restaurant 'Le Moulin des Eaux Vives'.

PRICE STRUCTURE

1 Bedroom

television, shower room with wc, washbasin, double bed, single bed: FF220 (2 people) FF275 (3 people)

Reduction: 7 nights

Capacity: 3 people

37.01 AMBOISE

Martine ALEKSIC

«La Chevalerie»
La Croix en Touraine
37150 BLERE

tel: (0) 2 47 57 83 64

Farm

This modernised farm has all modern comforts, an enclosed garden, full of flowers and animals to entertain the kids. It is situated on the edge of the Amboise forest. Ideal for ramblers and anglers, as well as for visits to the châteaux de Touraine.

PROPERTY

***

off street parking, garden, lounge, hosts have pets, pets not accepted, kitchen, babies welcome, free cot, hiking, fishing 4km, golf course 5km

PRICE STRUCTURE

4 Bedrooms

First & second rooms: shower room with wc, double bed, single bed: FF220 (2 people) FF320 (3 people)

Third room: shower room with wc, double bed: FF220

Fourth room: shower room with wc, twin beds: FF220

Extra bed: 80FF

Capacity: 10 people

10 km - S - AMBOISE LA CROIX DE TOURAINE: hosts can collect from station, railway station 3km airport 25km

Dominique DUPIN

«La Riveraine»
4, quai des Violettes
37400 AMBOISE

tel: (0) 2 47 57 34 27

Residence of character

AMBOISE
railway station 2km

PRICE STRUCTURE

2 Bedroom

bathroom with wc, shower, twin beds: FF260

bathroom, wc, double bed: FF240

Capacity: 4 people

37.17 AMBOISE

Dominique is charming. She loves tennis and music. Her house is on the edge of the River Loire with a view over the grounds between the two arms of the river. You are only 500m from the Château d'Amboise. There is a barbecue in the courtyard.

PROPERTY

off street parking, garden, tv lounge, hosts have pets, pets not accepted, babies welcome, free cot, fishing, sea or lake watersports 1km, river watersports 1km, hiking 2km, mushroom picking 2km, golf course 24km

Adequate English spoken

— In Amboise, from the N152, cross the bridge and turn left on to the D751 along by the Loire for 300m, after passing the hotel 'Choiseul'.

Claude FOURSAC

3, Rue de l'Europe
37150 CHISSEAUX

tel: (0) 2 47 23 90 87

Residence of character

20 km - S -
AMBOISE
CHISSEAUX:
railway station 1km

37.35 AMBOISE

The same family have lived in this impressive house for the last 150 years. With a bit of luck you will meet all four generations, all extremely likeable. It is 1km from Chenonceaux and near some of the most famous of the Loire Valley châteaux. On sale: Wine from their vineyard.

PROPERTY

***

private parking, garden, tv lounge, no pets, dinner available, packed lunch, riding, hiking, cycling, fishing, mushroom picking, river watersports

Fluent English spoken

PRICE STRUCTURE

2 Suites

First room: shower room with wc, bathroom, double bed, 3 single beds: FF400 (2 people) FF750 (5 people)

Second room: along corridor bathroom with wc, double bed, 2 single beds: FF300 (2 people) FF600 (4 people)

Reduction: 3 nights

Capacity: 9 people

— At Amboise take the D31 towards Bleré as far as La Croix en Touraine where you should take the D40 on the left towards Chenonceaux. The house is on the D40 going towards Montrichard.

Caroline MANIE

«Auberge Forestière Marcheroux»
Route de Chenonceaux
D81 37400 FORET D'AMBOISE

tel: (0) 2 47 57 27 57
fax: (0) 2 47 30 28 29

Residence of character

2 km - S - AMBOISE FORET D'AMBOISE:
railway station 5km
airport 30km
car essential

PRICE STRUCTURE

5 Bedrooms

N°1 & N°3: television, telephone, shower room with wc, washbasin, double bed, single bed: FF320 (2 people) FF400 (3 people)

N°2 & N°4 & N°5: television, telephone, shower room with wc, washbasin, double bed: FF320

Reduction: 15/10–30/03 and 3 nights and groups

Capacity: 12 people

37.38 AMBOISE

A former 17th century hunting lodge, this inn in the heart of the Amboise forest is an ideal base for day trips (2km from Amboise and 4km from Chenonceaux). Simple rooms, off the beaten track. Try some classic old-fashioned dishes in the restaurant. Helicopter trips over the châteaux can be arranged.

PROPERTY

✱✱✱

private parking, extensive grounds, tv lounge, hosts have pets, dinner available, swimming pool, hiking, mushroom picking, hunting 1km, cycling 2km, fishing 4km, river watersports 4km, golf course 10km

Adequate English spoken

— From Paris, take the A10, then the N18 Exit to Amboise. Near Amboise, on the D751, head towards Chenonceaux (D81). Take the first right after 2km. Follow the signs.

Michèle DUVIVIER

«Relais de la Herserie»
Château de la Herserie
37150 LA CROIX EN TOURAINE

tel: (0) 2 47 23 54 36
fax: (0) 2 47 64 56 85

Château

10 km - S - AMBOISE
LA CROIX DE TOURAINE: hosts can collect from station, railway station 3km
airport 30km
car essential

37.39 AMBOISE

This château overlooks a superb estate with a lake and 3 hectares of undulating grounds, containing a wildlife park with over 130 animals. Do not be surprised to see a kangaroo, a llama, deer or peacocks... a magical experience. The rooms are quite basic, but it is ideal for a group of friends.

PROPERTY

✱✱✱

private parking, extensive grounds, lounge, hosts have pets, telephone, babies welcome, free cot, riding, hiking, hunting, interesting flora, cycling 5km, golf course 10km, fishing 10km, sea or lake watersports 25km

Basic English spoken

— At Amboise, take the D31 towards La Croix de Touraine (from Tours, take the D140 towards Chenonceaux). From the centre of La Croix de Touraine, head in the direction of Chenonceaux, then take the second road on the left. The chateau is 700 m further on, on the right.

PRICE STRUCTURE

23 Bedrooms and 1 Suite

Rabelais: shower room with wc, double bed, twin beds: FF300 (2 people) FF460 (4 people)

(5 rooms) shower room with wc, double bed: FF300

Bayard: washbasin, single bed: FF150

La Palice: washbasin, double bed: FF250

Montmorency: double bed: FF250

Moncontour: twin beds: FF300

Pardaillan & Capitan: double bed, single bed: FF250 (2 people) FF300 (3 people)

Château N° 3: bathroom, double bed: FF300

Château N° 4, 7 & 8: shower, twin beds: FF300

Château N° 6b: shower room with wc, 4 single bed: FF300 (2 people) FF460 (4 people)

Château N° 9: shower, double bed, twin beds: FF300 (2 people) FF460 (4 people)

Château N° 10: shower, single bed: FF150

Château Suite: bathroom with wc, 3 double beds: FF250 (2 people) FF750 (6 people)

Extra bed: 80FF
Reduction: 01/10–01/04 and 7 nights and groups

Capacity: 58 people

Centre Val-de-Loire

AZAY LE RIDEAU

SALLES

«Château du Gerfaut»
Le Gerfaut
37190, AZAY LE RIDEAU

tel: (0) 2 47 45 40 16
fax: (0) 2 47 45 20 15

Château

AZAY LE RIDEAU
railway station 4km
airport 30km
car essential

PRICE STRUCTURE

7 Bedrooms

Verte: bathroom with wc, double bed, single bed: FF635 (2 people) FF775 (3 people)

Rouge: bathroom with wc, shower, twin beds: FF590

Jaune & Rose: bathroom with wc, double bed, single bed: FF560 (2 people) FF700 (3 people)

Blanche: shower, wc, double bed: FF450

Bleue: bathroom with wc, shower, double bed: FF635

Lilas: shower room with wc, twin beds: FF560

Extra bed: 140FF
Reduction: 4 nights and children

Capacity: 17 people

37.03 AZAY LE RIDEAU

A hunting lodge of the Kings of France, particularly favoured by Louis XI for falconry. The château was built at the beginning of the century. The rooms are rather sober but the location is so wonderful. Deer roam in the grounds. On sale: Honey, paté

1 self-catering apartment, rented weekly.

PROPERTY

✱✱✱✱

off street parking, extensive grounds, lounge, hosts have pets, no pets, telephone, packed lunch, babies welcome, free cot, tennis, closed: 1/11-31/03, hiking, cycling, golf course 12km

Fluent English spoken

— In Azay le Rideau, take the D751 towards Tours. At the 'Gendarmerie' and the supermarket, turn left towards Villandry then take the first road on the right.

Therèse & Daniel
BERNARD

«le Prieuré»
8, Cour de l'Abbaye
37220 TAVANT

tel: (0) 2 47 97 08 58
fax: (0) 2 47 97 08 59

Private home

15 km - S - AZAY LE RIDEAU
TAVANT: railway station 40km
car essential

Centre Val-de-Loire

AZAY LE RIDEAU

37.07 AZAY LE RIDEAU

These 17th century buildings are next to the abbey of Tavant. There are 2 apartments available around the pool, named after wine which is so close to the heart of Thérèse and Daniel! For golfers they have clubs you can borrow.

PROPERTY

✱✱✱

garden, tv lounge, hosts have pets, telephone, dinner available, kitchen, babies welcome, free cot, swimming pool, 3 nights minimum stay, hiking, cycling, fishing, river watersports 2km, golf course 30km

Adequate English spoken

PRICE STRUCTURE

2 Apartments

Bourgueil & Saumur Champigny: lounge, television, kitchen, shower room with wc, double bed: FF400

Reduction: 01/09–15/06

Capacity: 4 people

— From the A10, Exit St Maure de Touraine, towards l'Ile Bouchard where you take the road to Chinon, south of the Vienne river, for 2km. The house is 300m further on the right after you have entered the village, below the arch.

Jacky & Michèle COCHEREAU

«Ferme de La Persillerie»
37110 LES HERMITES

tel: (0) 2 47 56 32 04

Private home

16 km - N W - CHATEAU-RENAULT
LES HERMITES: airport 30km
car essential

37.19 CHATEAU-RENAULT

This is just as you imagine a farm should be, in the middle of the fields, and you will love the warm accent of Michèle and Jacky. You are mid–way between two rival tourist areas: the listed villages of the beautiful Loir valley and the châteaux of the Loire Valley. The choice is yours!

PRICE STRUCTURE

3 Bedrooms

Aliénor: shower, wc, double bed: FF200

Adélaïde: double bed: FF200

Alyssia: bathroom, wc, double bed, single bed: FF200 (2 people) FF250 (3 people)

Extra bed: 50FF

Reduction: 4 nights

Capacity: 7 people

PROPERTY

✸✸

off street parking, garden, hosts have pets, dinner available, babies welcome, free cot, hiking, cycling, fishing 5km, interesting flora 15km, sea or lake watersports 20km, golf course 23km, gliding 30km

— In Château-Renault, take the D766 towards Angers for 1km. Turn right towards Le Boulay. As you leave the village, turn right on to the D72 towards Monthodon, then Les Hermites. The farm is on the left, 4km after Monthodon.

Dany & Patricia
NIEDBALSKI

«La Maréchalerie»
6, rue des Rosiers - Le Sentier
37110 MONTHODON

tel: (0) 2 47 29 61 66

Residence of character

9 km - N W - CHATEAU-RENAULT
LE SENTIER:
airport 30km
car essential

37.28 CHATEAU-RENAULT

This friendly and dynamic couple will look after you well. You will enjoy your stay here, whether for a weekend or a longer holiday, whatever the time of the year. A warm, friendly atmosphere, very good food, and grandmother's hand-embroidered sheets... a real bargain.

PROPERTY

***

off street parking, garden, tv lounge, hosts have pets, dinner available, babies welcome, free cot, hiking, cycling, mushroom picking, fishing 2km, golf course 25km, interesting flora 25km sea or lake watersports 30km

Fluent English spoken

— At Château-Renault, head in the direction of Angers for 2km, and turn right on to the D54 towards Le Boulay. Le Sentier is 3km after leaving Le Boulay.

PRICE STRUCTURE

6 Bedrooms

First, second & fourth room: shower room with wc, double bed: FF210

Third room: shower room with wc, double bed, single bed: FF210 (2 people) FF260 (3 people)

Fifth room: shower room with wc, twin beds: FF210

Studio: bathroom with wc, 2 double beds, single bed: FF330

Extra bed: 50FF

Capacity: 16 people

Michel & Claudette
BODET

«la Butte de l'Epine»
37340 CONTINVOIR

tel: (0) 2 47 96 62 25

Residence of character

30 km - N -
CHINON
CONTINVOIR:
airport 40km
car essential

PRICE STRUCTURE

2 Bedrooms

(2 rooms) shower room with wc, washbasin, twin beds: FF290

Extra bed: 80FF

Capacity: 4 people

37.05 CHINON

This is an excellent address, well worth a detour. You will appreciate being on the edge of the woods in an exceptionally charming house. It is especially great in the spring, when the birds migrate, and in autumn the colours are magnificent. Michel knows a thing or two about Bourgeuil wine.

PROPERTY

***

private parking, extensive grounds, tv lounge, hosts have pets, no pets, no smoking, closed: 24/12-2/01, hiking, cycling, fishing 6km, sea or lake watersports 6km, golf course 16km

Fluent English spoken

— At Chinon, take the D749 towards Bourgeuil and then to Gizeux, where you turn right for Continvoir, then follow the signs.

Martine DESCAMPS

«Le Clos de Ligré»
22, rue du Rouillé
37500 LIGRE

tel: (0) 2 47 93 95 59

Residence of character

5 km - S E -
CHINON
LIGRE: hosts can collect from station, railway station 8km
airport 40km
car essential

37.42 CHINON

Martine will welcome you to her authentic Touraine farmhouse, dating from the 19th century. The old wine press sets off these ancient surroundings beautifully. The garden is quiet, and there is a music room available to you. The bedroom "Fruitier" is totally authentic, but watch the low ceiling!

PROPERTY

✱✱✱

private parking, garden, lounge, hosts have pets, dinner available, babies welcome, free cot, swimming pool, hiking, cycling, birdwatching, fishing 5km, hunting 5km, mushroom picking 6km, interesting flora 15km, golf course 20km, sea or lake watersports 40km

PRICE STRUCTURE

3 Bedrooms

Pressoir: television, bathroom with wc, double bed: FF450

Treille: television, bathroom with wc, double bed, single bed: FF450 (2 people) FF560 (3 people)

Fruitier: lounge, television, bathroom, twin beds, single bed: FF350 (2 people) FF440 (3 people)

Extra bed: 110FF

Capacity: 8 people

— At Chinon, cross the River Vienne and take the D749 towards lílle Bouchard. Turn right towards Ligr . 1km out of Ligr , head towards the hamlet of 'Le Rouilly'. There is then a sign to "Le Clos du Ligré".

Marie Christine PICARD

Allée du Bois Goulu
86200 POUANT

tel: (0) 5 49 22 52 05

Residence of character

22 km - S - CHINON POUANT: car essential — At Chinon head towards l'Isle-Bouchard then Richelieu (D749). At Champigny take the D113 for Pouant. The house is 800m from the church (going towards Richelieu) and 80m from the cross (avenue of lime trees).

86.12 CHINON

You approach this beautifully maintained house along an impressive avenue of lime trees. Top quality furniture and spacious, quiet bedrooms. Obviously you will want to visit the châteaux but the Chinon vineyards are also well worth a visit

PROPERTY

✱✱✱

private parking, extensive grounds, tv lounge, kitchen, babies welcome, free cot, hiking, hunting, mushroom picking, fishing 4km, golf course 35km

PRICE STRUCTURE

3 Bedrooms

shower room with wc, double bed: FF260

shower room with wc, double bed: FF260

bathroom, 2 single beds (Childrens size): FF120

Capacity: 6 people

Vicomte & Vicomtesse Hilaire Le ROUX de LENS

«Château du Puy d'Arçay» - Arçay
86200 LOUDUN

tel: (0) 5 49 98 29 11

Château

30 km - S W - CHINON
ARCAY: hosts can collect from station, railway station 50km
airport 70km
car essential

86.17 CHINON

Old world charm in a superb setting. This 17th century house contains furniture and a dining room in the style of the period. Your hostess loves to spoil her guests, and along with her husband will fill you in on all the local legends. This area contains many attractive villages.

PROPERTY

***

private parking, extensive grounds, tv lounge, hosts have pets, telephone, dinner available, babies welcome, free cot, closed: 01/12-01/02, hiking, mushroom picking, fishing 4km, sea or lake watersports 12km, river watersports 12km, golf course 30km

Fluent English spoken

— At Chinon take the D759 towards Loudun. Continue towards Thouars and then turn left on to the D19 towards Arçay. It is the first house on the right.

PRICE STRUCTURE

3 Bedrooms

Ménage: shower room with wc, washbasin, double bed: FF240

Second room: shower room with wc, washbasin, double bed, single bed: FF240 (2 people) FF280 (3 people)

Third room: along corridor bathroom, washbasin, single bed: FF160

Capacity: 6 people

Michel COUSIN

«Les Carrés»
1, rue du 11 Novembre
37460 GENILLÉ

tel: (0) 2 47 59 53 25

Residence of character

10 km - N E - LOCHES
GENILLE: railway station 10km
airport 50km
car essential

37.33 LOCHES

This 19th century house in large wooded grounds is in the heart of the Val d'Indrois and Le Lochois. The bedrooms are comfortable and well-appointed. The apartment is separate and well-equipped. Here their motto is: Welcome, comfort and freedom to go as you please.

PRICE STRUCTURE

4 Bedrooms and 1 Apartment

Kiwi: shower room with wc, twin beds: FF230

Milrose: bathroom with wc, double bed: FF270

Paille: bathroom with wc, double bed, single bed: FF270 (2 people) FF340 (3 people)

Fushia: shower room with wc, double bed: FF270

Le Menou: lounge, television, kitchen, bathroom with wc, double bed: FF300

Extra bed: 70FF
Reduction: 3 nights

Capacity: 11 people

PROPERTY

✸✸✸

private parking, extensive grounds, tv lounge, no pets, packed lunch, babies welcome, free cot, closed: 15/10-31/03, hiking, cycling, fishing, mushroom picking 2km, sea or lake water-sports 8km, golf course 30km

English spoken

— At Loches take the D764 towards Blois. At Genillé turn right on to the D10 towards Montrésor, and it is the first house on the right.

Michael REES

«Moulin de la Touche»
37240 LIGUEIL

tel: (0) 2 47 92 06 84
fax: (0) 2 47 59 96 38

Residence of character

18 km - S W -
LOCHES
LIGUEIL: railway station 18km
airport 55km
car essential

37.40 LOCHES

This 19th century water-mill, with it's garden and lovely swimming pool, has masses of charm. You will stay in the impressive Miller's House, completely and skillfully restored by this English couple. More restoration work is in progress. Ideal if you want peace and relaxation. On sale: Honey.

PROPERTY

✱✱✱

off street parking, extensive grounds, tv lounge, hosts have pets, no pets, dinner available, swimming pool, hiking, fishing, cycling 2km, sea or lake watersports 20km, river watersports 20km, golf course 25km, interesting flora 30km, birdwatching 30km

Fluent English spoken

PRICE STRUCTURE

5 Bedroom

First room: shower room with wc, double bed, single bed: FF410 (2 people) FF510 (3 people)

Second, third & fourth room: shower room with wc, double bed, single bed: FF360 (2 people) FF460 (3 people)

Fifth room: shower room with wc, double bed: FF330

Extra bed: 100FF
Reduction: 01/09–30/06

Capacity: 14 people

— Coming from Loches on the D31 and heading towards Ligueil, take the road on the left. The "Moulin de la Touche" is 2 km further on, on the left.

Malvina & Olivier
MASSELOT

«La Capitainerie»
37600 VERNEUIL SUR INDRE

tel: (0) 2 47 94 88 15
fax: (0) 2 47 94 70 75

Private home

7 km - S - LOCHES
VERNEUIL SUR INDRE:
railway station 7km
airport 35km
car essential

PRICE STRUCTURE

4 Bedrooms

Jaune: shower room with wc, twin beds: FF310

Bleue: shower room with wc, twin beds: FF290

Verte: shower room with wc, double bed, single bed: FF310 (2 people) FF370 (3 people)

Rouge: shower room with wc, twin beds, single bed: FF310 (2 people) FF370 (3 people)

Capacity: 10 people

37.43 LOCHES

Right in the heart of the Loire Valley castles and vineyards, Malvina welcomes you in her 18th property, surrounded by 8 hectares of fields. It is 7km from the quiet, small town of Loches, with its citadel, 11th century keep and 14th century château which bear witness to 1000 years of history. The three attic rooms have been tastefully restored, and they have a pleasant, cool garden with a swimming pool. Hiking in the forest, cycling, fishing, riding and tennis are all available close by. Fleur de Soleil member.

PROPERTY

❋❋❋

off street parking, garden, no pets, no smoking, swimming pool, hiking, cycling, fishing,

English spoken

— South of Loches, go towards Chateauroux on the N143 then the D41 to Verneuil sur Indre. On the village square, opposite the "Salle Communale", turn left and the Capitainerie is 400m further on.

Jacqueline GAY

«Les Hautes Gatinières»
7, chemin de Bois Soleil
37210 ROCHECORBON

tel: (0) 2 47 52 88 08
fax: (0) 2 47 52 85 90
e-mail:
jacquelinegay@minitel.

Private home

3 km - N E - TOURS
ROCHECORBON:
hosts can collect from station,
railway station 7km
airport 8km
car essential

37.24 TOURS

A new Touraine style house, on the hillside overlooking the village. All the rooms are spotlessly clean and have a beautiful view. You will be able to taste the Vouvray wine as Jacqueline lives beside a vineyard. Fleur de Soleil member.

PROPERTY

✱✱✱

private parking, garden, lounge, hosts have pets, telephone, babies welcome, free cot, closed: 15/01-15/02, hiking, cycling, fishing, river watersports, mushroom picking 4km, interesting flora 6km, golf course 10km, hunting 10km

Adequate English spoken

PRICE STRUCTURE

2 Bedrooms and 1 Suite

First room: television, bathroom with wc, double bed, 2 single beds: FF295 (2 people) FF480 (4 people)

Second room: television, bathroom with wc, double bed, single bed: FF295 (2 people) FF380 (3 people)

Third room: television, bathroom with wc, double bed: FF295

Extra bed: 85FF
Reduction: 01/10–30/04 and 6 nights and groups

Capacity: 9 people

— In Tours, take the N152 towards Vouvray. At the set of traffic lights, just after the information point 'l'observatoire', turn left into the 'rue des Clouets', then follow the signs 'chambres d'hotes'.

Françoise CHAINEAU

«Relais de la Martinière»
37, route de la Martinière
37510 SAVONNIERES

tel: (0) 2 47 50 04 46
fax: (0) 2 47 50 11 57

Residence of character

10 km - W - TOURS
SAVONNIERES: airport 20km
car essential
— In Tours, take the D7 towards Villandry. In Savonnières, take the road towards Ballan, by the 'Hotel du Faisan'. As you go up the hill take the road on the right.

37.25 TOURS

A marvellous setting for this 17th century farmhouse, which has been superbly restored. Peace and quiet, relaxation, simplicity and a convivial atmosphere... a swimming pool, tennis courts, a large conservatory, cycling and visits to the châteaux. Well worth a detour.

PROPERTY

❋❋❋

off street parking, garden, lounge, hosts have pets, kitchen, swimming pool, tennis, closed: 01/10-01/05, hiking, cycling, fishing, river watersports 2km, golf course 6km

Adequate English spoken

PRICE STRUCTURE

6 Bedrooms

Villandry & Azay: shower room with wc, twin beds: FF350

Langeais: shower room with wc, double bed: FF350

Amboise: shower room with wc, double bed, single bed: FF350 (2 people) FF410 (3 people)

New Forest: bridal room, washbasin, double bed: FF250

Connemara: washbasin, double bed, single bed: FF250 (2 people) FF310 (3 people)

Capacity: 14 people

Anne-Marie LARIÉ

«Le Clos du Paradis»
46, rue Descartes
37130 LANGEAIS

tel: (0) 2 47 96 65 37
fax: (0) 2 47 96 65 37

Private home

25 km - W - TOURS
LANGEAIS:
airport 30km

37.30 TOURS

This house is in quiet grounds, in the centre of the town with a view over the Château de Langeais, where Charles VIII and Anne de Bretagne were married. Many artists come to Le Clos in order to paint the view of the château from the bedroom called "Peintre".

PROPERTY

✱✱✱

private parking, extensive grounds, tv lounge, hosts have pets, babies welcome, free cot, wheelchair access, hiking, cycling, fishing, birdwatching, hunting 5km, interesting flora 5km, mushroom picking 5km, golf course 10km, river watersports 10km

Basic English spoken

PRICE STRUCTURE

3 Bedrooms and 1 Suite

Peintre: washbasin, double bed, cot: FF230

Vue: twin beds: FF230

Third room: twin beds: FF230

Rez de Chaussée: shower room with wc, 2 twin beds: FF270 (2 people) FF400 (4 people)

Extra bed: 70FF

Capacity: 10 people

— At Tours, take the N152 towards Saumur. In the town, turn right at the château. The street is immediately on the left after the church.

Jacques DESVIGNES

«Château de Montgouverne»
37210 ROCHECORBON

tel: (0) 2 47 52 84 59
fax: (0) 2 47 52 84 61

Château

3 km - N E - TOURS
ROCHECORBON:
railway station 7km
airport 7km

37.36 TOURS

This is one of those magical places where you want time to stand still. The charm, beauty and elegance of this château and its listed grounds, will make this a memorable stop. In this 18th century residence amongst the vineyards, Christine and Jacques love entertaining. On sale: antiques, wine.

PRICE STRUCTURE

4 Bedrooms and 2 Suites

Petits matins: television, telephone, bathroom with wc, double bed: FF590

A volets clos: television, telephone, bathroom with wc, double bed: FF690

A l'ombre des roses: television, telephone, bathroom with wc, twin beds: FF690

L'heure Bleue: television, telephone, bathroom with wc, twin beds: FF790

Couleur Lilas: lounge, television, telephone, bathroom with wc, double bed, single bed: FF790 (2 people) FF950 (3 people)

Parfum de Fleurs: television, telephone, bathroom with wc, twin beds, single bed: FF1050 (2 people) FF1210 (3 people)

Extra bed: 160FF

Capacity: 14 people

PROPERTY

✱✱✱✱

private parking, extensive grounds, tv lounge, hosts have pets, no pets, telephone, dinner available, swimming pool, closed: 21/12-04/01, hiking, cycling, fishing 1km, river watersports 1km, interesting flora 7km, golf course 16km

Fluent English spoken

— From the A10, take the Tours Sainte Radegonde Exit. Take the N521 and then the N152 towards Vouvray. Turn left at Saint-Georges.

Geneviève DEMERSON

16, rue de la Maulardière
37270 ST MARTIN LE BEAU

tel: (0) 2 47 50 23 18

Private home

18 km - E - TOURS
ST MARTIN LE BEAU: hosts can collect from station, railway station 12km
airport 3km
car essential

37.37 TOURS

Next to a large cave hollowed out of the rock-face, this house with mezzanine, American kitchen and bathrooms on the lower ground floor, is ideal for families. Good base for visiting the Loire Valley châteaux. At the bottom of the lush, green garden, the trickle of the stream will lull you to sleep...

PROPERTY

**

private parking, garden, tv lounge, telephone, kitchen, babies welcome, free cot, hiking, hunting, mushroom picking, river watersports, fishing 3km

Basic English spoken

PRICE STRUCTURE

1 Apartment

Studio Mezzanine: lounge, television, kitchen, bathroom with wc, double bed, 3 single beds: FF280 (2 people) FF480 (5 people)

Extra bed: 100FF
Reduction: 1/09–30/06 and 4 nights and groups and children

Capacity: 5 people

— In Tours, take the D140 towards Chenonceaux. At the church of St Martin le Beau, take Rue Raymond Sergent, and go up it for 600 metres.

Jean-Yves & Annie
PESCHARD

10, chemin de Paris
41500 SERIS

tel: (0) 2 54 81 07 83
fax: (0) 2 54 81 39 88

Farm

25 km - N E - BLOIS
SERIS: hosts can collect from station, railway station 7km
airport 160km

PRICE STRUCTURE

5 Bedrooms

Bleue: bathroom with wc, double bed, single bed: FF280 (2 people) FF350 (3 people)

Verte: shower room with wc, 2 double beds: FF280 (2 people) FF430 (4 people)

Rose: shower room with wc, double bed: FF270

Saumon: shower room with wc, 4 single beds: FF290 (2 people) FF450 (4 people)

Bleu Marine: television, shower room with wc, double bed: FF280

Extra Bed: 75FF
Reduction: 7 nights

Capacity: 15 people

41.05 BLOIS

Annie, who is very kind and always smiling, will welcome you, and invite you to try her delicious cooking based on her organic farm produce. As well as châteaux visits, she will introduce you to deer rearing, making dried flowers and jam making, French style. They are also keen on cycling. On sale: Home-made jam.

PROPERTY

✱✱✱

off street parking, garden, tv lounge, hosts have pets, no pets, dinner available, packed lunch, babies welcome, free cot, cycling, hiking 7km, fishing 7km, golf course 13km, river watersports 13km

Adequate English spoken

— In Blois, take the N152 towards Orléans. In Mer, turn left towards Talcy, then right towards Séris (D25). Follow the signs.

Marie-Claude
DENICHERE

«Manoir du Vieux
Cèdre»
5, rue Basse des Grouëts
41000 BLOIS

tel: (0) 2 54 78 24 29
fax: (0) 2 54 78 24 29

Residence of character

BLOIS
hosts can collect
from station,
railway station 3km
airport 60km

41.06 BLOIS

Mona's place is warm and lively. A charming and pretty bedroom is furnished so as to give you maximum privacy. In a very quiet street in the centre of Paris. An excellent address. Advance booking only

PROPERTY

✱✱✱

private parking, garden, tv lounge, hosts have pets, dinner available, packed lunch, babies welcome, free cot, swimming pool, closed: 15/11-15/02, hiking, fishing, golf course 4km, sea or lake watersports 7km

Adequate English spoken

— From the centre of Blois, take the N152 towards Tours. Follow the river Loire for 4km. The manor is on the right.

PRICE STRUCTURE

4 Bedrooms and 2 Suites

Bleue: television, bathroom with wc, double bed, single bed: FF280 (2 people) FF360 (3 people)

Boiserie: television, shower room with wc, double bed, single bed: FF280 (2 people) FF360 (3 people)

Verte: bathroom with wc, double bed: FF260

Tourelle: shower, wc, double bed: FF280

Suite second floor: bathroom with wc, 2 double beds, single bed: FF300 (2 people) FF580 (5 people)

Suite Jardin: television, bathroom with wc, 2 double beds, single bed: FF300 (2 people) FF580 (5 people)

Extra bed: 60FF
Reduction: groups and children

Capacity: 20 people

Bernard & Micheline POHU

5, Place de l'Eglise
Villeneuve-Frouville
41290 OUCQUES

tel: (0) 2 54 23 22 06

Farm

20 km - N - BLOIS VILLENEUVE FROUVILLE: airport 60km car essential — In Blois take the D924 towards Châteaudun-Chartres. In the village of Villeneuve-Frouville, the farm is near to the church

41.12 BLOIS

This simple farm is very clean and has a lovely courtyard. Situated in a quiet, charming and attractive village, it is equidistant from Blois and Vendome. You can visit both the châteaux of the Val de Loire and the romantic Vallée du Loire. (The stairs are quite steep). On sale: Honey, cheese, wine.

PROPERTY

✱✱

private parking, garden, tv lounge, hosts have pets, no pets, closed: 15/01-31/01, hiking 4km, cycling 4km, hunting 4km, sea or lake watersports 4km, golf course 6km, fishing 15km, birdwatching 15km, gliding 18km, interesting flora 20km, river watersports 20km

Basic English spoken

PRICE STRUCTURE

3 Bedrooms

Ecossaise: along corridor shower, washbasin, twin beds: FF230

Clémentine: along corridor shower, washbasin, double bed, cot: FF230 FF280

Pervenche: shower, washbasin, twin beds, 2 single beds: FF250 (2 people) FF320 (4 people)

Capacity: 8 people

41.14 BLOIS

A large detached house in grounds where ducks and peacocks roam. There are several fishing lakes, and thoughtfully, Denise and Marcel have installed a small bar next to them. Also be sure to let Marcel take you to the neighbouring vineyards. You will not be disappointed. On sale: Goat's cheese, asparagus, strawberries.

Marcel PARPEIX

Le Gros Chêne - Couddes
41700 CONTRES

tel: (0) 2 54 71 56 11

Private home

PROPERTY

✸✸✸

private parking, extensive grounds, tv lounge, hosts have pets, no pets, babies welcome, free cot, fishing, interesting flora, cycling 3km, sea or lake watersports 5km, river watersports 5km, mushroom picking 8km, golf course 10km, gliding 19km

27 km - S - BLOIS
COUDDES: airport 180km
car essential
— At Blois, D765 towards Romorantin-Vierzon. At Cour-Cheverny, turn right on to the D102 towards Contres, then Couddes There, turn right towards Thésée (D11). Le Gros Chêne is on this road.

PRICE STRUCTURE

5 Bedrooms

First & second rooms: shower room with wc, double bed, single bed: FF250 (2 people) FF320 (3 people)

Third, fourth & fifth rooms: shower room with wc, double bed: FF250

Reduction: groups

Capacity: 12 people

Brice & Patricia DELOISON

«Le Béguinage»
41700 COUR CHEVERNY

tel: (0) 2 54 79 29 92
fax: (0) 2 54 79 94 59
e-mail: le.beguinage@wanadoo.

Residence of character

14 km - S E - BLOIS
COUR CHEVERNY: hosts can collect from station, railway station 15km
airport 65km

PRICE STRUCTURE

5 Bedrooms and 1 Suite

Verte: shower room with wc, twin beds: FF340

Suite Bleue: television, shower room with wc, double bed, 2 single beds: FF340 (2 people) FF500 (4 people)

Rouge: shower room with wc, double bed: FF290

Jaune: shower room with wc, double bed, 2 single beds: FF340 (2 people) FF480 (4 people)

Bouton d'Or: lounge, bathroom with wc, double bed: FF360

Lavande: bathroom with wc, double bed: FF360

Extra bed: 80FF
Reduction: 11/11–11/03 and children

Capacity: 16 people

41.15 BLOIS

Brice and Patricia are an absolutely charming young couple. We really like the atmosphere in their house and the garden is full of old world charm. Try the "Bleue" suite, which is restrained and refined and full of light and brightness.

PROPERTY

✱✱✱

private parking, extensive grounds, lounge, hosts have pets, telephone, dinner available, babies welcome, free cot, hiking, cycling, fishing, hunting, mushroom picking, golf course 1km, river watersports 4km, sea or lake watersports 13km

Basic English spoken

— At Blois, D765 towards Romorantin-Vierzon. Enter Cour-Cheverny, the house is on this road, on the right.

41.22 BLOIS

This couple of wine-growers will welcome you warmly to their simple farmhouse. This is the ideal spot for a family to experience real rural life. You will be able to visit the vineyards, and the Loire châteaux are all around. On sale: Local wines, goat's cheese.

Josette & Pierre MARTEAU

«Domaine La Croix des Corbillières»
Les Corbillières
41700 OISLY-CONTRES

tel: (0) 2 54 79 55 34

Farm

PROPERTY

✷

private parking, hosts have pets, no pets, kitchen, cycling, fishing, mushroom picking, hiking 2km, golf course 10km, river watersports 15km

Basic English spoken

PRICE STRUCTURE

1 Bedroom
along corridor shower room with wc, double bed, 2 single beds: FF200 (2 people) FF360 (4 people)

Capacity: 4 people

27 km - S - BLOIS
LES CORBILLIERES:
railway station 30km
airport 60km
car essential
— At Blois take the D956 towards Contres and St Aignan. At Contres turn right on to the D30 towards Pontlevoy. Les Corbillières is 6km further on.

Marie Claude
NAVAR-DENICHERE

«Les Chercherelles»
1, Voie du Petit Moulin
41700 COUR CHEVERNY

tel: (0) 2 54 79 93 63
fax: (0) 2 54 78 24 29

Private home

14 km - S E - BLOIS
COUR CHEVERNY:
car essential

PRICE STRUCTURE

5 Bedrooms

1, 2 and 3: telephone, bathroom with wc, washbasin, double bed: FF270

4 and 5: telephone, bathroom with wc, washbasin, double bed: FF250

Extra bed: 50FF
Reduction: groups

Capacity: 10 people

41.25 BLOIS

Nicole will welcome you to her sparkling new detached house in the country. This is a nice, comfortable stop, quiet and relaxing in the heart of Sologne, yet also near to the Loire Valley châteaux (Cheverny....). A very handy overnight stop.

PROPERTY

✸✸

off street parking, garden, lounge, hosts have pets, dinner available, packed lunch, babies welcome, free cot, wheelchair access, closed: 3/11-25/03, hiking, fishing, hunting, interesting flora, cycling 1km, golf course 1km

— At Blois, take the D765 towards Romorantin-Vierzon. As you leave Cour Cheverny, take Les Chercherelles on the left, then follow the signs.

Jocelyne BRUMEL-JOUAN

«La Guibruyère»
7, rue de la Croix
41220 THOURY EN SOLOGNE

tel: (0) 2 54 87 01 32

Residence of character

23 km - E - BLOIS
THOURY EN SOLOGNE: railway station 12km
airport 25km
car essential

41.26 BLOIS

Typical, pleasant Sologne farmhouse. A friendly home, where Jocelyne's love of entertaining shines through. Add the charm of the garden, the walking and bike rides: theirs is a life dedicated to the outdoors and the history of France. On sale: Honey, asparagus, wine, cheese.

PROPERTY

✸✸✸

private parking, extensive grounds, tv lounge, hosts have pets, no pets, telephone, dinner available, babies welcome, free cot, hiking, cycling, mushroom picking, fishing 4km, birdwatching 6km, golf course 10km, hunting 10km, sea or lake watersports 18km, gliding 20km

Fluent English spoken

PRICE STRUCTURE

4 Bedrooms

First room: television, telephone, along corridor bathroom with wc, double bed: FF250

Second room: television, along corridor shower room with wc, double bed: FF250

Third room: television, along corridor bathroom with wc, double bed: FF250

Chambre des Enfants: single bed, childrens size, cot: FF200

Extra bed: 100FF

Capacity: 7 people

— From Blois, take the D33 to Thoury. Once you reach the village, turn right at the "Stop" sign and head towards Dhuizon, then take the first left. This is Rue de la Croix (in the centre of the village).

Jean-Pierre & Inge TARTIERE

«Château du Bois Minhy»
Chèmery
41700 CONTRES

tel: (0) 2 54 79 51 01
fax: (0) 2 54 79 06 26

Château

Centre Val-de-Loire

27 km - S - BLOIS
CHEMERY: railway station 25km
airport 200km
car essential

BLOIS

41.27 BLOIS

This charming little château in Renaissance style is on a 7 hectare estate, with a swimming pool, a large terrace and a barbecue. Here, you will find perfect peace and quiet. This is the ideal spot to visit the Loire Valley Châteaux, only between 15km and 40km away. It is possible to rent the whole château if required.

PRICE STRUCTURE

3 Bedrooms and 1 Apartment

First room: bathroom with wc, double bed, twin beds, single bed: FF300 (2 people) FF570 (5 people)

Fifth room: bathroom with wc, double bed, single bed: FF300 (2 people) FF390 (3 people)

Seventh room: shower room with wc, double bed, single bed: FF280 (2 people) FF350 (3 people)

Grande Suite: lounge, television, kitchen, shower room with wc, 2 double beds, single bed: FF450 (2 people) FF720 (5 people)

Extra bed: 90FF

Capacity: 16 people

PROPERTY

✱✱✱

private parking, extensive grounds, tv lounge, hosts have pets, dinner available, kitchen, babies welcome, free cot, swimming pool, hiking, cycling, mushroom picking, fishing 5km, river watersports 12km, golf course 15km, sea or lake watersports 25km

Fluent English spoken

— At Blois, take the D956 towards Contres, then Selles sur Cher. The château is just before Chèmery.

Anita & Didier MERLIN

«Ferme des Saules»
41700 CHEVERNY

tel: (0) 2 54 79 26 95
fax: (0) 2 54 79 97 54
e-mail: merlin.cheverny@infonie.fr http: www.cher.com/fermedessaules

Residence of character

15 km - S E - BLOIS
CHEVERNY: railway station 20km
airport 200km
car essential

41.28 BLOIS

This house is situated 2km from the Château de Cheverny, in a pastoral setting. You can wander at will through the forest of Cheverny (there are walking and cycling trails marked). In the evening, you will really enjoy taking dinner with your hosts: quality cuisine!

PROPERTY

✱✱✱

off street parking, extensive grounds, no pets, dinner available, packed lunch, babies welcome, free cot, swimming pool, closed: 15/12-15/01, hiking, fishing, mushroom picking, golf course 2km, hunting 2km, sea or lake watersports 15km, river watersports 15km

Fluent English spoken

PRICE STRUCTURE

4 Bedrooms and 1 Apartment

First room: bathroom with wc, double bed, single bed: FF320 (2 people) FF450 (3 people)

Second room: shower room with wc, double bed: FF295

Third room: bathroom with wc, twin beds, single bed: FF320 (2 people) FF450 (3 people)

Anne: bathroom with wc, twin beds: FF320

Studio: television, kitchen, bathroom with wc, double bed, single bed: FF320 (2 people) FF450 (3 people)

Extra bed: 70FF

Capacity: 13 people

— At Blois, take the D765 towards Romorantin-Vierzon. At Cheverny, head towards the château and then take the D102 towards Contres, and follow signs to "La Ferme des Saules".

Dominique & Thierry
COUTON

«La Petite Maison»
Nocfond
41320 LANGON

tel: (0) 2 54 98 16 21

Private home

10 km - S E - ROMORANTIN NOCFOND: hosts can collect from station, car essential

41.20 ROMORANTIN

This is an old Sologne farmhouse, quietly situated in extensive grounds. Typical of La Sologne, there is an abundance of woods, lakes and countryside full of game... Dominique and Thierry will help you discover the real Sologne. You can also visit some beautiful châteaux in this region.

PRICE STRUCTURE

4 Bedrooms

La Varende & Guernazelles: shower room with wc, double bed: FF280

Combles : Berthe St James: bathroom with wc, double bed: FF330

Combles : Bagatelle: bathroom with wc, twin beds: FF330

Extra bed: 60FF
Reduction: 7 nights

Capacity: 8 people

PROPERTY

✸✸✸

private parking, extensive grounds, tv lounge, hosts have pets, packed lunch, babies welcome, free cot, hiking, cycling, hunting, mushroom picking, birdwatching, fishing 6km

Basic English spoken

— In Romorantin, take the D724 towards Salbris. At Selles St Denis turn right on to the D123 towards Mennetou sur Cher. Nocfond is 200m on the right before the bridge over La Petite Réré. Follow the lane to the very end; it is the last house on the left.

Caroline & Emmanuel
QUINTIN

«Les Atelleries»
41300 SELLES ST DENIS

tel: (0) 2 54 96 13 84
fax: (0) 2 54 96 13 84
e-mail:
Caroline.Quintin@wanadoo.fr
www.perso.wanadoo.fr/caroline.quintin/

Farm

16 km - E -
ROMORANTIN
SELLES ST DENIS:
railway station 5km
airport 70km
car essential

41.23 ROMORANTIN

Caroline and Emmanuel are a dynamic young couple who have completely restored this old farm house in Sologne with great taste. It is a pleasure to stay here for several days.

PROPERTY

✸✸✸

off street parking, extensive grounds, tv lounge, kitchen, hiking, cycling, hunting, mushroom picking 2km, fishing 5km, interesting flora 8km, birdwatching 8km, river watersports 15km, golf course 35km

Adequate English spoken

PRICE STRUCTURE

3 Bedrooms

RDC-Boulangerie: bathroom with wc, double bed: FF280

Colombage: shower room with wc, 3 single beds: FF280 (2 people) FF330 (3 people)

ETAGE-Boulangerie: bathroom with wc, double bed, single bed: FF280 (2 people) FF330 (3 people)

Extra bed: 50FF
Reduction: 4 nights

Capacity: 8 people

— On the A71 take the Salbris Exit and then take the D724 towards Romorantin. At Selles St Denis take the D123 on the right towards Marcilly en Gault. "Les Atelleries" are on your right.

André & Odette COLAS

«St Nicolas»
25, route de St Nicolas
41800 ST RIMAY

tel: (0) 2 54 85 03 89

Residence of character

15 km - W - VENDOME ST RIMAY: hosts can collect from station, railway station 10km airport 45km — At Vendome, take the D917 towards Montoire sur Loire. St. Nicolas is just before Les Roches: after the St. Rimay turning, turn left 200m before the bridge over le Loir.

41.08 VENDOME

The bedrooms are in a converted chapel, dating from the 11th century, next to the farmhouse. You are on the Route St. Jacques de Compostelle and in the heart of the Vallée du Loir. It is a romantic area, with picturesque villages such as Lavardin and extensive vineyards. On sale: Wine, eggs, asparagus, vegetables.

PROPERTY

✱✱✱

private parking, garden, no pets, dinner available, kitchen, hiking 3km, fishing 3km, cycling 5km, river watersports 15km

English spoken

PRICE STRUCTURE

3 Bedrooms

First room: twin beds: FF230

Second room: twin beds: FF230

Third room: shower room with wc, washbasin, double bed, 2 single bed: FF230 (2 people) FF400 (4 people)

Extra bed: 75FF

Capacity: 8 people

Brigitte BECQUELIN

«Château de la Volonière»
72340 PONCE sur LE LOIR

tel: (0) 2 43 79 68 16
fax: (0) 2 43 79 68 18

Château

35 km - W - VENDOME
PONCE SUR LE LOIR: airport 45km
car essential

72.08 VENDOME

This 15th century château, in the village of craftsmen, accommodates up to 12 people. Each bedroom is in a different theme. The restoration has been done so skilfully that you would expect the poet Ronsard to appear at any moment. Superb lake. Very good value for money. There is an inn nearby. On sale: Paintings and sculptures.

PROPERTY

****

off street parking, extensive grounds, tv lounge, hosts have pets, telephone, packed lunch, babies welcome, free cot, closed: 1/12-15/03, hiking, cycling, fishing, sea or lake watersports 7km

Basic English spoken

— In Vendome, take the D917 towards Montoire sur Loir - Troo -Poncé sur Loir.

PRICE STRUCTURE

3 Bedrooms and 2 Suites and 2 Apartments

Roméo: lounge, television, kitchen, shower room with wc, twin beds: FF480

Juliette: shower room with wc, double bed: FF370

Louis XIII: shower room with wc, twin beds: FF370

Barbe Bleue: bathroom with wc, double bed: FF370

Mille et une nuits: bathroom with wc, 2 double beds, 2 single beds: FF370 (2 people) FF570 (4 people)

Apartment: lounge, television, kitchen, bathroom with wc, twin beds, 2 single beds: FF600 (2 people) FF800 (4 people)

Extra bed: 100FF
Reduction: 2 nights

Capacity: 18 people

Monique DEAGE

«Les Patis du Vergas»
72310 LAVENAY

tel: (0) 2 43 35 38 18
fax: (0) 2 43 35 38 18

Private home

35 km - W - VENDOME
LAVENAY: railway station 25km
airport 40km
car essential

72.09 VENDOME

Chez Monique, you are surrounded by beauty. The rooms are in a separate house with its own barbecue, in beautiful grounds with a private lake well stocked with fish. (Barbecue, games, sauna, billiards). 1/11–30/03 : advance booking only

PRICE STRUCTURE

5 Bedrooms

Paquerette: television, shower room with wc, double bed: FF330

Iris: shower room with wc, twin beds: FF270

Bleuet: shower room with wc, double bed: FF270

Primevère & Jasmin: shower room with wc, double bed, single bed: FF270 (2 people) FF330 (3 people)

Reduction: 2 nights

Capacity: 12 people

PROPERTY

✱✱✱

off street parking, extensive grounds, tv lounge, dinner available, kitchen, packed lunch, wheelchair access, closed: 1/01-1/03, cycling, fishing, river watersports, hiking 3km, sea or lake watersports 15km

Fluent English spoken

— At Vendome, take the D917 towards Montoire sur Loir-Troo-Pont de Braye where you turn right on to the D303 towards St Calais. Then turn left towards Lavenay.

Pierre & Patricia
FOURNIER

«Le Clos de PontPierre»
115, rue des Eaux Bleues
45190 TAVERS

tel: (0) 2 38 44 56 85
fax: (0) 2 38 44 58 94

Residence of character

2 km - S W -
BEAUGENCY
TAVERS: railway
station 3km
airport 150km

45.05 BEAUGENCY

An ideal stop on the route of the châteaux of the Loire Valley: near to the autoroute and on the N512, but quite quiet. This old stone farmhouse has been restored with great taste. The garden is enormous and Patricia & Pierre are very welcoming. Pierre is a chef.

PROPERTY

✱✱✱

private parking, garden, tv lounge, hosts have pets, no pets, dinner available, babies welcome, free cot, no smoking, swimming pool, closed: 01/02 -28/02, hiking, cycling, mushroom picking, fishing 1km, river watersports 3km, golf course 7km, interesting flora 7km, hunting 10km, sea or lake watersports 30km

Basic English spoken

— On the A10, take the Exit Meung sur Loire and take the N152 towards Blois. The entrance is on the N152 (follow the signs).

PRICE STRUCTURE

4 Bedrooms

Arabesque: television, shower room with wc, twin beds: FF290

Eglantine: television, shower room with wc, double bed: FF290

L'Oiseau: lounge, television, shower room with wc, 2 double beds: FF290 (2 people) FF450 (4 people)

Aubépine: shower room with wc, 3 single beds: FF290 (2 people) FF370 (3 people)

Extra bed: 80FF
Reduction: 5 nights

Capacity: 11 people

Olivier & Mireille TANT

«Fermette de la Sainte Rose»
45210 CHEVANNES

tel: (0) 2 38 90 92 23
fax: (0) 2 38 90 92 23

Private home

10 km - E - DORDIVES
CHEVANNES:
airport 80km
car essential
— On the A6, take the Exit Dordives, where you turn left on to the D43 towards Bransles and the D315. Then turn left towards Chevannes.

45.03 DORDIVES

A small farm, pleasantly renovated, in the heart of this Gâtinais village, only 1 hour from Paris. Mireille and Olivier will suggest some unusual excursions, such as visits to beaver, snail or ostrich farms. Do not miss Montargis and its canals.

PROPERTY

***

private parking, garden, lounge, no pets, dinner available, kitchen, packed lunch, babies welcome, free cot, cycling, hiking 7km, fishing 10km, sea or lake watersports 10km

Adeqate English spoken

PRICE STRUCTURE

3 Bedrooms

Rouge & Verte: shower room with wc, double bed, single bed: FF230 (2 people) FF295 (3 people)

Jaune-Mezzanine: shower room with wc, double bed, 2 single beds: FF230 (2 people) FF360 (4 people)

Extra bed: 60FF
Reduction: children

Capacity: 2 people

45.04 MALESHERBES

Why not spend a weekend here and enjoy Francine's warm welcome in the quiet of this little Gâtinais town. Ideal for shooting weekends. The bedrooms on the ground floor overlook the internal courtyard where breakfast can be served. Le gâtinais is famous for its honey. On sale: Honey.

Francine HYAIS

3, cour du Château
45390 ECHILLEUSES

tel: (0) 2 38 33 60 16

Private home

PROPERTY

✱✱✱

off street parking, hosts have pets, dinner available, closed: 01/11-01/02, golf course 20km, sea or lake watersports 20km

20 km - S - MALESHERBES ECHILLEUSES: hosts can collect from station, railway station 20km airport 70km
— From the A6, take the "Ury" Exit. Head towards Malesherbes (N152). At la Chapelle la Reine, take the D36 towards Piseaux, and continue towards Bellegarde (D948). DO NOT taket the first road to Echilleuses D28), but the second on the right and follow the arrows. On entering the village, take the first small road on the right.

PRICE STRUCTURE

2 Bedrooms

First & second room: shower room with wc, double bed: FF230

Extra bed: 80FF

Capacity: 4 people

Denise & Pierre DURIN

9, Chemin du Pleu
45730 ST BENOIT sur LOIRE

tel: (0) 2 38 35 72 68
fax: (0) 2 38 35 72 68
e-mail: durin.pierre@wanadoo.fr

Residence of character

30 km - S E - ORLEANS
ST BENOIT sur LOIRE: railway station 25km
airport 150km
car essential

Centre

ORLEANS

45.09 ORLEANS

This couple took early retirement and have put their hearts into renovating this farm-house without losing any of its character. You may think you are going to stay for just one night but by the time Denise has served you her delicious meals you will certainly extend your stay much longer. On sale: Watercolour courses.

PRICE STRUCTURE

1 Bedroom and 1 Suite

Suite: along corridor bathroom with wc, shower, double bed, twin beds: FF260 (2 people) FF460 (4 people)

Mansardée: shower, wc, double bed, 2 single beds: FF260 (2 people) FF380 (4 people)

Extra bed: 60FF

Reduction: 3 nights

Capacity: 8 people

PROPERTY

✱✱✱

off street parking, garden, tv lounge, hosts have pets, no pets, dinner available, babies welcome, free cot, closed: 01/10-01/04, cycling, fishing, river watersports, hiking 5km, golf course 10km, interesting flora 10km, mushroom picking 10km, hunting 15km, sea or lake watersports 20km

English spoken

— At Orléans Exit Orléans-Nord on A11, take the N60 towards Montargis as far as Châteauneuf sur Loire. There, take D60 towards St Benoit. The house is midway between St Benoit and St Père in hamlet of Les Places (head towards ULM and enter on garden side).

45.11 ORLEANS

Romantic atmosphere in this partially restored manor house, split into small rooms. Relax and chat in the lounge, in the sophisticated company of your hostess. There is also a semi-detached lodge, separate, but still close to the main house. A charming, classy place to stop.

Muguette BERNARD

4, route de Clémont
45620 ISDES

tel: (0) 2 38 29 12 10/ 10 89
fax: (0) 2 38 29 10 00

Residence of character

PROPERTY

✹✹✹

off street parking, garden, tv lounge, no smoking, hiking, fishing, golf course 12km, hunting 12km, sea or lake watersports 12km

Fluent English spoken

35 km - S E - ORLEANS
ISDES: railway station 20km
car essential
— Exit 3 on the A71 (Lamotte Beuvron). Head towards Vouzon, Souvigny, Isdes on the D101. The house is in centre of the village.

PRICE STRUCTURE

3 Bedrooms

Jaune: bathroom with wc, double bed: FF270

Rose: along corridor bathroom with wc, washbasin, double bed: FF270

Petit pavillon: kitchen, shower room with wc, double bed: FF270

Capacity: 6 people

Géraldine NIVET

8, rue de Chanzy
28140 LOIGNY LA BATAILLE

tel: (0) 2 37 99 70 71

Farm

28.06 ORLEANS

Géraldine has completely restored this house. The pretty, spacious bedrooms are very comfortable and the bathrooms attractive. Everything has been re-done, but she has not raised her prices. A bargain not to be missed, along with the farm produce on sale. 40km from Chartres and its cathedral. On sale: Home-made jam, eggs, vegetables and fruit.

PROPERTY

✱✱

private parking, garden, tv lounge, hosts have pets, dinner available, hiking 5km, cycling 5km. fishing 5km

35 km - N W - LOIGNY LA BATAILLE: car essential — From the A10, Exit Artenay, then the D10 towards Poupry and then the D3-9 towards Loigny la Bataille.

PRICE STRUCTURE

4 Bedrooms

First room: shower room with wc, twin beds: FF190

Second, third & fourth rooms: shower room with wc, double bed: FF190

Extra bed: 50FF

Capacity: 8 people

BELGIUM
GERMANY
LUXEMBOURG
62
Valenciennes
Douai
Arras
NORD
PAS-DE-
CALAIS
59
St. Quentin
Charleville-Mézières
Sedan
02
08
PICARDIE
Laon
Rethel
Compiègne
Soissons
Reims
Thionville
Verdun
METZ
57
Meaux
CHÂLONS
51
LORRAINE
55
Bar-le-Duc
Vitry
Nancy
Lunéville
ILE DE FRANCE
St. Dizier
54
77
CHAMPAGNE-
ARDENNE
Melun
Fontainebleau
Neufchâteau
Troyes
10
88
Èpinal
Sens
52
Chaumont
Montargis
Langres
Auxerre
89
70
Vesoul
BOURGOGNE
FRANCHE-
COMTE
21
58
DIJON

Sylvie & Régis GOULDEN

«Les Sources»
Route de Saulces aux Tournelles
08270 SAULCES MONCLIN

tel: (0) 3 24 38 59 71
fax: (0) 3 24 72 74 60
e-mail: sources@club-internet.fr

Private Home

12 km - N E - RETHEL
SAULCES MONCLIN: hosts can collect from station,
railway station 12km

08.01 RETHEL

This place used to be an old people's home in the middle of extensive grounds with a river, a lake, and a waterfall. Sylvie and Régis are most friendly. Be sure to try their apple juice which is excellent, and they will introduce you to organic food, yoga, even the Internet!

PROPERTY

**

off street parking, extensive grounds, tv lounge, hosts have pets, telephone, dinner available, packed lunch, fishing,

Adequate English spoken

— From Rethel take the N51 Reims-Charleville road, towards Charleville-Mézières. At Saulces Monclin follow the signs to Les Sources.

PRICE STRUCTURE

8 Bedrooms

Rose & Pervenche & Rossignol: bathroom with wc, washbasin, 3 single beds: FF250 (2 people) FF330 (3 people)

Anémone: bathroom with wc, washbasin, 4 single beds: FF250 (2 people) FF420 (4 people)

Pinson: bathroom, 3 single beds: FF250 (2 people) FF330 (3 people)

Bleuet & Jonquille & Coquelicot: washbasin, 2 single beds: FF230

Reduction: 2 nights and children

Capacity: 22 people

acques & Nicole SONGY

«La Grosse Haie»
Chemin de St Pierre
51150 MATOUGUES

tel: (0) 3 26 70 97 12
fax: (0) 3 26 70 12 42

Farm

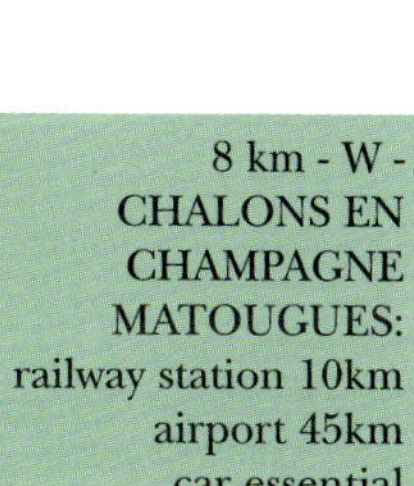

8 km - W -
CHALONS EN CHAMPAGNE
MATOUGUES:
railway station 10km
airport 45km
car essential

51.01 CHALONS EN CHAMPAGNE

Between the vineyards and the river, discover the charm of this land. Choose from mountain bikes, car touring, and visits to the Champagne cellars in Epernay. The meals are really gastronomic and local produce is on sale. 4km from autoroute A26. On sale: Home-made jam, meringues.

PRICE STRUCTURE

3 Bedrooms

Rose: along corridor bathroom with wc, washbasin, double bed: FF255

Blanche: shower room with wc, double bed, twin beds: FF275 (2 people) FF345 (4 people)

Bleue: shower room with wc, 2 double beds: FF275 (2 people) FF345 (4 people)

Reduction: 3 nights

Capacity: 10 people

PROPERTY

✱✱✱

off street parking, garden, tv lounge, hosts have pets, no pets, dinner available, packed lunch, babies welcome, free cot, cycling, hiking 4km, fishing 4km, golf course 18km

Basic English spoken

— On the A26, Exit N° 27 'St Gilbrien' and turn left on to the D3 towards Epernay. The farm has a large hedge. It is on the road on the left, 100m from the bus-stop (sign posted).

Christian & Christine
DAMBRON

Montbayen
51530 ST MARTIN
D'ABLOIS

tel: (0) 3 26 59 95 16
fax: (0) 3 26 51 67 91

Farm

12 km - S W -
EPERNAY
ST MARTIN
D'ABLOIS:
airport 45km
car essential

51.07 EPERNAY

An excellent welcome in this modern house in a very pleasant setting. It overlooks a beautiful village and the nearby forest. Yours hosts produce their own champagne in their cellars below the house. Be sure to see their breakfast museum. They can also advise on wine-tasting tours. On sale: Their own champagne.

PROPERTY

✱✱

private parking, garden, tv lounge, hosts have pets, kitchen, babies welcome, free cot, hiking, cycling, mushroom picking, golf course 20km, birdwatching 50km, sea or lake watersports 50km

Adequate English spoken

PRICE STRUCTURE

4 Bedrooms and 1 Suite

Suite: television, shower room with wc, washbasin, double bed, single beds, twin beds: FF270 (2 people) FF580 (5 people)

First room: shower room with wc, double bed, single bed: FF270 (2 people) FF360 (3 people)

Second, & third room: shower room with wc, double bed: FF270

Extra bed: 50FF
Reduction: 25.11 – 15.02 and 4 nights and children

Capacity: 12 people

— In Epernay, take the D51 towards Sézanne for 7km. Turn right on to the D11 towards St Martin d'Ablois. Turn right on to the D22 towards Vauciennes (2nd street on the right after the 'Place de la Mairie').

Anne-Laure
GUILLEPAIN

«Le Domaine du Village»
14, rue René Baudet
51160 CHAMPILLON

tel: (0) 3 26 51 65 75
fax: (0) 3 26 52 84 94

Residence of Character

8 km - N - EPERNAY
CHAMPILLON:
railway station 5km
airport 25km
car essential

51.16 EPERNAY

This is a wine-growing estate, in a prestigious area: from the terrace of this beautiful property, refurbished in typical Champagne style, you can admire the view over Epernay - the home of Champagne. Near the vineyard, have a look at the 19th century wine press, capable of handling 4 tons of grapes and manually operated. On sale: local wine.

PRICE STRUCTURE

2 Bedrooms

Vignoble: television, telephone, shower room with wc, bathroom, double bed: FF500

Village: television, telephone, shower room with wc, bathroom, twin beds: FF400

Extra bed: 80FF

Capacity: 4 people

PROPERTY

❋❋❋

private parking, extensive grounds, tv lounge, hosts have pets, no pets, telephone, hiking, cycling, interesting flora, mushroom picking 1km, fishing 3km, hunting 3km, golf course 20km

Basic English spoken

— From Epernay, take the N51 towards Reims until you get to Dizy . From there, take the scenic route (N2051) as far as Champillon.

51.03 REIMS

This village house next to the farm is at the gateway to the vineyards of Champagne and only a few minutes from the A4. This is a land of woods and valleys. The bedrooms are beautiful and really comfortable. An excellent address, and still only one hour from Disneyland!

Eric & Nathalie
LELARGE

«Ferme du Grand Clos»
Route de Jonquery
51170 VILLE EN TARDENOIS

tel: (0) 3 26 61 83 78

Farm

PROPERTY

private parking, tv lounge, no pets, babies welcome, free cot

English spoken

PRICE STRUCTURE

4 Bedrooms

Bleue: lounge, television, shower room with wc, double bed, single bed: FF290 (2 people) FF370 (3 people)

Pêche: lounge, television, shower room with wc, 2 double beds: FF290 (2 people) FF450 (4 people)

Juliette: lounge, television, shower room with wc, 2 double beds: FF290 (2 people) FF450 (4 people)

Mezzanine: lounge, television, shower room with wc, double bed: FF290

Reduction: 05.01 – 30.04

Capacity: 13 people

22 km - S W - REIMS
VILLE EN TARDENOIS:
airport 22km
car essential
— On the A4, take the Exit 21 to Dormans and the D380 towards Reims. In the town, turn right at the bank 'Crédit Agricole'. The house is opposite the bank.

51.06 REIMS

Annie-France
MALISSART

9, rue Thiers
51500 MAILLY
CHAMPAGNE

tel: (0) 3 26 49 43 47
fax: (0) 3 26 49 43 47

Farm

Here they produce "Grand Cru" Champagne. There is also plenty to do in this beautiful part of the "Montagne de Reims": forest walking, hiking (GR14), visits to sulphur quarries, the River Marne, 'Les Faux de Verzy' and the "Route du Champagne". On sale: Their own Champagne ('Grand Cru classé 100%'). 1 gite for groups : capacity 25 people: 65 FF per pers.

PROPERTY

✸✸

private parking, tv lounge, hosts have pets, hiking

Fluent English spoken

10 km - S - REIMS
MAILLY CHAMPAGNE:
car essential
— At Reims, on the A4, take the Exit 26 to Cormentreuil. In Cormentreuil, take the D9 towards Louvois. There, turn left on to the D26 towards Mailly-Champagne.

PRICE STRUCTURE

3 Bedrooms

(2 rooms) washbasin, double bed: FF200

(1 room) washbasin, double bed, single bed: FF200 (2 people) FF300 (3 people)

Extra bed: 100FF

Capacity: 7 people

51.10 REIMS

Jean ROBION

8, rue de la Barbe aux Cannes
51170 BLIGNY

tel: (0) 3 26 49 27 79

Private Home

This quiet, retired couple of wine growers have now let their son take over the running of their vineyard. Attractive new house, quiet, yet in the centre of the village. On the Paris - Reims road: convenient for Disneyland, and the «Route du Champagne». Good regional restaurant (3km). On sale: their own Champagne.

PROPERTY

✸✸✸

off street parking, garden, tv lounge, babies welcome, free cot, hiking, mushroom picking 2km, fishing 7km, golf course 10km

Basic English spoken

15 km - S W - REIMS
BLIGNY: airport 25km
car essential
— On the A4 Reims-Paris, take the Exit 21 towards Dormans. Then take the D980 on the left towards Reims. Follow the sign «chambres d'hotes» as you enter the village.

PRICE STRUCTURE

1 Bedroom and 1 Suite

Suite: shower room with wc, double bed, 2 single beds: FF270 (2 people) FF470 (4 people)

bathroom with wc, double bed: FF270

Capacity: 6 people

Michel & Chantal LE VARLET

«Ferme du Temple»
51700 PASSY GRIGNY

tel: (0) 3 26 52 90 01
fax: (0) 3 26 52 18 86

Farm

30 km - S W - REIMS
PASSY GRIGNY:
railway station 10km
airport 110km
car essential

51.11 REIMS

This is a cereal growing farm, but there are still remnants of the period of the knights Templar here. It is very well situated, convenient to an exit from the A4 (without any of the noise), 1 hour from Disneyland and near to the 'Route de Champagne'. The rooms are very practical on the first floor.

PROPERTY

✸✸✸

off street parking, garden, tv lounge, hosts have pets, no pets, dinner available, babies welcome, free cot, golf course 2.5km, hiking 8km, cycling 8km, fishing 10km

Adequate English spoken

PRICE STRUCTURE

4 Bedrooms

Bleu: shower room with wc, twin beds: FF300

Rose & Jaune: shower room with wc, double bed, cot: FF300

Rez de Chaussée- Abricot: shower room with wc, twin beds, single bed, cot: FF300 (2 people) FF400 (3 people)

Capacity: 9 people

— On the A4 Reims-Paris, take the Exit 21 towards Dormans. Then take the D980 on the right, and continue for 1km towards Dormans. Then take the second unmade road, which descends on the right, lined with walnut trees.

Joy & Laurent LAPIE

2, Rue du Calvaire
51360 VAL DE VESLE

tel: (0) 3 26 03 92 88
fax: (0) 3 26 03 92 88

Private Home

18 km - S E - REIMS
VAL DE VESLE:
railway station 1km
airport 20km
car essential

Champagne-Ardenne

REIMS

PRICE STRUCTURE

3 Bedroom

First room: television, bathroom with wc, double bed: FF260

Second room: shower room with wc, double bed, single bed: FF260 (2 people) FF340 (3 people)

Third room: shower, wc, double bed: FF260

Extra bed: 80FF

Capacity: 7 people

51.14 REIMS

This house is well-furnished, the bedrooms are very comfortable and beautifully decorated. The welcome is warm and here you are at the foot of the Champagne vineyards and near to the Faux de Verzy.

PROPERTY

✱✱✱

off street parking, garden, tv lounge, babies welcome, free cot, fishing, cycling 4km, hiking 5km, interesting flora 5km, mushroom picking 5km

Adequate English spoken

— From the A4 Exit 26 Reims-Cormentreuil. Then take the N44 towards Chalons and then the second road on the left after Beaumont sur Vesle. (Coming from the A26 Exit Chalons la Veuve take the N44 towards Reims).

Christine MALARD

17, Grande Rue
51230 CONNANTRE

tel: (0) 3 26 81 07 42

Private Home

18 km - E -
SEZANNE
CONNANTRE:
airport 70km
car essential

51.12 SEZANNE

Very easy to find from the N4. This is a restored barn, with 2 self- contained rooms above the doctor's surgery. They have billiards and table-tennis, etc. It is near to the famous Lac du Der, about 1 hour from Disneyland and on the doorstep of the Champagne country. On sale: Champagne

PROPERTY

✱✱

off street parking, extensive grounds, tv lounge, hosts have pets, kitchen, babies welcome, free cot, hiking, hunting, sea or lake watersports, fishing 15km

Fluent English spoken

PRICE STRUCTURE

2 Bedroom

First room: television, wash-basin, twin beds: FF280

Second room: television, twin beds, single bed: FF200 (2 people) FF290 (3 people)

Extra bed: 45FF

Capacity: 5 people

— At Sézanne, take the N4 towards Vitry le François as far as Connantre. Turn right 1.5km from the main road, and take the D5. Pass the sugar factory and the house is in the centre of the village, near to the shops.

Denis & Michelle GEOFFROY

16, rue de Hancourt
51290 MARGERIE-HANCOURT

tel: (0) 3 26 72 48 47
fax: (0) 3 26 72 48 47

Farm

20 km - S - VITRY LE FRANÇOIS MARGERIE HANCOURT: hosts will collect from station, railway station 20km

51.05 VITRY FRANÇOIS

A working farm, with pigeons everywhere. An excellent overnight stop with a warm and friendly welcome. Only 15km from the Der lake, famous for its migratory birds and fishing. Do not miss the unusual wooden churches.

PRICE STRUCTURE

3 Bedrooms and 1 extra room

Bas: shower room with wc, washbasin, double bed: FF200

Etage - first room: shower room with wc, 2 double beds: FF200 (2 people) FF270 (4 people)

Etage - third room: shower room with wc, double bed, single bed: FF200 (2 people) FF250 (3 people)

Extra bed: 50FF

Capacity: 9 people

PROPERTY

***

off street parking, garden, tv lounge, hosts have pets, dinner available, kitchen, babies welcome, free cot, closed: 15/12-15/01, fishing 2km, birdwatching 15km, sea or lake watersports 15km

— In Vitry, take the D396 towards Brienne le Château. Just before Margerie, turn left, then right. Follow the sign 'Ferme de Hancourt'.

MEDITERRANEAN SEA

Bastia

Calvi

2B

CORSE

Corte

AJACCIO

2A

Propriano

Sartène

Porto Vecchio

Bonifacio

MEDITERRANEAN SEA

Dominique SALICETI

Lano
20244 SAN LORENZO

tel: (0) 4 95 48 41 51

Private Home

18 km - S E - PONTE LECCIA
LANO: railway station 18km,
car essential
— At Ponte Leccia take the N193 towards Ajaccio for 4.5km. Left on to the D239 towards San Lorenzu for 11km. Go down on the right towards the river, cross the bridge. Signs to Lano on the left. After 300m take the hairpin right. Go right to the top of the village, past the church.

20.07 PONTE LECCIA

This is where the beaten track ends. This comfortable studio is perched high up in deepest Corsica. If you love the countryside, peace and quiet, and the heady perfume of the maquis, you will find no other place like this. 18km to the nearest shop or restaurant.

PROPERTY

lounge, hosts have pets, pets not accepted, babies welcome, free cot, wheelchair access, 3 nights minimum stay, hiking, cycling, fishing, hunting, interesting flora, mushroom picking, river watersports 30km, sea or lake watersports 50km

PRICE STRUCTURE

1 Apartment
lounge, kitchen, along corridor shower room with wc, double bed: FF240

Reduction: 7 nights

Capacity: 4 people

Christian & Claudine PERRIER

«Domaine de Croccan
Km 3 route de Granac
20100 SARTENE

tel: (0) 4 95 77 11 37
fax: (0) 4 95 73 42 89
e-mail: christian.perrie wanadoo.fr
http:www.corsenet.com pub/m/madun/madu html

Residence of Characte

SARTENE
hosts will collect from station,
ferry 15km,
airport 40km,
car essential

20.06 SARTENE

This exceptional spot is ideal for riding and romantic hiking excursions. Spend wonderful evenings in this old house, off the beaten track, but with a view over the sea. This is the real Corsica ... "Heaven on Earth!" Room 2 has bath & WC in the room. Fleur de Soleil member. On sale: Home-made jam.

PROPERTY

✱✱✱

private parking, extensive grounds, hosts have pets, telephone, dinner available, babies welcome, free cot, no smoking, closed: 1/12-31/12, riding, hiking, cycling, fishing, hunting, interesting flora, mushroom picking, birdwatching, sea or lake watersports 10km, river watersports 20km

Fluent English spoken

PRICE STRUCTURE

4 Bedrooms

Bonifacio & Cote Sauvage: twin beds, single bed: FF38 (2 people) FF570 (3 people)

Campo Moro: bathroom with wc, washbasin, twin beds: FF380

Alta Rocca: bathroom with wc, washbasin, 2 single beds: FF380

Reduction: 01.09 – 30.06 and groups and children

Capacity: 10 people

— On the square by the church in Sartène, turn left towards the “Maison de l’Artisanat”. At the intersection, take the road on the right towards Granace for 3km. The entrance is on the left and the house is 300m further down, at the end of the unmade road.

Roanne
69
01
CLERMONT-
FERRAND
Thiers
RHÔNE-
ALPES
LYON
63
42
Vienne
38
St.-Etienne
19
Tulle
15
43
Brive
LIMOUSIN
le Puy
Aurillac
Valence
07
Privas
46
26
Mende
48
Cahors
Rodez
12
84
82
Alès
Carpentras
Millau
MIDI-PYRÉNÉES
30
Avignon
Albi
LANGUEDOC-
ROUSSILLON
Nimes
81
13
Arles
TOULOUSE
Castres
MONTPELLIER
Béziers
31
34
Carcassonne
Narbonne
11
Foix
09
MEDITERRANEAN
SEA
Perpignan
66
ANDORRA
SPAIN

Gabrielle DHOMS

«Le Siestou»
11800 LAURE
MINERVOIS

tel: (0) 4 68 78 30 81
fax: (0) 4 68 78 30 81

Farm

20 km - N E - CARCASSONNE LAURE MINERVOIS: hosts will collect from station, railway station 20km airport 20km

11.07 CARCASSONNE

Very warm welcome on this large estate which produces Minervois wine. The farmhouse is surrounded by woods, an ideal spot for children. Bedrooms are tastefully decorated in Provençal style. There is tennis and a swimming pool nearby. On sale: their own Minervois wine.

PROPERTY

***

private parking, extensive grounds, lounge, hosts have pets, dinner available, packed lunch, babies welcome, free cot, no smoking

PRICE STRUCTURE

4 Bedrooms

Verte & Bleue: bathroom with wc, double bed: FF250

Rose: shower room with wc, double bed, 2 single beds (Childrens size): FF250 (2 people) FF400 (4 people)

Jaune: shower room with wc, 2 single beds: FF250

Extra bed: 80FF
Reduction: 3 nights

Capacity: 10 people

— In Carcassonne, take the N113 towards Narbonne. Turn left on to the D610 towards Trèbes then the D135 towards Laure-Minervois where you turn right on to the D111 towards Puichéric. Continue for 3km.

11.13 CARCASSONNE

Nicole GALINIER

«La Maison sur la Colline»
Mas de Ste Croix
11000 CARCASSONNE

tel: (0) 4 68 47 57 94

Private Home

This house is peacefully situated amongst the vines, 1km from the medieval city of Carcassonne. Your hosts are retired gardeners and Nicole loves plants. The interior of the house has a great deal of character and you will be well looked after here.

PROPERTY

✱✱✱

off street parking, garden, tv lounge, hosts have pets, dinner available, packed lunch, babies welcome, free cot, swimming pool, hiking, cycling, fishing, interesting flora, sea or lake watersports, golf course 3km, mushroom picking 15km

CARCASSONNE
hosts will collect from station,
railway station 3km,
airport 6km,
car essential
— In Carcassonne, head for the cemetery which is on the left of the entrance to the Place du Prado. Follow it round, keeping on the left, and DO NOT take the Chemin des Anglais, which descends. The house is 1km on, after you have gone under the bridge.

PRICE STRUCTURE

5 Bedrooms

Bleue: bridal room, television, bathroom with wc, shower, double bed, 2 single beds: FF450 (2 people) FF520 (4 people)

Jaune: shower room with wc, double bed: FF300

Beige: television, along corridor shower room with wc, double bed, single bed: FF400

Rez de jardin- Blanche: television, shower room with wc, double bed: FF350

Coquelicot: lounge, shower room with wc, double bed, 3 single beds: FF350 (2 people) FF65 (5 people)

Extra bed: 80FF Reduction: 3 nights

Capacity: 16 people

Vanessa, Jérome &
Nathalie, Alain
YAGER & GRANDIN

«Domaine de la Bonde
11390
CUXAC-CABARDÈS

tel: (0) 4 68 26 57 16
fax: (0) 4 68 26 59 94
http: www.labonde-cuxac.com

Residence of Character

11.23 CARCASSONNE

Vanessa, Jérome, Nathalie and Alain have just taken over this establishment and are preparing to receive their first guests with great enthusiasm. The setting is really pleasant and the rooms spacious, with large bathrooms. A lovely village - you will have an excellent holiday.

25 km - N - CARCASSONNE CUXAC CABARDES: hosts will collect from station,
railway station 25km
airport 25km
car essential

PROPERTY

✱✱✱

off street parking, extensive grounds, lounge, hosts have pets, pets not accepted, dinner available, packed lunch, babies welcome, free cot, swimming pool, closed: 01/11-01/03, hiking, mushroom picking, fishing 1km, cycling 4km, golf course 25km, sea or lake watersports 25km

Fluent English spoken

PRICE STRUCTURE

5 Bedrooms

First room: bridal room, shower room with wc, double bed, 2 single beds: FF380 (2 people) FF540 (4 people)

Second, third, fourth & fifth rooms: shower room with wc, double bed: FF350

Extra bed: 90FF

Capacity: 12 people

— At Carcassonne, take the D118 towards Castres and Mazamet. At Cuxac Cabardés, follow the signs "chambres d'hotes".

Isabelle CLAYETTE

Domaine des Castelles»
11170 CAUX ET
SAUZENS

tel: (0) 4 68 72 03 60
fax: (0) 4 68 72 03 60

Residence of character

5 km - W - CARCASSONNE CAUX ET SAUZENS: hosts will collect from station, railway station 5km airport 4km car essential

11.26 CARCASSONNE

A beautiful house in a former vineyard surrounded by an oasis of green. The rooms are comfortable and bear evocative names such as "Suite Palmier" and "Laurier Rose", full of exotic and pastoral charm. Isabelle will tell you all you need to know about the area and its riches. Fleur de soleil member. Apartment for 5 people also available.

PRICE STRUCTURE

2 Bedrooms and 1 Suite

Suite Palmier: shower room with wc, double bed, twin beds, single bed: FF350 (2 people) FF620 (5 people)

Laurier Rose: shower room with wc, double bed, single bed: FF350 (2 people) FF440 (3 people)

Tournesol: shower room with wc, double bed: FF300

Extra bed: 90FF

Capacity: 10 people

PROPERTY

✱✱✱

off street parking, extensive grounds, tv lounge, pets not accepted, dinner available, babies welcome, free cot, hiking 3km, fishing 3km, cycling 5km, sea or lake watersports 6km, golf course 8km

Fluent English spoken

— From Carcassonne, head towards Salvaza airport, then take the D119 towards Montréal for 4km. The property is on the left; follow the signs.

Jérôme & Olivia
JOSEPH

«La Bastide Saint Louis»
42, rue Barbès
11000 CARCASSONNE

tel: (0) 4 68 72 34 81
fax: (0) 4 68 72 09 88

Flat/Apartment

11.28 CARCASSONNE

In the town centre, near to the medieval cité, this home has an interesting history. It is an ancient convent dating from the Middle Ages, which was destroyed by the Black Prince and rebuilt as a "hotel particulier" in the 18th century. Your hosts manage to combine the traditional building with modern decor. On sale: Wine.

CARCASSONNE
hosts will collect
from station
airport 3km

PROPERTY

✱✱✱

lounge, hosts have pets, telephone, babies welcome, free cot, golf course 2km, fishing 5km, hunting 5km, hiking 10km, cycling 10km, mushroom picking 15km, birdwatching 50km, sea or lake watersports 50km, river watersports 50km

English spoken

PRICE STRUCTURE

2 Bedrooms and 1 Suite

Grise: television, bathroom with wc, shower, washbasin, double bed, single bed: FF350 (2 people) FF430 (3 people)

Bleue: television, along corridor shower room with wc, double bed, single bed: FF300 (2 people) FF380 (3 people)

Suite Ocre: television, bathroom with wc, shower, washbasin, double bed, 2 single beds: FF300 (2 people) FF500 (4 people)

Extra bed: 80FF
Reduction: 15.10 – 15.02 and 7 nights

Capacity: 10 people

— At Carcassonne, head towards the "Centre-ville" and Place Carnot. The rue Barbès is a one-way street and in continuation of the rue Victor Hugo, parallel to the rue Verdun. It crosses the only pedestrianised sreet. At the end, park in one of the many free parking spaces.

Aimé & Laétitia
OURLIAC

«Le Château d'Aragon»
11600 ARAGON

tel: (0) 4 68 77 19 62
fax: (0) 4 68 77 19 62

Château

12 km - N -
CARCASSONNE
ARAGON: railway
station 14km
airport 16km
car essential

PRICE STRUCTURE

4 Bedrooms and 1 Suite

Mabilia: lounge, shower room with wc, double bed: FF290

Azalaïs & Effante: bathroom with wc, shower, double bed: FF290

Guillaume-Roger: bathroom with wc, shower, double bed, single bed: FF340 (2 people) FF420 (3 people)

Eliazar: bathroom with wc, shower, double bed, twin beds: FF290 (2 people) FF440 (4 people)

Extra bed: 80FF

Reduction: 3 nights and groups

Capacity: 2 people

11.29 CARCASSONNE

This medieval château, watching over this typical Mediterranean village, is a beautiful home dating from the 12th century, and is listed amongst France's historic monuments. On sale: their own wine, jam, Aragon honey, wine preserves.

PROPERTY

✱✱✱✱

off street parking, garden, tv lounge, hosts have pets, pets not accepted, dinner available, closed: 15/10-01/04, hiking, cycling, interesting flora, fishing 6km, golf course 14km, sea or lake watersports 40km

Adequate English spoken

— From Carcassonne, take the N113 towards Toulouse. 2km after the Carcassonne Exit, turn right on to the D203 towards Pennautier and then Aragon. Before arriving in the village, turn right and follow the signs to the wine "Coopérative" and then more signs.

Sarah WORTHINGTON

«Carrefour»
1, rue de l'Etang
11700 PEPIEUX

tel: (0) 4 68 91 69 29
fax: (0) 4 68 91 69 29
e-mail: sally.worthington@wanadoo.fr

Residence of character

26 km - E - CARCASSONNE
PEPIEUX: railway station 40km
airport 40km
car essential

11.30 CARCASSONNE

Your hostess is English and welcomes you to her home, in what was formerly a 17th century coaching inn. It is 25 minutes from Carcassonne and 5 minutes from the Canal du Midi, between the Montagne Noire and Les Corbières. There is so much to see in this area, and your hostess will be delighted to show you around personally, if you wish. Credit cards accepted.

PROPERTY

✱✱✱

off street parking, garden, tv lounge, pets not accepted, telephone, dinner available, packed lunch, 12 years old minimum age, no smoking, cycling, sea or lake watersports 2km, hiking 5km, fishing 8km, interesting flora 15km, mushroom picking 15km, golf course 20km, river watersports 20km, gliding 70km

Fluent English spoken

PRICE STRUCTURE

3 Bedrooms and 1 Suite

Jaune: bathroom with wc, shower, double bed: FF350

Bleu: bathroom with wc, shower, double bed: FF350

Vert: bathroom with wc, shower, double bed, twin beds: FF350 (2 people) FF650 (4 people)

Reduction: 7 nights

Capacity: 8 people

— At Carcassone, take the N113 towards Narbonne. Then turn left on to the D610 towards Trèbes Puichéric, Olonzac on the left and then Pépieux. The house is to the left of the church.

81.06 CASTELNAUDARY

Philippe & Martine DUPRESSOIR

«Château de Gandels»
81700 GARREVAQUES

tel: (0) 5 63 70 27 67
fax: (0) 5 63 70 27 67

Château

23 km - N - CASTELNAUDARY GARREVAQUES: airport 50km, car essential — From the A61, Exit Castelnaudary. Take the D624 and then the D622 as far as Revel. Then go towards Castres and as you leave the town, at the roundabout, turn left towards Garrevaques, and continue for 2.4km. The château is on the right.

Martine knows all about quality, and this is reflected in the large salons and stylish bedrooms. She also loves cooking and bakes her own bread. The landscaped gardens were designed by the famous architect Lenotre (fountains, pools, waterlillies...).

PROPERTY

✱✱✱✱

off street parking, extensive grounds, tv lounge, hosts have pets, dinner available, babies welcome, free cot, swimming pool, riding, hiking, fishing, hunting, birdwatching, interesting flora 1km, mushroom picking 1km, cycling 5km, sea or lake watersports 5km, river watersports 5km

English spoken

Price structure

4 Bedrooms and 1 Suite and 1 Apartment

Rétro: television, bathroom with wc, double bed: FF550

Chambres Tour & Baldaquin: television, bathroom with wc, double bed: FF650

Chambre Terrasse: television, bathroom with wc, twin beds: FF600

Suite Eugénie: television, bathroom with wc, 2 double bed: FF1200

Suite Empereur: television, kitchen, bathroom with wc, 2 double beds, twin beds: FF1200

Extra bed: 100FF Reduction: groups

Capacity: 18 people

11.24 NARBONNE

This is an old vinegrower's house in the process of being restored. Serge and Marie offer a warm welcome, and you must try their delicious cooking in their magnificent dining room decorated with wine vats. This place really has the atmosphere of a typical old farmhouse.

Serge MAYEN

«Domaine du Petit Fidèle»
Ancienne route de Coursan
11100 NARBONNE

tel: (0) 4 68 32 18 12

Private Home

PROPERTY

✱✱✱

off street parking, garden, lounge, pets not accepted, dinner available, packed lunch, babies welcome, free cot, fishing, golf course 2km, hiking 15km, interesting flora 15km, mushroom picking 15km, birdwatching 15km, sea or lake watersports 15km

Basic English spoken

NARBONNE: railway station 5km, airport 30km, car essential — Take the Exit Narbonne-Sud on the A9. Go straight on along the bypass. At the fourth roundabout turn right, turn left immediately and left again (the old road to Coursan). Continue for 2.5km. The house is a reddish-ochre colour.

PRICE STRUCTURE

3 Bedrooms and 1 Suite

shower room with wc, double bed: FF200

shower room with wc, double bed: FF20

shower room with wc, 2 single beds: FF220

Suite: shower room with wc, double bed, 2 single beds: FF330 (2 people) FF440 (4 people)

Reduction: 16.09 – 30.06 and 7 nights

Capacity: 10 people

Philippe GRILLERE

«Les Hauts de Cabanoule»
Chemin du Bruel
30140 GENERARGUES

tel: (0) 4 66 61 84 60
fax: (0) 4 66 61 84 60

Private Home

30.30 ALES

Close to the largest bamboo wood in Europe, this elegant house is perched high up, with an uninterrupted view of the valley. This goes perfectly with breakfast on the terrace, and then you must decide whether to enjoy the heated swimming pool or a walk in the beautiful forest.

10 km - S W - ALES
GENERARGUES:
hosts will collect from station,
railway station 10km
airport 50km
car essential

PROPERTY

✱✱✱

private parking, extensive grounds, tv lounge, hosts have pets, telephone, dinner available, babies welcome, free cot, wheelchair access, swimming pool, closed: 01/01–31/01, hiking, cycling, mushroom picking, birdwatching, interesting flora 2km, fishing 3km, hunting 5km, golf course 10km, sea or lake watersports 70km

Fluent English spoken

PRICE STRUCTURE

5 Bedrooms

La Clède: television, shower room with wc, twin beds: FF330

Cévenole & Bambouseraie: television, shower room with wc, double bed, single bed: FF330 (2 people) FF400 (3 people)

Tornac: television, shower room with wc, double bed: FF330

Bastide: shower room with wc, twin beds: FF330

Extra bed: 100FF
Reduction: 4 nights

Capacity: 12 people

— At Alès, take the N110 towards Montpellier, and then the D910 on the right as far as Anduze. Then take the D129 for Génerargues. When you reach the exit sign as you leave Génerargues, continue for 400m and then turn right. Follow the signs to "Les Hauts de Cabanoule".

Maryvonne & Richard ROUDIER-VILLARD

«Château d'Isis»
30440 ST JULIEN DE LA NEF

tel: (0) 4 67 73 56 22
fax: (0) 4 67 73 56 22

Château

13 km - S E - LE VIGAN
ST JULIEN DE LA NEF: railway station 50km
airport 50km
car essential

30.22 LE VIGAN

The château is is the process of being restored, but you will love the peace and quiet that pervades this place along with the cool shade of the trees and the babbling brook. What an ideal spot to relax! Be sure to ask to see the trout farm. On sale: Vegetables, jam, wine, vinegar.

PROPERTY

✸✸✸

private parking, extensive grounds, lounge, hosts have pets, dinner available, packed lunch, closed: 10/01-31/01, hiking, hunting, interesting flora, mushroom picking, birdwatching, cycling 5km, river watersports 5km, golf course 20km, fishing 50km

Fluent English spoken

— At Le Vigan take the D999 towards Montpellier. At St Julien de la Nef follow the signs for 1km along by the river Hérault.

PRICE STRUCTURE

4 Bedrooms and 2 Apartments

Bleu: bathroom with wc, double bed: FF300

Rose: bathroom with wc, twin beds: FF320

Verte: bathroom with wc, 2 double beds, 2 single beds: FF380 (2 people) FF780 (4 people)

Suite: lounge, bathroom with wc, double bed: FF320F

St Bresson & Thaurac: kitchen, shower room with wc, 2 double beds, 2 single beds: FF360 (2 people) FF540 (4 people)

Reduction: children

Capacity: 24 people

Régis & Corinne
BURCKEL de TELL

48, Grande rue
30420 CALVISSON

tel: (0) 4 66 01 23 91
fax: (0) 4 66 01 42 19

Residence of character

15 km - S W - NIMES
CALVISSON: railway station 15km
airport 15km
car essential

PRICE STRUCTURE

4 Bedrooms and 2 Suites

First floor-l'Espagnole: bathroom with wc, single bed: FF230

First floor-le Patio: bathroom with wc, double bed: FF280

First floor-Duchesse: shower room with wc, double bed, single bed: FF280 (2 people) FF350 (3 people)

Second floor-la Provençale: shower room with wc, double bed: FF280

Second floor-la Camarguaise: bathroom with wc, twin beds: FF280

Second floor-la Terrasse: bathroom with wc, shower, double bed, single bed: FF280 (2 people) FF350 (3 people)

Capacity: 13 people

30.05 NIMES

At the heart of this old village in the midi, Régis & Corinne have restored this 15th century "hotel particulier". Admire the fountains, the fireplaces and terraces, and the focal point of the patio. There is a music room and exposed beams. A good address near Nîmes and Arles. Private parking: 30FF

PROPERTY

✱✱✱

off street parking, lounge, dinner available, hiking, cycling, interesting flora, hunting 2km, fishing 10km, mushroom picking 10km, golf course 15km, birdwatching 15km, sea or lake watersports 25km, river watersports 25km

Fluent English spoken

— From A9 Exit Gallargues. Take the N113 towards Nîmes, then the D1 towards Calvisson. The house is next to the town hall (Mairie).

30.06 NIMES

Françoise GUILLERY

«la Crémade»
30190 AUBUSSARGUES

tel: (0) 4 66 81 22 62

Private Home

Françoise's house is between the garrigue and the vines, where you get the wonderful flavour of the scented Provençal air. The bedroom is in a separate little house, on a mezzanine floor with the lounge below. You will enjoy the wilderness feel of this part of Provence and the Aquatic Park at Uzès is well worth a visit.

PROPERTY

✱✱

off street parking, garden, hosts have pets, pets not accepted, 18 years old minimum age, swimming pool, 2 nights minimum stay 1/05-31/10, hiking, cycling 8km, golf course 9km, river watersports 10km

Fluent English spoken

45 km - N W - NIMES
AUBUSSARGUES:
airport 35km
car essential
— At Nîmes, take the N106 towards Alès for 11km, then the D225 towards Dions and the D22 towards Aubussargues. At the STOP sign, turn left towards Collorgues and turn right at the sign "Quartier la Crémade". It is the first house on the left after the fire hydrant.

PRICE STRUCTURE

1 Bedroom
lounge, television, bathroom with wc, double bed: FF370

Reduction: 03.10 – 24.06

Capacity: 2 people

30.07 NIMES

Eliette COUSTON

«La Mazade»
12, rue de la Mazade
30730 ST MAMERT

tel: (0) 4 66 81 17 56

Residence of character

Eliette is an artist and her studio is part of the house. She has cleverly combined modern art and the charms of this 19th century house. She is a mine of information on places to visit, festivals and local artists and exhibitions. On sale: Hand-made leather garments

PROPERTY

✱✱

off street parking, extensive grounds, tv lounge, hosts have pets, pets not accepted, dinner available, packed lunch, hiking, fishing 18km, river watersports 25km, birdwatching 40km

Basic English spoken

14 km - N W - NIMES
ST MAMERT: hosts will collect from station, railway station 14km
airport 20km
— On the A9, Exit 'Nîmes-Ouest'. Go towards Alès and turn left on to the D999 towards Le Vigan for 10km. Turn right on to the D1 towards St Mamert for 4km. In the village, the house is at the corner by the 'coiffeur' (butchers).

PRICE STRUCTURE

3 Bedroom
shower room with wc, twin beds: FF300

(2 rooms) shower room with wc, double bed: FF300

Extra bed: 70FF

Capacity: 6 people

Gérard CRISTINI

«La Terre des Lauriers»
Rive Droite Pont
du Gard
30210 REMOULINS

tel: (0) 4 66 37 19 45
fax: (0) 4 66 37 19 45

Residence of character

20 km - W - NIMES
REMOULINS:
railway station 20km
airport 20km
car essential

30.20 NIMES

Gérard's spacious bastide is only 800m from the famous Pont du Gard. Enjoy the cool shade of their grounds, the peaceful forest, the river, the swimming pool and the brunch style breakfast. You may never have dreamed of such a holiday! 30/10–01/04 : advance bookings only. Self-catering apartment rented weekly

PRICE STRUCTURE

3 Bedrooms and 1 Suite

Exotique: bathroom with wc, shower, double bed: FF420

Rétro: shower room with wc, double bed: FF420

Romantique: shower room with wc, twin beds, single bed: FF420 (2 people) FF570 (3 people)

Provençale: shower room with wc, double bed, 3 single beds: FF420 (2 people) FF720 (5 people)

Extra bed: 150FF
Reduction: 3 nights

Capacity: 12 people

PROPERTY

***

private parking, extensive grounds, tv lounge, hosts have pets, pets not accepted, babies welcome, free cot, swimming pool, closed: 01/10-01/03, hiking, cycling, fishing, interesting flora, river watersports 1km, golf course 12km

Adequate English spoken

— Exit Remoulins from the A9. At Remoulins, cross the river Gardon and take the right bank to Pont du Gard. The house is on the right.

Eric & Mercédes
BREL-THIANGE

«Le Clos de Vic»
2, rue du Temple
30260 VIC LE FESQ

tel: (0) 4 66 80 52 01
fax: (0) 4 66 80 59 77

Private Home

24 km - W - NIMES
VIC LE FESQ: hosts will collect from station,
railway station 25km
airport 30km
car essential

30.26 NIMES

In the heart of a peaceful village, the very welcoming Mercédes has made sure to give her rooms the personal touch, Provençal stylę. You are at the foot of the Cévennes, close to numerous interesting towns as well as historic sites that you absolutely must visit.

PROPERTY

✱✱✱

off street parking, garden, lounge, hosts have pets, dinner available, packed lunch, no smoking, swimming pool, 2 nights minimum stay 01/07-31/08, riding, cycling, fishing, hunting, hiking 1km, golf course 25km, sea or lake watersports 40km, mushroom picking 60km, winter sports 60km

Fluent English spoken

PRICE STRUCTURE

3 Bedrooms

Pagnol: television, telephone, shower room with wc, double bed, single bed: FF380 (2 people) FF480 (3 people)

Mistral: television, shower room with wc, twin beds: FF380

Daudet: television, bathroom with wc, double bed: FF380

Extra bed: 100FF

Capacity: 7 people

— From Nîmes, head towards Guissac on the D999. Take the second exit for Vic le Fesq. In the village, take the first road on the left. It is the last house on the right (wall topped with railings).

Michèle
DELCOR CLAMENS

«Les Pins de Jol»
St Quentin la Poterie
30700 UZES

tel: (0) 4 66 03 16 84
fax: (0) 4 66 03 16 84

Private Home

30 km - N - NIMES
ST QUENTIN LA POTERIE: railway station 30km
airport 40km
car essential

30.27 NIMES

If you are visiting the Gard area, you really must stop at Michèle's place. You will fall in love with her hospitality, her house, so calm in the heart of a pine forest, and her swimming pool. Michèle is more than happy to talk about the local pottery as well as the superb Roman sites nearby.

PRICE STRUCTURE

3 Bedrooms

(1 room) bathroom, wc, double bed, single bed: FF300 (2 people) FF375 (3 people)

(2 rooms) shower room with wc, double bed, single bed: FF350 (2 people) FF425 (3 people)

Extra bed: 75FF

Capacity: 9 people

PROPERTY

✸✸✸

off street parking, extensive grounds, pets not accepted, no smoking, swimming pool, 2 nights minimum stay, hiking, cycling 2km, golf course 5km, fishing 15km, sea or lake watersports 15km

English spoken

— From Nîmes, take the D979 to Uzès. Continue towards Lussan then turn right on to the D125 in the direction of St Quentin-la-Poterie for 700 metres. Turn right to "Les Pins de Jol"

30.29 NIMES

This large and imposing 19th century house with well decorated, comfortable rooms is situated near Uzès. This is the Midi with its little villages, vineyards and châteaux. You will stay on for the beauty of the surroundings as well as the genuine welcome of your hosts, Michel and John.

John KARAVIAS

«Les Marronniers»
Place de la Mairie
30580 LA BRUGUIERE

tel: (0) 4 66 72 84 77
fax: (0) 4 66 72 85 78
e-mail: les.marronniers@hello.to

Residence of character

PROPERTY

✱✱✱✱

garden, lounge, pets not accepted, telephone, dinner available, 15 years old minimum age, swimming pool, 3 nights minimum stay, hiking, cycling, mushroom picking, golf course 11km, river watersports 15km

Fluent English spoken

39 km - N - NIMES
LA BRUGUIERE: railway station 39km, airport 82km, car essential
— From Nîmes, take the D979 to Uzès. Continue towards Lussan for 8km. Turn right on to the D238 as far as La Bruguière. The house can be found in the main village square, next to the town hall and the château.

PRICE STRUCTURE

4 Bedrooms

1: television, shower room with wc, double bed: FF500

2: television, shower room with wc, twin beds: FF500

3: television, shower room with wc, bathroom, twin beds: FF600

4: television, shower room with wc, double bed: FF500

Capacity: 8 people

Carole & Claude
DUFFOUR

«Mas de l'Argile»
30190 ST CHAPTES

tel: (0) 4 66 81 27 58
fax: (0) 4 66 81 27 58
e-mail: duffour@mnet.fr

Private Home

20 km - S E - NIMES
ST CHAPTES:
railway station 25km
airport 35km
car essential

PRICE STRUCTURE

1 Bedroom
television, shower room with wc, bathroom, double bed: FF450

Capacity: 2 people

30.31 NIMES

This pretty mas is set amongst the trees and has a large swimming pool. They have just one large room, which is air conditioned. There is cycling and golf 15km away and a tennis court in the village. You are only 15km from Uzès, 20km from the famous Pont du Gard, 40km from Arles, 50km from Avignon and 75km from the coast. Fleur de Soleil member.

PROPERTY

***

off street parking, extensive grounds, pets not accepted, no smoking, swimming pool, closed: 01/10-14/06, cycling 15km, golf course 15km

English spoken

— From the Autoroute, Exit Nîmes Ouest. Head towards Alès and after 16km, turn right and go through the village of St. Chaptes. At the roundabout turn left, then right, and the entrance is on the left.

34.04 BEZIERS

Very friendly family atmosphere in this vineyard in the heart of the village where they produce the Faugères wine. Comfortable rooms. Near to beaches, Les Gorges d'Héric and numerous typical villages, abbeys, watermills... On sale: Wine. 3 self-catering apartments.

Josette HORTER

«La Coquillade»
Rue du 8 Mai 1945
34480 AUTIGNAC

tel: (0) 4 67 90 24 05

Farm

PROPERTY

✱✱

off street parking, garden, tv lounge, hosts have pets, dinner available, packed lunch, hiking, cycling, fishing 8km, river watersports 10km, interesting flora 15km, golf course 20km, sea or lake watersports 35km

18 km - N - BEZIERS AUTIGNAC: hosts will collect from station, railway station 20km airport 35km,
— In Béziers, take the D909 towards Bédarieux for 23km. Turn left towards Autignac. Go to the church square and turn on the left of the church. Continue for 100m.

PRICE STRUCTURE

3 Bedrooms

First & second room: shower room with wc, twin beds: FF240

Third room: shower room with wc, double bed: FF240

Extra bed: 50FF
Reduction: 7 nights

Capacity: 6 people

Alain & Catherine POISSON

‹Domaine Fon de Rey»
Route de Pézenas
34810 POMÉROLS

tel: (0) 4 67 77 08 56
fax: (0) 4 67 77 08 56

Residence of character

20 km - N E - BEZIERS
POMEROLS: hosts will collect from station,
railway station 10km
airport 20km
car essential

34.05 BEZIERS

You will be enthralled by Catherine, Alain and the plentiful and refined cooking of their daughters Céline and Aurélie. This wonderfully restored, 17th century residence is now the cosy home of an artist, amongst the vines, near the beaches and forest.

PROPERTY

✱✱✱

private parking, extensive grounds, tv lounge, hosts have pets, telephone, dinner available, packed lunch, swimming pool, closed: 11/11-15/03, 3 nights minimum stay 1/07-31/08, cycling, hiking 2km, golf course 10km, fishing 10km, sea or lake watersports 10km, river watersports 15km

Fluent English spoken

PRICE STRUCTURE

6 Bedrooms and 1 Suite

Suite: bridal room, bathroom with wc, twin beds, double bed, single bed: FF385 (2 people) FF770 (5 people)

Royale: kitchen, shower room with wc, twin beds: FF440

First room: shower room with wc, twin beds: FF275

Second & third rooms: shower room with wc, double bed: FF75

Fourth room: bathroom with wc, double bed, 2 single beds: FF330 (2 people) FF440 (4 people)

Fifth room: shower room with wc, twin beds, single bed: FF330 (2 people) FF385 (3 people)

Extra bed: 100FF
Reduction: 01.09 – 30.06

Capacity: 20 people

— On the A9, take the Exit 'Agde' and go towards Pézenas for 3km. Turn right on to the D18 towards Florensac and at Pomerols, go towards Pézenas for 1km.

Andrew & Jennifer
VINER

7, Rue de la Fontaine
34420 VILLENEUVE L
BEZIERS

tel: (0) 4 67 39 87 15
fax: (0) 4 67 39 87 15

Residence of character

5 km - S - BEZIERS
VILLENEUVE LES BEZIERS: hosts will collect from station, railway station 5km airport 65km

34.06 BEZIERS

Jennifer is Australian and her passion is her guests. She will introduce you to her wonderful 15th century home in the heart of a peaceful village, with its beautiful staircase, comfortable rooms and remarkable frescoes. Near to the beaches.

PROPERTY

✱✱✱

lounge, hosts have pets, pets not accepted, dinner available, packed lunch, babies welcome, free cot, hiking, cycling, fishing 2km, birdwatching 5km, sea or lake watersports 5km, gliding 5km, golf course 15km

Fluent English spoken

PRICE STRUCTURE

4 Bedrooms

Pois de Senteur: shower room with wc, twin beds: FF270

Baldaquin: bathroom with wc, double bed: FF270

Provençale: bathroom with wc, shower, double bed: FF270

Rose: bathroom with wc, shower, 2 single beds: FF27

Extra bed: 70FF
Reduction: 01.10 – 31.05 and 7 nights

Capacity: 2 people

— On the A9, take the Exit Béziers-Est. Go towards Sérignan. The house is opposite the 'Mairie', in the centre of Villeneuve.

Ann Marie HIGGINS

5, rue René Soulette
34490 THÉZAN LES BÉZIERS

tel: (0) 4 67 36 31 42
fax: (0) 4 67 35 25 17

Private Home

12 km - N - BEZIERS
THEZAN LES BEZIERS: railway station 10km
airport 25km
car essential

34.09 BEZIERS

Overlooking the Vallée de l'Orb, in the heart of the Béziers vineyards, this place has a superb view. Either relax beside the pool or on the beach or visit Cathar castles and vineyards.

PRICE STRUCTURE

3 Bedrooms

Bleu: along corridor shower room with wc, double bed: FF275

Vert: along corridor bathroom with wc, twin beds: FF275

Jaune: shower room with wc, double bed: FF275

Extra bed: 75FF

Capacity: 6 people

PROPERTY

***

private parking, garden, lounge, hosts have pets, pets not accepted, dinner available, kitchen, 5 years old minimum age, swimming pool, tennis, hiking, cycling, fishing 3km, river watersports 10km, golf course 15km, sea or lake watersports 25km

Fluent English spoken

— Take Exit Béziers-Est from the A9, then the D909 towards Bédarieux. Then, left on to the D33 towards Pailhès-Thézan.

Pierre&Linda BLANPA
VANDERMOSTEN

«L'Hacienda des Roucans»
Route des Réals -
Les Roucans
34490 MURVIEL
LES BEZIERS

tel: (0) 4 67 32 90 10
fax: (0) 4 67 32 90 81

Private Home

12 km - N W -
BEZIERS
MURVIEL LES BEZIERS: railway station 20km
airport 70km
car essential

34.10 BEZIERS

This is a small corner of Belgium beside the river. You can spend a wonderful holiday here, and choose between canoeing, sunbathing beside the pool, the sauna, or just sitting in the shade of the garden. On sale: Wine, Muscat, charcuterie.

PROPERTY

✱✱✱

private parking, extensive grounds, tv lounge, hosts have pets, telephone, dinner available, 6 years old minimum age, swimming pool, 7 nights minimum stay 1/07-31/08, hiking, cycling, fishing, river watersports 1km, interesting flora 15km, mushroom picking 15km

Fluent English spoken

— A9 to Béziers-Centre. After 2.8km, at roundabout go towards Montpellier-Bédarieu. Signs St Pons-Bédarieu, Lignan & Murviel (D19). Then follow signs to Cessenon (D19 then D36). After les Roucans left after the first house. Then down the hill to the car-park.

PRICE STRUCTURE

7 Bedrooms

Casa Pitou: lounge, television, shower room with wc, bathroom, 2 double beds: F525 (2 people) FF685 (4 people)

Gourmande: television, shower room with wc, bathroom, double bed: FF420

Casa Irène: television, shower room with wc, bathroom, double bed: FF367

Montjoie: television, shower room with wc, double bed: FF367

Mickey: television, bathroom with wc, double bed: FF367

Larissa + Gémeaux: 2 twin beds: FF523

Extra bed: 80FF
Reduction: 7 nights

Capacity: 16 people

ndré & Jeanne CRISIAS

«Résidence Le Clot»
111-113, Quai Cornu
La Tamarissière 34300
AGDE

tel: (0) 4 67 94 21 78
fax: (0) 4 67 94 19 32

Private Home

20 km - S E - BEZIERS
AGDE: hosts will collect from station,
railway station 3km
airport 6km
car essential
— At Béziers take the N112 towards Agde then turn right on to the N32 towards Sète. Then right towards Le Grau d'Agde/La Tamarissière. Le Clot is on the right-hand side of the road.

34.13 MONTPELLIER

Here the accommodation is in very basic studio-cabins which are 100m from the river Hérault and 1km from the sea. You are free to explore the 10 hectare wooded estate and there are many games provided for children. 4/07–29/08 : Flats are also available to rent on a weekly basis.

PROPERTY

✱✱

off street parking, garden, hosts have pets, swimming pool, closed: 1/10-31/03, hiking, fishing, sea or lake watersports, golf course 4km, birdwatching 6km

Basic English spoken

PRICE STRUCTURE

3 Apartments

Le Coquillage & l'Etoile de Mer & l'Hippocampe: kitchen, shower room with wc, double bed, 2 single beds, childrens size: FF230 (2 people) FF330 (4 people)

Capacity: 12 people

34.12 MONTPELLIER

Elisabeth NOUALHAC

«Domaine du Pous»
Le Pous
34380 NOTRE DAME DE
LONDRES

tel: (0) 4 67 55 01 36

Manor House

In this old house dating from the 17th and 18th century situated amidst the woods and garrigue, everything exudes quality. The welcome of your hostess, the care and attention she lavishes upon you, the furniture and the decor are all of a high standard. Quite a discovery.

PROPERTY

✱✱✱✱

off street parking, extensive grounds, lounge, pets not accepted, dinner available, gliding 5km

30 km - N W - MONTPELLIER
LE POUS: railway station 30km
airport 40km
car essential
— At Montpellier take the D986 towards Le Vigan. After St Martin de Londres take the second on the right towards Notre Dame de Londres, and continue as far as Le Pous.

PRICE STRUCTURE

6 Bedrooms

shower room with wc, washbasin, double bed, single bed: FF280 (2 people) FF330 (3 people)

(2 rooms) shower room with wc, washbasin, double bed: FF280

shower room with wc, washbasin, 2 single beds: FF280

bathroom with wc, washbasin, 2 single beds: FF280

bathroom with wc, washbasin, double bed: FF350

Extra bed: 50FF

Capacity: 13 people

Huguette FAIDHERBE

«Domaine Le Bel Air»
76 rue Serge Lifar -
Bat. E
34080 MONTPELLIER

tel: (0) 4 67 03 27 53

Flat

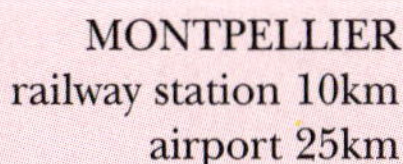

MONTPELLIER
railway station 10km
airport 25km

34.18 MONTPELLIER

Near the Municipal Buildings of Montpellier, this is a small, cosy ground floor apartment with a garage. There is a kitchen area, terrace and private garden looking out on to an olive grove. Huguette is a small, friendly lady full of energy but you will still find peace and quiet here. Very convenient for the city.

PRICE STRUCTURE

1 Bedroom
television,
double bed: FF310

Extra bed: 120FF
Reduction: 15.09 – 30.06

Capacity: 2 people

PROPERTY

✱✱

off street parking, garden, tv lounge, hosts have pets, kitchen, 3 years old minimum age, wheelchair access, no smoking

Basic English spoken

— Take Exit 31 from the A9 and head north towards Montpellier. Les Cévennes or Celleneuve/Hotel du département. Follow the sign 'Hotel du département, ENTREE ADMINISTRATIVE'. The 'Domaine du Bel Air' is on the right of the Rue Serge Lifar. Ring the Entryphone.

Marie Claude DEMAILI

2, rue du Vieux Pont
34670 ST BRES

tel: (0) 4 67 70 62 75
fax: (0) 4 67 70 62 75
e-mail:
mcdemail@mnet.fr

Residence of character

15 km - E -
MONTPELLIER
ST BRES: railway
station 15km
airport 14km
car essential

34.19 MONTPELLIER

This was originally an old 17th century coaching inn, in this village between the famous towns of Montpellier and Nîmes. You will be captivated immediately. The setting is magnificent and the bedrooms comfortable. There is an indoor swimming pool and you are only 30 minutes from the beaches. You are also near to the Camargue and the Cévennes. Fleur de soleil member.

PROPERTY

✱✱✱

off street parking, garden, lounge, hosts have pets, 6 years old minimum age, babies welcome, free cot, swimming pool, golf course 3km, birdwatching 20km, sea or lake watersports 20km

Fluent English spoken

PRICE STRUCTURE

2 Bedrooms and 1 Suite

Suite: lounge, kitchen, along corridor bathroom, wc, double bed, 2 twin beds: FF400 (2 people) FF800 (4 people)

Jaune & Bleue: shower room with wc, double bed: FF350

Extra bed: 100FF

Reduction: 7 nights

Capacity: 10 people

— From the A9, take Exit 28. Head towards Nîmes on the N113. After Baillargues, go towards St Bres on the left. The house is just after the little bridge, No. 2.

Monique
SYKES-MAILLON

«La Ciboulette»
221, Rue de l'Eglise
34400 ST CHRISTOL

tel: (0) 4 67 86 81 00
fax: (0) 4 67 86 81 00
e-mail: cibou@aol.com

Private Home

24 km - N E -
MONTPELLIER
ST CHRISTOL

PRICE STRUCTURE

2 Bedrooms

shower room with wc, twin beds: FF370

bathroom with wc, double bed: FF370

Capacity: 4 people

34.20 MONTPELLIER

This impressive old residence, with a garden and a beautiful view over the vines, is in the centre of a small wine-producing village. It is on the route to Spain, between Nîmes and Montpellier, and is only half an hour from beaches, the Cévennes and the golf courses of Massane and La Grande-Motte. Fleur de Soleil member.

PROPERTY

✱✱✱

off street parking, garden, pets not accepted, closed: 1/11-28/02, golf course 20km, sea or lake watersports 20km

English spoken

— On the autoroute A9 (E15), Exit Lunel towards Sommière. Contact your host for more detailed directions.

Hubert & Anne-Sylvie PFISTER

«Château de Cauvel»
48110 ST MARTIN DE LANSUSCLE

tel: (0) 4 66 45 92 75
fax: (0) 4 66 45 94 76

Château

65 km - S E - MENDE
LANSUSCLE: hosts will collect from station,
railway station 50km
airport 100km
car essential

48.05 MENDE

In the heart of the Cévennes, the out-buildings of this 17th century château form a small hamlet in their own right. In this conservation area (impressively a 'world Biosphere Reserve') there are deer and wild boar. Anne-Sylvie's local dishes are a delight.

PROPERTY

✱✱✱

off street parking, extensive grounds, tv lounge, hosts have pets, telephone, dinner available, kitchen, packed lunch, babies welcome, free cot, hiking, cycling, hunting, interesting flora, mushroom picking, river watersports, fishing 5km

English spoken

— In Mende, N88 & N106 towards Alès. 19km after Florac, right onto D62 towards Barre des Cévennes then left on to D162 towards 'Col de Fontmort'. Left on to D13 towards St Germain de Calberte for 2km.

PRICE STRUCTURE

12 Bedrooms and 1 Suite and 1 Apartment

Chambre de prestige Bonheur: shower room with wc, double bed, single bed Childrens size

Chambre de prestige Rétro-Louis Philippe: bathroom with wc, double bed, twin beds

Chambre de prestige Anglaise (château): bathroom with wc, twin beds

Clématite: bathroom with wc, double bed

Pellegrine: shower room with wc, double bed, single bed

Provence/Lavande: shower room with wc, double bed, 2 single beds

Maison La Clède: lounge, kitchen, shower room with wc, double bed, 2 single bed

Chambres de séjour (5 rooms): shower room with wc, 2 single beds

Chambre de randonneurs Amaryllis: shower room with wc, 4 single beds

Danielle & Pierre
MEJEAN PARENTINI

«La Maison de Marius»
8, rue du Pontet
48320 QUEZAC

tel: (0) 4 66 44 25 05

Private Home

30 km - S - MENDE
QUEZAC: railway station 40km
airport 100km
car essential

PRICE STRUCTURE

2 Bedrooms

Rivière & Pontet: shower room with wc, double bed: FF300

Extra bed: 100FF

Capacity: 4 people

48.06 MENDE

This typical, Languedoc village house is in the Cevennes National Park, at the beginning of the Gorges du Tarn. The welcome is warm and attentive, the decor refined and the local food healthy and colourful. The region offers a wealth of sporting activities. Fleur de Soleil member.

PROPERTY

✱✱✱

off street parking, dinner available, hiking

— From the A75, Exit Marvejols. Then take the N88 to Monde and the N106 towards Alès. The house is on the right in Ispagnac.

Marie-Christine DONA

Pla de l'Ous - Fetges
66210 SAUTO

tel: (0) 4 68 04 20 89

Private Home

8 km - E - FONT-ROMEU
FETGES: railway station 25km
airport 90km
car essential

66.05 FONT-ROMEU

Marie-Christine's typical little mountain house proudly stands 1700 metres up, facing the Pyrenees and the Spanish border. There is a view over the Mont- Louis fortifications. The ideal starting point for some wonderful excursions. There are two large ski resorts less than 5km away.

PROPERTY

✱✱

off street parking, garden, tv lounge, hosts have pets, wheelchair access, 2 nights minimum stay, mushroom picking, cycling 2km, fishing 2km, hunting 2km, winter sports 2km, gliding 2km, sea or lake watersports 8km, golf course 10km, interesting flora 10km

Adequate English spoken

PRICE STRUCTURE

2 Bedrooms

Rez de Chaussée: television wc, double bed: FF250

Mini-Suite: television, wc, double bed, 2 single beds: FF250 (2 people) FF290 (4 people)

Capacity: 6 people

— At Perpignan, take the N116 towards Font-Romeu. 10km before Font-Romeu, cross the village of Fetges, then take the 1st right (opposite the bridge over the river Têt). This is a small road heading to Pla de l'Ous. 600 metres on the left, take the steep road and then follow the signs.

Helena-Shelagh MICHIE

«La Belle Auriole»
66600 OPOUL

tel: (0) 4 68 29 19 26
fax: (0) 4 68 29 19 26

Private Home

66.01 PERPIGNAN

Helena who is English loves this region, where she put down her roots 17 years ago. Her mas is typical of the Roussillon area. Here you are surrounded by vines and the garrigues, wilderness all around you. Helena organises themed stays, and hiking trips.

35 km - N - PERPIGNAN
OPOUL: railway station 30km
airport 30km
car essential
— On the A9, take the Exit Perpignan Nord. Then take the D12 towards Vingrau and turn right on to the D9 towards Opoul. Go through Opoul and follow the signs "Château de Périllos" and after 1.5km, take the little made-up lane on the left, which descends towards an electricity pylon.

PROPERTY

✷

off street parking, garden, hosts have pets, pets not accepted, dinner available, packed lunch, closed: 30/10-15/04, hiking, cycling, sea or lake watersports 25km, gliding 25km, interesting flora 30km, mushroom picking 30km, birdwatching 30km, winter sports 50km

Fluent English spoken

PRICE STRUCTURE

2 Suites

Mezzanine-1: double bed, twin beds, 2 single beds: FF240 (2 people) FF840 (6 people)

Mezzanine-2: lounge, double bed, 3 single beds: FF240 (2 people) FF690 (5 people)

Extra bed: 75FF
Reduction: 4 nights

Capacity: 1 people

Jacques&Annelies VISSENAEKEN-VAES

«Domaine du Mas Cammas»
Auberge des Comédien
Mas Cammas 66300
CAIXAS

tel: (0) 4 68 38 82 27
fax: (0) 4 68 38 83 67

Residence of character

Languedoc-Roussillon

PERPIGNAN

66.03 PERPIGNAN

Everything is beautiful in this mas, which dominates the Roussillon plain...the bedrooms, the dining room, the swimming pool, the silence. We advise you to request the most expensive rooms because they are amazing and cut out of rock. Excellent value for money. Completely quiet.

25 km - S W - PERPIGNAN
CAIXAS: hosts will collect from station, railway station 26km
airport 32km
car essential

PROPERTY

✱✱✱✱

private parking, extensive grounds, lounge, hosts have pets, pets not accepted, telephone, dinner available, packed lunch, swimming pool, closed: 01/12-31/01, hiking, cycling, hunting, interesting flora, mushroom picking, birdwatching, golf course 20km, sea or lake watersports 20km, fishing 30km

Fluent English spoken

PRICE STRUCTURE

3 Bedrooms and 3 Suites

Vigneron: shower room with wc, washbasin, double bed, single bed: FF460 (2 people) FF690 (3 people)

Suite Patrons, Suite Pigeonnier & Suite Berger: shower room with wc, double bed, twin beds: FF490 (2 people) FF800 (4 people)

Cour: shower room with wc twin beds: FF550

Jardin: shower room with wc, double bed: FF500

Extra bed: 90FF

Capacity: 15 people

— On the A9 take Exit Perpignan-Sud. 50m after the toll booths (péage) turn left to Thuir. Before Thuir turn left towards Fourques (D615) and D2 towards Caixas par Montauriol. Entrance on the D2 road (look for the sign Mas Cammas and large barrels).

CENTRE
POITOU CHARENTES
LIMOUSIN
AUVERGNE
AQUITAINE
MIDI-PYRÉNÉES
LANGUEDOC-ROUSSILLON
SPAIN
ANDORRA
Cholet
Châtellerault
Châteauroux
Bourges
Nevers
POITIERS
Moulins
Montluçon
La Rochelle
Guéret
Vichy
Rochefort
Saintes
Cognac
Royan
Angoulême
LIMOGES
CLERMONT-FERRAND
Thiers
Périgueux
Tulle
Brive
Aurillac
Libourne
BORDEAUX
Bergerac
Cahors
Mende
Villeneuve
Rodez
Agen
Millau
Montauban
Albi
Mont-de-Marsan
Auch
TOULOUSE
Castres
Béziers
Pau
Tarbes
Carcassonne
Narbonne
St.Gaudens
Foix
Perpignan
37
58
36
18
86
03
87
23
17
16
63
19
15
43
33
24
46
48
47
12
82
40
81
32
31
34
64
65
09
11
66

12.06 RODEZ

Michel & Mireille
BEDOS

12290 PONT DE
SALARS

tel: (0) 5 65 46 84 14
fax: (0) 5 65 46 84 14
e-mail: michel.bedes@
fnac.net

Private home

You will love Michel and Mireille. She is a professional guide and can organise, depending on your interest, various tours or activities to introduce you to the Aveyron, which she adores and knows so well. Do not miss les Gorges du Tarn 45 minutes away and Conques.

PROPERTY

✱✱✱

off street parking, garden, tv lounge, dinner available, packed lunch, babies welcome, free cot, hiking, cycling, mushroom picking, sea or lake watersports, fishing 1km, hunting 3km, golf course 20km, gliding 40km

Basic English spoken

20 km - S E - RODEZ
PONT DE SALARS:
railway station 20km
airport 30km
car essential
— At Rodez, take the N88 towards Albi. At La Primaube, take the D911 on the left towards Millau as far as Pont de Salars. The house is opposite the gendarmerie.

PRICE STRUCTURE

3 Bedrooms

First room: lounge, television, shower room with wc, double bed: FF270

Second room: television, shower room with wc, twin beds: FF270

Third room: television, shower room with wc, double bed: FF270

Extra bed: 100FF
Reduction: 1/09–30/05 and 3 nights and children

Capacity: 6 people

Valérie BALANSA

«La Manufacture»
2, rue des Docteurs Basset
31190 AUTERIVE

tel: (0) 5 61 50 08 50
fax: (0) 5 61 50 08 50

Residence of character

30 km - S - TOULOUSE
AUTERIVE: railway station 1km
airport 35km

31.05 TOULOUSE

This magnificent building has been in the same family for five generations. It was originally a small 18th century sheet factory, right in the centre of the village. Now you can enjoy the swimming pool and the large pleasant garden.

PROPERTY

✱✱✱

private parking, extensive grounds, tv lounge, hosts have pets, babies welcome, free cot, swimming pool, closed: 1/11-31/03, hiking, cycling, fishing, hunting 5km, sea or lake watersports 15km, golf course 30km

English spoken

PRICE STRUCTURE

4 Bedrooms

Noire: bathroom with wc, double bed, single bed: FF380 (2 people) FF490 (3 people)

Empire: shower room with wc, twin beds: FF380

de Claude: bathroom with wc, double bed: FF380

du Parc: bathroom with wc, twin beds, single bed: FF380 (2 people) FF490 (3 people)

Extra bed: 90FF

Capacity: 10 people

— In Toulouse take the N20 towards Foix. At Auterive turn left at the second traffic lights towards the Centre-Ville. Cross the river Ariège and the canal and it is the first street on the left opposite the Post Office. First house on the right.

Geneviève LANSIAUX

Le Village
31290 MONTGAILLARD-
LAURAGAIS

tel: (0) 5 61 27 27 90

Private home

Midi-Pyrénées

TOULOUSE

30 km - S E -
TOULOUSE
MONTGAILLARD:
railway station 5km
airport 40km
car essential

PRICE STRUCTURE

1 Bedroom and 1 Suite and 1 Apartment

Glycine: along corridor shower room with wc, wash-basin, double bed: FF250

Chartreuse: lounge, television, kitchen, shower room with wc, double bed, 2 single beds: FF400 (2 people) FF700 (4 people)

Perroquet: bathroom with wc, double bed, 2 single beds: FF300 (2 people) FF550 (4 people)

Extra bed: 100FF
Reduction: 3 nights

31.07 TOULOUSE

This charming residence is in a very quiet village amongst the undulating hills of the Cathar country, 30 minutes from Carcassone and Toulouse. There is a swimming pool to cool off in, the private terrace of the charter house plus Genevi's boundless enthusiasm for the history of art.

PROPERTY

✱✱✱

private parking, garden, tv lounge, hosts have pets, pets not accepted, babies welcome, free cot, swimming pool, closed: 01/10-30/04 & 01/07-31/07, riding, hiking, cycling, fishing, interesting flora, mushroom picking, gliding 5km, golf course 10km, sea or lake watersports 10km, winter sports 80km

Basic English spoken

— On the A61, Exit Villefranche de Lauragais. Then take the N113 towards Toulouse, and after 3km turn right. The village of Montgaillard is on top of a hill, and the house is on the square with the war memorial.

32.02 AUCH

Near the main Auch-Toulouse road, you will find this old farm which is in the process of being restored by a charming English couple. They have an organic orchard and Claudette makes her own bread with organic flour. Enjoy it with Victor's jam for breakfast, or at dinner. The medieval festival in August should not be missed.

PROPERTY

✱✱

off street parking, extensive grounds, tv lounge, hosts have pets, pets not accepted, dinner available, 14 years old minimum age, no smoking, closed: 31/10-14/03, hiking, hunting, mushroom picking, fishing 1km, cycling 5km, sea or lake watersports 13km, river watersports 20km, golf course 25km, gliding 25km

Fluent English spoken

PRICE STRUCTURE

1 Bedroom

shower room with wc, twin beds: FF240

Capacity: 2 people

Victor & Claudette HORLEY

«La Hurre-Tanière»
Montiron
32200 GIMONT

tel: (0) 5 62 67 83 80
fax: (0) 5 62 67 83 80
e-mail:
hurrebab@aol.com

Private home

24 km - E - AUCH
GIMONT: hosts will collect from station
railway station 10km
airport 50km,
car essential
— At Auch, take the N124 towards Toulouse. As you leave Gimont, turn right on to the D4 towards Samatan, and continue for 6km. The turn is the first on the right, after the road to Montiron and the "B & B France" sign. The house is the first on the left.

Frédérique & Thierry ALBERT

«Au Cardenau»
32390 STE CHRISTIE

tel: (0) 5 62 64 33 33
fax: (0) 5 62 64 30 17

Residence of character

13 km - N - AUCH
STE CHRISTIE:
hosts will collect from station,
railway station 12km
airport 70km
car essential

32.04 AUCH

This vast 18th century pile is typical of Gascony, d'Artagnan country! It combines peace and quiet with a respect for tradition. Peacocks roam in the two hectares of grounds, and the enormous rooms contain beautiful furniture. The welcome is warm and numerous music festivals are held in the area.

PRICE STRUCTURE

3 Bedrooms

La Belle Matinée: shower room with wc, double bed, 2 single beds,(1=Childrens size): FF280 (2 people) FF375 (4 people)

Le Cardenau: lounge, television, bathroom with wc, double bed, cot: FF310

Les Voiles de la Liberté: bathroom with wc, shower, washbasin, double bed, twin beds, cot: FF310 (2 people) FF500 (4 people)

Extra bed: 95FF

Reduction: 5 nights and children

Capacity: 10 people

PROPERTY

✱✱✱

private parking, extensive grounds, lounge, hosts have pets, babies welcome, free cot, swimming pool, hiking, fishing, hunting, interesting flora, mushroom picking, gliding 5km, cycling 10km, sea or lake watersports 10km, golf course 12km

Basic English spoken

— At Auch take the N21 towards Agen for 12.5km, then turn right on to the D172 towards Ste Christie.

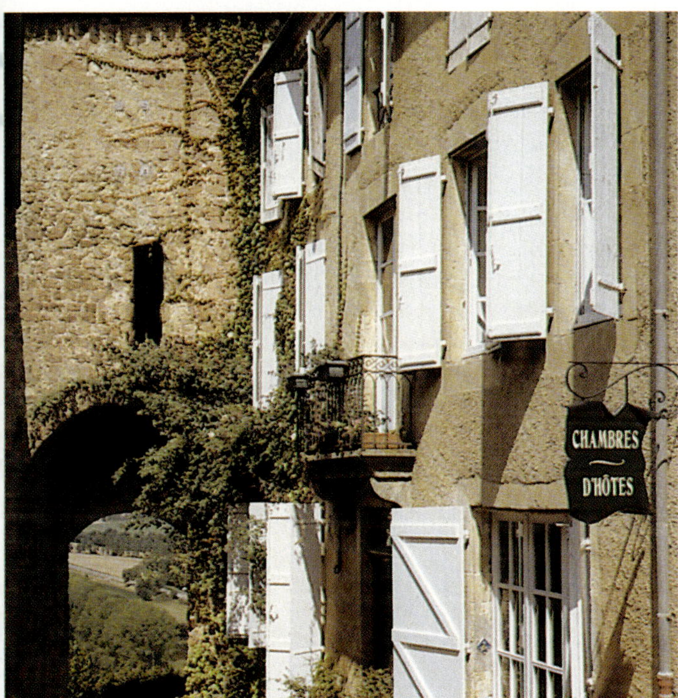

Marie-Thérèse KOVACS

«Maison de la Porte Fortifiée»
32320 MONTESQUIOU

tel: (0) 5 62 70 97 59
fax: (0) 5 62 70 97 59

Residence of character

27 km - S W - AUCH
MONTESQUIOU:
railway station 27km
airport 90km
car essential

32.08 AUCH

This house is built on to the walls of the 13th century fortified gate, in a quiet village full of flowers. There is a panoramic view from the terrace. You are in the heart of Gascony, Musketeer country and Marie-Thérèse can provide you with information on the area. An unforgettable place...

PROPERTY

✵✵✵

garden, lounge, hosts have pets, pets not accepted, packed lunch, babies welcome, free cot, closed: 06/01-06/02, bird-watching, hiking 1km, fishing 1km, hunting 1km, mushroom picking 5km, sea or lake watersports 5km, golf course 10km, river watersports 20km

Fluent English spoken

— From Auch, go to Mirande on the N21 where you join the D137 for Montesquiou. In the village, follow the signs 'Chambres d'hotes'/ 'Porte Fortifiée'. The house is built on to the walls.

PRICE STRUCTURE

4 Bedrooms and 1 Apartment

Bleu: shower room with wc, twin beds: FF280

Baldaquin: shower room with wc, double bed: FF280

Verte: shower room with wc, double bed, single bed: FF270 (2 people) FF390 (3 people)

Apartment: lounge, kitchen, shower room with wc, double bed: FF430

Crème: bathroom with wc, twin beds: FF320

Reduction: 5 nights and children

Capacity: 11 people

Eduard & Nel VOS

«La Méline»
Route de Sauzet
46140 ALBAS

tel: (0) 5 65 36 97 25
fax: (0) 5 65 36 97 25

Residence of character

25 km - W - CAHORS
ALBAS: hosts will collect from station, railway station 25km
airport 140km
car essential

46.01 CAHORS

PRICE STRUCTURE

3 Bedrooms

First room: wheelchair access, television, bathroom with wc, shower, twin beds: FF275

Sous-pente second room: television, shower room with wc, double bed, single bed: FF275 (2 people) FF345 (3 people)

Sous-pente third room: television, shower room with wc, double bed: FF275

Reduction: 7 nights

Capacity: 7 people

'La Méline' is on a hillside in the middle of the countryside, a few kilometres from a very picturesque village overlooking the river Lot. Beautiful views over forests and vines, in this peaceful, relaxing and refreshing spot. Visit neighbouring farms and vineyards. On sale: Cahors wine. Vegetarian meals also available

PROPERTY

***

off street parking, extensive grounds, tv lounge, hosts have pets, pets not accepted, dinner available, wheelchair access, closed: 01/10-31/03, hiking, cycling, mushroom picking, fishing 4km, river watersports 9km, golf course 25km, gliding 25km

Fluent English spoken

— In Cahors, take the D911 to Castelfranc. In Castelfranc, take the D45 and then the D8 towards Albas. In Albas take the D37 towards Sauzet. After 3.8km, "La Méline" is on the right. It is signposted from Albas

46.02 CAHORS

A comfortable house, near the village in the heart of this verdant, undulating countryside. Wild orchids grow at the roadside in this unspoilt area. Within 30km there is a wide selection of places of interest.

PROPERTY

✱✱✱

off street parking, extensive grounds, tv lounge, hosts have pets, dinner available, packed lunch, babies welcome, free cot, swimming pool, tennis, hiking, cycling, mushroom picking, fishing 3km, golf course 20km, river watersports 20km

PRICE STRUCTURE

3 Bedrooms

Pistache: lounge, shower, wc, twin beds: FF250

Noisette/la Tour: lounge, shower room with wc, double bed, 2 single beds: FF250 (2 people) FF430 (4 people)

Extra bed: 90FF
Reduction: 7 nights

Capacity: 2 people

Guy NODON

«Domaine de Montsalvy»
Montsalvy
46340 DEGAGNAC

tel: (0) 5 65 41 51 57
fax: (0) 5 65 41 51 57

Private home

25 km - N - CAHORS
DEGAGNAC: railway station 13km
airport 80km
car essential
— From Cahors, take the D911 towards Villeneuve sur Lot. After Espère, turn right on to the D6 towards Degagnac. From the village square, go towards the railway station then turn right after the sports ground. At the top of the hill, turn right.

Ferme Auberge

«Aux Délices de La Serpt»
46250 FRAYSSINET-LE-GELAT

tel: (0) 5 65 36 66 15
fax: (0) 5 65 36 60 34

Farm

35 km - N W - CAHORS
FRAYSSINET LE GELAT:
railway station 35km
airport 150km
car essential
— At Cahors, take the D911 towards Villeneuve sur Lot for 15.5km as far as Rostassac. Turn right on to the D660 towards Frayssinet. At the roundabout, go towards Villefranche, Périgueux. Follow the signs.

46.04 CAHORS

You are sure of a friendly, family welcome from Annick and Marie-France in this 18th century 'ferme-auberge', typical of le Quercy, in the middle of the country, full of flowers. Admire their beautiful old dovecot and taste the local produce.On sale: Foie-gras, confits, rillettes, patés.

PROPERTY

✱✱✱

off street parking, garden, lounge, hosts have pets, dinner available, packed lunch, babies welcome, free cot, hiking, cycling, mushroom picking, fishing 4km, river watersports 30km

Adequate English spoken

PRICE STRUCTURE

1 Bedroom

shower room with wc, double bed, single bed: FF200 (2 people) FF240 (3 people)

Capacity: 3 people

Mireille PINATEL

«La Grange de Marcillac»
MARCILLAC
46800 ST CYPRIEN

tel: (0) 5 65 22 90 73 / 42
fax: (0) 5 65 24 91 05

Farm

24 km - S W - CAHORS
MARCILLAC: hosts will collect from station,
railway station 25km
airport 100km

46.07 CAHORS

You will be overcome by Mireille's kindness, as she welcomes you to her stone house, typical of the Quercy Blanc. She will introduce you to music, flowers and wildlife, truffles, foie-gras and the local cuisine... as one does on holiday. New for 99: a swimming pool so we advise you to book. On sale: Duck conserves, jam.

PROPERTY

✱✱✱

off street parking, garden, lounge, hosts have pets, pets not accepted, telephone, dinner available, packed lunch, babies welcome, free cot, swimming pool, closed: 20/12-28/12, hiking, cycling, fishing 3km, golf course 5km, sea or lake watersports 7km, river watersports 40km

Basic English spoken

— At Cahors, N20 towards Caussade (3km). Right on to D653 then left on to D7 towards Lascabanes. Cross St Cyprien towards Montcuq. As you leave the village, left towards Marcillac (2.5km) (signposted).

PRICE STRUCTURE

5 Bedrooms and 1 Suite and 1 Apartment

First room: shower room with wc, double bed: FF270

Second room: shower room with wc, 3 single beds: FF270 (2 people) FF340 (3 people)

Third room: shower room with wc, 2 single beds: FF270

Fourth room: shower room with wc, 3 single beds: FF300 (2 people) FF370 (3 people)

Fifth room: shower room with wc, double bed, single bed: FF300 (2 people) FF370 (3 people)

Apartment: kitchen, shower room with wc, double bed, twin beds: FF550 (2 people) FF700 (4 people)

Suite: shower room with wc, shower, double bed, twin beds: FF300 (2 people) FF440 (4 people)

Extra bed: 70FF
Reduction: 3 nights and groups

Capacity: 21 people

Marcelle HOURRIEZ

«Château de Roussillon»
46090 ST PIERRE
LAFEUILLE

tel: (0) 5 65 36 87 05
fax: (0) 5 65 36 82 34

Château

12 km - N -
CAHORS
ST PIERRE
LAFEUILLE: railway
station 10km
airport 120km
car essential

46.15 CAHORS

An authentic feudal château in complete peaceful surroundings. The ideal place for a relaxing holiday, and a complete change of scene. Here, originality is the byword and the atmosphere is quite unique. Marcelle started restoring this place 40 years ago, and the interior contrasts strongly with the exterior. 1 self-catering apartment

PRICE STRUCTURE

1 Bedroom

Chapelle: lounge, television, telephone, shower room with wc, double bed, 2 single beds, FF450 (2 people) FF650 (4 people)

Extra bed: 100FF
Reduction: 2 nights
Capacity: 4 people

PROPERTY

****

off street parking, extensive grounds, pets not accepted, telephone, closed: 01/11-31/03, hiking, fishing 10km, river watersports 10km

Basic English spoken

— At Cahors, take the N20 towards Brive for 12km. The château is at St Pierre Lafeuille, on the right after the church.

Dominique BRUN

«Château d'Uzech»
46310 ST GERMAIN DU BEL AIR

tel: (0) 5 65 22 75 80
fax: (0) 5 65 22 75 80

Château

25 km - N -
CAHORS
ST GERMAIN DU BEL AIR:railway station 20km
airport 110km
car essential

Midi-Pyrénées

CAHORS

46.16 CAHORS

In this ancient castle, you will be enthralled by the welcome of your hosts, their sense of style and their inventive cooking, both pleasant to the eye and even more delicious. You will have an unforgettable stay. Also a visit to Rocamadour and Sarlat should not be missed. 25 FF per animal

PROPERTY

****

off street parking, extensive grounds, tv lounge, hosts have pets, dinner available, kitchen, babies welcome, free cot, swimming pool, closed: 30/11-30/01, hiking, mushroom picking, sea or lake watersports 7km, golf course 20km, river watersports 30km

Fluent English spoken

— At Cahors, take the D911 towards Villeneuve sur Lot. At Espère, turn right on to the D12 towards Nuzejouls, St Denis Catus and Uzech.

PRICE STRUCTURE

1 Bedroom and 3 Apartments

Bergerie: lounge, television, kitchen, shower room with wc, double bed, single bed: FF500 (2 people) FF600 (3 people)

Remparts: lounge, television, kitchen, bathroom with wc, double bed, single bed: FF500 (2 people) FF600 (3 people)

Tour: lounge, television, kitchen, bathroom with wc, double bed: FF500

Petite Tour: shower room with wc, single bed: FF300

Capacity: 9 people

Barbara SZILÀGYI

«La Charrue»
Engrange
46090 FRANCOULÈS

tel: (0) 5 65 36 84 21
fax: (0) 5 65 36 84 21

Residence of character

Midi-Pyrénées

15 km - N - CAHORS
ENGRANGE: railway station 17km
airport 160km
car essential

CAHORS

46.18 CAHORS

PRICE STRUCTURE

4 Bedrooms

(4 rooms) shower room with wc, washbasin, double bed: FF250

Reduction: 01/09–30/06 and 7 nights

Capacity: 2 people

Very friendly English couple, who know this area very well. They have restored this ancient stone farmhouse, which is typical of the Dordogne. They cook with great enthusiasm, and really love receiving their guests. Special weekly half-board rates.

PROPERTY

off street parking, garden, tv lounge, hosts have pets, pets not accepted, dinner available, 15 years old minimum age, closed: 01/11-01/03, hiking, sea or lake watersports 8km, fishing 17km, golf course 50km

Fluent English spoken

— Take the N20 towards Limoges. Engrange is on the right, 1km after Pelacoy.

André et Jacqueline
CHRISTOPHE

«Trespécoul»
46310 PEYRILLES

tel: (0) 5 65 31 00 91
fax: (0) 5 65 31 00 91

Farm

30 km - N -
CAHORS
PEYRILLES: railway station 15km
airport 150km
car essential

46.19 CAHORS

You will find a very warm welcome in this farm, where you can experience rural life at close hand ... the young calves really are adorable. There is a small kitchen available. This place is very quiet and well placed for visiting Rocamadour, Cahors and Sarlat. They offer very good weekly rates.

PROPERTY

✸✸

off street parking, garden, hosts have pets, kitchen, babies welcome, free cot, closed: 01/11-01/04, hiking, fishing, hunting, mushroom picking, cycling 15km, sea or lake watersports 15km, river watersports 30km

English spoken

PRICE STRUCTURE

3 Bedrooms

First room: bathroom with wc, double bed, single bed: FF230 (2 people) FF300 (3 people)

Second & third rooms: shower room with wc, double bed: FF200

Extra bed: 30FF
Reduction: 7 nights

Capacity: 7 people

— At Cahors, take the N20 towards Brive. At Pont de Rhodes, left on the D23 towards St Germain de Bel Air. Cross the village towards Concorès, and as you enter the village of Concorès, left on to the D12 towards Cahors. Trespécoul is 1.5km on the left before Peyrilles (signposted).

46.20 CAHORS

Christian MONCOUTIÉ

«Les Graves»
46090 ST PIERRE
LAFEUILLE

tel: (0) 5 65 36 83 12

Private home

Near to the main road, this old farmhouse also has a camp-site. The rooms have independent entrances and are simple, with basic bathrooms. The welcome is warm and a kitchenette is available, but you will also be tempted by the village inn. Credit cards accepted

PROPERTY

✸

off street parking, tv lounge, telephone, dinner available, wheelchair access, swimming pool, hiking, fishing 7km, sea or lake watersports 15km

Adequate English spoken

12 km - N - CAHORS
ST PIERRE LAFEUILLE:
railway station 12km
airport 110km
car essential
— At Cahors, take the N20 towards Brive. Then take the Exit "Nord" for St Pierre Lafeuille.

PRICE STRUCTURE

3 Bedrooms

First & second rooms: shower room with wc, washbasin, double bed: FF250

Third room: bathroom with wc, washbasin, double bed, 2 single beds: FF240 (2 people) FF350 (4 people)

Reduction: 01/10–31/05

Capacity: 8 people

46.23 CAHORS

You will have a great time with this very friendly English couple. After a swim in the superb pool surrounded by flowers, your appetite will be ready for Judy's delicious dishes.

Richard & Judy STIBBON

«La Sagesse»
Brouelles
46090 MAXOU

tel: (0) 5 65 36 81 90

Residence of character

PROPERTY

off street parking, garden, tv lounge, no pets, dinner available, packed lunch, 18 years minimum age, no smoking, swimming pool, closed: 01/10-31/05, hiking, fishing 12km

Fluent English spoken

PRICE STRUCTURE

5 Bedrooms

First room: shower room with wc, double bed, single bed: FF300 (2 people) FF350 (3 people)

Second room: lounge, shower room with wc, double bed: FF300

Third room: lounge, shower room with wc, twin beds: FF300

Fourth & fifth rooms: bathroom with wc, shower, double bed: FF300

Extra bed: 50FF

Capacity: 11 people

8 km - N - CAHORS
BROUELLES: railway station 12km
airport 120km
car essential
— At Cahors take the N20 northwards. At St Pierre La Feuille take the D47 on the left towards Maxou. 1km from Maxou turn right towards Brouelles. It is the second house on the left as you enter the village.

46.24 CAHORS

Carmen & Pierre
NOUYRIT

«Les Mazuts»
46090 ARCAMBAL

tel: (0) 5 65 23 95 29
fax: (0) 5 65 23 95 29

Residence of character

This old farm has 3 hectares of land, a little pond and a beautiful view over the Lot Valley. Pierre and Carmen are retired, and their genuine welcome is complemented by the charm of this farm: little beamed corridors, narrow staircases, pigeon loft... Fleur de Soleil member.

PROPERTY

✸✸

private parking, garden, hosts have pets, dinner available, packed lunch, babies welcome, free cot, hiking, fishing 4km, river watersports 6km, cycling 11km, golf course 20km

11 km - E - CAHORS
ARCAMBAL: railway station 11km
airport 100km
car essential
— From Cahors, take the DN11 as far as Arcambal and then head towards St. Cirq Lapopie. Follow the signs as far as Les Mazuts.

PRICE STRUCTURE

4 Bedrooms

Bleu: double bed, single bed: FF200 (2 people) FF250 (3 people)

Rose: 3 single beds: FF200 (2 people) FF250 (3 people)

Vert: double bed: FF200

Mediterranée: along corridor shower room with wc, double bed, 2 single beds: FF250 (2 people) FF350 (4 people)

Extra bed: 50FF
Reduction: 6 nights

Capacity: 12 people

Caroline & Knud
KRISTOFFERSEN

«Domaine Lapèze»
46800 MONTCUQ

tel: (0) 5 65 24 91 97
fax: (0) 5 65 24 91 98

Private home

28 km - S W -
CAHORS
MONTCUQ: railway
station 24km
airport 100km
car essential

46.25 CAHORS

Eat your heart out Peter Mayle! Caroline and Knud, a delightful Anglo-Danish couple, have cracked it. Recently settled in this wonderful area, they have tastefully renovated this impressive stone house on the slopes, overlooking their vines and fruit trees. Peace and quiet, and a swimming pool on the terrace. Do not miss the Sunday market in the village with the dodgy name..

PROPERTY

✱✱✱

off street parking, extensive grounds, hosts have pets, dinner available, babies welcome, free cot, swimming pool, hiking, cycling, fishing, sea or lake watersports 2km, golf course 15km

Fluent English spoken

PRICE STRUCTURE

3 Bedrooms

Les Pruniers: telephone, bathroom with wc, shower, twin beds: FF400

Les Vignes & Le Jardin: telephone, shower room with wc, double bed: FF350

Studio: telephone, kitchen, shower room with wc, twin beds: FF450

Extra bed: 100FF

Capacity: 8 people

— In Cahors, take the N20 towards Caussade for 3 km Then take the D653 on the right to Montcuq. Look for the sign on the main road, turn off and keep going until you see the mill-stone.

Carin & Occo
BINNENDIJK

«La Cabane»
Poudens
46340 DEGAGNAC

tel: (0) 5 65 41 49 74
fax: (0) 5 65 41 49 74

Private home

25 km - N -
CAHORS
DEGAGNAC: railway station 6km
airport 80km
car essential

Midi-Pyrénées

CAHORS

46.28 CAHORS

PRICE STRUCTURE

3 Bedrooms

First room: bathroom with wc, double bed: FF395

Second room: shower room with wc, double bed: FF300

Third room: shower room with wc, 2 single beds: FF360

Extra bed: 50FF

Capacity: 6 people

Your Dutch hosts, Carin and Occo, welcome you to their 18th century residence, which has been completely restored. In the summer they serve a varied and interesting breakfast on the beautiful terrace, with its panoramic view over the Céou valley. This place is quiet and rural and has a swimming pool, as well as spacious, comfortable bedrooms. You can just relax here, or enjoy visiting the numerous places of interest in the area. Fleur de Soleil member.

PROPERTY

✱✱✱

off street parking, extensive grounds, no pets, swimming pool

English spoken

— On the N20 Brive - Gourdon road, Exit Gourdon. Head towards Cahors on the D12 and after 6km, at the bridge over the river, look for the signs "La Cabane".

Martine & Michel
VILLEDIEU

Boussac
46100 FIGEAC

tel: (0) 5 65 40 06 63
fax: (0) 5 65 40 09 22
http: www.villedieu.com

Farm

10 km - W - FIGEAC
BOUSSAC: railway station 10km

46.27 FIGEAC

This working farm has adopted eco-tourism. The bedrooms are in the barns and stables, which have been converted with great skill. An ideal spot for nature lovers, as this region is rich in nature reserves. On sale: Foie-gras, cassoulet.

PROPERTY

✵✵✵

off street parking, extensive grounds, lounge, hosts have pets, telephone, dinner available, packed lunch, swimming pool, hiking, fishing 3km, river watersports 3km, cycling 10km

Adequate English spoken

— At Figeac, take the D13 towards Cahors for 6km. Then turn left on to the D41 towards Boussac and follow the signs.

PRICE STRUCTURE

4 Bedrooms

Bleue: shower room with wc, double bed: FF270

Suite: lounge, shower room with wc, double bed, 2 single beds: FF500 (2 people) FF680 (4 people)

Fourniol: shower room with wc, 2 single beds: FF310

Nouveau Fourniol: shower room with wc, double bed: FF380

Extra bed: 70FF

Capacity: 10 people

Midi-Pyrénées

ROCAMADOUR

Gérard & Claude
RAMELOT

«Moulin de Fresquet»
46500 GRAMAT

tel: (0) 5 65 38 70 60
fax: (0) 5 65 38 70 60

Residence of character

9 km - S E -
ROCAMADOUR
GRAMAT: hosts will collect from station, railway station 1km
airport 65km

PRICE STRUCTURE

5 Bedroom

Le Rocher: television, shower room with wc, double bed: FF349

La Meunière: television, shower room with wc, double bed: FF319

Le Meunier & Le Bief: television, shower room with wc, double bed: FF319

Les Meules: television, shower room with wc, 2 double beds: FF419 (2 people) FF528 (4 people)

Extra bed: 60FF
Reduction: 1/10–1/06

Capacity: 12 people

46.11 ROCAMADOUR

This authentic 17th century Quercy water-mill is situated in beautiful gardens full of flowers, through which a river flows. In the evening, the ambiance is perfect, as by candle-light you sample delicious regional cuisine in this beautiful home.

PROPERTY

✱✱✱✱

private parking, extensive grounds, tv lounge, no pets, telephone, dinner available, closed: 01/11-01/04, hiking, cycling, fishing, hunting 2km, mushroom picking 2km, golf course 15km, river watersports 15km, sea or lake watersports 30km

Adequate English spoken

— From Rocamadour head in the direction of the N140 and turn right towards Figeac. 500m after Gramat, turn left on to the little lane for 300m.

Christian PETERS

«Le Grand Cèdre»
6, rue du Barry
65270 ST PE DE BIGORRE

tel: (0) 5 62 41 82 04
fax: (0) 5 62 41 85 89
e-mail:
grand.cedre@sudfr.com
www.sudfr.com/grand.cedre

Residence of character

7 km - W -
LOURDES
ST PE DE BIGORRE: hosts will collect from station, railway station 1km
airport 20km
car essential

Midi-Pyrénées

LOURDES

65.03 LOURDES

In spite of their name, this is a French family who are in love with their 17th century home. Be sure to see the 400 year old cedar tree in the grounds. It is well worth dressing up for a candlelit dinner in the splendid dining room. On sale: Mountain ham, Pyrenees cheese, confit de canard, foie-gras.

PROPERTY

✱✱✱

private parking, extensive grounds, tv lounge, hosts have pets, telephone, dinner available, babies welcome, free cot, hiking, cycling, fishing, mushroom picking, river watersports, hunting 1km, interesting flora 2km, birdwatching 3km, golf course 7km, sea or lake watersports 7km

Fluent English spoken

PRICE STRUCTURE

2 Bedrooms and 1 Suite

Art Déco: shower room with wc, double bed: FF320

Henri II: bathroom with wc, double bed, single bed: FF320 (2 people) FF400 (3 people)

Louis XV: bathroom with wc, double bed, cot: FF320

Louis Philippe: shower room with wc, double bed: FF320

Extra bed: 80FF
Reduction: 30/10–30/03 and 6 nights

Capacity: 2 people

— At Lourdes take the D937 for St Pé de Bigorre.

Bernadette & Bruno
HAURINE ALBERT

«La Grange»
65120 VIZOS

tel: (0) 5 62 92 87 41

Private home

32 km - S -
LOURDES
VIZOS: hosts will collect from station, railway station 30km
airport 35km
car essential

65.06 LOURDES

PRICE STRUCTURE

2 Bedrooms

First & second rooms: telephone, double bed: FF180

Extra bed: 60FF
Reduction: 7 nights

Capacity: 4 people

This little barn is 830 metres up in the hills in a village of only 37 inhabitants, with a wonderful view over the route of the Tour de France. The location, the warm welcome and the reasonable price will tempt you to spend a lot of time here. Mountain treks where you can learn about the shepherds way of life, as well as skiing and spa treatments. On sale: rabbits, chickens, cheese, eggs.

PROPERTY

✸✸

off street parking, garden, tv lounge, hosts have pets, dinner available, packed lunch, babies welcome, free cot, hiking, cycling, interesting flora, mushroom picking, fishing 2km, winter sports 7km, gliding 9km, river watersports 12km, golf course 30km

Basic English spoken

— From Lourdes, go to Luz St Saveur (N21 to Argelès then the D921 to Luz. From here, turn left on to the D172 towards Vizos and continue for 2km. The house is at the beginning of the village (slightly down the mountain side).

Ingrid & Jean Louis
ROBAIN

«Karinou»
L'Ayous
65400 GAILLAGOS

tel: (0) 5 62 97 41 29
fax: (0) 5 62 97 41 29

Private home

24 km - S W -
LOURDES
GAILLAGOS: hosts will collect from station,
railway station 24km
airport 30km
car essential

65.07 LOURDES

This is a converted sheepfold, now a family home, 1100m up in the Pyrenees. This sunny valley is full of villages and footpaths to discover, and Jean Louis and Ingrid have no shortage of ideas and suggestions for your stay: hiking, mountain biking, paragliding...

PROPERTY

✱✱✱

off street parking, extensive grounds, tv lounge, hosts have pets, telephone, dinner available, kitchen, packed lunch, babies welcome, free cot, no smoking, 7 nights minimum stay, 01/07-31/08, hiking, cycling, fishing, hunting, mushroom picking, birdwatching, winter sports 7km, interesting flora 8km, river watersports 10km, golf course 35km

Adequate English spoken

— At Lourdes, head towards Argelès Gazost (N21). At Argelès, go towards Col de l'Aubisque (D918). Cross Arras en Lavedan, then take the second road on the right as far as Gaillagos. Go up to and pass the church, and then turn left and continue to the end of the road.

PRICE STRUCTURE

1 Bedroom and 1 Apartment

Bergerie karinou: television, telephone, kitchen, shower room with wc, 7 single beds,(2 childrens size), cot: FF280 (2 people) FF630 (7 people)

Chambre 3: 3 single beds: FF280 (2 people) FF350 (3 people)

Maison: shower room with wc, twin beds: FF280

Extra bed: 70FF
Reduction: 01/01–31/01 and 01/05–31/05 and 7 nights and groups and children

Capacity: 12 people

Claudie & Xavier BOLAC

«Château de Tail»
Route de Goux
65700 CASTELNAU
RIVIERE BASSE

tel: (0) 5 62 31 93 75
fax: (0) 5 62 31 93 26
e-mail:
chateaudutail@sudfr.com
http:
www.sudfr.com/chateaudutail

Château

40 km - N - TARBES
CASTELNAU
RIVIERE BASSE:
hosts will collect from station,
railway station 45km
airport 53km
car essential

Midi-Pyrénées

TARBES

65.04 TARBES

This is a special place, and as you will discover, everything possible is done to ensure a pleasant stay. The decor is a labour of love created by Claudie. Here you have four-poster beds, comfort, excellent value for money and above all an outstanding welcome from your charming hosts.

PROPERTY

✱✱✱✱

extensive grounds, tv lounge, hosts have pets, no pets, telephone, dinner available, packed lunch, babies welcome, free cot, swimming pool, cycling, mushroom picking, fishing 1km, hunting 1km, sea or lake watersports 20km, golf course 40km

Fluent English spoken

PRICE STRUCTURE

4 Bedrooms and 1 Suite

Anglaise: shower room with wc, twin beds: FF350

Suite: bathroom with wc, double bed, 2 single beds: FF450 (2 people) FF550 (4 people)

Bleue: shower, bathroom, wc, double bed, single bed: FF350 (2 people) FF450 (3 people)

Chambres aux Simples & aux Anges: bathroom with wc, double bed: FF350

Extra bed: 75FF

Capacity: 13 people

— At Tarbes take the D935 towards Mont de Marsan. 14km after Maubourguet turn left towards Castelnau. In the centre of Castelnau follow the road to Goux and follow the signs.

Marie COLOMBIER

«Domaine de Jean-Pierre»
20, route de Villeneuve
65300 PINAS

tel: (0) 5 62 98 15 08
fax: (0) 5 62 98 15 08
e-mail:Marie.Colombier@wanadoo.fr

Private home

35 km - S E - TARBES
PINAS: railway station 5km
airport 45km
car essential

65.08 TARBES

This splendid house, full of character, surrounded by wooded grounds, is 600m up on the Lannemezan plateau, in the foothills of the Pyrenees. The bedrooms are very charming, furnished with antiques. Your hostess will give you the warmest of welcome and also serves an excellent breakfast on the terrace. There are plenty of visits in the surrounding area, as well as restaurants offering regional and gastronomic cuisine. Lourdes is 50km away. Fleur de Soleil member.

PROPERTY

✱✱✱

off street parking, extensive grounds, hiking, golf course 3km

English spoken

— From the A64, Exit 16 towards Toulouse on the N117. At Pinas, 5km from Lannemezan, take the D158 by the church towards Villeneuve. It is 800m on, on the right. Follow the signs.

PRICE STRUCTURE

3 Bedrooms

(3 rooms) bathroom with wc, double bed: FF250

Extra bed: 70FF

Capacity: 6 people

Hans Peter& Madeleine CAMENZIND

«Le Château de Fourès»
St Marcel Campes
81170 CORDES

tel: (0) 5 63 56 13 55
fax: (0) 5 63 56 13 55

Château

25 km - N W - ALBI
CORDES: railway station 4km
airport 75km
car essential

81.09 ALBI

PRICE STRUCTURE

2 Bedrooms and 1 Suite

Rez de Chaussée: bathroom with wc, double bed: FF350

Etage-Suite: along corridor shower room with wc, 2 double beds, cot: FF350 (2 people) FF620 (4 people)

Etage-Chambre: along corridor shower room with wc, double bed: FF350

Extra bed: 70FF
Reduction: 7 nights

Capacity: 8 people

Madame is French and Monsieur Swiss. Their walled garden is as romantic as you could wish, with a pond, water lillies, a tennis court, a sheltered swimming pool...an idyllic spot. The house is quiet with a nice view and furnished with style and good taste. It is at the foot of the beautiful village of Cordes which dates from the 13th century.

PROPERTY

✱✱✱

off street parking, extensive grounds, hosts have pets, no pets, telephone, babies welcome, free cot, swimming pool, tennis, hiking, fishing, interesting flora, birdwatching, river watersports, golf course 30km

English spoken

— At Albi take the D600 as far as Cordes. Continue along the D922 towards Carmaux for 1km and then turn right towards Campes fot 1km. At the church, turn left and continue for 300m.

Monique, Raymond & Christiane ZIDI & AIRAUDO

«Villa Akwaba»
81140 LE VERDIER

tel: (0) 5 63 33 94 72
fax: (0) 5 63 33 96 58

Private home

30 km - W - ALBI
LE VERDIER: hosts will collect from station,
railway station 14km
airport 75km
car essential

81.12 ALBI

Raymond and Monique have travelled the world and, in their very comfortable, modern villa, have managed to show off beautifully their collection of African sculptures and other souvenirs. It is quiet, with a beautiful view, and the two donkeys are just waiting for you to make a fuss of them. Christiane's cooking is pretty good too.

PROPERTY

✱✱✱

private parking, extensive grounds, tv lounge, hosts have pets, no pets, telephone, dinner available, packed lunch, babies welcome, free cot, swimming pool, closed: 15/12-15/01, hiking, cycling, fishing 1km, hunting 2km, mushroom picking 3km, sea or lake watersports 3km, river watersports 20km, golf course 25km

Fluent English spoken

— At Albi, head towards Toulouse and then take the N2088 for Gaillac and join the D964 towards Castelnau de Montmirail. Then take the D15 towards Le Verdier for 4km. At the bottom of the village, turn left towards Castelnau de Montmirail (300m), then take the first little road on the right towards Ste Cécile-Domaine des Trois Moineaux for 1.5km. Continue straight on, as far as the modern house with the swimming pool.

PRICE STRUCTURE

3 Bedrooms

Verdi: lounge, television, telephone, bathroom with wc, shower, double bed, single bed: FF600 (2 people) FF720 (3 people)

Chopin: television, telephone, bathroom with wc, double bed, single bed: FF500 (2 people) FF620 (3 people)

Mozart: television, telephone, shower room with wc, double bed: FF400

Extra bed: 120FF
Reduction: 01/10–31/03 and 7 nights and children

Capacity: 8 people

Lyne & Denis SOULIE

«Domaine de Gradille»
Route de Montauban
81310 LISLE sur TARN

tel: (0) 5 63 41 01 57
fax: (0) 5 63 57 43 73
e-mail:
lynesoulie@wanadoo.
fr

Farm

27 km - W - ALBI
LISLE SUR TARN:
railway station 5km
airport 55km
car essential

81.13 ALBI

This impressive large house is in pastoral surroundings near Albi and Cordes. Perfectly quiet, your sleep will be undisturbed. During the day, relax under the trees in the grounds, or walk through the vineyards to the lake and have a go at fishing. Alternatively, make use of the swimming pool...what a choice! Be sure to try the Vin de Gaillac. On sale: Their own wine.

PRICE STRUCTURE

5 Bedrooms

First room: bathroom with wc, double bed: FF250

2 & 3: shower, double bed, single bed: FF180 (2 people) FF250 (3 people)

4 & 5: bathroom with wc, double bed, single bed: FF250 (2 people) FF320 (3 people)

Extra bed: 50FF

Capacity: 14 people

PROPERTY

✸✸✸

off street parking, extensive grounds, tv lounge, hosts have pets, no pets, dinner available, swimming pool, riding, hiking, fishing, hunting, mushroom picking, sea or lake watersports, cycling 5km, golf course 25km, river watersports 25km

Adequate English spoken

— At Albi, head towards Toulouse and then take the N2088 for Gaillac. At Gaillac, take the D999 towards Montauban. Continue for 5km as far as the crossroads. The house is opposite the hamlet called "La Grouillère", near to the bus stop. Then follow the signs.

Fons & Ben PESSERS & WILKE

«Hotel Domaine de Rasigous»
Rasigous
81290 ST AFFRIQUE LES MONTAGNES

tel: (0) 5 63 73 30 50
fax: (0) 5 63 73 30 51

Residence of character

10 km - S - CASTRES
ST AFFRIQUE LES M.: railway station 15km
airport 65km
car essential

81.07 CASTRES

We really fell in love with this unassuming house, nestling at the foot of the Montagne Noire. It has been furnished with great taste and much character and the beautiful landscaped garden contains some very old trees. The rustic dining room and the comfortable salon have a fireplace.

PROPERTY

✱✱✱✱

off street parking, extensive grounds, lounge, dinner available, wheelchair access, swimming pool, riding, cycling, interesting flora, mushroom picking, birdwatching, hiking 5km, fishing 5km, gliding 10km, hunting 20km

Fluent English spoken

— At Castres, take the D85 towards Revel via Dourgne. St Affrique is on the right-hand side of the road. The property is on the left of the road, 2.5km from St Affrique.

PRICE STRUCTURE

8 Bedrooms

First room: lounge, television, telephone, bathroom with wc, double bed: FF510

Second room: lounge, television, telephone, bathroom with wc, double bed: FF610

Third room: lounge, television, telephone, bathroom with wc, twin beds: FF510

Fourth room: lounge, television, telephone, bathroom with wc, single bed: FF280

Suite Bleue: lounge, television, telephone, bathroom with wc, twin beds: FF910

Suite Eliane Reberga: lounge, television, telephone, bathroom with wc, shower, double bed: FF860

Seventh room: lounge, television, telephone, bathroom with wc, twin beds: FF610

Suite en duplex: lounge, television, telephone, bathroom with wc, double bed: FF880

Reduction: 15/10–5/04

Capacity: 15 people

Etienne & Rose-Marie BELVÈZE

«La Coste du Milieu»
Rue de St Pierre Livron
82160 CAYLUS

tel: (0) 5 63 67 05 85
fax: (0) 5 63 67 05 85

Private home

44 km - N E - MONTAUBAN
CAYLUS: hosts will collect from station, railway station 22km

Midi-Pyrénées

MONTAUBAN

82.06 MONTAUBAN

PRICE STRUCTURE

3 Bedrooms

Grand Mère Pélagie: television, kitchen, bathroom with wc, 2 double beds: FF280 (2 people) FF560 (4 people)

Rez de Chaussée-Tante Simone: television, kitchen, shower room with wc, 2 single beds: FF280

Extra bed: 70FF

Capacity: 6 people

Rose Marie is very warm hearted, and bends over backwards to make you comfortable. This is an old family home, which is full of souvenirs. Etienne, who is a doctor, will take you on hiking trips, and is extremely knowledgeable about this region. Caylus is a medieval village, inhabited since ancient times.

PROPERTY

✱✱

off street parking, garden, tv lounge, hosts have pets, telephone, babies welcome, free cot, wheelchair access, closed: 15/10-01/06, hiking, cycling, fishing, interesting flora, mushroom picking, sea or lake watersports, river watersports 11km, golf course 40km, birdwatching 44km

Basic English spoken

— At Montauban, N20 towards Cahors, then at Caussade, take the D926 towards Villefranche de Rouergue. As you leave Caylus, head in the direction of St Pierre de Livron and follow the signs.

82.07 MONTAUBAN

Lisanne is a painter and gives you a warm welcome to her bastide perched on a hill. There are two apartments of a high standard, as well as a shaded terrace. You will enjoy her unusual and colourful dinners.

Lisanne ASHTON

«Les Chimères»
Avenue Louis Bessières
82240 PUYLAROQUE

tel: (0) 5 63 31 25 71

Private home

PROPERTY

✱✱✱

off street parking, garden, lounge, hosts have pets, dinner available, kitchen, babies welcome, free cot, river watersports, hiking, cycling, fishing, hunting,

Fluent English spoken

PRICE STRUCTURE

2 Bedrooms and 2 Apartments

Lounge, kitchen, shower room with wc, twin beds, cot: FF280

Lounge, kitchen, shower room with wc, double bed: FF280

Romantique: bathroom with wc, double bed, single bed: FF320

Rustique: bathroom with wc, double bed, single bed: FF300

Extra bed: 40FF
Reduction: 7 nights and children

Capacity: 10 people

35 km - N E - MONTAUBAN
PUYLAROQUE: hosts will collect from station, railway station 14km airport 100km
— At Montauban take the N20 as far as Caussade and then the D17 towards Limogne. It is the first house on the right in Puylaroque.

NETHERLANDS
BELGIUM
ENGLISH CHANNEL
Dunkerque
Calais
St. Omer
Boulogne
NORD
PAS-DE-
CALAIS
LILLE
59
62
Valenciennes
Douai
Arras
Abbeville
AMIENS
80
Dieppe
St. Quentin
Charleville-Mézières
Sedan
02
PICARDIE
Laon
08
Rethel
Le Havre
76
ROUEN
Compiègne
Beauvais
60
Soissons
Reims
Senlis
Lisieux
HAUTE
NORMANDIE
95
Pontoise
27
Evreux
Mantes
93
Meaux
51
CHÂLONS
55
PARIS
92
75
Versailles
ILE DE FRANCE
Bar-le-Duc
BASSE
NORMANDIE
Vitry
Dreux
78
94
Evry
77
St. Dizier
61
28
Melun
Chartres
91
CHAMPAGNE-
ARDENNE
Alençon
Fontainebleau
52
Troyes
Sens
CENTRE
72
Chaumont
10
Châteaudun
Le Mans
Montargis
PAYS
DE LA LOIRE
ORLÉANS
45
BOURGOGNE
21
Vendôme
Auxerre
89

59.01 LILLE

This place is about a 1 hour 30 minutes drive from Calais on the road to Brussels, yet you are in a village only 6 minutes by metro from the centre of Lille. Your charming hostess has given up teaching English in order to look after her guests and her beloved association of "Aides Volontaires".

Yves & Chantal LE BOT

59, Rue Faidherbe
59139 WATTIGNIES

tel: (0) 3 20 60 24 51

Private Home

PROPERTY

✱✱

private parking, garden, hosts have pets, dinner available, kitchen, packed lunch, babies welcome, free cot, cycling, hiking 2km, fishing 10km, interesting flora 10km, mushroom picking 10km, golf course 15km, sea or lake watersports 50km

Fluent English spoken

PRICE STRUCTURE

3 Bedrooms

First & second rooms: shower room with wc, double bed: FF260

Third room: bathroom with wc, 2 single beds: FF260

Extra bed: 50FF

Reduction: 5 nights and groups

Capacity: 6 people

3 km - S - LILLE
WATTIGNIES: hosts will collect from station, railway station 8km
airport 10km
— Take Exit 19 off the A1. Take the D549 towards Wattignies (7km). At the chemist (pharmacie), turn left towards the centre. The house is on the left just before the church.

Béatrice & Bernard
QUILLEROU

«Chez B&B»
78, rue Caumartin
59000 LILLE

tel: (0) 3 20 06 95 04

Private Home

3 km - N - LILLE
LA MADELEINE:
railway station 2km
airport 10km

PRICE STRUCTURE

1 Bedroom

Suite: television, bathroom with wc, double bed: FF255

Extra bed: 100FF
Reduction: 3 nights

Capacity: 2 people

59.03 LILLE

This place is in an ideal spot, in a quiet part of central Lille. You will get on well with Béatrice and be charmed by the decor of her home. This house dates from 1870, and she has kept its authentic style. They love to talk about literature over a glass of Bernard's wonderful wine.

PROPERTY

✱✱✱

off street parking, garden, tv lounge, no pets, dinner available, packed lunch, babies welcome, free cot, hiking, cycling, interesting flora, golf course 8km, birdwatching 8km

Fluent English spoken

— When coming from Calais on the A25, Exit 3 to "Lille-Centre, Ronchin". At the roundabout, take the third street on the right (Rue des Postes). When you reach the roundabout at the Place de la Solidarité, go straight on and then take the first right in to Rue B. Delespoul. It is the fourth street on the left. When coming from Paris or Brussels, head towards Dunkerque, then "Lille-Sud", then left to "Lille-Wazemmes". At the first roundabout, go towards Béthune-Dunkerque. At the second roundabout, take the second on the right (Rue des Postes).

Jeannine HULIN

28, rue des Hannetons
59000 LILLE

tel: (0) 3 20 53 46 12
fax: (0) 3 20 53 46 12

Private Home

LILLE
hosts will collect from station,
railway station 3km
airport 5km

59.07 LILLE

This charming little house is in a quiet street, 10 minutes from the centre of Lille. The conservatory is full of light, full of class and the paintings and period furniture add a cosy, warm feeling to this place. Jeannine is full of life. The bed is a bit small; not for giants!

PROPERTY

✸✸

off street parking, garden, lounge, hosts have pets, no pets, dinner available, 3 years minimum age, golf course 15km, gliding 70km

English spoken

PRICE STRUCTURE

1 Bedroom
2 single beds (1 Childrens size): FF240

Extra bed: 60FF

Capacity: 2 people

— From the Place de la Garde, take the Rue Nationale, and turn left into Rue Solférino, then Rue de Douai, and then Armand Caret as far as a bridge which crosses the road. Turn right under the bridge, then second on the left, left again and then left once more into the Rue des Hannetons.

Annie & Daniel
LEFEVRE

Rue du Quesnoy - Lieu-dit la Maison Rouge, N°1
59990 ROMBIES ET MARCHIPONT

tel: (0) 3 27 26 26 50

Private Home

8 km - E - VALENCIENNES
ROMBIES: hosts will collect from station, railway station 12km
airport 55km
car essential
— On the A2 towards Brussels, Exit 24 Onnaing. follow signs to Le Quesnoy-Rombiés on the D101. 1500 m after leaving the village, you will come to the hamlet "Maison Rouge". The property is right by the sign.

59.06 VALENCIENNES

Daniel and Annie take great pleasure in offering a simple, warm welcome in their home. The large living room has bay windows, overlooking their wooded garden. Valenciennes is 10 minutes away, and Belgium is just over the garden fence! Practical and friendly.

PROPERTY

✷

private parking, extensive grounds, tv lounge, hosts have pets, telephone, dinner available, packed lunch, babies welcome, free cot, hiking, sea or lake watersports 12km, river watersports 12km, golf course 20km

Basic English spoken

PRICE STRUCTURE

2 Bedroom

First room: double bed, 2 single beds (1 Childrens size): FF200 (2 people) FF250 (4 people)

Second room: double bed: FF200

Extra bed: 50FF

Capacity: 6 people

Chantal de SAULIEU

«Chateau de Grand Rullecourt»
62810 GRAND RULLECOURT

tel: (0) 3 21 58 06 37

Château

24 km - S W - ARRAS
GRAND RULLECOURT: hosts will collect from station, railway station 24km airport 70km

62.07 ARRAS

The Viscount makes the jam and his wife brings you your breakfast. You will really enjoy their company and their sense of humour. They need it, because for 10 years, they have been restoring this château, where the lady in waiting of Marie, Queen of Scots was born.

PROPERTY

✹✹✹

private parking, extensive grounds, lounge, no pets, packed lunch, no smoking, hiking, interesting flora, mushroom picking, fishing 7km, hunting 8km, cycling 20km, golf course 20km, gliding 24km, birdwatching 40km

Adequate English spoken

— At Arras, take the N39 towards Le Touquet. Then turn left on to the D75 towards Avesnes le C. and a further 4km to Doullens.

PRICE STRUCTURE

4 Bedrooms and 1 Suite

Polonaise: bridal room, lounge, shower room with wc, double bed: FF400

Second room: lounge, bathroom with wc, twin beds: FF400

Baldaquin: bathroom with wc, 2 double beds: FF500 (2 people) FF900 (4 people)

Suite: bathroom with wc, double bed, single bed, twin beds: FF500 (2 people) FF1100 (5 people)

Fifth room: lounge, bathroom with wc, double bed: FF500

Extra bed: 50/100FF
Reduction: children

Capacity: 15 people

Gina BULOT

«Les Cohettes»
28, rue de Pernes
62190 AUCHY-AU-BOIS

tel: (0) 3 21 02 09 47
fax: (0) 3 21 02 81 68
e-mail: temps-libre-evasion@wanadoo.fr

Residence of character

25 km - W - BETHUNE
AUCHY AU BOIS: hosts will collect from station, railway station 8km
airport 75km
car essential

62.08 BETHUNE

Here you are only 45 minutes from Calais. This restored farmhouse is full of flowers, which are Gina's great passion. She and her children guarantee you a kind, smiling welcome, and you will enjoy her traditional French cuisine. The British and Canadian military cemetery at Vimy is 20km away. 2 apartments for 6/12 people available to rent by the week.

PRICE STRUCTURE

5 Bedrooms

Rose & Verte: shower room with wc, double bed: FF240

Bleue: shower room with wc, double bed, single bed: FF280 (2 people) FF350 (3 people)

Jonquille: bathroom with wc, double bed: FF220

Lilas: bathroom with wc, double bed, single bed: FF240 (2 people) FF310 (3 people)

Extra bed: 70FF

Capacity: 12 people

PROPERTY

✱✱✱

off street parking, extensive grounds, tv lounge, hosts have pets, no pets, dinner available, kitchen, babies welcome, free cot, hiking, cycling, fishing 10km, golf course 20km, sea or lake watersports 45km

Adequate English spoken

— From the A26, take Exit No. 4 (Thérouanne). Then take the D341 towards Arras. 1km after Rely, turn right towards Auchy. Then take the first on the left (Rue des Pernes) and continue for 1km.

Marie-Lou VANDE-WALLE

25 rue des Martyrs
de la Résistance
59630 BOURBOURG

tel: (0) 3 28 22 21 41

Residence of character

30 km - E - CALAIS
BOURBOURG:
hosts will collect from station,
railway station 18km
airport 20km
car essential

59.02 CALAIS

Marie-Lou knows what the word welcome means! Her 18th century house is decorated in a half Flemish, half British style, and is right in the middle of this little town, 7km from the sea. The garden is full of flowers and a real oasis. An excellent address.

PROPERTY

✱✱✱

private parking, garden, lounge, no pets, kitchen, babies welcome, free cot, fishing 3km, hiking 7km, interesting flora 7km, sea or lake watersports 7km, river watersports 7km

Basic English spoken

PRICE STRUCTURE

2 Bedrooms

Louis XV-Rose: television, shower room with wc, double bed: FF270

Campagnarde bleue: television, shower room with wc, double bed, twin beds: FF270 (2 people) FF350 (4 people)

Extra bed: 100FF
Reduction: 3 nights and groups and children

Capacity: 6 people

— On the A16 going towards Dunkerque take Exit number 23b to Bourbourg. Follow signs to Bourbourg Centre and take the Rue de La Mairie (Rue des Martyrs de la Résistance). Look for the B&B France sign on the door (no.25).

Nathalie DUVIVIER

«Le Château»
287, route de la Bistade
59630 ST PIERRE
BROUCK

tel: (0) 3 28 27 50 05
fax: (0) 3 28 27 50 05

Residence of character

35 km - E - CALAIS
ST PIERRE
BROUCK: railway
station 6km
airport 80km
car essential

Nord

CALAIS

PRICE STRUCTURE

2 Bedrooms and 1 Suite

Myosotis: bathroom with wc, twin beds: FF290

Rose: shower room with wc, double bed: FF290

Jonquille: shower room with wc, double bed, single bed: FF350 (2 people) FF390 (3 people)

Extra bed: 50FF

Capacity: 7 people

59.05 CALAIS

A charming residence, situated in grounds of 2 hectares. You will appreciate the refined decor, the beautiful furniture and the quality of service offered by Nathalie. Be sure to visit the Cote d'Opale just 15km away. Superb accommodation at a very reasonable price. Extra bed for a child: 50FF.

PROPERTY

****

private parking, extensive grounds, lounge, hosts have pets, no pets, dinner available, babies welcome, free cot, no smoking, riding, hiking, cycling, fishing, golf course 6km, mushroom picking 6km, interesting flora 15km, sea or lake watersports 15km, hunting 20km, birdwatching 20km

Adequate English spoken

— At Calais, take the A16 towards Dunkerque. Take Exit 24 and go on to the D600 towards St Omer. St Pierre Brouck is on the D1, on the right between Bourbourg and Watten.

62.02 LILLE

You will feel at home in their simple, old farmhouse. Jean–Jacques does not hesitate to travel 10km to make sure you have fresh baguettes for breakfast. You will be captivated by the good humour of his wife, a school teacher. We have added a 2nd Sun, as recommended by past guests. 2 self-catering apartments, rented weekly.

PROPERTY

✸✸

off street parking, extensive grounds, hosts have pets, no pets, kitchen, babies welcome, free cot, hiking, fishing, golf course 5km, sea or lake watersports 5km, interesting flora 18km, bird-watching 18km

Adequate English spoken

PRICE STRUCTURE

3 Bedrooms

Grande: shower room with wc, washbasin, double bed, 2 single beds (childrens size): FF230 (2 people) FF370 (4 people)

Mansardes 1 & 2: shower, washbasin, double bed, single bed: FF210 (2 people) FF280 (3 people)

Extra bed: 50FF

Capacity: 10 people

Jean-Jacques
BEHAGHEL

«La Ferme de Wolphus»
N° 39 RN43 - Wolphus
62890 ZOUAFQUES

tel: (0) 3 21 35 61 61
fax: (0) 3 21 35 61 61

Private Home

15 km - S E - CALAIS
ZOUAFQUES: railway station 9km
airport 80km
— On the A26, take Exit 2. At the 'Stop', turn right towards Calais for 500m. At the next 'Stop', turn left on to the N43 for 1km. The house is on the left (20min from Eurotunnel).

62.12 CALAIS

Thérèse de
LAMARLIÈRE

693, Rue du Parc
62890 AUDREHEM

tel: (0) 3 21 35 06 30

Private Home

They are experts on the history of the Channel Tunnel and this friendly couple love to make friends. There are hiking (GR168) and mountain bike trails nearby. A washing machine and tumble dryer are available for serious walkers. Here you will find peace and quiet in the heart of the country. On sale: Honey, foie-gras, poultry, bread.

27 km - S E - CALAIS
AUDREHEM: hosts will collect from station, railway station 15km
airport 25km
car essential
— Take Exit 2, Ardres, from the A26. Follow the D217 towards Licques, Zouafques, Tournehem and Bonningues les Ardres. As you leave the village on the D223 towards Audrehem, it is the first road on the right.

PROPERTY

✹✹

off street parking, garden, lounge, no pets, telephone, dinner available, kitchen, packed lunch, babies welcome, free cot, no smoking, fishing, hiking 1km, cycling 1km, golf course 17km, birdwatching 20km, sea or lake watersports 20km

Basic English spoken

PRICE STRUCTURE

3 Bedrooms

First room: shower room with wc, double bed: FF210

Second room: shower, washbasin, double bed: FF180

Third room: shower, washbasin, double bed: FF180

Extra bed: 50FF
Reduction: groups

Capacity: 6 people

62.13 LE TOUQUET PARIS PLAGE

This place is right in the centre of the well-known resort of Le Touquet, between the sea and the forests. This is a large Anglo-Norman family villa, nestling at the bottom of a sloping garden. Georges, tall with a white beard, and his wife Marie really know the meaning of the word "welcome". Children under 5 are free.

Georges & Marie
VERSMÉE

«Villa Birdy Land»
Av Foch
62520 LE TOUQUET

tel: (0) 3 21 05 31 46
fax: (0) 3 21 05 95 07

Residence of character

PROPERTY

✸✸✸

private parking, extensive grounds, lounge, hosts have pets, telephone, babies welcome, free cot, closed: 11/11-01/04, hiking, cycling, golf course, fishing, hunting, interesting flora, sea or lake watersports, river watersports 10km, birdwatching 20km

Adequate English spoken

PRICE STRUCTURE

2 Bedrooms

Jaune: television, telephone, bathroom with wc, twin beds: FF350

Bleue: telephone, bathroom with wc, double bed: FF350

Reduction: 2 nights and children

Capacity: 4 people

LE TOUQUET PARIS PLAGE
hosts will collect from station,
railway station 4km
airport 2km
— Follow signs to Le Touquet-Centre and then signs to "Holiday Inn". The house is opposite this hotel.

Elena DESPREZ

«La Crête des Dunes»
Av. Blériot
62520 LE TOUQUET

tel: (0) 3 21 05 04 98
fax: (0) 3 21 05 04 98

Private Home

LE TOUQUET PARIS PLAGE
hosts will collect from station,
railway station 5km
airport 2km

62.15 LE TOUQUET PARIS PLAGE

Elena and Fred are a really enthusiastic and welcoming young couple, who will welcome you to this special place, from which you can enjoy all the attractions of Le Touquet. They serve a hearty breakfast, either in the garden or in the conservatory with its panoramic view. You are only a few steps from the sand dunes and the sea.

PRICE STRUCTURE

4 Bedrooms

Ecoute triple: shower, wash-basin, double bed, single bed: FF330 (2 people) FF360 (3 people)

Capelage: along corridor bathroom with wc, double bed: FF330

Cabestan 1: twin beds: FF290

Cabestan 2: double bed: FF290

Reduction: 31.10 – 31.03 and 7 nights and children

Capacity: 9 people

PROPERTY

✱✱✱

private parking, garden, tv lounge, hosts have pets, no pets, kitchen, babies welcome, free cot, closed: 24/12-2/01, riding, hiking, cycling, golf course, interesting flora, sea or lake water-sports, gliding 2km, fishing 6km, hunting 10km, river water-sports 10km

Fluent English spoken

— On the A16, as you enter Le Touquet, follow the signs to "Base nautique Sud - chars à voiles". Just before you reach the sea front, take the Rue de Paris on the left. Continue straight on, heading towards the sand dunes. "La Crête des Dunes" is at the top of the hill.

Geneviève GYSELINCK

«Ferme Auberge du Vieux Puits»
5 bis, Rue de L'Abbaye
02420 BONY

tel: (0) 3 23 66 22 33
fax: (0) 3 23 66 25 27

Farm

15 km - N - ST QUENTIN
BONY
airport 100km
car essential

02.01 ST QUENTIN

You eat well chez Geneviève. This is also a relaxing stop in a beautiful area, convenient for the A26 autoroute. The American military cemetery from the First World War is only 1km away. On sale: regional farm produce.

PROPERTY

pool, tennis, hiking, cycling, fishing 5km, golf course 15km, hunting 15km

Basic English spoken

— In St Quentin, take the N44 towards Cambrai. Bony is on the left, 1km from the N44.

PRICE STRUCTURE

5 Bedrooms

First Auberge: television, telephone, shower room with wc, double bed, 2 single beds (childrens size): FF310 (2 people) FF420 (4 people)

Second Auberge: television, telephone, shower room with wc, twin beds: FF310

Third Auberge: television, telephone, kitchen, bathroom with wc, double bed, single bed: FF310 (2 people) FF420 (3 people)

Fourth & fifth rooms: television, telephone, shower room with wc, double bed: FF310

Extra bed: 110FF

Capacity: 13 people

Jacques & Nicole
MAURICE

«Ferme de Léchelle»
02200 BERZY LE SEC

tel: (0) 3 23 74 83 29
fax: (0) 3 23 74 82 47

Farm

10 km - S -
SOISSONS
BERZY LE SEC:
railway station 15km
airport 80km
car essential

02.03 SOISSONS

Staying at this large, traditional 13th century farm, with Nicole as your lively hostess, you will relax and enjoy the open country. From the terrace garden, admire the views over the surrounding countryside with its springs and groves. After a large, traditional Picardie breakfast, the region of Flanders, with its abbeys and Roman churches, is waiting to be explored. On sale: chickens, eggs.

PRICE STRUCTURE

5 Bedrooms

Benoite: bathroom with wc, double bed: FF250

Quentin: shower room with wc, twin beds: FF250

double bed: FF230

double bed: FF230
twin beds: FF230

Extra bed: 80FF

Capacity: 10 people

PROPERTY

✱✱✱

private parking, garden, lounge, hosts have pets, telephone, dinner available, babies welcome, free cot, closed: 23/12-02/01, hiking, cycling, interesting flora, hunting 15km, mushroom picking 15km, golf course 30km

Fluent English spoken

— At Soissons, take the N2 towards Paris, then left on to the D172 towards Chaudun. Pass through Chaudun, and after 2km turn left and take the D177 towards Lechelle. You will find the farm just as you enter the village.

60.01 BEAUVAIS

This 18th century sheep farm in the Bray region also has a beautiful dovecote. Here you should walk; around the area or from farm to farm. Beauvais is a very interesting town, and the cathedral is well worth a visit.

PROPERTY

✱✱✱

private parking, hosts have pets, telephone, dinner available, kitchen, packed lunch

Adequate English spoken

PRICE STRUCTURE

4 Bedrooms

Rez de Chaussée: shower room with wc, double bed: FF230

Etage : First room: shower room with wc, double bed, cot: FF230

Etage : Second & third rooms: shower room with wc, double bed, single bed: FF230 (2 people) FF290 (3 people)

Extra bed: 60FF
Reduction: 3 nights and children

Capacity: 10 people

Jean-Claude & Annick LETURQUE

«La Ferme du Colombier»
14, rue du Four Jean Legros
60650 SAVIGNIES

tel: (0) 3 44 82 18 49
fax: (0) 3 44 82 53 70

Flat/Apartment

8 km - N W - BEAUVAIS
SAVIGNIES: hosts will collect from station, railway station 8km
car essential
— In Beauvais, take the N31 towards Rouen. As you leave Beauvais, take the D1 on the right towards Savignies. The farm is near to the church.

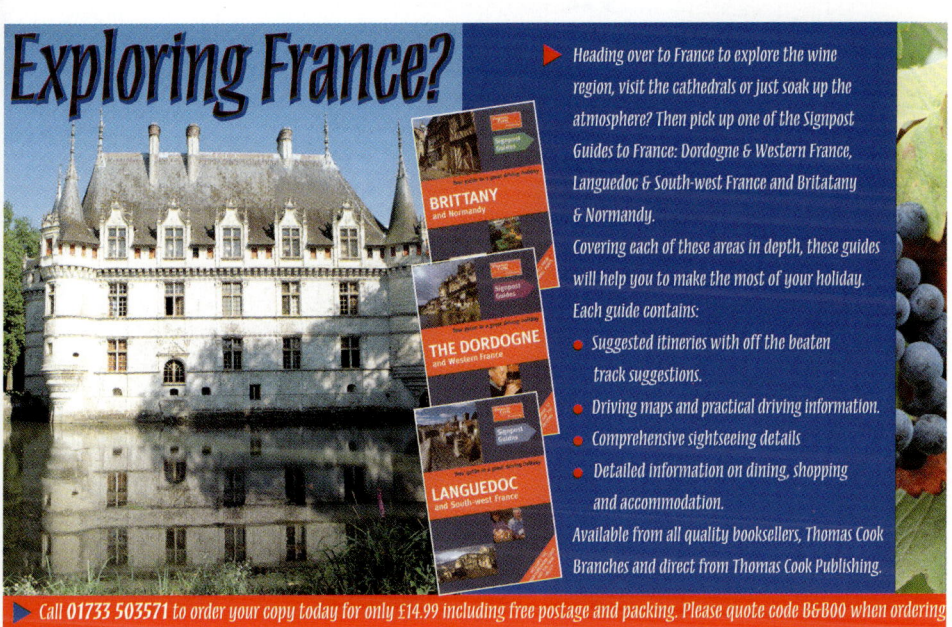

Annie FRÉMAUX

«La Ferme des 3 Bouleaux»
154, rue de Clermont
60480 MONTREUIL sur BRECHE

tel: (0) 3 44 80 44 85
fax: (0) 3 44 80 08 52

Farm

20 km - N E - BEAUVAIS
MONTREUIL SUR BRECHE: railway station 20km
airport 20km
car essential

60.04 BEAUVAIS

This farmhouse has character and is full of interest as it was a 17th century barn, restored in the old style. Aurélie, the daughter, will show you around the farm. The welcome is warm, there is a good fire in the hearth and excellent cooking. 30% reduction if you stay two nights or more.

PRICE STRUCTURE

4 Bedrooms

Narcisse & Lilas & Myosotis: television, shower room with wc, washbasin, double bed: FF230

Fougères: lounge, television, shower room with wc, washbasin, double bed, cot: FF230

Extra bed: 50FF

Reduction: 2 nights

Capacity: 8 people

PROPERTY

***

private parking, garden, tv lounge, hosts have pets, no pets, dinner available, kitchen, packed lunch, babies welcome, free cot, wheelchair access, hiking, cycling, fishing

Adequate English spoken

— At Beauvais head in the direction of Amiens and turn right to Froissy on the D151.

Pauline BRUNGER

«Ferme-Hotel de Bellerive»
492, Rue de Bellerive
60170 CAMBRONNE LES RIBECOURT

tel: (0) 3 44 75 02 13
fax: (0) 3 44 76 10 34

Residence of character

60.03 COMPIEGNE

This old farmhouse near the A1 has been restored with great charm. It is on the edge of the forest and the rooms have a delightful view over the canal. This is also a restaurant, and Pauline is a very good chef. Dishes to take-away.

15 km - N - COMPIEGNE
CAMBRONNE LES RIBECOURT: hosts will collect from station,
railway station 2km
airport 50km

PROPERTY

✱✱✱

off street parking, garden, tv lounge, hosts have pets, dinner available, packed lunch, babies welcome, free cot, hiking, cycling, fishing, hunting, interesting flora, mushroom picking, golf course 5km, sea or lake watersports 5km, river watersports 5km

Fluent English spoken

PRICE STRUCTURE

5 Bedrooms

First, fourth & fifth rooms: shower room with wc, double bed: FF275

Second room: shower room with wc, twin beds: FF275

Third room: bathroom with wc, twin beds: FF275

Extra bed: 100FF
Reduction: 4 nights

Capacity: 10 people

— In Compiègne, take the N32 towards Noyon. In Ribécourt, turn right on to the D66. (From Calais: A1, Exit 12 ROYE then follow directions for Noyon. Then take the N32 towards Compiègne. After Ribécourt turn left on to D66). Cross the canal, and the house is immediately on the right after the bridge.

René & Christiane AUGUSTIN

«Chateau de Drucas»
Beauvoir-Wavans
62390 AUXI-LE-CHÂTEAU

tel: (0) 3 21 04 01 11

Château

25 km - N E - ABBEVILLE BEAUVOIR WAVANS: car essential

62.06 ABBEVILLE

This small château is about 200 years old. It is reached via an avenue of lime trees, leading to magnificent grounds, through which a river flows. Madame's welcome is charming. The decor is simple, unpretentious rococo style.

PRICE STRUCTURE

2 Bedrooms and 1 Suite

First room: double bed, single bed (childrens size): FF220 (2 people) FF300 (3 people)

Second room: double bed: FF220

Suite: kitchen, bathroom with wc, 2 double beds, single bed: FF250 (2 people) FF500 (5 people)

Extra bed: 50FF

Capacity: 10 people

PROPERTY

***

private parking, extensive grounds, lounge, hosts have pets, telephone, babies welcome, free cot, riding, hiking, cycling, fishing, mushroom picking, interesting flora 2km, sea or lake watersports 2km, golf course 25km, birdwatching 25km, gliding 40km

Basic English spoken

— In Abbeville, take the D925 towards St Riquier and the D941 towards Auxi le Château. In Auxi, turn right on to the D938.

Brigitte BOUVET

«Fermette du Marais»
Route d'Abbeville -
Lannoy
80120 RUE

tel: (0) 3 22 25 06 95
fax: (0) 3 22 25 89 45

Private Home

20 km - N W -
ABBEVILLE
LANNOY: railway
station 2km
airport 150km

80.01 ABBEVILLE

This restored old farmhouse is a favourite spot for hunting and fishing. It is very well organised and ideal for children, who can enjoy many activities in complete safety. Brigitte is a dynamic host, with a very warm welcome.

PROPERTY

***

off street parking, extensive grounds, lounge, hosts have pets, telephone, 7 nights minimum stay, 01/07-31/08, cycling, fishing 1km, hunting 1km, hiking 2km, interesting flora 4km, mushroom picking 4km, golf course 7km, birdwatching 7km, sea or lake watersports 7km

Adequate English spoken

— On the A16, Exit 24 towards Rue for 4.5km. The house is 500m on the left before the roundabout as you enter Rue.

PRICE STRUCTURE

3 Bedrooms and 6 Apartments

First room: television, telephone, shower room with wc, double bed, 2 single beds (1 childrens size): FF360 (2 people) FF490 (4 people)

Second room: television, telephone, shower room with wc, double bed: FF360

Third room: television, telephone, kitchen, shower room with wc, double bed, single bed(childrens size): FF360 (2 people) FF420 (3 people)

Fourth room: lounge, television, telephone, kitchen, shower room with wc, 2 double beds, 2 single beds (1 childrens size): FF480 (2 people) FF780 (6 people)

Fifth room: television, telephone, kitchen, shower room with wc, double bed, single bed: FF480 (2 people) FF610 (3 people)

Sixth room: television, telephone, kitchen, shower room with wc, double bed, 2 single beds, (1 childrens room): FF480 (2 people) FF650 (4 people)

Seventh and eighth rooms: lounge, television, telephone, kitchen, shower room with wc, double bed: FF480

Ninth room: television, telephone, kitchen, bathroom with wc, double bed, single bed: FF480 (2 people) FF610 (3 people)

Reduction: 01.09 – 30.06 and 2 nights

Capacity: 2 people

Jacques BUISSON

«La Buissonière»
9, Chemin Blanc
80135 BUSSUS
BUSSUEL

tel: (0) 3 22 28 07 23
fax: (0) 3 22 28 02 28

Private Home

12 km - E -
ABBEVILLE
BUSSUS BUSSUEL:
airport 80km
car essential

80.05 ABBEVILLE

Here they have 2 comfortable bedrooms leading on to the terrace and the quiet of the garden. A modern house near the forest of Crécy make friends with Jacque's 2 shire horses. The breakfast speciality is home-made bread and "gateau battu".

PRICE STRUCTURE

2 Bedrooms

First & second rooms: television, shower room with wc, double bed: FF220

Extra bed: 80FF
Reduction: 3 nights

Capacity: 4 people

PROPERTY

✱✱

off street parking, garden, no pets, telephone, babies welcome, free cot, no smoking, hiking, cycling, mushroom picking, fishing 6km, golf course 12km, hunting 20km, interesting flora 20km, sea or lake watersports 20km, river watersports 20km, birdwatching 30km

English spoken

— From the A16 Calais-Paris, take Exit to Abbeville-Nord. Then head in the direction of St Riquier, and cross Bussus Bussuel, taking the last street on the right.

Catherine & Etienne STEVENS

«Le Gui Nel»
80130 TULLY

tel: (0) 3 22 26 41 13
fax: (0) 3 22 30 28 31

Residence of character

80.09 ABBEVILLE

A 19th century mansion house in the heart of a quiet little village, 6 km from the sea. Etienne is a doctor, and Catherine breeds Welsh ponies. The rooms are unusual and spotlessly clean, with a feel of the beach! Your top-quality breakfast will be served in the conservatory.

25 km - W - ABBEVILLE
TULLY: hosts will collect from station, railway station 12km
airport 160km
car essential

PROPERTY

***

private parking, garden, tv lounge, hosts have pets, no pets, dinner available, packed lunch, wheelchair access, hiking, hunting 6km, interesting flora 6km, birdwatching 6km, sea or lake watersports 6km, gliding 8km, fishing 10km, mushroom picking 10km, river watersports 15km, golf course 17km

Fluent English spoken

PRICE STRUCTURE

2 Bedrooms

Bleue & Verte: television, shower room with wc, double bed: FF270

Extra bed: 50/100FF
Reduction: 4 nights

Capacity: 4 people

— From Abbeville, follow the D925 towards Eu/Le Tréport for 25 km, then turn right after Friville Escarbotin towards Tully, on the D229. The house is in the centre of the village.

Alain & Maryse SAGUEZ

2, Rue Grimaux
80480 DURY

tel: (0) 3 22 95 29 52
fax: (0) 3 22 95 29 52

Residence of character

80.03 AMIENS

Be sure to let Alain take you for a ride in one of the carriages he makes himself. Add to this an excellent welcome, a high standard of comfort and an outstanding breakfast. There is also an impressive choice of restaurants. Be sure to visit Amiens cathedral.

PROPERTY

✱✱✱

private parking, extensive grounds, tv lounge, hosts have pets, no pets, babies welcome, free cot, no smoking, riding, hiking, hunting, mushroom picking, cycling 1km, golf course 2km, fishing 4km, sea or lake watersports 10km

English spoken

5 km - S - AMIENS
DURY: 5km
airport 100km
car essential
— Close to the A16. In Amiens, take the N1 towards Paris. On entering Dury, turn right into the first street towards St Fuscien.

PRICE STRUCTURE

4 Bedrooms

First room: kitchen, shower room with wc, double bed: FF310

Second room: bathroom with wc, double bed, twin beds: FF310 (2 people) FF500 (4 people)

Third room: bathroom with wc, double bed, single bed: FF310 (2 people) FF390 (3 people)

Rez de Chaussée: bathroom with wc, twin beds: FF310

Extra bed: 60FF

Capacity: 11 people

ENGLISH CHANNEL
Guernsey (to UK)
Jersey (to UK)
Dunkerque
Calais
St. Omer
Boulogne
62 NORD PAS-DE-CALAIS
Abbeville
80
AMIENS
Dieppe
Cherbourg
76
PICARDIE
Le Havre
ROUEN
Beauvais
60
HAUTE NORMANDIE
CAEN
Lisieux
Senlis
St. Lô
95
Pontoise
50
14
27
Evreux
Mantes
BASSE NORMANDIE
93
Vire
92
PARIS
75
78
St. Malo
Argentan
Dreux
ILE DE FRANCE
94
Avranches
Evry
Dinan
61
28
Alençon
Chartres
91
Fougères
22
BRETAGNE
53
RENNES
35
72
Laval
Châteaudun
45
Le Mans
ORLÉANS
56
Vendôme
Redon
Châteaubriant
41
Blois
PAYS DE LA LOIRE
44
Angers
49
Tours
St. Nazaire
NANTES
Saumur
37
Vierzon
Cholet
Bourges
CENTRE
18
Châtellerault
36
Châteauroux
La Roche
85

14.03 BAYEUX

An old stone farmhouse-inn, dating from 1830, which has been converted into 6 apartments and 6 bedrooms. It is by the sea, right by the Normandy beaches. You must try the local specialities.

Michel & Frédérique LEGRAND

«La Ferme du Colombier»
Rue Marcel Destors
14450 GRANDCAMP MAISY

tel: (0) 2 31 22 68 46
fax: (0) 2 31 22 14 33

Farm

PROPERTY

off street parking, garden, tv lounge, hosts have pets, telephone, dinner available, packed lunch, hiking, sea or lake watersports,

Basic English spoken

PRICE STRUCTURE

6 Bedrooms

First, second & third rooms: shower room with wc, double bed: FF220

Fourth room: shower room with wc, twin beds: FF240

Fifth room: shower room with wc, 2 double beds: FF220 (2 people) FF350 (4 people)

Sixth room: shower room with wc, double bed, 2 single beds: FF220 (2 people) FF300 (4 people)

Extra bed: 75FF

Capacity: 16 people

27 km - N W - BAYEUX
GRANDCAMP MAISY:
railway station 30km
airport 60km
car essential
— At Bayeux, take the N13 towards Cherbourg. At Osmanville, turn right on to the D514 towards Grandcamp-Maisy. Signposted.

Dominique & Alain
MARION

Le Chateau
14450 GRANDCAMP
MAISY

tel: (0) 2 31 22 66 22
fax: (0) 2 31 22 66 22

Private Home

27 km - N W -
BAYEUX
GRANDCAMP
MAISY: railway
station 30km
car essential

14.37 BAYEUX

Ideally located in the middle of the landing beaches at 3km from the old town Bayeux and its famous tapestry. You'll be welcome in a XVII century farmhouse by Alain and Dominique and their family. Fleur de Soleil member.

PRICE STRUCTURE

3 Bedrooms

Camélia & Jonquille: shower room with wc, double bed: FF300

Glycine: shower room with wc, 2 single beds: FF300

Extra bed: 100FF

Capacity: 6 people

PROPERTY

***

off street parking, garden, dinner available, closed: 01/11-31/03, sea or lake watersports,

English spoken

— Contact your host for detailed directions.

14.04 BAYEUX

A renovated farmhouse in a quiet spot, near to the sea and the Normandy beaches. The ideal place to recharge your batteries and let it all hang out! They even run Yoga and massage courses. On sale: honey, vegetables, cider. 2 self-catering apartments, rented weekly.

Cécile & Thérèse
GRENIER & DESSEAUX

«Le Vallon» - Hottot les Bagues
14250 TILLY sur SEULLES

tel: (0) 2 31 08 11 85
fax: (0) 2 31 08 11 85

Private home

PROPERTY

off street parking, garden, tv lounge, no smoking,
Basic English spoken

12 km - S - BAYEUX
HOTTOT LES BAGUES:
hosts will collect from station,
railway station 15km
airport 15km
— At Bayeux, take the D6 towards Tilly sur Seulles. Turn right on to the D9 towards Caumont. At Hottot les Bagues, after the "Mairie" and opposite the school (école), turn left. The house is on the left, just before the château.

PRICE STRUCTURE

5 Bedrooms

shower room with wc, double bed: FF220

shower room with wc, twin beds: FF220

shower room with wc, 4 single beds: FF220 (2 people) FF380 (4 people)

shower room with wc, 3 single beds: FF220 (2 people) FF300 (3 people)

shower room with wc, single beds: FF140

Extra bed: 60FF
Reduction: groups

Capacity: 12 people

Catherine GUY

«Le Clos St Jean»
Route de la Mer
14520 Ste HONORINE
DES PERTES

tel: (0) 2 31 21 79 34
fax: (0) 2 31 34 60 51

Private home

13 km - N W -
BAYEUX
STE HONORINE
DES PERTES: car
essential

14.16 BAYEUX

This large, modern, elegant stone house is only 300m from the sea, and the invasion beaches. The garden has views over the large lawn to the sea. The bedrooms lead out on to the balcony. The American military cemetery at Omaha Beach is 2km away, and Bayeux is also well worth a visit.

PRICE STRUCTURE

1 Bedroom and 2 Apartments

Bleue: television, shower room with wc, double bed, single bed: FF290 (2 people) FF340 (3 people)

Verte-Apartment: shower room with wc, double bed, twin beds: FF270 (2 people) FF470 (3 people)

Apartment: lounge, television, shower room with wc, double bed, twin beds: FF280 (2 people) FF500 (4 people)

Capacity: 2 people

PROPERTY

✵✵✵

off street parking, extensive grounds, television, babies welcome, free cot, wheelchair access, hiking, fishing, sea or lake watersports, cycling 2km, golf course 2km, interesting flora 10km, birdwatching 40km

English spoken

— At Bayeux, take the D6 for Port en Bessin. Then turn left on to the D514. Ste Honorine is just after Huppain (signposted).

Bertrand & Catherine GIRARD

«Le Relais de la Vignet
Route de Crouay
14400 TOUR EN BESS

tel: (0) 2 31 21 52 83
fax: (0) 2 31 21 52 83

Residence of character

14.25 BAYEUX

This farm-house, typical of the area, has been restored to a good standard with excellent taste. A pleasant family atmosphere reigns and Catherine is a good cook. Near the D-day beaches and Bayeux, an excellent base for visiting Normandy.

5 km - N W - BAYEUX
TOUR EN BESSIN: hosts will collect from station, railway station 6km
airport 30km
car essential

PROPERTY

✱✱✱

off street parking, garden, tv lounge, hosts have pets, dinner available, babies welcome, free cot, hiking, cycling, hunting, fishing 3km, golf course 6km, sea or lake watersports 6km, interesting flora 10km, mushroom picking 10km, birdwatching 10km

English spoken

PRICE STRUCTURE

3 Bedrooms

Rose: lounge, television, shower room with wc, double bed, 2 single beds: FF250 (2 people) FF370 (4 people)

Verte - Rez de chaussée: bridal room, television, shower room with wc, double bed, single bed: FF250 (2 people) FF310 (3 people)

Blanche-Annexe: along corridor shower room with wc, double bed, 2 single beds: FF250 (2 people) FF370 (4 people)

Extra bed: 60FF

Capacity: 11 people

— From Bayeux head towards Cherbourg on N13 for 6km, as far as the village of Tour en Bessin. As you leave the village turn left on the road towards Crouay. Continue for 1.5km and follow the signs.

Odile & Jean-Claude
LENOURICHEL

«Ferme du Mouchel»
14710 FORMIGNY

tel: (0) 2 31 22 53 79
Fax: (0) 2 31 21 56 55

Farm

15 km - N W -
BAYEUX
FORMIGNY: railway
station 15km
airport 45km
car essential

14.29 BAYEUX

This restored stone farm-house offers good standards of comfort on a working farm. Odile is your lively hostess, and full of enthusiasm for the area and attentive to all details that make your stay that extra bit enjoyable.

PRICE STRUCTURE

3 Bedrooms and 1 Suite

(2 rooms) shower room with wc, double bed, single bed: FF240 (2 people) FF300 (3 people)

along corridor bathroom with wc, double bed, 2 single beds: FF240 (2 people) FF320 (4 people)

Indépendante: shower room with wc, double bed, twin beds: FF260 (2 people) FF420 (4 people)

Extra bed: 50FF

Capacity: 14 people

PROPERTY

✱✱✱

off street parking, garden, hosts have pets, no pets, telephone, sea or lake watersports 5km

— From the N13 from Bayeux towards Cherbourg turn right after about 15km to Formigny (D517). Turn right after the church and then left, following signs to Ferme du Mouchel.

14.30 BAYEUX

Let Chantal's exuberant 'joie de vivre' sweep you into her farmhouse, full of character, in this quiet village close to the sea. On returning from sight-seeing or swimming, try the local dishes cooked with local farm produce. On sale: farm produce, jam.

PROPERTY

✱✱

off street parking, extensive grounds, lounge, hosts have pets, dinner available, babies welcome, free cot, cycling,

Fluent English spoken

PRICE STRUCTURE

3 Bedrooms

Jaune: along corridor shower, wc, double bed: FF250

Blanche: double bed, single bed: FF250 (2 people) FF350 (3 people)

double bed, 3 single beds: FF250 (2 people) FF500 (5 people)

Extra bed: 100FF
Reduction: 3 nights and groups

Capacity: 10 people

Chantal KLEIN

«Ferme de la Houlotte»
14400 NONANT

tel: (0) 2 31 92 50 29
fax: (0) 2 31 92 50 29

Farm

4 km - S E - BAYEUX
NONANT: railway station 6km
airport 20km
car essential
– In Bayeux, take the N13 towards Caen, then the D33 towaeds Nonant. Turn right at the church and go under the bridge. The farm is situated 1.6km further down the road. Follow the signs.

Annick SIMONIN

«Ferme Mahyas»
14330 STE
MARGUERITE D'ELLE

tel: (0) 2 31 92 98 15

Farm

25 km - S W - BAYEUX
STE MARGUERITE D'ELLE: railway station 7km
airport 60km
car essential
— At Bayeux, take the D752 towards St. Lo. In the forest, when you reach the roundabout turn right and go as far as Cerisay la Forêt. At the STOP sign, turn right and 200m further on turn left. At the crossroads, head in the direction of St. Jean de Savigny on the left and the farm is 300m further on, on the left.

14.36 BAYEUX

This former coaching inn, over 300 years old, has been transformed into a farmhouse with great character on a 37 hectare property. They produce their own fresh milk, veal and pork. This is the real rural experience, in the country with the river nearby. Add to this their Pommeau and Calvados, and you have the complete image of picture-postcard Normandy.

PROPERTY

**

off street parking, garden, lounge, hosts have pets, dinner available, babies welcome, free cot, closed: 01/10-01/04, fishing, hunting, hiking 5km, cycling 7km, sea or lake watersports 25km, golf course 30km

Basic English spoken

PRICE STRUCTURE

3 Bedrooms

(2 rooms) double bed: FF200

Second room: shower room with wc, washbasin, double bed, single bed: FF250 (2 people) FF280 (3 people)

Extra bed: 80FF

Capacity: 7 people

Caroline RITCHIE

«le Muthier»
4, Hameau la Vieille
50680 ST GEORGES D'ELLE

tel: (0) 2 33 71 99 27
fax: (0) 2 33 71 99 27

Private home

50.15 BAYEUX

Caroline and Geoffrey have just bought this delightful old country house, quietly situated amongst the fields. They are in the process of completely renovating the interior and still find time to organise "theme days" and visits to the invasion beaches. When Geoffrey was a top chef, he won many accolades when he was working in some of the top hotels of the world, and still manages to bake his own bread.

25 km - S E - BAYEUX
ST GEORGES D'ELLE: railway station 8km
airport 45km

PROPERTY

✱✱✱

private parking, extensive grounds, hosts have pets, no pets, dinner available, packed lunch, babies welcome, free cot, hiking, cycling, fishing, hunting, interesting flora, mushroom picking, sea or lake watersports 40km, gliding 40km

Fluent English spoken

PRICE STRUCTURE

3 Bedrooms

television, along corridor bathroom with wc, double bed: FF250

television, shower room with wc, double bed: FF25(

Familiale: television, showe room with wc, double bed, 2 single beds: FF300 (2 pec ple) FF400 (4 people)

Extra bed: 50FF

Capacity: 8 people

— At Bayeux, take the D572 to St. Lo. Then turn right towards St. Georges d'Elle and follow the signs.

Michel & Dany
BERNARD

Le Clos de St Laurent»
St Laurent du Mont
14340 CAMBREMER

tel: (0) 2 31 63 47 04
fax: (0) 2 31 63 46 92

Residence of character

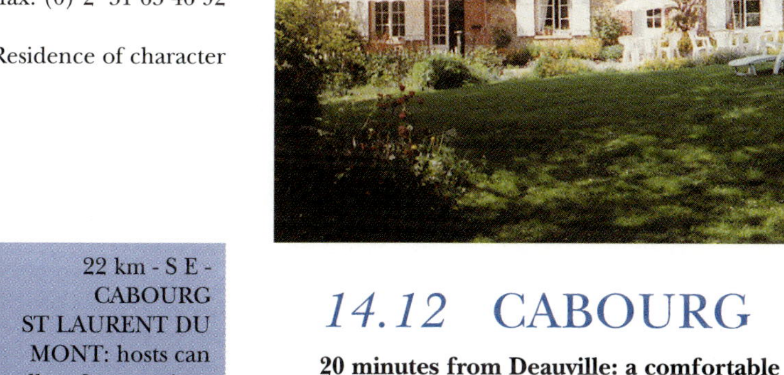

22 km - S E - CABOURG
ST LAURENT DU MONT: hosts can collect from station, station 12km airport 28km

14.12 CABOURG

20 minutes from Deauville: a comfortable 18th century house, furnished with exquisite taste. From the garden there is a panoramic view over the valley and 'la Suisse Normande'. Excursions, delicious home-made jam, and pleasant hours spent at the table with Michel and Dany will add to your enjoyment.

PRICE STRUCTURE

2 Bedrooms and 1 Suite and 1 Apartment

Jaune: television, bathroom with wc, double bed: FF280

Orange/Rose: television, along corridor bathroom with wc, 2 double beds, single room: FF280 (2 people) FF660 (5 people)

Bleuet: television, shower room with wc, double bed: FF280

La Maison de José: bridal room, lounge, television, kitchen, shower room with wc, double bed, twin beds, single bed: FF380 (2 people) FF700 (5 people)

Capacity: 2 people

PROPERTY

***

off street parking, extensive gardens, tv lounge, hosts have pets, no pets, dinner available, babies welcome, free cot, 2 nights minimum stay 01/07-31/08, golf course 25km, sea or lake watersports 25km

Basic English spoken

— Exit Cabourg, on the A13. Take the D49 towards Carrefour St Jean (N13) where you turn left on to the D50 towards Cambremer. The house is on the bend as you go up the hill, on the right.

14.18 CAEN

Jacques LARSON

«Le Cottage»
2, Chemin du Longrais
14930 MALTOT

tel: (0) 2 31 26 96 10
fax: (0) 2 31 26 83 82

Private Home

This beautiful modern villa is quiet, with a shaded garden and very pleasant. They also have a little dog and a parrot. For room no. 3, you have a shower in the bedroom. Even though Caen was devastated during the war, it still keeps its unique cachet as William the Conqueror's town.

PROPERTY

✱✱

off street parking, garden, hosts have pets, sea or lake water-sports 6km, hiking 8km, cycling 8km, fishing 8km, mushroom picking 8km, golf course 12km, birdwatching 20km

6 km - S W - CAEN
MALTOT:
airport 6km
— In the centre of Caen, at the roundabout by the Zenith, head in the direction of Louvigny. At the next roundabout, go towards Maltot (D212) and follow the signs "chambres d'hotes" and "B&B France".

PRICE STRUCTURE

3 Bedrooms

First room: along corridor shower room with wc, double bed, single bed: FF200 (2 people) FF280 (3 people)

Second room: shower room with wc, double bed, single bed: FF200 (2 people) FF280 (3 people)

Third room: shower room with wc, double bed: FF200

Capacity: 8 people

ené & Monique LEROY

«Le Pré Boulard»
Route de Caen
14430 ANNEBAULT

tel: (0) 2 31 64 80 86
fax: (0) 2 31 64 80 86

Private home

14 km - S - DEAUVILLE ANNEBAULT: airport 30km
car essential
— From Deauville, head for Pont l'Evêque, where you should take the N175 towards Caen. It is the 3rd house on the right, after the Annebault roundabout. (If you are coming from Rouen, on the A13, take the Exit towards Villers sur Mer, and then take the N175 towards Caen).

14.19 DEAUVILLE

Situated right on the N175, this beautiful house is very practical and only 12km from Pont l'Evêque, 14km from Deauville, and 20km from Honfleur. There is a kitchen available, and the rooms are spacious, pleasant and comfortable

PROPERTY

✱✱

private parking, extensive gardens, tv lounge, hosts have pets, kitchen, babies welcome, free cot, golf course 10km, sea or lake watersports 12km

PRICE STRUCTURE

5 Bedrooms

Bordeaux: along corridor bathroom, double bed, single bed: FF220 (2 people) FF270 (3 people)

Verte & Rose: along corridor shower, double bed: FF220

Bleue: washbasin, double bed: FF200

Jardin: double bed, single bed: FF220 (2 people) FF270 (3 people)

Extra bed: 50FF
Reduction: groups

Capacity: 12 people

Pascal & Janneke MARI

«Manoir de la Plane»
14130 ST GATIEN
DES BOIS

tel: (0) 2 31 89 08 47

Manor house

11 km - E -
DEAUVILLE
ST GATIEN DES
BOIS: hosts can
collect from station,
station 10km
airport 5km

14.34 DEAUVILLE

Janneke and Pascal, a Franco-Dutch couple, welcome you to their large manor house, dating from the turn of the century, between Honfleur and Deauville. The setting is quite special, and you will enjoy the space, quiet and relaxing atmosphere of this place, which is nicely set in two hectares of ancient woodland and fruit trees. A collection of watercolours has been used to decorate the bedroom walls. On sale: Paintings.

PROPERTY

✱✱✱

private parking, extensive gardens, babies welcome, free cot, riding, hiking, cycling, golf course, hunting, fishing 4km, sea or lake watersports 4km

Fluent English spoken

PRICE STRUCTURE

1 Bedroom

First room: bathroom with wc, double bed: FF350

Second room: bathroom with wc, double bed, single bed: FF400 (2 people) FF450 (3 people)

Third room: lounge, bathroom with wc, double bed: FF400

Fourth room: bathroom with wc, double bed: FF400

Apartment: lounge, kitchen, bathroom with wc, shower room with wc, 2 double beds, 5 single beds: FF600 (2 people) FF1200 (9 people)

Extra bed: 50FF
Reduction: 3 nights

Capacity: 18 people

— From the A13, Exit Deauville - Honfleur. Head towards "Honfleur Hopital" for 8km. The manor is the first property on the left before the hospital.

Jean Luc & Ariane LEBAILLY

«La Colombière»
143, Av Michel d'Ornano
14910 BLONVILLE SUR MER

tel: (0) 2 31 98 59 51

Residence of character

2 km - S W - DEAUVILLE BLONVILLE SUR MER: hosts can collect from station, station 2km airport 15km

14.35 DEAUVILLE

This half-timbered house, typical of the last century, is situated between the sea and the countryside, near to Deauville and its racecourses. Some of the bedrooms are on the second floor, with sloping ceilings. On one side, there is the English Channel (beach is only 100m away) and on the other, a nature reserve which protects many species of birds. Apartment to rent weekly in July and August.

PRICE STRUCTURE

2 Bedrooms

Apartment: kitchen, double bed: FF230

Second room Mezzanine: double bed, single bed: FF230 (2 people) FF380 (3 people)

Capacity: 2 people

PROPERTY

✱✱

private parking, garden, hosts have pets, kitchen, babies welcome, free cot, no smoking, riding, hiking, cycling, fishing, birdwatching, sea or lake watersports, golf course 8km

English spoken

— From Deauville, on the D513, go through Bionville. L'Avenue d'Ornano follows the coast. The house is No.143.

Patricia WALLIS

«Domaine de la Hamberie»
Fresné la Mère
14700 FALAISE

tel: (0) 2 31 90 34 61
fax: (0) 2 31 90 34 61

Private Home

14.20 FALAISE

Here, a very friendly English couple from Yorkshire, welcome you to their restored farmhouse. You will spend pleasant hours around their dinner table. They also have a large swimming pool and sand-pit for children, plus 3 gîtes on the farm.

5 km - E - FALAISE
FRESNE LA MERE:
airport 45km
car essential

PROPERTY

✱✱✱

off street parking, garden, lounge, hosts have pets, dinner available, babies welcome, free cot, hiking 3km, fishing 6km, golf course 25km, river watersports 35km, sea or lake watersports 40km

Fluent English spoken

PRICE STRUCTURE

2 Bedrooms and 1 Suite

Double: shower room with wc, double bed: FF275

Twin: shower room with wc, twin beds: FF275

Family Suite: shower room with wc, 2 twin beds: FF300 (2 people) FF440 (4 people)

Extra bed: 50FF
Reduction: groups

Capacity: 8 people

— At Falaise, take the D63 towards Trun. As you enter Fresné la Mère, turn right before the level-crossing, and then take the 2nd on the left. Cross the level-crossing, and continue right to the end.

Vicky GRAN

«La Drouetterie»
Marolles
14100 LISIEUX

tel: (0) 2 31 62 73 93

Residence of character

12 km - E - LISIEUX
MAROLLES: hosts can collect from station,
station 12km
airport 30km
car essential

14.22 LISIEUX

Your hosts and their two sons will welcome you to this beautiful, timbered, Normandy house. Peace and quiet is guaranteed. Each of the two bedrooms has beautiful exposed beams, and a separate entrance. They produce their own honey. On sale: honey, cider, Calvados.

PRICE STRUCTURE

2 Bedrooms

(2 rooms) television, shower room with wc, double bed, single bed: FF250 (2 people) FF320 (3 people)

Extra bed: 70FF

Capacity: 6 people

PROPERTY

✱✱✱

off street parking, extensive gardens, tv lounge, hosts have pets, babies welcome, free cot, fishing 5km, golf course 12km, hunting 20km, sea or lake watersports 22km

English spoken

— At Lisieux, take the N13 towards Paris for 8km. At the crossroads of Le May, turn right towards Marolles. As you enter the village, turn right on to the D75B, and head in the direction of Courtonne. The house is on the D75B, down a slope on the right.

Pierre HENDRYCKS

«Ferme du Chalet»
27210 BERVILLE SUR MER

tel: (0) 2 32 57 21 24/ 69 49
fax: (0) 2 32 56 53 64

Residence of character

27.04 HONFLEUR

An unusual B & B. These hotel-type studios have been created in a 17th century thatched farmhouse, 82 m long. This unique building is on the edge of the Seine, and Deauville is only 20 minutes away. Fleur de soleil member. On sale: Regional produce.

9 km - E - HONFLEUR BERVILLE SUR MER: hosts can collect from station, station 25km airport 20km

PROPERTY

✱✱✱

private parking, extensive gardens, tv lounge, dinner available, packed lunch, 2 nights minimum stay, hiking, fishing, sea or lake watersports, golf course 15km

English spoken

PRICE STRUCTURE

14 Apartments

(7 apartments) lounge, kitchen, shower room with wc, 2 double beds: FF410 (2 people) FF620 (4 people)

(7 apartments) lounge, kitchen, shower room with wc, 3 double beds: FF510 (2 people) FF780 (6 people)

Reduction: children

Capacity: 70 people

— In Honfleur or at the Pont de Normandie, take the D180 towards Toutainville. In Rivière St Sauveur turn left towards Berville. The house is opposite the church.

acques & Marie-Hélène
DECARSIN

«Le Prieuré des Fontaines»
les Préaux
7500 PONT AUDEMER

Tel: (0) 2 32 56 07 78
Fax: (0) 2 32 42 88 23

Residence of character

5 km - S W - PONT AUDEMER
LES PREAUX:
airport 25km
car essential

27.05 PONT AUDEMER

Jacques has wonderfully restored this 17th century building, with its ground floor that opens on to a swimming pool and a garden, landscaped with great skill. A great place to stop in Normandy.

PRICE STRUCTURE

4 Bedrooms and 1 suite

Rez de Chaussée-Nénuphar: bridal room, telephone, bathroom with wc, double bed, single bed: FF340 (2 people) FF440 (3 people)

Capucine: telephone, bathroom with wc, double bed: FF340

Marmotte: telephone, bathroom with wc, double bed, single bed: FF340 (2 people) FF440 (3 people)

Cendrillon: telephone, bathroom with wc, double bed: FF340

Familiale: telephone, bathroom with wc, washbasin, shower, double bed, 2 single beds: FF400 (2 people) FF590 (4 people)

Extra bed: 40/100FF

Capacity: 14 people

PROPERTY

✱✱✱

private parking, garden, tv lounge, hosts have pets, no pets, telephone, dinner available, no smoking, cycling, mushroom picking, sea or lake watersports 5km, golf course 20km

Basic English spoken

— In Pont Audemer, take the D139 towards Lisieux. The house is on this road (signposted).

Normandie

PONT AUDEMER

Michel & Françoise
LETELLIER

le Village
27350 ROUGEMONTI

tel: (0) 2 32 56 84 80
fax: (0) 2 32 56 84 80

Residence of character

20 km - E - PONT AUDEMER ROUGEMONTIER: airport 40km car essential

27.06 PONT AUDEMER

A lovely welcome awaits in this substantial house with antique furniture, in very pleasant grounds. It is on the edge of the forest of Brotonne where you can go hiking or riding. Easy to find on the N175. Home-made jam and cakes. On sale: Home-made jam.

PROPERTY

✱✱✱

private parking, extensive gardens, tv lounge, hosts have pets, no pets, dinner available, babies welcome, free cot, closed: 25/12&1/01, hiking, fishing 3km, golf course 18km

Adequate English spoken

PRICE STRUCTURE

2 Bedrooms

Rose: shower room with wc double bed: FF300

Verte: bathroom with wc, double bed: FF300

Extra bed: 70FF
Reduction: 1/10–31/03 an 5 nights

Capacity: 4 people

— In Pont Audemer, take the N175 towards Rouen for 15km. In the village, the house is on the left.

Jacqueline MESNIL

«Le Château»
27230 ST AUBIN DE SCELLON

tel: (0) 2 32 46 85 41

Château

25 km - S - PONT AUDEMER
ST AUBIN DE SCELLON
airport 25km
car essential

Normandie

PONT AUDEMER

PRICE STRUCTURE

2 Bedrooms

Abricot: bridal room, bathroom with wc, double bed: FF320

Soleil Levant: shower, wc, double bed: FF290

Extra bed: 50FF

Capacity: 4 people

27.07 PONT AUDEMER

A small, 19th century château, surrounded by delightfully verdant grounds, situated in a small village. Ideal for a stopover to and from Britain. There are also plenty of historic places, manors and châteaux to be visited.

PROPERTY

✱✱✱

private parking, extensive gardens, tv lounge, dinner available, babies welcome, free cot, closed: 15/09-01/04, sea or lake watersports 15km, golf course 20km

Basic English spoken

— In Pont Audemer, take the D810 towards Bernay. In Lieurey, take the D28 towards Thiberville. In St Aubin de Scellon, the château is near to the church, opposite the D41.

Gaston & Michelle Le PLEUX

«La Clé des Champs»
27500 TRIQUEVILLE

tel: (0) 2 32 41 37 99

Residence of character

10 km - S W - PONT AUDEMER
TRIQUEVILLE:
airport 15km
car essential

27.08 PONT AUDEMER

Near to the A13, and the Vernier marches and Honfleur. The house is an old cider press, dating from 1789, which has been restored with great taste and charm. There is a beautiful, quiet garden. The old staircase that leads to the bedrooms is rather steep. The breakfast is beautifully served. On sale: Cider.

PRICE STRUCTURE

2 Bedrooms

Rose & Jaune: shower room with wc, double bed: FF270

Extra bed: 50FF

Capacity: 4 people

PROPERTY

✱✱✱

private parking, garden, tv lounge, no pets, dinner available, hiking, cycling, fishing, hunting, mushroom picking, bird-watching, river watersports 6km, golf course 20km, sea or lake watersports 20km

Basic English spoken

— At Pont-Audemer take the D87 towards St Germain-Village. Continue straight on until the sign Triqueville (CV19). Follow the signs to La Clé des Champs.

50.26 AVRANCHES

Claude & Patrice
WAGNER

«Manoir de la Croix»
Le Gros Chêne
50530 MONTVIRON

tel: (0) 2 33 60 68 30
fax: (0) 2 33 60 69 21

Residence of character

8km - NW - Avranches
Montviron:
station 9km
airport 35km
car essential
— From Avranches, take the D973 towards Granville. From the village of Montviron cross the level crossing, and after 1km the 'manoir' is at the cross-roads. Take the road to the left of the property and turn right into the car park.

Claude and Patrice have just finished restoring their manor house dating from 1839, to the highest standards with flair and excellent taste. The bedrooms are spacious and most have individual sun terraces. Ideal base for a holiday. Their infectious enthusiasm will ensure that you get the very best from your stay in this area.

PROPERTY

✱✱✱✱

off street parking, extensive gardens, tv lounge, hosts have pets, no pets, no smoking, hiking 8km, sea or lake watersports 8km

Fluent English spoken

PRICE STRUCTURE

2 Bedrooms and 2 Suites

Rebecca: lounge, television, bathroom with wc, shower, double bed, single bed: FF400 (2 people) FF500 (3 people)

Marie-Louise: lounge, television, bathroom with wc, shower, double bed, single bed: FF400 (2 people) FF500 (3 people)

Eugénie & Pauline: television, bathroom with wc, shower, double bed: FF300

Extra bed: 80FF

Capacity: 10 people

Normandie

AVRANCHES

Geneviève & Jean PICO

«La Ramade»
2, route de la Cote
Marcey les Grèves 5030
AVRANCHES

tel: (0) 2 33 58 27 40

Private home

3 km - N W -
AVRANCHES
MARCEY LES
GREVES: hosts can
collect from station,
airport 70km
car essential

50.28 AVRANCHES

This large house in pink granite is situated between the Normandy beaches and the Mont St Michel. It is easy to find (on the main road). The beautiful rooms have been completely renovated and are all sound-proofed. Geneviève is an attentive hostess.

PROPERTY

✱✱✱

private parking, extensive gardens, tv lounge, no pets, telephone, babies welcome, free cot, closed: 3/11-1/03, hiking, cycling, fishing 10km, interesting flora 10km, mushroom picking 10km, birdwatching 10km, gliding 18km, sea or lake watersports 20km

Adequate English spoken

— In Avranches head towards Granville. Just after the bridge take the CD911 towards Jullouville. The property is on the right.

PRICE STRUCTURE

5 Bedrooms

First room: shower, bathroom, wc, double bed, twin beds: FF320 (2 people) FF400 (4 people)

Second room: shower, twin beds: FF300

Third room: shower, double bed: FF300

Fourth room: shower room with wc, double bed, single bed: FF300 (2 people) FF350(3 people)

Fifth room: shower room with wc, double bed: FF300

Extra bed: 70FF

Reduction: 5 nights

Capacity: 2 people

Marilyn & Richard
TUBBS

«La Basse Grezilière»
St Georges de
Reintembault
35420 LOUVIGNÉ du
DESERT

tel: (0) 2 99 97 10 19

Residence of character

27 km - S -
AVRANCHES
ST GEORGES DE
R.: station 20km
airport 80km
car essential

PRICE STRUCTURE

2 Bedrooms

First and second rooms: along corridor bathroom with wc, double bed, twin beds: FF250 (2 people) FF500 (4 people)

Capacity: 4 people

35.34 AVRANCHES

On the border between Brittany and Normandy, this is a beautiful 17th century farmhouse which your English hosts have renovated with good taste. They have preserved the original oak beams, the fireplace and the bread oven. Take a good road map so that you are sure to find it, as it really is a wonderful place to stay!

PROPERTY

✱✱✱

private parking, garden, tv lounge, hosts have pets, no pets, telephone, 5 years old minimum age, no smoking, hunting 2km, fishing 10km, sea or lake watersports 10km, interesting flora 14km, golf course 70km

Fluent English spoken

— At Avranches, take the N175 and the D998 as far as St James. From there, head towards St Hilaire de Harcouët on the D30. As you leave St James, take the D230 for St Georges de Reintembault. Near the centre, go left on the D115 towards Hamelin. Take the 2nd road on the left, signposted to La Basse Grézilière.

50.04 CHERBOURG

Here at Jacqueline's place, you will find the atmosphere of the nice little family guest houses of old. Biville is a small town, known for its beautiful sandy beaches. Public tennis courts are opposite the house.

Charles & Jacqueline RENET

Le Bourg - Biville
50440 BEAUMONT LA HAGUE

tel: (0) 2 33 52 76 62

Private home

PROPERTY

private parking, garden, tv lounge, hosts have pets, dinner available, kitchen, packed lunch, babies welcome, free cot, hiking, sea or lake watersports,

Adequate English spoken

PRICE STRUCTURE

6 Bedrooms

A & B: washbasin, double bed: FF200

C: shower, wc, washbasin, double bed: FF250

E: shower, wc, washbasin, double bed, single bed: FF250 (2 people) FF330 (3 people)

D: shower, washbasin, double bed: FF220

F: shower, wc, washbasin, twin beds: FF200

Extra bed: 80FF
Reduction: 10 nights and groups

Capacity: 13 people

18 km - W - CHERBOURG
BIVILLE: hosts can collect from station, station 18km
airport 30km
— At Cherbourg, take the D901 towards Beaumont. Turn left on to the D37 towards Vasteville then right on to the D118 towards Biville. The house is on the left, opposite the school (sign posted).

Marie-France CAILLET

«Le Manoir de la Fèverie»
Ste Geneviève
50760 BARFLEUR

tel: (0) 2 33 54 33 53
fax: (0) 2 33 22 12 50

Manor house

25 km - E - CHERBOURG
BARFLEUR: station 25km, airport 15km
car essential
— At Cherbourg, take the D901 towards Barfleur. 1km after Tocqueville, turn right on to the D10 and follow the signs.

50.17 CHERBOURG

If you are going to Normandy, be sure to do whatever it takes to spend a few days chez Marie-France. This old manor will live up to your wildest dreams....the bedrooms are fantastic, Marie-France is charming and, if you love horses, there is an added bonus as they are horse breeders.

PROPERTY

✱✱✱

private parking, garden, tv lounge, hosts have pets, babies welcome, free cot, no smoking, hiking, cycling, mushroom picking, fishing 3km, sea or lake watersports 3km, golf course 25km

PRICE STRUCTURE

1 Bedroom and 1 Suite

La Tour: television, shower room with wc, double bed: FF300

Coquelicot: television, shower room with wc, twin beds: FF350

Madras: television, bathroom with wc, twin beds: FF350

Reduction: 1/10–30/05 and 2 nights

Capacity: 6 people

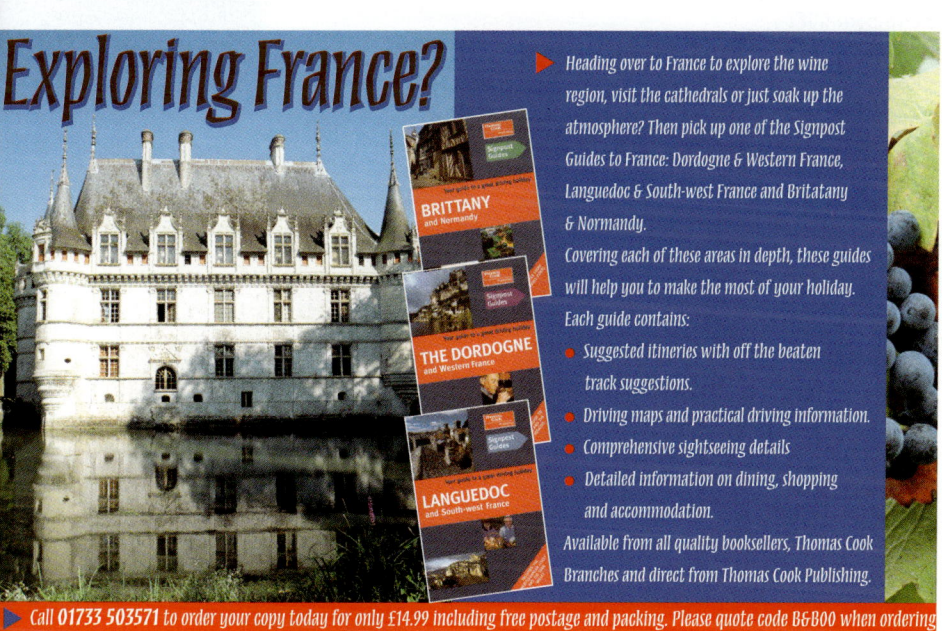

50.32 CHERBOURG

This young couple welcome you to their family manor house, only 300 metres from the sea. Climb the impressive staircase to reach your well-equipped room, with a view over the sea and garden. There is a ferry to the Channel Islands 2 km away. Excellent value for money.

PROPERTY

✹✹

off street parking, garden, hosts have pets, dinner available, babies welcome, free cot, hiking, cycling, fishing, sea or lake watersports, interesting flora 15km, gliding 15km, golf course 22km

Basic English spoken

PRICE STRUCTURE

1 Bedroom and 3 Apartments

Tourelle: bathroom with wc, double bed: FF250

Bureau: kitchen, bathroom with wc, double bed: FF210

Les Meurtrières: kitchen, shower room with wc, double bed, single bed: FF250 (2 people) FF280 (3 people)

La Mansarde: lounge, kitchen, bathroom with wc, double bed: FF300

Extra bed: 50FF
Reduction: 01/09–20/12 and 05/01–30/06 and 4 nights

Capacity: 2 people

Laurence LE COUTOU

«Le Valciot»
14 Chemin des Costils
50340 SIOUVILLE-HAGUE

tel: (0) 2 33 52 93 15

Manor house

25 km - S W - CHERBOURG
SIOUVILLE HAGUE:
station 22km
airport 40km
car essential
— From Cherbourg take the D904 as far as Les Pieux, and then the D23 towards Siouville. In this village, facing the cemetery turn left and then turn right at the "Stop" sign. Then take the first on the right. The house is 500 m further on, on the right.

Patricia BROOKER

«Le Perchoir»
St Croix
0630 TEURTHEVILLE
BOCAGE

tel: (0) 2 33 54 67 57
fax: (0) 2 33 54 67 57

Private home

18 km - S E - CHERBOURG TEURTHEVILLE BOCAGE: station 12km

PRICE STRUCTURE

3 Bedrooms

First room: double bed, 2 single beds: FF300 (2 people) FF500 (4 people)

Second room: double bed, single bed: FF300 (2 people) FF400 (3 people)

Third room: double bed: FF300

Capacity: 9 people

50.34 CHERBOURG

Only 30 minutes from Cherbourg, Le Perchoir is the ideal place for an overnight stop. Your hosts are English, and their house, in the heart of the country, is full of owls....stone owls, wooden owls and even some real ones in the barn. Children will love playing with the chickens and goats. There is wonderful seafood to be enjoyed only 5 minutes away. On sale: Eggs.

PROPERTY

✱✱

private parking, garden, tv lounge, hosts have pets, no pets, telephone, dinner available, babies welcome, free cot, no smoking, hiking, fishing 6km, sea or lake watersports 7km, river watersports 10km, cycling 12km, golf course 18km

Fluent English spoken

— From Cherbourg, D911 towards St Pierre Eglise. At Hamel, turn right on to the D24 to Le Theil for 5km. Turn left on to the D56 towards Quéthou for 7km. Follow signs to "Le Perchoir" for 2.5km. (From Valognes, take the D902 towards Quethou for 10km. Turn left on to the D119 towards Teurtheville.)

Hélène POSLOUX

«La Moinerie de Haut
Les Hauts Champs
50200 NICORPS

tel: (0) 2 33 45 30 56

Residence of character

4 km - S -
COUTANCES
NICORPS: hosts can collect from station, station 5km
airport 80km
car essential

50.21 COUTANCES

Hélène is sweet and pleasant. She bakes delicious croissants and muffins, and her husband takes part in gymkhanas. The farmhouse has been restored with excellent taste. Make sure you can handle the rather steep staircase and if you can, stay several days to really get the most out of this wonderful place.

PROPERTY

✱✱✱

off street parking, garden, tv lounge, hosts have pets, dinner available, babies welcome, free cot, riding, hiking, cycling, hunting, mushroom picking, river watersports 6km, golf course 10km, fishing 10km, sea or lake watersports 10km, gliding 10km

English spoken

— At Coutances, follow signs to Villedieu les Poëles (D7) for 2km. Then turn left on to the D27 towards Nicorps. Continue for 2km as far as the signpost 'Les Hauts Champs'.

PRICE STRUCTURE

3 Bedrooms

Franck: along corridor shower room with wc, twin beds: FF180

Nicolas: shower room with wc, double bed: FF200

Sous les toits-Frédérique: twin beds, single bed(childrens size): FF150 (2 people) FF180 (3 people)

Extra bed: 50FF
Reduction: 1/11–1/03 and 2 nights

Capacity: 2 people

Emile YVON

25, route du Vaudroulin
50400 GRANVILLE

tel: (0) 2 33 90 86 00

Private home

GRANVILLE:
station 3km
airport 100km

PRICE STRUCTURE

2 Bedrooms

First room: shower room with wc, washbasin, double bed, 2 single beds: FF200 (2 people) FF300 (4 people)

Second room: shower, washbasin, double bed: FF200

Reduction: 4 nights

Capacity: 6 people

50.33 GRANVILLE

Yvon and his wife are a lovely, retired couple. From their terrace, there is a view over the sea, which is only 125m away. There is a lot to do in Granville, including excursions to Jersey and Guernsey. You are also only 50km from Mont St. Michel.

PROPERTY

private parking, garden, no pets, babies welcome, free cot, hiking, fishing, birdwatching, golf course 3km, sea or lake watersports 3km, river watersports 3km

— Coming from Avranches on the D973, take the second road on the left after the town name sign for "Granville". You are on the Route de Vaudrolin. The house is No.125.

Madeleine
STRACQUADANIO

«Le Vieux Presbystère»
35610 VIEUX VIEL

tel: (0) 2 99 48 65 29
fax: (0) 2 99 48 65 29

Residence of character

13 km - S - MONT ST MICHEL
VIEUX VIEL: hosts can collect from station,
station 20km
airport 50km
car essential

35.06 MONT ST MICHEL

In the heart of the Bay of Mont St Michel, Jean and Madeleine will welcome you with charm and kindness to their 17th century presbytery, with its beautiful interior furnished with antiques. It is well worth the detour, not least for the wonderful cooking (their "canard en cocotte" is a masterpiece). On sale: Wine.

PROPERTY

✱✱✱

private parking, garden, tv lounge, hosts have pets, no pets, dinner available, packed lunch, babies welcome, free cot, closed: 15/01-30/01, mushroom picking 4km, hiking 5km, cycling 5km, golf course 15km, sea or lake watersports 30km

Basic English spoken

— In Pontorson, take the N176 towards Dol de Bretagne, then turn left on to the D219 towards Sougéal where you turn right towards Vieux-Viel. The house is by the church.

PRICE STRUCTURE

5 Bedrooms

Rez de Chaussée: shower room with wc, washbasin, 2 double beds, FF250 (2 people) FF420 (4 people)

Baldaquin: shower room with wc, washbasin, double bed, single bed: FF260 (2 people) FF450 (3 people)

Aile droite: shower room with wc, washbasin, double bed, single bed: FF250 (2 people) FF380 (3 people)

Fourth room: along corridor bathroom with wc, double bed: FF250

Fifth room: along corridor bathroom with wc, 2 single beds: FF250

Extra bed: 70FF

Capacity: 14 people

M. F. & Alain BARRÈRE & SCHROTTER

«Château de La Ballue»
35560 BAZOUGES LA PÉROUSE

tel: (0) 2 99 97 47 86
fax: (0) 2 99 97 47 70

Château

35.25 MONT ST MICHEL

From the windows, you will admire the beautiful gardens "à la française". The large bedrooms are spacious and very comfortable. Your hosts will let you try some very refined 17th century dishes, and in the summer, famous artists exhibit their work here. On sale: Books, modern art.

PROPERTY

****

private parking, extensive gardens, tv lounge, hosts have pets, no pets, babies welcome, free cot, closed: 01/01-31/01, 2 nights minimum stay, hiking, cycling, hunting, mushroom picking, interesting flora 15km, golf course 18km, fishing 20km, sea or lake watersports 20km, birdwatching 25km

English spoken

20 km - S - MONT ST MICHEL BAZOUGES LA PEROUSE: hosts can collect from station, station 12km airport 30km — From the Mont St Michel, take the N175 towards Rennes, and at Antrain, follow the signs to the château (Monument Historique).

PRICE STRUCTURE

4 Bedrooms and 1 Suite

Victor Hugo: shower room with wc, double bed, 2 single beds: FF750 (2 people) FF1050 (4 people)

Diane: bathroom with wc, double bed, single bed: FF650 (2 people) FF800 (3 people)

Perse: bathroom with wc, twin beds, single bed: FF650 (2 people) FF800 (3 people)

France: lounge, bathroom with wc, double bed, 2 single beds, twin beds: FF950 (2 people) FF1300 (6 people)

Florence: bathroom with wc, double bed, 2 single beds: FF750 (2 people) FF1050 (4 people)

Extra bed: 150FF

50.07 MONT ST MICHEL

François & Catherine
TIFFAINE

«la Gautrais»
50240 ST JAMES

tel: (0) 2 33 48 31 86
fax: (0) 2 33 48 58 17

Farm

This old house has been beautifully restored with old beams and an open fireplace in the living room. Furnished with antiques, one of the bedrooms has a balcony. The terrace overlooks a large garden and the green valley beyond. Cycles may be hired.

PROPERTY

✵✵✵

private parking, garden, tv lounge, hosts have pets, no pets, dinner available, kitchen, babies welcome, free cot, riding, hiking, cycling, fishing, sea or lake watersports 10km

Adequate English spoken

PRICE STRUCTURE

4 Bedrooms

Bleue: shower room with wc, bathroom, double bed, single bed: FF200 (2 people) FF270 (3 people)

Verte: shower room with wc, bathroom, double bed: FF200

Balcon: shower room with wc, bathroom, 2 double beds: FF230 (2 people) FF300 (4 people)

Frisette: kitchen, shower room with wc, bathroom, double bed, single bed: FF200 (2 people) FF300 (3 people)

Extra bed: 50FF
Reduction: 5 nights

Capacity: 12 people

20 km - S E - MONT ST MICHEL
ST JAMES: airport 60km
car essential
— On the A84, Exit 32-St James. Follow signs to the supermarket "SuperU" (on the D12), then after 900m you will see the sign "Ferme la Gautrais".

Roger & Renée BOURGUENOLLE

«La Basse Guette»
50300 LE VAL ST PERE

tel: (0) 2 33 58 24 35

Farm

50.05 MONT ST MICHEL

This is a pleasant, restored, stone farmhouse. The bedrooms are on the upper floors. It is near to the Mont St Michel and Avranches. The war museum is 1km away and a good restaurant a little further.

PROPERTY

***

private parking, garden, tv lounge, no pets, kitchen, packed lunch, wheelchair access, swimming pool, tennis, hiking, fishing 2km, interesting flora 6km, river watersports 6km, sea or lake watersports 15km

Basic English spoken

30 km - E - MONT ST MICHEL
LE VAL ST PERE: hosts can collect from station, station 6km
airport 65km
— Leaving the Mont St Michel, go towards Avranches. On the N175, take the Exit 'Cromel - Le Val St Père'

PRICE STRUCTURE

5 Bedrooms

First room: bathroom with wc, double bed: FF210

Second room: shower room with wc, double bed: FF210

Fourth room: shower room with wc, 2 double beds: FF230 (2 people) FF320 (4 people)

Third & fifth room: shower room with wc, double bed, 2 single beds: FF230 (2 people) FF320 (4 people)

Reduction: groups and children

Capacity: 16 people

Michel & Marie-Thérès GUESDON

«Au Jardin Fleuri»
Route de Servon - La Mottaiserie
50220 CEAUX

tel: (0) 2 33 70 97 29
e-mail: michelguesdon@minitel.net

Private home

10 km - E - MONT ST MICHEL
CEAUX: station 10km
airport 65km
car essential

50.06 MONT ST MICHEL

Your charming hostess will make you want to spend several nights here, in her stone built house. Near to the Mont St Michel and Avranches, and with a restaurant 100m away, the surroundings are relaxing with a beautiful view.

PROPERTY

✱✱✱

off street parking, garden, tv lounge, hosts have pets, hiking, cycling, mushroom picking, sea or lake watersports, fishing 3km, birdwatching 5km

Adequate English spoken

PRICE STRUCTURE

5 Bedrooms

First floor: First room: shower room with wc: FF200

First floor: Second room: bathroom with wc, double bed: FF200

First floor: Third room & Second floor fifth room: shower room with wc, double bed: FF200

Second floor: Fourth room: television, shower room with wc, double bed: FF200

Extra bed: 30FF

Capacity: 10 people

— Leaving the Mont St Michel, turn left on to the D275 towards Courtils then Ceaux. Opposite the 'hotel du Petit Quinquin'. Go in the direction of Servon for 50m. 1st entrance on the right

Lucette BOUTELOUP

«Les Vallées»
St Quentin sur le Homme
50220 DUCEY

tel: (0) 2 33 60 61 51

Farm

25 km - E - MONT ST MICHEL ST QUENTIN SUR LE HOMME: airport 50km
car essential

PRICE STRUCTURE

4 Bedrooms

First room: shower room with wc, 2 double beds: FF200 (2 people) FF290 (4 people)

Second room: along corridor bathroom with wc, double bed, single bed: FF180 (2 people) FF260 (3 people)

Third & fourth rooms: shower, wc, double bed: FF200

Extra bed: 50FF
Reduction: 8 nights

Capacity: 11 people

50.08 MONT ST MICHEL

A very attractive house, recently built of stone, 500m from the village. A peaceful, leafy place, which is only 15 minutes from the Mont St Michel and 5km from Avranches. There is a swimming pool, tennis and riding nearby. Fresh milk and home-made jam. On sale: Foie-gras, rillettes de canard, cider.

PROPERTY

✱✱

private parking, garden, tv lounge, hosts have pets, no pets, dinner available, kitchen, closed: 20/06-30/06, sea or lake watersports 1km, cycling 3km, interesting flora 5km, river watersports 5km

Adequate English spoken

— Leaving the Mont St Michel, go towards Avranches. On the dual-carriageway take the Exit to St Quentin sur Le Homme. In the village, opposite the church, take the small road between the 'Boulangerie' and the Post Office. The house is 300m from the village.

Marie-Pierre
LEMOULAND

«La Ferme de la Ruette
50220 DUCEY

tel: (0) 2 33 70 95 90
fax: (0) 2 33 70 95 90

Farm

8 km - E - MONT ST MICHEL BAS COURTILS:
airport 70km
car essential

50.11 MONT ST MICHEL

We love Marie-Pierre, who is a kind, strong character. A classic, Normandy stone farmhouse on a working farm specialising in rearing live, salt sheep. Well worth seing. Ideal for families on a budget. They are members of a cycling club. On sale: cider.

PROPERTY

✸

off street parking, garden, tv lounge, no pets, kitchen, closed: 25/10-02/11, cycling, sea or lake watersports 1km

Basic English spoken

PRICE STRUCTURE

5 Bedrooms

First floor: First & second rooms: shower, washbasin, double bed: FF180

Second floor Mansardées fourth room: along corridor bathroom, washbasin, double bed: FF180

Second floor Mansardées third and fifth rooms: shower, washbasin, 2 double beds: FF180 (2 people) FF250 (4 people)

Extra bed: 50FF

Capacity: 14 people

— Leaving the Mont St Michel, turn left on to the D275 towards Courtils. In Bas Courtils, take the D288 towards Roche-Torin for 200m. The farm is on the right.

14.15 VILLEDIEU LES POELES

Daniel GUEZET

La Plaine Postel
14380 COURSON

tel: (0) 2 31 68 83 41
fax: (0) 2 31 68 83 41

Farm

This friendly and dynamic young couple will welcome you to their modern, spacious and very comfortable farm. Do not miss dinner round the fire. Billiard room and swimming pool. On sale: cider, Calvados.

15 km - E - VILLEDIEU LES POELES
LA PLAINE POSTEL: hosts can collect from station, station 17km airport 75km — At Villedieu les Poëles, take the D924 then D524 towards Vire. In St Sever, turn left on to the D81 towards 'Landelles et Coupigny', then follow the signs.

PROPERTY

✱✱✱

off street parking, garden, tv lounge, hosts have pets, dinner available, packed lunch, babies welcome, free cot, swimming pool

English spoken

PRICE STRUCTURE

5 Bedrooms

Verdure & Mimosa: television, shower room with wc, twin beds: FF220

Bleuet: television, shower room with wc, double bed: FF220

Verdoyante & Rose: shower room with wc, washbasin, double bed, 2 single beds: FF165 (2 people) FF255 (4 people)

Extra bed: 50FF

Capacity: 14 people

Hervé & Annick
LAGADEC

«Manoir de la Porte»
50870 STE PIENCE

tel: (0) 2 33 68 13 61
fax: (0) 2 33 68 29 54

Manor house

10 km - S W - VILLEDIEU LES POELES
STE PIENCE: station 10km
airport 90km
car essential

50.12 VILLEDIEU LES POELES

This house was originally an old priory, dating from the 15th century. It is situated in a pleasant spot with beautiful grounds and a lake. The whole family is charming! Barbecue available in summer.

PROPERTY

✱✱✱✱

off street parking, extensive gardens, tv lounge, no pets, dinner available, no smoking, hiking, cycling, mushroom picking, fishing 10km, interesting flora 10km, river watersports 10km, golf course 20km, sea or lake watersports 20km

Fluent English spoken

— At Villedieu les Poëles, take the N175 towards Avranches. At the cross-roads 'Le Parc', turn right towards Ste Pience and follow the signs.

PRICE STRUCTURE

2 Bedrooms

lounge, bathroom with wc, double bed, 2 single beds: FF230 (2 people) FF330 (4 people)

Extra bed: 50FF

Capacity: 4 people

Daniel & Mary-Claude DUCHEMIN

«Le Cottage de la Voisinière»
La Voisinière
50410 PERCY

tel: (0) 2 33 61 18 47
fax: (0) 2 33 61 43 47

Private home

10 km - N - VILLEDIEU LES POELES
PERCY: car essential

50.23 VILLEDIEU LES POELES

Stop at Mary-Claude's and admire her extraordinary English garden. She has a passion for flower-arranging, as well as her ornamental pond and water lilies...For the children there are sheep and a temperamental donkey. Delicious and unusual home-made jams. Very close to Hambie Abbey. On sale: honey, Calvados.

PRICE STRUCTURE

5 Bedrooms

First floor-Lavande: shower room with wc, double bed, single bed(childrens size): FF215 (2 people) FF285 (3 people)

First floor-Fuschia: shower room with wc, twin beds: FF215

Dépendances-ground floor-Magnolia & first floor-Camélia: shower room with wc, double bed: FF215

First floor-Cyclamen: shower room with wc, double bed: FF255

Extra bed: 70FF

Capacity: 11 people

PROPERTY

✱✱✱

off street parking, garden, hosts have pets, kitchen, fishing 1km, hiking 5km, interesting flora 8km, golf course 30km, sea or lake watersports 30km, river watersports 30km

Basic English spoken

— A84:Exit 38. At Villedieu les Poeles, go towards Percy. At Percy, turn left on to the D98 towards Sourdeval, and continue for 1.5km.

50.27 VILLEDIEU LES POELES

An avenue of chestnut trees leads up to this 19th century house in a beautiful valley. Here you are free to enjoy peace and quiet and space. The rooms are tastefully furnished and you will certainly spend some pleasant moments chatting to Liliane and Christian in the evening.

Liliane & Christian JAMARD

«La Vaucelle»
50410 VILLEBAUDON

tel: (0) 2 33 61 18 61

Farm

PROPERTY

✱✱

off street parking, garden, tv lounge, hosts have pets, babies welcome, free cot, hiking, fishing, hunting, river watersports 15km, golf course 30km, sea or lake watersports 30km

Adequate English spoken

15 km - N - VILLEDIEU LES POELES
VILLEBAUDON: station 15km
airport 70km
car essential
— Villebaudon is at the intersection of the D999 Villedieu les Poëles to Cherbourg road and the D13 Caen to Granville road. Take the D13 towards Bréhal and the house is 500m on the left.

PRICE STRUCTURE

4 Bedrooms

Eglantine: double bed: FF200

Glycine: washbasin, double bed: FF200

Giroflée: double bed: FF200

Campanule: double bed, single bed: FF200 (2 people) FF250 (3 people)

Extra bed: 50FF

Capacity: 9 people

Nathalie DE DROUAS

«Les Boulais»
50800 ST MARTIN LE BOUILLANT

tel: (0) 2 33 60 32 20
fax: (0) 2 33 60 45 20

Château

12 km - S - VILLEDIEU LES POELES
ST MARTIN LE BOUILLANT:hosts can collect from station,
station 13km
airport 110km
car essential

PRICE STRUCTURE

3 Bedrooms

Carnière: bathroom with wc, double bed: FF395

Chant d'oiseau: bathroom with wc, double bed: FF350

Bain de Mer: shower room with wc, single bed: FF250

Extra bed: 100FF

Capacity: 5 people

50.30 VILLEDIEU LES POELES

The rooms in this château are in unusual, bright colours. It is surrounded by spacious grounds on a hill, near to the beaches. Your hostess is lively and her three beautiful Labrador dogs are even more lively! Outside the main season the château is also used as a language school.

PROPERTY

✱✱✱

off street parking, extensive gardens, lounge, hosts have pets, dinner available, packed lunch, babies welcome, free cot, hiking, fishing, hunting, mushroom picking, interesting flora 20km, birdwatching 20km, cycling 25km, golf course 25km, sea or lake watersports 25km

Fluent English spoken

— From Villedieu take the N175 then the D924 towards Viré. Then take the D999 towards Brécey. After Chérencé le Héron follow signs to St Martin le Bouillant. When you reach this village continue as far as the saw mill (Scierie Norgeot). Then turn right towards Loges-sur-Brécey. After 1km before the Mairie and the church, take the drive up to the château which is on the left.

61.07 L'AIGLE

A vast château in beautifully landscaped grounds with a lake. The rooms are spacious and comfortable, with modern bathrooms. In spite of a slightly impersonal atmosphere, children will love it, and you will all feel at ease.

PROPERTY

✱✱✱

private parking, extensive gardens, tv lounge, hosts have pets, telephone, babies welcome, free cot, fishing, mushroom picking, hiking 40km, golf course 50km

PRICE STRUCTURE

6 Bedrooms

(4 rooms) television, telephone, kitchen, bathroom with wc, double bed: FF395

201: television, telephone, kitchen, bathroom with wc, twin beds: FF395

210: television, telephone, kitchen, bathroom with wc, 2 single beds: FF395

Extra bed: 50FF
Reduction: 7 nights

Capacity: 12 people

Michel THANOS

«Le Château»
61550 LA FERTE FRESNEL

tel: (0) 2 33 24 23 23
fax: (0) 2 33 24 50 19

Château

14 km - N W - L'AIGLE
LA FERTE FRESNEL:
station 12km
airport 170km
car essential
— At L'Aigle, turn right on to the D12 (from the N26) towards Vimoutiers. Head for the centre of the village, and when you are facing the château grounds, turn left and the entrance is immediately after the round Dovecot on the right.

Patrick REBULARD

«Le Village du Cheval»
61140 BAGNOLES DE L'ORNE

tel: (0) 2 33 37 12 79
fax: (0) 2 33 31 15 50

Private home

61.05 ALENCON

You are in a riding centre (50 horses and ponies). Patrick is a European champion of carriage driving. Enjoy an apéritif in the fantastic carriage museum. Here, the rooms are designed for practicality and are brand new. The accommodation is particularly ideal for children and groups. Bagnoles is a jewel surrounded by wonderful countryside.

PROPERTY

✱✱

off street parking, hosts have pets, telephone, dinner available, packed lunch, riding, hiking, cycling, interesting flora, golf course 1km, fishing 1km, hunting 1km, mushroom picking 1km, sea or lake watersports 2km, river watersports 6km

Fluent English spoken

45 km - N W - ALENCON BAGNOLES DE L'ORNE: hosts can collect from station, station 2km airport 220km — At Alençon, take the N12 towards Laval and at Pré-en-Pail, take the N176 towards Flers. At Couterne, turn right on to the D916 towards La Ferté Macé - Flers, then left on to the D935 towards Bagnoles de l'Orne. Follow the signs to "Village du Cheval".

PRICE STRUCTURE

2 Bedrooms and 6 Suites

(1 room) - Family 4: shower room with wc, twin beds, 2 single beds: FF250 (2 people) FF380 (4 people)

(2 rooms) - Family 5: shower room with wc, twin beds, 3 single beds: FF250 (2 people) FF475 (5 people)

(1 room) - Family 6: shower room with wc, twin beds, 4 single beds: FF250 (2 people) FF570 (6 people)

(1 room) - Family 7: shower room with wc, twin beds, 7 single beds: FF250 (2 people) FF665 (9 people)

(1 room) - Family 9: shower room with wc, twin beds, 7 single beds: FF250 (2 people) FF855 (9 people)

(2 rooms) - Dormitory: shower, wc, washbasin, 8 single beds: FF190 (2 people) FF760 (8 people)

Reduction: groups

Capacity: 52 people

72.19 ALENCON

Roland & Nina JUGLET

«Les Terres Noires»
ST REMY DES MONTS
72600 MAMERS

tel: (0) 2 43 97 79 27

Farm

You will find peace and quiet at Nina and Rolands' place. This is an excellent spot, very comfortable and ideal for an overnight stop. You cannot fail to feel at home here and children will love the sheep.

PROPERTY

**

private parking, garden, hosts have pets, no pets, wheelchair access, 2 nights minimum stay, hiking, fishing 1km, cycling 3km, mushroom picking 9km, golf course 15km, sea or lake watersports 25km, interesting flora 45km

PRICE STRUCTURE

1 Bedroom

lounge, television, along corridor bathroom with wc, double bed: FF240

Extra bed: 80FF
Reduction: 7 nights

Capacity: 2 people

30 km - S E - ALENCON
ST REMY DES MONTS:
hosts can collect from station,
station 25km
airport 180km
car essential
— At Alençon take the D311 as far as Mamers then the D2 towards La Ferté Bernard as far as St Rémy des Monts.

61.10 ARGENTAN

Nicole & Michel HUET des AUNAY

Le Val de Baize
18, rue de Mauvaisville
61200 ARGENTAN

tel: (0) 2 33 67 27 11
fax: (0) 2 33 35 39 16

Farm

A warm, professional welcome awaits you in this beautiful 18th century house at the heart of a cereal farm, where Michel is assisted by his daughters. Ask him to show you his collection of American baseball cane. Excellent value for money. On sale: Cider, jam.

PROPERTY

private parking, garden, tv lounge, no pets, telephone, packed lunch, hiking, fishing, interesting flora, gliding 1km, cycling 2km, golf course 15km, sea or lake watersports 25km

Basic English spoken

PRICE STRUCTURE

3 Bedrooms and 1 Apartment

Jaune: along corridor shower room with wc, washbasin, double bed: FF210

Rose & Bleu: along corridor shower room with wc, washbasin, twin beds: FF210

Apartment: kitchen, shower room with wc, washbasin, double bed: FF250

Extra bed: 40FF

Capacity: 8 people

ARGENTAN
hosts can collect from station,
station 2km
airport 60km
car essential
— At Argentan head towards Alençon on the N158. 2km after Mauvaisville turn right and follow the signs for 500m.

Joseph Le MOTHEUX du PLESSIS

«La Miotière»
61400 LE PIN LA GARENNE

tel: (0) 2 33 83 84 01

Farm

10 km - S -
MORTAGNE AU PERCHE
LE PIN LA GARENNE:
station 30km
car essential

61.03 MORTAGNE AU PERCHE

Madame du Plessis is charming. You will stay in a little house within this working farm. It has a lot of class and has been furnished with great taste and character. In September, there is a programme of cultural events. A region with beautiful forests.

PROPERTY

***

off street parking, extensive gardens, lounge, hosts have pets, no pets, dinner available, babies welcome, free cot, wheelchair access, hiking, mushroom picking, golf course 10km

Basic English spoken

PRICE STRUCTURE

3 Suites

Maison 1: lounge, shower room with wc, double bed, 3 single beds: FF400 (2 people) FF650 (5 people)

Maison 2: lounge, kitchen, bathroom with wc, double bed, twin beds: FF400 (2 people) FF650 (4 people)

Maison 3: lounge, bathroom with wc, double bed, single bed: FF400 (2 people) FF600 (3 people)

Reduction: groups and children

Capacity: 12 people

— In Mortagne, take the D938 towards Le Pin la Garenne. In the village, turn right on to the D256 towards St Jouin de Blavou for about 1km. First lane on the left.

Geneviève BONNIAU-STADELMANN

«La Champinière»
61190 BUBERTRÉ

tel: (0) 2 33 83 34 77
fax: (0) 2 33 83 34 77

Residence of character

10 km - N - MORTAGNE AU PERCHE
BUBERTRE: hosts can collect from station,
station 18km
airport 130km
car essential

61.08 MORTAGNE AU PERCHE

A simple but professional welcome awaits you in this superb house, situated in the heart of Le Perche Natural Park, on the edge of the forest. An excellent atmosphere and very good food. The brand new bedrooms are pleasantly decorated and very quiet. The museum PERCHE-CANADA and the château of the Comtesse de Ségur are nearby. On sale: Regional produce. Half-board available.

PRICE STRUCTURE

4 Bedrooms

Soléiado: shower room with wc, double bed: FF290

Mistral: shower room with wc, double bed, 2 single beds: FF290 (2 people) FF490 (4 people)

Capéo: shower room with wc, twin beds: FF290

Ventoux: along corridor bathroom with wc, double bed: FF290

Extra bed: 100FF

Capacity: 2 people

PROPERTY

✱✱✱✱

off street parking, garden, tv lounge, hosts have pets, no pets, telephone, dinner available, packed lunch, babies welcome, free cot, wheelchair access, hiking, cycling, interesting flora, mushroom picking, fishing 4km, sea or lake watersports 4km, hunting 5km, gliding 12km, golf course 15km

Fluent English spoken

— From Mortagne turn right on to the N12 towards Paris as far as the Exit to Tourouvre. Then take the D32 towards Moulins de la Marche and Bubertré. Follow the signs to 'chambre d'hotes'.

Madeleine FAUQUET

169, rue du Colombier - D108
76730 AUPPEGARD

tel: (0) 2 35 85 20 43

Private home

12 km - S - DIEPPE
AUPPEGARD: car essential

76.01 DIEPPE

If you are looking for a typical little timbered Normandy cottage, 10km from Dieppe, just for you, then this is the address. Breakfast is served in the rustic dining room, a wonderful experience.

PROPERTY

✱✱✱

private parking, garden, lounge, hosts have pets, no pets, dinner available, sea or lake watersports 10km

Adequate English spoken

— At Dieppe, take the N27 towards Rouen for 12km. Turn right on to the D108 towards Auppegard and continue for 2km. The house is on the right.

PRICE STRUCTURE

1 Bedroom

lounge, shower room with wc, double bed, 3 single beds,childrens size, cot: FF220 (2 people) FF470 (5 people)

Extra bed: 70FF

Capacity: 5 people

Annick & Henri
FAUVILLE

«La Maison Blanche»
Le Bourg
76270 NESLE-HODENG

tel: (0) 2 35 94 57 79
fax: (0) 2 35 94 57 79

Private home

40 km - S E - DIEPPE
NESLE HODENG:
station 15km
airport 140km
car essential
— On the A28 Rouen-Abbeville Exit 9 Neufchatel. At Neufchatel take the D134 towards Forges les Eaux for 5km. Then the D135 towards Beauvais and left towards Nesle-Hodeng. From Dieppe go to Neuchatel (D915 & D48).

76.15 DIEPPE

Annick and Henri are delighted to share their home and their meals with you. In a green and leafy setting there is a good choice of walks. The beautiful, large conservatory overlooks the garden. An ideal spot for peace and quiet. You are also on the Neufchatel cheese trail.

PROPERTY

✱✱✱

private parking, extensive gardens, lounge, hosts have pets, dinner available, kitchen, closed: 01/03-31/03, hiking, cycling, mushroom picking 2km, fishing 6km, interesting flora 12km, sea or lake watersports 35km, birdwatching 50km

Adequate English spoken

PRICE STRUCTURE

2 Bedrooms and 1 Suite

Romantique: television, shower room with wc, double bed, single bed (childrens size): FF250 (2 people) FF310 (3 people)

Campagnarde: along corridor shower room with wc, double bed: FF220

Contemporaine: shower room with wc, double bed, single bed (childrens size): FF250 (2 people) FF350 (3 people)

Extra bed: 60FF

Capacity: 8 people

Catherine DEMARQUET

«Manoir de Beaumont»
Beaumont
76260 EU

tel: (0) 2 35 50 91 91
fax: (0) 2 35 50 19 45

Residence of character

30 km - N E - DIEPPE
EU: hosts can collect from station, station 3km
airport 100km
car essential

75.38 DIEPPE

This is a former hunting lodge, beautifully restored and in a quiet location. Catherine gives a very special welcome in this really authentic setting, and is a mine of information to help you plan your visits. One of our most inviting stops...

PROPERTY

****

off street parking, garden, lounge, hosts have pets, no pets, babies welcome, free cot, hiking, cycling, interesting flora, mushroom picking, birdwatching, fishing 2km, sea or lake watersports 2km, river watersports 3km, golf course 30km

Fluent English spoken

— From Dieppe, take the D925 towards Le Tréport/Eu. As you leave Eu, before you reach the D49 towards Ponts and Marais, take the Beaumont road on the right and follow the signs "Chambres d'hotes" for 2 km

PRICE STRUCTURE

2 Bedrooms and 1 Suite

Louis XVI: lounge, shower room with wc, double bed, 2 single beds: FF270 (2 people) FF370 (4 people)

Pitou: kitchen, shower room with wc, double bed, twin beds, single bed: FF270 (2 people) FF420 (5 people)

Entente Cordiale: shower room with wc, double bed: FF270

Extra bed: 50FF
Reduction: 15/11–15/12 and 08/01–30/01

Capacity: 11 people

76.06 ETRETAT

Alain & Claudine RAS

«Ferme des Quatre Brouettes»
76280 TURRETOT

tel: (0) 2 35 20 23 73
fax: (0) 2 35 20 23 73

Farm

You will be charmed by Claudine's warm welcome, and this traditional Normandy house and flower garden. It is 10km from Etretat, 2km from the main Le Havre - Fécamp road, and 7km from the equestrian centre. You will love the fireside dinners. On sale: farm produce.

PROPERTY

✱✱✱

private parking, garden, tv lounge, hosts have pets, dinner available, kitchen, packed lunch, babies welcome, free cot, hiking, cycling, sea or lake watersports 7km, golf course 10km

Fluent English spoken

10 km - S - ETRETAT
TURRETOT: hosts can collect from station, station 7km
airport 15km
— In Etretat, take the D940 towards Le Havre. Turn left on to the D32 towards Gonneville la Mallet. Cross the village and take the D125 towards Turretot. Cross two junctions, the farm is on this road, 1km on the left, towards Hermeville.

PRICE STRUCTURE

4 Bedrooms and 1 Apartment

Coquelicot: lounge, kitchen, shower room with wc, double bed: FF240

Pervenche: kitchen, shower room with wc, double bed: FF220

Camélia: kitchen, shower room with wc, double bed, single bed: FF220

Myosotis: shower room with wc, double bed, single bed: FF220 (2 people) FF270 (3 people)

Rose: along corridor shower room with wc, double bed, single bed: FF200 (2 people) FF260 (3 people)

Extra bed: 60FF
Reduction: 3 nights

Capacity: 13 people

76.18 LE HAVRE

Claude & Béatrice LEROU[illegible]

8, route de la Marguerite
76133 ST MARTIN DU BEC

tel: (0) 2 35 20 26 20

Private home

This place is a thatched house on a farm, in a typical village between Le Havre and Etretat, close to the sea. Claude and Béatrice are retired farmers, and will welcome you as only the Normans know how, that is to say in a warm, open and friendly way. On sale: Orange juice, jam, cheese.

PROPERTY

✱✱

off street parking, garden, tv lounge, hosts have pets, telephone, kitchen, babies welcome, free cot, hiking, fishing 4km, sea or lake watersports 5km, golf course 10km, river watersports 10km

15 km - N - LE HAVRE
ST MARTIN DU BEC: hosts can collect from station, station 2km
airport 8km
car essential
— From Le Havre, head towards Montvilliers, Epouville. Then take the D32 towards Rolleville, Turretot. Follow signs to Rolleville. At St Martin du Bec, near the château, take the first turn on the left and follow the old road. Follow signs "chambres d'hotes".

PRICE STRUCTURE

3 Bedrooms

Rose: along corridor shower room with wc, washbasin, double bed, single bed: FF200 (2 people) FF260 (3 people)

Fleurs & Jaune: washbasin, double bed: FF200

Extra bed: 60FF
Reduction: 1/09–31/03 and 5 nights and groups

Capacity: 7 people

Luc & Paulette DEMAEGDT

«Domaine de la Coudraye»
27370 LA HAYE DU THEIL

tel: (0) 2 32 35 52 07
fax: (0) 2 32 35 17 21

Farm

15 km - S - ROUEN
LA HAYE DU THEIL: car essential

Normandie

ROUEN

PRICE STRUCTURE

2 Bedrooms

Rose: shower room with wc, double bed, single bed: FF240 (2 people) FF280 (3 people)

Bleue: shower room with wc, bathroom, double bed, single bed: FF240 (2 people) FF280 (3 people)

Extra bed: 20FF

Capacity: 6 people

27.09 ROUEN

This farmhouse has been built on the site of a château destroyed during the war. All that remains is the chapel, where breakfast is served. The rooms are very comfortable. Convenient location, only 20 minutes from the A13. They also produce their own patés and foie gras. On sale: Foie-gras, confits, rillettes.

PROPERTY

✱✱✱

off street parking, extensive gardens, tv lounge, hosts have pets, babies welcome, free cot, tennis, hiking,1km fishing,1km mushroom picking 1km, cycling 3km, golf course 7km, sea or lake watersports 15km

— On the A13, take the Exit Maison Brulée. Then take the N138 towards Alençon, and turn left on to the D80 as far as La Haye du Theil. The farm is on the D26, heading towards St Pierre des Fleurs.

Marie-Cécile LAMBERT

«La Ferme de Vivier»
88, route de Duclair
76150 ST JEAN DU CARDONNAY

tel: (0) 2 35 33 80 42

Farm

7 km - N W - ROUEN
ST JEAN DU CARDONNAY: station 6km

76.07 ROUEN

17th century timbered Norman farmhouse in the heart of the country with a duck pond. You could visit the abbeys in the region but you are more likely to decide to stay and be enthralled by the warm smile and welcome of Marie-Cécile. On sale: Cider, home-made jam.

PROPERTY

✱✱✱

off street parking, garden, lounge, hosts have pets, telephone, kitchen, wheelchair access, no smoking, river watersports 4km, golf course 15km, sea or lake watersports 45km

Basic English spoken

—At Rouen, take the A15 towards Dieppe sur Le Havre for 3km. Take the Exit to Maromme and keep to the right. On the roundabout take the 3rd road, the D43 towards Duclair. Continue for 4km.

PRICE STRUCTURE

5 Bedrooms

Rose: television, shower room with wc, double bed: FF220

Bleue: wheelchair access, television, shower room with sc, twin beds: FF220

Iris: television, shower room with wc, double bed, single bed: FF220 (2 people), FF320 (3 people)

Palmiers: television, shower room with wc, double bed, 2 single beds: FF220 (2 people) FF420 (4 people)

Rhododendron: television, shower room with wc, washbasin, double bed: FF220

Extra bed: FF45/100
Reduction: children

Capacity: 13 people

Annie & Roger
AUDIBERT

Cidex 21
76690 FRICHEMESNIL

Tel: (0) 2 35 33 59 13

Residence of character

25 km - N - ROUEN
FRICHEMESNIL:
station 3km
airport 40km
car essential
— From Rouen, take the A28 towards Abbeville. Take Exit 11 and take the N29 towards Totes. After 6km, turn left on to the D151 towards Bosc le Hard, and then Frichmesnil. The cottage is the third house after the church.

76.16 ROUEN

This is an authentic, 350 year-old Normandy half-timbered cottage, in a landscaped garden. The little village has a listed church, and from here you can travel the roads of Haute-Normandie. On sale: farm produce.

PROPERTY

private parking, garden, tv lounge, no pets, dinner available, babies welcome, free cot, hiking, cycling 3km, interesting flora 3km, golf course 8km, sea or lake watersports 30km

Adequate English spoken

PRICE STRUCTURE

1 Bedroom

bathroom with wc, double bed, twin beds: FF250 (2 people) FF460 (4 people)

Extra bed: 100FF
Reduction: 3 nights

Capacity: 4 people

ENGLISH CHANNEL
Guernsey (to UK)
Jersey (to UK)
ATLANTIC OCEAN
Cherbourg
Dieppe
Le Havre
ROUEN
76
HAUTE NORMANDIE
CAEN
Lisieux
St. Lô
50
14
BASSE NORMANDIE
27
Evreux
Vire
Lannion
Argentan
St. Malo
Avranches
Guingamp
Dreux
St. Brieuc
Dinan
61
28
Alençon
22
BRETAGNE
Fougères
Chartres
53
Pontivy
RENNES
72
35
Laval
Châteaudun
56
Le Mans
Lorient
Vannes
Vendôme
Redon
Châteaubriant
41
Blois
PAYS DE LA LOIRE
44
Angers
CENTRE
49
Tours
St. Nazaire
NANTES
Saumur
37
Cholet
36
Châtellerault
Châteauroux
85
La Roche
POITIERS
les Sables-d'Olonne
79
86
Niort
POITOU CHARENTES
La Rochelle
87
Rochefort
16
Saintes
LIMOGES
Cognac
Royan
17
Angoulême
LIMOUSIN

Josiane BELORDE

«Chateau du Plessis»
44860 PONT SAINT
MARTIN

tel: (0) 2 40 26 81 72
fax: (0) 2 40 32 76 67
http://www.chateaux-france.com/-plessis

Château

10 km - S - NANTES PONT SAINT MARTIN: hosts can collect from station, station 15km, airport 5km car essential

44.04 NANTES

An austere and authentic looking Breton château, dating from the 15th century, with a magnificent rose garden. Inside it is cosily furnished with antiques. Madame Belorde is a lovely person and typical of the modern French aristocracy. Near to the airport, but no noise problem.

PRICE STRUCTURE

4 Bedrooms

Anne de Bretagne: bathroom with wc, twin beds: FF900

Napoléon: bathroom with wc, twin beds: FF600

Duchesse de Berry: bathroom with wc, double bed: FF800

Enfants: twin beds: FF300

Extra bed in room: 150/200FF Reduction: 2 nights and children

Capacity: 10 people

PROPERTY

****

private parking, extensive gardens, tv lounge, hosts have pets, no pets, telephone, dinner available, babies welcome, free cot, hiking, cycling, fishing 1km, golf course 15km

Adequate English spoken

— At Nantes, take the N137 towards Bordeaux. Turn right on to the D65 towards Pont St Martin. The château is after Pont St Martin, on the left (follow the signs 'Monument Historique').

Antonio FALANGA

«Château de St Thomas
44360 ST ETIENNE DE
MONTLUC

tel: (0) 2 40 85 90 60
fax: (0) 2 40 86 97 62

Château

25 km - N W -
NANTES
ST ETIENNE DE
MONTLUC:
airport 20km
car essential

44.05 NANTES

A peaceful 19th century château surrounded by woods with a lake. You will be captivated by the charms of this young Italian host and his French wife. There are stables and archery in the grounds. An ideal place for playing golf and discovering the marshlands.

PROPERTY

****

private parking, extensive gardens, tv lounge, hosts have pets, no pets, dinner available, babies welcome, free cot, riding, hiking, cycling, fishing, golf course 8km, birdwatching 30km

PRICE STRUCTURE

5 Bedrooms

Saumon: television, bathroom with wc, double bed: FF650

Verte; bathroom with wc, twin beds: FF650

Bleue: bathroom with wc, double bed: FF650

Rouge & Romantique: bathroom with wc, double bed: FF650

Extra bed in room: 100FF
Reduction: 01.10–31.05

Capacity: 10 people

— At Nantes, take the N165 towards Vannes and leave it at St Etienne de Montluc. In the village, after the large town hall square ('Mairie'), take the 2nd road on the left.

Gérard & Annick
BOUSSEAU

«Domaine de La
Penissière»
44690 CHATEAU-
THEBAUD

tel: (0) 2 40 06 51 22
fax: (0) 2 40 06 51 22

Private home

25 km - S E -
NANTES
CHATEAU
THEBAUD:
airport 15km
car essential

44.06 NANTES

This is a wine grower's house, quietly situated amongst the vines. It goes without saying that you will be able to taste their own wines free of charge in the cellar. You will enjoy the kindness of Annick and her delicious fireside dinners. On sale: Their own Muscadet wine.

PRICE STRUCTURE

4 Bedrooms

Blanche, Jaune & Rose: television, shower room with wc, double bed: FF230

Rez de chaussée: shower room with wc, double bed: FF230

Extra bed in room: 70FF

Capacity: 9 people

PROPERTY

✱✱✱

private parking, garden, tv lounge, hosts have pets, dinner available, babies welcome, free cot, hiking 1km, fishing 1km, sea or lake watersports 40km

— At Nantes, take the N137 towards Bordeaux. Turn left on to the D63 then D58 towards Château-Thébaud. Follow the signs 'Chambres d'hotes' then 'Domaine de la Pénissière'.

Marcel & Yvonne
PINEAU

«La Mercerais»
44130 BLAIN

tel: (0) 2 40 79 04 30

Private house

30 km - N - NANTES
BLAIN: Nearest
airport 35km
car essential

44.08 NANTES

From the welcoming apéritif on arrival, Marcel and Yvonne will receive you like friends of the family and give you tips on the attractions of their region. The house has a beautiful flower garden and is near the forest of Gâvre and La Baule.

PROPERTY

Private parking, extensive grounds, lounge, no pets, no smoking, cycling, fishing 1km, birdwatching 25km, sea or lake watersports 30km

PRICE STRUCTURE

3 Bedrooms

Rose: bathroom with shower, 2 double beds, single bed: FF265 (2 people) FF460 (5 people)

Bleue: bathroom with shower, double bed, single bed: FF265 (2 people) FF330 (3 people)

Bas: double bed: FF265 (2 people)

Extra bed in room: 15/65FF

Capacity: 10 people

Directions:- At Nantes, take the N137 towards Rennes for 22km. Turn left on to the D164 towards Blain - Redon. At Blain, turn right on to the N171 towards Nozay. After 3km at the cross, turn right twice.

Madeleine & Marcel HECAUD

«Le Gravier»
44130 BLAIN

tel: (0) 2 40 79 10 25

Private house

44.14 NANTES

Just a few minutes from Nantes, La Baule and Vannes, Madeleine and Marcel invite you to the peace and quiet of her longhouse near the Nantes-Brest canal. The centre of Blain is close by and you are only a short walk away from the restaurants and the medieval château.

PROPERTY

✱✱

off street parking, garden, hosts have pets, kitchen available, babies free, cot supplied, cycling, fishing, mushroom picking 4km, river watersports 5km, golf course 17km

Basic English spoken

30 km - N - NANTES
BLAIN:
Railway station 18km
Nearest airport 30km
Directions:- In Nantes, take the N137 towards Rennes, then the D164 towards Redon. In Blain, head towards St. Nazaire and Le Château. After crossing the canal bridge, take the first right. It is the second house on the right.

PRICE STRUCTURE

2 Bedrooms

Bathroom, double bed: FF235

Telephone, bathroom with shower, double bed, 2 single beds: FF235(2 people) FF355 (4 people)

Extra bed in room: 60FF
Reduction: 6 nights

Capacity: 6 people

Françoise
LEBARILLIER

«Le Relais de la Rinière»
44430 LE LANDREAU

tel: (0) 2 40 06 41 44
lariniere@chez.com

Private house

10 km - E - NANTES
LE LANDREAU:
Hosts will collect from station
Nearest airport 25km
car essential

44.15 NANTES

Your charming hostess will welcome you to her new house, having moved from Normandy, where she wowed her guests, particularly with her home-made jam! Now on the main Nantes to Cholet road, she welcomes you to her 19th century house with a large garden.

PROPERTY

***

Private parking, garden, tv lounge, hosts have pets, babies free, cot supplied

Adequate English spoken

PRICE STRUCTURE

3 Bedrooms

(2) Television, bathroom with shower, double bed: FF260

(1) Television, bathroom with shower, 2 single beds: FF260

Extra bed in room: 60FF

Capacity: 6 people

Directions:- On the Nantes-Cholet dual carriageway (N249), Exit Vallet and take the D37 towards Landrau. 1km before you reach Landrau, turn right towards La Renouère, and then La Rinière.

Claude-Anne &
Jean-Noël LEAUTE

«Le Rêve Bleu»
10, impasse Arc en Ciel
44210 PORNIC

tel: (0) 2 40 82 92 22

Private house

18 km - S -
ST NAZAIRE
PORNIC: Hosts will collect from station
Rail station 2km
Nearest airport 45km
car essential

44.16 ST NAZAIRE

This large, new house full of light is near to Pornic, a pleasant seaside resort. Breakfast is served in the spacious, sparkling dining room, and the "Romantique" bedroom is much appreciated by guests. They plan to have a large conservatory finished by the summer of 2000, which will make it even more attractive.

PRICE STRUCTURE

3 Bedrooms

La Romantique: Television, Telephone, Bathroom with bath, Double bed: FF340

Merisier & Chambre: 3 Lounge, Telephone, Kitchen, Double bed: FF250

Extra bed in room: 30FF
Reduction: 01.03–30.06

Capacity: 6 people

PROPERTY

***

off street parking, garden, tv lounge, hosts have pets, telephone, babies free, cot supplied, hiking 1km, cycling 2km, fishing 2km, interesting flora 2km, golf course 4km, sea or lake watersports 4km, birdwatching 7km, river watersports 26km

Basic English spoken

Directions:- Coming from Nantes on the D751, 3km before Pornic, just after the level crossing, turn left towards La Fontaine aux Bretons. Then follow the signs.

Pays-de-la-Loire

ANGERS

Noël VANDENBERGHE LEBBE

«Château de la Beuvrière»
49220 GREZ-NEUVILLE

tel: (0) 2 41 37 67 67
fax: (0) 2 41 95 24 16

Château

20 km - N W - ANGERS
GREZ NEUVILLE:
Rail station 25km
Nearest airport 20km
car essential

49.01 ANGERS

Your hosts are charming. This imposing 19th century château is surrounded by 36 hectares of wooded grounds. They have their own 9 hectare lake with an island that you can reach by boat. You will be impressed by the superb Gothic chapel. Large bedrooms.

PROPERTY

****

off street parking, extensive grounds, TV lounge, hosts have pets, no pets, dinner available, hiking, golf course 10km

English spoken

Directions:- At Angers, take the N162 towards Laval for 18km. Turn left on to the D291.

PRICE STRUCTURE

11 Bedrooms

Gothique: bathroom with shower, double bed: FF870

14: bathroom with shower, 2 single beds: FF640

26 & 24: bathroom with shower, double bed: FF585

34: bathroom with shower, double bed: FF485

16: bathroom with shower, double bed, single bed: FF740 (2 people) FF785 (4 people)

4 & 12: Bathroom with bath, double bed: FF870

2 & 8: Bathroom with bath, double bed: FF740

36: Bathroom with bath, twin beds, single bed: FF840

Extra bed in room: 65FF

Capacity: 23 people

Jacqueline & Auguste BAHUAUD

«La Croix d'Etain»
2, rue de l'Ecluse
49220 GREZ NEUVILLE

tel: (0) 2 41 95 68 49

Manor House

20 km - N W - ANGERS
GREZ NEUVILLE:
Hosts will collect from station
Rail station 25km
Nearest airport 20km

PRICE STRUCTURE

4 Bedrooms

Verte: Bathroom, 2 single beds: FF450

Bleue: Bathroom, Double bed: FF380

Rose: Bathroom, Double bed, Single bed: FF380 (2 people) FF480 (4 people)

Blanche: Bathroom, 2 single beds: FF450

Extra bed in room: 100FF
Reduction: 01.11–30.03 and 3 nights and groups

Capacity: 9 people

49.02 ANGERS

This manor house from the Directoire period is beside the Mayenne, in a conservation area. The rooms are spacious and cosy. Unique decor. A delightful area, full of châteaux and vineyards. Do not miss a visit to the slate mine or hire a cruiser on the river (no permit required).

PROPERTY

✱✱✱

private parking, extensive grounds, TV lounge, hosts have pets, telephone, dinner available, babies free, cot supplied, hiking, fishing, golf course 10km

Adequate English spoken

Directions:- At Angers, take the N162 towards Laval for 20km. Turn right towards Grez-Neuville and continue for 1.5km. The property is between the church and the river.

49.04 ANGERS

Susan and Peter, a friendly English couple, have painstakingly restored this 1850's farmhouse, situated in 18 hectares of grounds. It is 15km from a race-course and in a region that counts no less than 8 golf courses. In each room there are tea and coffee making facilities. There is a full size snooker table in the lounge and Russian billiards. English Breakfast: + 35FF/Pers.

Peter & Susan-Ann SCARBORO

«La Chaufournaie»
49500 CHAZE sur ARGOS

tel: (0) 2 41 61 49 05
fax: (0) 2 41 61 49 05

Residence of character

PROPERTY

***

off street parking, extensive grounds, TV lounge, hosts have pets, no pets, dinner available, fishing 4km, mushroom picking 12km, hiking 15km, cycling 15km, river watersports 20km, golf course 25km, bird-watching 30km, sea or lake watersports 30km

Fluent English spoken

PRICE STRUCTURE

5 Bedrooms

Mme de Fontenay & Miss France: bathroom with shower, double bed: FF240

Miss Guadeloupe & Miss Orléanais: bathroom with shower, 2 single beds: FF240

Miss Paris: bathroom with shower, double bed, single bed; FF240 (2 people) FF320 (3 people)

Extra bed in room: 90FF

Capacity: 11 people

35 km - N W - ANGERS
CHAZE SUR ARGOS: rail station: 35km
nearest airport: 100km
car essential
Directions:- At Angers, take the N162 towards Laval. At Le Lion d'Angers, turn left on to the D770 towards Candé. The house is on this road, 3km after Vern d'Anjou.

49.12 ANGERS

Totally authentic. Not a 'château-hotel' but a real château whose floors creak and which has been lived in by the same family for 6 generations. The grounds are magnificent with a lake, swans and charming little nooks and crannies. Real class, relaxation, luxury... sheer pleasure. On sale: Anjou wine and honey.

François de VALBRAY

«Château des Briottières»
49330 CHAMPIGNÉ

tel: (0) 2 41 42 00 02
fax: (0) 2 41 42 01 55
briottieres@wanadoo.fr
www.briottieres.com

Château

PROPERTY

****

private parking, extensive grounds, TV lounge, no pets, telephone, dinner available, packed lunch, babies free, cot supplied, swimming pool, horse riding, hiking, cycling, fishing, golf course 3km, river watersports 7km, hunting 60km

English spoken

PRICE STRUCTURE

15 Bedrooms and 3 suites and 2 apartments

Château-Rose: Bridal room, Television, Telephone, Bathroom, Shower room, Double bed: FF1620

Château-Etang: Telephone, Bathroom, Shower room, 2 single beds: FF1320

Château-Petite Rose: Telephone, Bathroom, Shower room, Double bed: FF1020

Amis: Telephone, Bathroom, Shower room, Double bed: FF870

Fruitière-Cottage: Telephone, Bathroom, Shower room, Double bed: FF770

Fruitière-Cottage-2: Telephone, Bathroom, Shower room, twin beds, Single bed: FF570

Extra bed in room: 150FF

Capacity: 13 people

25 km - N - ANGERS
CHAMPIGNE:
Rail station 25km
Nearest airport 110km
Car essential
Directions:- From the A11, Exit 11 (Durtal). Head towards Châteauneuf sur Sarthe and Champigné, where you follow the signs. (From Angers, take the N162 towards Laval. Turn right on to the D768 towards Champigné.)

Michel & Françoise
TOUTAIN

«Le Prieuré de
Vendanger»
D62 - Vendanger
49150 LE GUEDENIAU

tel: (0) 2 41 67 82 37
fax: (0) 2 41 67 82 43
toutainf.wanadoo.fr

Residence of character

40 km - E - ANGERS
VENDANGER:
Hosts will collect from station
Rail station 40km
Nearest airport 40km
Car essential

49.13 ANGERS

This 16th century priory converted into a "gentilhommière" in the 19th century, has been restored by your hosts, with an original, baroque decor. Surrounded by high woods, there is a lake where you can fish. Billiards, golf lessons, hunting, themed holidays, candle-lit dinners, a piano, a swimming pool... What a delight! On sale: Coffee, home-made jam, sculptures. 1 self-catering apartment, rented weekly.

PROPERTY

✱✱✱

off street parking, extensive grounds, TV lounge, hosts have pets, no pets, telephone, dinner available, packed lunch, babies free, cot supplied, swimming pool, hiking, cycling, fishing, hunting, mushroom picking, golf course 12km

Adequate English spoken

Directions:- At Angers, take the N147 towards Longué. At Beaufort, turn left on to the D7 towards Mouliherne and then take the D62 at the Bois Mandet crossroads. The house is on this road, 5km along on the left, before Mouliherne, after the woods.

PRICE STRUCTURE

4 Bedrooms

Chantepleure: Bathroom, Double bed, 3 Single beds: FF395 (2 people) FF650 (5 people)

Cannelle: Bathroom, Double bed, Single bed: FF340 (2 people) FF425 (3 people)

Jabloir: Bathroom, Double bed: FF340

Cascaret: Bathroom, Double bed: FF340

Clairette: Bathroom, 2 Single beds: FF340

Extra bed in room: 85FF
Reduction: 3 nights and children

Capacity: 14 people

Jeanne CHARPENTIER

«La Rousselière»
49170 LA
POSSONNIERE

tel: (0) 2 41 39 13 21
fax: (0) 2 41 39 13 21

Residence of character

20 km - S W - ANGERS
LA POSSONNIERE: Rail station 3km
Nearest airport 80km
Car essential
Directions:- At Angers, take the N23 towards Nantes. In St Georges sur Loire, turn left on to the D961 towards Chalonnes for 3km. Just before the railway bridge, turn left on to the D111 towards La Possonnière. Continue for 1.5km and then turn left.

49.15 ANGERS

This beautiful 18th century residence on the slopes of La Loire has kept its olde-worlde charm. Enjoy breakfast and dinner on the terrace or a siesta by the pool. An excellent address due to its location, the atmosphere and, above all, Jeanne's welcome.

PROPERTY

***

off street parking, extensive grounds, TV lounge, hosts have pets, telephone, dinner available, babies free, cot supplied, swimming pool closed 12/11-12/12, cycling, hiking 3km, fishing 3km, birdwatching 3km, river watersports 4km, mushroom picking 6km, hunting 7km, interesting flora 8km, golf course 18km, gliding 20km

Basic English spoken

PRICE STRUCTURE

6 Bedrooms

Les Roses: Television, Telephone, Bathroom , 2 single beds: FF400

Les Oiseaux: bathroom with shower, 2 single beds: FF300

Rêve Bleu: Television, Telephone, Bathroom, Double bed: FF400

Fleurs Bleues: Television, Bathroom, Double bed, 2 Single bed: FF400 (2 people) FF580 (4 people)

Les Marroniers & Les Clématites: bathroom with shower, Double bed, Single bed: FF300 (2 people) FF390 (3 people)

Extra bed in room: 90FF
Reduction: 7 nights

Capacity: 16 people

Marie-Hélène & François de ROCQUIGNY

«La Cotinière»
Le Clos d'Aligny 49320
GREZILLE

tel: (0) 2 41 59 72 21
fax: (0) 2 41 59 72 21

Residence of character

20 km - SE - ANGERS
GREZILLE: Railway station 30 km,
airport: 100km,
car essential
At Angers, go towards Niort-Poitiers. At Les Alleuds (on the D761), turn left towards Grezille. At Grezille, take the D161 towards Louerre. Le Clos d'Aligny is 2 km from the village.

49.23 ANGERS

The welcome is warm and attentive, like old friends in this old Anjou farmhouse. Choose between the rooms with white stone walls or the old vine press (with a very unusual staircase), right next to the cellars carved out of the rock

PROPERTY

***

private parking, garden, TV lounge, hosts have pets, telephone, dinner available, babies welcome, cot free, hiking, interesting flora, cycling, fishing, sea or lake watersports, golf course

English spoken

PRICE STRUCTURE

3 Bedrooms

(2) telephone, double bed, single bed: FF290 (2 people) FF360 (3 people)

Pressoir: telephone, bathroom with wc, double bed, 4 single beds: FF290 (2 people) FF530 (6 people)

Extra bed 90FF
Reduction: 5 nights

Capacity: 12 people

72.16 ANGERS

his dynamic young couple have 17 rooms available in this arge house, all of which are equally comfortable and pleasnt. Le Haras de la Potardière is also ideal for wedding receptions or special events etc. It is near the Loire Valley hâteaux, with the mild Anjou weather as a bonus.

PROPERTY

****

private parking, extensive grounds, lounge, hosts have pets, telephone, kitchen available, babies free, cot supplied, wheelchair access, swimming pool, tennis court, hiking, cycling, interesting flora, mushroom picking, birdwatching, fishing 3km, sea or lake watersports 9km, river watersports 9km, gliding 10km

English spoken

RICE STRUCTURE

Bedrooms

Ihât.-1°: Rose: Television, Telephone, Bathroom, Double bed: FF630

Ihât.-1°: Bleue: Television, Telephone, Bathroom, 2 single beds: FF630

Ihât.-1°: Verte: Television, Telephone, bathroom with shower, bath, Double bed: FF630

Ihât.-1°: Saumon: Television, Telephone, bathroom with shower, bath, Double bed, Single bed: FF680 (2 people) FF720 (3 people)

Ihât.-2°: Giverny: Lounge, Television, Telephone, bathroom with shower, bath, Double bed, 2 Single beds: FF980 (2 people) FF1060 (4 people)

Ihât.-2°: Néogothique: Lounge, Television, Telephone, bathroom with shower, bath, Double bed, Single bed: FF980 (2 people) FF1020 (3 people)

Haras-RDC: 1°: Television, Telephone, bathroom with shower, 2 single beds: FF480

Haras-RDC: 2°: Television, Telephone, Bathroom, 2 single beds: FF530

Haras-RDC: 3°: Television, Telephone, Bathroom, Double bed: FF530

Haras-1°: 4°: Television, Telephone, bathroom with shower, bath, twin beds, 2 single beds: FF680 (2 people) FF760 (4 people)

Haras-1°: 5°: Television, Telephone, Bathroom, Double bed: FF530

Haras-1°: 6°& 7°& 8°: Television, Telephone, bathroom with shower, bath, Double bed: FF530

Haras-1°: 9°: Television, Telephone, bathroom with shower, bath, twin beds, Single bed: FF580 (2 people) FF620 (3 people)

Haras : 10°: Lounge, Television, Telephone, Bathroom, Double bed: 2 single beds: FF680 (2 people) FF760 (4 people)

Extra bed in room: 150FF

Capacity: 41 people

François & Marie BENOIST

«Haras de la Potardière»Route de Bazouges-sur-le-Loir
72200 CROSMIÈRES

tel: (0) 2 43 45 83 47
fax: (0) 2 43 45 81 06

Manor House

45 km - N E - ANGERS
CROSMIERES: Rail station 18km
Nearest airport 45km
Car essential
Directions:- At Angers on the A11 towards Le Mans take Exit Sablé. Then follow the D306 towards La Flèche for 5km. In Crosmières turn right towards Bazouges. It is the second residence on the right after 3km.

Pays-de-la-Loire

SAUMUR

Christine DIGUET

«Le Moulin de Couché-La Ponote»
49260 LE PUY NOTRE DAME

tel: (0) 2 41 38 87 11
fax: (0) 2 41 38 86 99

Residence of character

20 km - S W - SAUMUR
LE PUY NOTRE DAME: Rail station 20km
Nearest airport 140km
Car essential

PRICE STRUCTURE

7 Bedrooms and 2 suites

Coquelicot & Géranium: Television, bathroom with shower, Double bed: FF350

Lilas & Pensée: Lounge, Television, Shower room, wc, Double bed: FF320

Primevère + Dahlia: television, bathroom with shower, 2 double beds: FF440 (2 people) FF560 (4 people)

Cyclamen + Jacinthe: television, bathroom with shower, 2 double beds, FF490 (2 people) FF560 (4 people)

Violette: Television, bathroom with shower, Double bed: FF350

Hortensia: Television, bath, wc, Double bed: FF350

Bleuet: Lounge, Television, bathroom with shower, 2 Double bed: FF490 (2 people) FF560 (4 people)

Extra bed in room: 95FF

Capacity: 24 people

49.08 SAUMUR

Impossible to describe until you have experienced it. The wonderful, friendly atmosphere at this water mill dating from 15th century, in the heart of the Saumur wine country has convinced us that you must stop here! Christine can advise you on the best wine cellars in the area. The restaurant is in the restored barn, and the bedrooms are in the old mill house.

PROPERTY

private parking, extensive grounds, TV lounge, hosts have pets, telephone, dinner available, packed lunch, Closed 15/10-01/04, hiking, cycling, river watersports 7km, sea or lake watersports 20km

Fluent English spoken

Directions:- At Saumur, take the N147 towards Loudun-Poitiers. At the 2nd roundabout at Montreuil-Bellay, take the D938 towards Thouars for 4km. Turn right on to the D158 towards Passais-Sanziers. The 'Moulin' is on the left, after the bridge on the river. (Signposted).

Dominique & Rosine
DAUGE

«Le Domaine de Mestré»
49590 FONTEVRAUD
L'ABBAYE

tel: (0) 2 41 51 72 32
fax: (0) 2 41 51 71 90

Residence of character

15 km - S E -
SAUMUR
FONTEVRAUD
L'ABBAYE: Nearest airport 150km
Car essential

49.16 SAUMUR

This farming estate has been in the same family since the 18th century, and in fact the whole family will welcome you. Comfort, elegance and excellent cuisine. Be sure to bring back some of their pure soap made from an old recipe. On sale: Soap.

PROPERTY

✱✱✱

off street parking, extensive grounds, TV lounge, telephone, dinner available, packed lunch, babies free, cot supplied, Closed 20/12-1/02, fishing, hunting, mushroom picking, hiking 5km, golf course 6km, cycling 15km, sea or lake watersports 15km, river watersports 15km, gliding 15km

English spoken

PRICE STRUCTURE

11 Bedrooms and 1 suite

1° & Sissi: Bathroom, Single bed: FF280

Rouge & Lits blancs & Oiseaux: Bathroom, 2 single beds: FF405

Bleue & Kinette & Abricot & Pommes: Bathroom, Double bed: FF405

La Suite: Bathroom, 2 Single bed: FF750

Les raisins: Bathroom, 2 Double bed: FF405 (2 people) FF730 (4 people)

8° Bathroom, Double bed, Single bed (childrens size): FF510

Extra bed in room: 85FF
Reduction: 5 nights

Capacity: 29 people

Directions:- In Saumur, take the D947 towards Chinon - Montsoreau where you turn right towards Fontevraud. Continue for 2km. The property is on the right.

François-Charles &
Annick WILLIOT

«Château du Bas du Gast»
6, rue de la Halle aux Toiles
53000 LAVAL

tel: (0) 2 43 49 22 79
fax: (0) 2 43 56 44 71

Château

LAVAL
Hosts will collect from station
Rail station 1km
Nearest airport 5km

53.01 LAVAL

A quiet, historic house, right in the centre of the town. The spacious bedrooms have a lot of class. Your hosts have conserved the ancient box trees that date from the 18th century. You will enjoy meeting these hosts, who speak perfect English. English Breakfast : + 30 FF/Person.

PROPERTY

✸✸✸✸

private parking, extensive grounds, lounge, hosts have pets, closed 1/12-31/01, cycling, golf course 4km

Fluent English spoken

PRICE STRUCTURE

3 Bedrooms

Napoléon: Bathroom, Shower room, Double bed, Single bed: FF750 (2 people) FF1050 (3 people)

Jaune: Bathroom, Double bed: FF650

Jouy: Bathroom, 2 single beds: FF700

Bleue + Verte: bathroom, shower, double bed, 2 single beds: FF570 (2 people) FF1350 (4 people)

Extra bed in room: 200/300FF

Capacity: 11 people

Directions:- In the centre of Laval, Follow signs to the 'Salle Polyvalente' or the 'Bibliothèque Municipale'. Le Bas du Gast is close by.

53.03 LAVAL

Lionel & Françoise
RABOURG

«La Charbonnerie»
53320 LOIRON

tel: (0) 2 43 02 44 74
fax: (0) 2 43 02 44 74

Working Farm

If you are near Laval, do not miss this farm. Although in the depths of the countryside, is not far off the main road. The two bedrooms are in a charming little house, separate from the main farm. The welcome is warm and sincere. On sale: Cider, Pommeau.

PROPERTY

✱✱

off street parking, TV lounge, hosts have pets, dinner available, kitchen available, babies free, cot supplied, fishing 4km, hiking 8km, golf course 15km, sea or lake watersports 15km, gliding 20km

PRICE STRUCTURE

2 Bedrooms

Charme Bridal room: Bathroom, 2 single beds, Single bed: FF260 (2 people) FF310 (3 people)
bathroom with shower Double bed: FF230

Extra bed in room: 50FF

Capacity: 5 people

13 km - W - LAVAL
LOIRON: Nearest airport 20km
car essential
Directions:- At Laval, take the N157 towards Rennes. 7km after St Berthevin, turn left (there is a sign) and continue for 3km. From Rennes, on the right, 2 km after the "Loiron" crossroads.

Geneviève THIBAULT

«le Grand Perray»
72500 LA BRUERE

tel: (0) 2 43 46 72 65
fax: (0) 2 43 46 72 65

Château

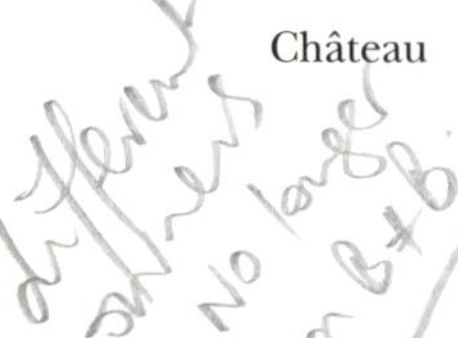

40 km - S - LE MANS
LA BRUERE:
Hosts will collect from station
Rail station 8km
Nearest airport 40km

72.03 LE MANS

You can easily imagine the ghost of the Knight Duguesclin's mistress waiting at the window in the 13th century tower of this château. Even the peacocks have their secrets. Yet these are happy memories, and so will your stay be, in this quiet and restful place.

PRICE STRUCTURE

9 Bedrooms

Tour: bathroom with shower, Double bed: FF500

2° & 3°: Television, Bathroom, Shower room, Double bed, Single bed: FF480 (2 people) FF520 (3 people)

4°: Bathroom, Shower room, 2 single beds: FF480

5°: Bathroom, Shower room, Double bed: FF400 (2 people) FF520 (3 people)

6°: Television Bathroom, Shower room, Double bed: FF380

7°: Television, Bathroom, Shower room, 2 single beds: FF380

8°: bathroom with shower, 2 single beds: FF380

Reduction: 5 nights

Capacity: 18 people

PROPERTY

✸✸✸

off street parking, extensive grounds, TV lounge, hosts have pets, dinner available, babies free, cot supplied, fishing, sea or lake watersports 12km, golf course 20km

Basic English spoken

Directions:- At Le Mans, take the N138 towards Tours. After Château du Loir at La Croix de Bonlieu, turn right on to the D7 towards La Bruère. When you reach Gué de Mézières, follow the signs.

Margaret ALLENET

«Château de la Vivantière»
72510 ST JEAN DE LA MOTTE

tel: (0) 2 43 45 29 15
fax: (0) 2 43 45 29 15
oallenet@aol.com

Château

30 km - S - LE MANS
ST JEAN DE LA MOTTE: Hosts will collect from station
Rail station 30km
Nearest airport 30km
Car essential

72.11 LE MANS

This château, built in the 17th century, was restored under Napoleon III. Delightful rooms make the choice extremely difficult. Such cooking, charm, kindness and the warm welcome of Margaret are sure to make you extend your stay. On sale: Goat's cheese.

PROPERTY

✱✱✱✱

private parking, extensive grounds, TV lounge, hosts have pets, telephone, dinner available, packed lunch, babies free, cot supplied, mushroom, picking, hiking 3km, cycling 3km, fishing 3km, sea or lake watersports 3km, river watersports 3km, gliding 12km, golf course 15km, hunting, 15km

English spoken

PRICE STRUCTURE

3 Bedrooms and 1 suite

Le Printemps: Lounge, Television, Telephone, Bathroom, Double bed: FF450

L'été: Television, Telephone, bathroom with shower, Double bed: FF350

L'Automne: Television, Telephone, Bathroom, Double bed: FF550

L'Hiver: Television, Telephone, bathroom with shower, Single bed: FF400

Reduction: 6 nights and groups and children

Capacity: 8 people

Directions:- At Le Mans, take the N23 towards Angers. At 'Point du jour', take the D54 on the left, towards St Jean de la Motte and continue for 2 km towards Mansigné.

72.13 LE MANS

Francis & Christine BERNAUD

«Ferme des Petites Landes»
72510 MANSIGNÉ

tel: (0) 2 43 46 16 96
fax: (0) 2 43 46 16 96

Working Farm

35 km - S - LE MANS
MANSIGNE: Hosts will collect from station
Rail station 35km
car essential
Directions:- At Le Mans, take the N23 towards Angers. At Le Chêne Vert, turn left and cross La Fontaine St Martin towards Mansigné. The farm is on the right, 5km after La Fontaine St Martin.

A friendly young couple with 3 children. The large bedrooms are very bright and comfortable, and the bathrooms spacious. Only 10min. from the famous Château de Lude. 30min. from Le Mans. Christine and Francis can also organise cycling tours (bikes can be hired).

PROPERTY

✸

private parking, garden, television, hosts have pets, dinner available, packed lunch, babies free, cot supplied, hiking, cycling, interesting flora, mushroom picking, birdwatching, sea or lake watersports 4km, river watersports 8km, golf course 10km

English spoken

PRICE STRUCTURE

2 Bedrooms

Kitchen, bathroom with shower, washbasin, Double bed, 2 Single beds: FF260 (2 people) FF320 (4 people)

Kitchen, bathroom with shower, washbasin, Double bed, 3 Single beds: FF260 (2 people) FF380 (5 people)

Extra bed in room: 50FF

Capacity: 9 people

Eliane & Jean-Louis
BRAZILIER

«Les 14 Boisselées»
Route de Château
du Loir
72800 LE LUDE

tel: (0) 2 43 94 90 65

Private house

30 km - S - LE MANS
LE LUDE: Rail station 10km
Nearest airport 160km
Car essential

72.17 LE MANS

Eliane and Jean-Louis are teachers and adore conversation. There is a family atmosphere here and you will certainly feel at home. Their cooking is refined and of a high quality. There are many trails for hikers and mountain bikers in the Vallée du Loir, and the Château de Lude should not be missed!

PROPERTY

✱✱

private parking, extensive grounds, lounge, no pets, dinner available, babies free, cot supplied, no smoking, hiking, fishing, mushroom picking, cycling 2km, golf course 40km

Adequate English spoken

Directions:- From Le Mans go to La Flèche via the A11 or the N23 towards Angers. Then take the D306 towards Le Lude and the D305 towards Château du Loir for 2km.

PRICE STRUCTURE

2 Bedrooms

Rez de chaussée: (corridor) bathroom with shower, Double bed: FF250

Etage: (corridor) Bathroom with bath, Double bed: FF250

Extra bed in room: 80FF

Capacity: 4 people

Pays-de-la-Loire

LE MANS

Laura ESQUIVEL

«Manoir du Riablay»
Rue St Jean
72500 CHATEAU DU LOIR

tel: (0) 2 43 44 20 20
fax: (0) 2 43 44 20 20
riablay@wanadoo.fr
perso.wanadoo.fr/riablay

Manor House

35 km - S E - LE MANS
CHATEAU DU LOIR:
Rail station 2km
Nearest airport 220km

PRICE STRUCTURE

6 Bedrooms

Améthyste & Ambre & Emeraude & Malaquite: Bathroom, washbasin, Double bed: FF420

Manoir : Saphir & Rubis: Lounge, Bathroom, Double bed: FF470

Extra bed in room: 100FF
Reduction: 2 nights and groups

Capacity: 12 people

72.18 LE MANS

This listed Renaissance manor house is haunted by the ghosts of Ronsard and Henri IV. The bedrooms are the ultimate in luxury in period style. The cave villages and the châteaux of the Loir valley are well worth a visit. Excellent value for the standards offered.

PROPERTY

***

off street parking, extensive grounds, hosts have pets, no pets, dinner available, wheelchair access, swimming pool, tennis court, hiking, cycling, fishing 3km, hunting 5km, sea or lake watersports 10km, mushroom picking 15km, golf course 18km

Fluent English spoken

Directions:- At Le Mans take the N138 towards Tours. There is a sign to the manor on the right of the town hall (Mairie). At the end of the rue St Jean, level with the square François Verrier, turn left into the road leading to the rue Verte.

Geneviève DALMONT

3, rue Jahard
72500 CHATEAU DU LOIR

tel: (0) 2 43 44 21 26
fax: (0) 2 43 44 56 86

Residence of character

35 km - S E - LE MANS
CHATEAU DU LOIR: Rail station 1km
Nearest airport 40km
Car essential

72.23 LE MANS

This beautiful, late 19th century residence, listed as an historic monument, is very quiet yet situated in the centre of the town. It has a superb, wrought iron staircase lit by stained glass windows and bathrooms furnished with period pieces. You will appreciate Geneviève's courtesy. A place to stop, full of character on the Loire Valley châteaux run.

PROPERTY

✱✱✱

private parking, garden, hosts have pets, no pets, babies free, cot supplied, closed 01/10-01/04, hiking, cycling, fishing 2km, hunting 5km, mushroom picking 5km, sea or lake watersports 6km, golf course 18km

PRICE STRUCTURE

2 Bedrooms

Bleue: Telephone, bathroom with shower, Double bed, 2 Single bed: FF325 (2 people) FF575 (4 people)

Rose: Bathroom, Double bed, 2 Single bed: FF325 (2 people) FF575 (4 people)

Extra bed in room: 75FF
Reduction: 3 nights

Capacity: 8 people

Directions:- In Le Mans , take the N138 towards Tours. In the town centre, take the road on the left by the town hall, and then the first left. Rue Jahard is a one-way street.

Evelyne BLOUERE

«Gripouce»
72250 CHALLES

tel: (0) 2 43 75 81 16
fax: (0) 2 43 75 20 08

Residence of character

20 km - S E - LE MANS
CHALLES:
Rail station 20km
Car essential

Pays-de-la-Loire

LE MANS

PRICE STRUCTURE

1 Suite

Suite: Lounge, Kitchen, Bathroom, Double bed, Single bed, cot: FF500 (2 people) FF650 (4 people)

Capacity: 3 people

72.24 LE MANS

This old house is in a calm location, surrounded by woodland. It is only 15km from the famous Bugatti circuit at Le Mans. You can wander in the woods or visit the old town of Le Mans with its cathedral. This is a good base for visiting The Châteaux of the Loire Valley. On sale: Hand-painted Limoges china.

PROPERTY

***

off street parking, extensive grounds, hosts have pets, no pets, kitchen available, babies free, cot supplied, tennis court, hiking, golf course 20km

Fluent English spoken

Directions:- At Le Mans, take the D304 as far as Parigné l'Evêque. Then, take the D90 on the left towards Challes. Continue towards Volnay for 1km, then take the little road on the left.

85.08 FONTENAY LE COMTE

Daniel & Christiane MONTALT

«Château de la Cacaudière»
Thouarsais-Bouildroux
85410 LA CAILLÈRE

tel: (0) 2 51 51 59 27
fax: (0) 2 51 51 30 61

Château

Well worth a stop between Roscoff or St Malo and the Périgord. The bedrooms are very pretty, spacious and decorated in excellent taste. It is a pleasure to stop here. You could say English style 'à la Française'.

PROPERTY

✱✱✱✱

private parking, extensive grounds, TV lounge, babies free, cot supplied, swimming pool, hiking, cycling, fishing 15km, hunting 15km, golf course 50km

Fluent English spoken

20 km - N - FONTENAY LE COMTE
THOURSAIS: Nearest airport 105km
Car essential
Directions:- At Fontenay, take the D938T towards Bressuire and continue for 4km. At Pisotte, turn left on to the D904 towards Sérigné. Then take the D23 towards St Cyr des Gâts.-La Caillère St Hilaire. 2km before La Caillère, turn right towards Thouarsais and continue for 500m.

PRICE STRUCTURE

5 Bedrooms and 2 suites

Héloïse: Television, Telephone, Bathroom, Double bed: FF450

Adrienne: Television, Telephone, Bathroom, Double bed, single bed: FF580 (2 people) FF680, (3 people)

Alice: Television, Telephone, Bathroom, 2 single beds: FF580

Joséphine: Bathroom, 2 single beds: FF580

Victoria: Bathroom, Double bed: FF480

Rosalie: Bathroom, Double bed: FF450

Olivia: Bathroom, Double bed, 3 single beds: FF540 (2 people), FF750 (5 people)

Capacity: 18 people

85.10 FONTENAY LE COMTE

Josette GOURON

7, rue de Lattre de Tassigny -
L'Anglée
85770 LE POIRÉ
sur VELLUIRE

tel: (0) 2 51 52 35 95

Private house

Josette and her husband are very friendly and will give you a warm welcome to their house which they have completely restored themselves. Josette also has 20 years experience of making goat's cheese. You will enjoy chatting to this couple and listening to their wonderful stories.

PROPERTY

✱

off street parking, garden, TV lounge, dinner available, babies free, cot supplied, closed 30/09 - 10/11, 4 nights minimum stay, hiking, cycling, fishing 1km, mushroom picking 1km, birdwatching 1km, hunting 13km, sea or lake watersports 15km, river watersports 15km, interesting flora 35km

13 km - S W - FONTENAY LE COMTE
L'ANGLEE:
Rail station 50km
Nearest airport 50km
Car essential
Directions:- At Fontenoy le Comte take the D938 towards La Rochelle. Then take the D68 on the right for Velluire, Le Poiré sur Velluire then L'Anglée.

PRICE STRUCTURE

4 Bedrooms

Rez de Chaussée: 1: Double bed: FF200

Etage: 2 & 3: Double bed, Single bed: FF200 (2 people) FF300 (3 people)

Etage: 4: 2 single beds FF200

Extra bed in room: 100FF

Capacity: 10 people

Michèle BONNISSEAU

9, impasse de la Fosse
85420 BOUILLE-COUR-
DAULT

tel: (0) 2 51 52 42 17

Private house

10 km - S E - FONTENAY LE COMTE
BOUILLE COURDAULT: Rail station 17km
Car essential

85.11 FONTENAY LE COMTE

Michèle has wonderfully combined the typical characteristics of this region in the dining room, with modern functional bedrooms. The Japanese style bedroom is very unusual and attractive. This is a comfortable place to stop, and excellent value for money.

PROPERTY

***

garden, lounge, no pets, kitchen available, closed 15/09-15/06, hiking, cycling, fishing, interesting flora 6km, river watersports 10km, sea or lake watersports 50km

Fluent English spoken

PRICE STRUCTURE

2 Bedrooms

Chambre 1: Bathroom, washbasin, Double bed: FF210

Japon: Bridal room, Shower room, wc, washbasin, Double bed: FF240

Extra bed in room: 80FF
Reduction: 6 nights

Capacity: 4 people

Directions:- Between Niort and Fontenay le Comte (on the N148 or from the A83, Exit Oulmes). Head towards Courdault. In the village, take the road towards the harbour. Then take the cul-de-sac which leads off this road on the right.

Monique FAVRE

«La Pérotine»
23, rue Jean Moulin
85770 LE POIRE SUR VELLUIRE

tel: (0) 2 51 52 35 00

Private house

9 km - S W - FONTENAY LE COMTE
LE POIRE SUR VELLUIRE: Rail station 25km
Nearest airport 35km
Car essential

PRICE STRUCTURE

5 Bedrooms

Lavande: Lounge, Bathroom, 2 Double bed: FF370 (2 people) FF740 (4 people)

Rose & Lilas & Muguet & Pensée: Double bed: FF370

Extra bed in room: 100FF

Capacity: 12 people

85.12 FONTENAY LE COMTE

Monique's house is warm and friendly, and tastefully decorated. She welcomes you to this house, typical of La Vendée, in the heart of the Marais Poitevin. They have their own fishing, or will take you on a boat trip through the Venise Verte, or guide you in rambles in the nearby wildlife reserve. On sale: Honey, antiques.

PROPERTY

✱✱

off street parking, garden, TV lounge, no pets, babies free, cot supplied, hiking, cycling, fishing, interesting flora, mushroom picking, birdwatching, gliding 15km, sea or lake watersports 30km, golf course 35km

Basic English spoken

Directions:- From the A83 or from Fontenay le Comte, head towards La Rochelle on the D938. After 7km, turn right towards Velluire, La Poiré sur Velluire. The house is in the centre of this village.

George & Jane TREPT

«La Haute Rivoire»
85470 BRETIGNOLLES
SUR MER

tel: (0) 2 51 33 80 34
fax: (0) 2 51 33 80 34

Private house

20 km - N W - LES SABLES D'OLONNE BRETIGNOLLES SUR MER: Hosts will collect from station Rail station 6km Nearest airport 80km

85.06 LES SABLES D'OLONNE

This friendly British couple have restored this 18th century farmhouse, meticulously respecting the style of the Vendée. It is easy to find, but nevertheless quiet. Excellent surfing beaches are 1.5km away and there is riding nearby.

PROPERTY

✱✱

private parking, garden, lounge, hosts have pets, no pets, dinner available, packed lunch, extensive grounds, swimming pool, closed 01/11-15/04, 3 nights minimum stay 16/06-15/09, hiking, cycling, sea or lake watersports 2km, golf course 10km, birdwatching 12km

Fluent English spoken

Directions:- At Les Sables d'Olonne, go towards Olonne - St Gilles Croix de Vie. After Brétignolles, turn right on to the D12 towards La Chaize Giraud for 1km, then turn right and follow the signs.

PRICE STRUCTURE

3 Bedrooms and 2 apartments

1°: bathroom with shower, Double bed: FF380

2°: bathroom with shower, 2 Single bed: FF400

3°: Lounge, bathroom with shower, Double bed: FF400

Studio 1: 7 nights minimum stay, Lounge, Kitchen, Bathroom, Double bed: FF450

Studio 2: 7 nights minimum stay, Lounge, Kitchen, bathroom with shower, Double bed: FF425

Extra bed in room: 60FF
Reduction: 15.09–15.06

Capacity: 10 people

RENNES
Laval
72
Châteaudun
Le Mans
Vendôme
PAYS
DE LA LOIRE
Blois
Angers
44
41
49
Tours
St. Nazaire
Saumur
37
NANTES
Cholet
PAYS DE
LA LOIRE
Châtellerault
36
La Roche
85
POITIERS
les Sables-
d'Olonne
79
86
Niort
Ile de Ré
La Rochelle
POITOU
CHARENTE
87
Ile d`Oléron
Rochefort
16
LIMOGES
Saintes
LIMOUSIN
Cognac
Royan
17
Angoulême
ATLANTIC
OCEAN
Périgueux
Brive
24
AQUITAINE
33
Libourne
BORDEAUX
Bergerac
Arcachon
47
46
Villeneuve
Cahors

Françoise HOMO

«La Croix»
16320 EDON

tel: (0) 5 45 64 75 44

Private house

16.07 ANGOULEME

On the edge of the Dordogne, this picturesque little hamlet on the main Angoulème-Périgueux road, boasts a listed church. Françoise welcomes you to her modern house, with very large bedrooms with shower and WC in the room. On sale: Pineau.

PROPERTY

✱✱

private parking, garden, television, hosts have pets, dinner available, babies free, cot supplied, wheelchair access, no smoking, swimming pool, closed 31/10-01/04, hiking, mushroom picking, fishing 1.5km

25 km - S E - ANGOULEME EDON:
Nearest airport 25km
car essential
Directions:- At Angoulème, take the D939 towards Périgueux as far as Edon.

PRICE STRUCTURE

3 Bedrooms

1: bathroom with shower, washbasin, Double bed, 2 Single beds: FF170 (2 people) FF250 (4 people)

2 & 3: bathroom with shower, washbasin, Double bed: FF170

Extra bed in room: 40FF

Capacity: 8 people

Catherine & Patrick SCHEURER

«L'Art Vert»
16170 AUGE

tel: (0) 5 45 21 63 28
fax: (0) 5 45 21 63 28

Residence of character

35km - N W - ANGOULEME
AUGE : Hosts will collect from station
Rail station 25km
Car essential

16.09 ANGOULEME

You are in the heart of Cognac Country. This friendly couple will chat to you about their travels and are full of information on this region and its Roman architecture. In their 18th century farmhouse, there is a brand-new, spacious and comfortable studio and an art gallery with regular exhibitions. On sale: Pineau des Charentes.

PROPERTY

✱✱

private parking, garden, TV lounge, hosts have pets, telephone, dinner available, babies free, cot supplied, hiking, cycling, mushroom picking, interesting flora 3km, fishing 8km, river watersports 10km, golf course 15km, sea or lake watersports 20km

Adequate English spoken

PRICE STRUCTURE

1 Bedroom

Lounge, bathroom with shower, Double bed, Single bed: FF300 (2 people) FF50 (3 people)

Reduction: 8 nights

Capacity: 3 people

Directions:- At Angoulème, take the D939 towards St Jean d'Angely for 28 km. Then right on the D75 towards Verdille. The house is on the D90 towards St Médard.

Henri & Monique
GEFFARD

La Chambre
16130 VERRIERES

tel: (0) 5 45 83 02 74
fax: (0) 5 45 83 01 82

Working Farm

16.04 COGNAC

Here the whole family will look after you, and always with a smile. They will invite you to taste their own production of Pinot and Cognac and to visit their distillery and vineyard. They can also arrange for you to meet local craftsmen, if you wish. On sale: Premier Cru Cognac, Pineau...

PROPERTY

✸✸✸

off street parking, extensive grounds, TV lounge, hosts have pets, kitchen available, hiking, cycling, hunting, fishing 1km, mushroom picking 1km, golf course 15km, river watersports 15km, gliding 15km, sea or lake watersports 50km

Adequate English spoken

18 km - S - COGNAC
VERRIERES: Nearest airport 100km
car essential
Directions:- On the A10, Exit 36 Pons-Cognac. Take the D732 towards Cognac. At Pons, take the D700 towards Barbezieux. At Archiac, turn left towards Verrières. Follow the signs.

PRICE STRUCTURE

5 Bedrooms

1 & 2: bathroom with shower, Double bed, Single bed: FF220 (2 people) FF290 (3 people)

3: bathroom with shower, washbasin, 2 Double beds, Single bed: FF220 (2 people) FF450 (5 people)

4 & 5: bathroom with shower, washbasin, 2 single beds: FF220

Extra bed in room: 95FF
Reduction: groups

Capacity: 15 people

Geneviève & Roland MATIGNON

Les Collinauds
16130 LIGNIERES SON-NEVILLE

tel: (0) 5 45 80 51 23

Working Farm

8 km - S E - COGNAC
LIGNIERES: Hosts will collect from station
Rail station 12km
Nearest airport 100km
Car essential

Poitou-Charentes

COGNAC

16.11 COGNAC

In this impressive house, you will relive the best of the good old days with Roland and Geneviève. The house is comfortable and furnished in the old style. Your hosts will introduce you to making cognac and the old agricultural instruments that they have restored. This place is excellent value for money. On sale: Pineau des Charentes.

PROPERTY

✱✱✱

private parking, extensive grounds, TV lounge, hosts have pets, dinner available, kitchen available, packed lunch, babies free, cot supplied, hiking, cycling, hunting, mushroom picking, fishing 2km, river watersports 20km, sea or lake watersports 80km

Adequate English spoken

PRICE STRUCTURE

4 Bedrooms

Grenier & Bonne & Rustique: bathroom with shower, Double bed: FF230

Bleue: bathroom with shower, Double bed, 2 Single beds: FF230 (2 people) FF300 (4 people)

Extra bed in room: 50FF

Capacity: 10 people

Directions:- At Cognac, take the D24 towards Ségonzac, and then the D1 towards Barbezieux for 8km. Take the D699 to the left towards Angoulême for 1km. Then, take a small lane on the left, signposted "Les Collinauds".

Arlette LAFUSTE

«Beaupréau»
48, Av Louise Pichon - Rompsay
17180 PERIGNY

tel: (0) 5 46 27 02 65
fax: (0) 5 46 27 02 65

Residence of character

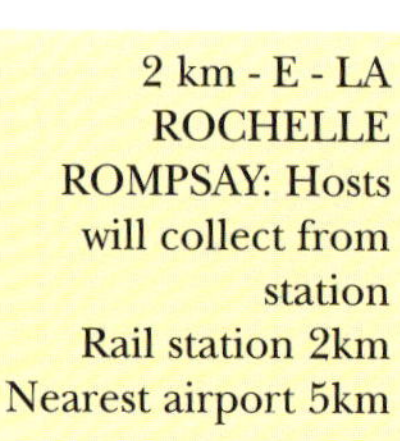

2 km - E - LA ROCHELLE ROMPSAY: Hosts will collect from station
Rail station 2km
Nearest airport 5km

17.13 LA ROCHELLE

This is a family home surrounded by attractive grounds of 1 hectare. It is only a few minutes from the beautiful town of La Rochelle, where you should not miss the "Francofolies" and other festivals in the summer.

PRICE STRUCTURE

3 Bedrooms

Verte & Rouge: Bathroom, Double bed, Single bed: FF290 (2 people) FF375 (3 people)

Bleue: (corridor) bathroom with shower, 2 Single beds: FF270

Extra bed in room: 65FF
Reduction: 01.11–01.05 and 4 nights

Capacity: 8 people

PROPERTY

✹✹✹

off street parking, extensive grounds, TV lounge, hosts have pets, telephone, kitchen available, babies free, cot supplied, wheelchair access, 2 nights minimum stay 1/07-31/08, hiking, cycling, sea or lake watersports 2km, golf course 3km

Basic English spoken

Directions:- At La Rochelle station go towards Niort (Avenue Foch) then take the first road on the right (Rue de Périgny) and follow the canal for 2km. The house is on the left.

17.16 LA ROCHELLE

)pposite Fort Boyard of TV fame, le Chalet is situated in the ıeart of the town, 300 metres from the beaches in a leafy ,ocation. With its bird reserves and oyster farms, Fouras is a ively resort. Francoise, president of the local radio station, cnows her region very well. On sale: seafood, wine, cheese.

PROPERTY

✱✱

private parking, garden, hosts have pets, telephone, hiking, cycling, fishing, interesting flora, mushroom picking, sea or lake watersports, golf course 6km

Fluent English spoken

PRICE STRUCTURE

5 Bedrooms

Boyard & Ré: Television, bathroom with shower, washbasin, Double bed: FF340

Aix & Loti: Television, Shower room, washbasin, Double bed: FF300

Passerose: Shower room, washbasin, 2 single beds: FF310

Oléron: Shower room, washbasin, Double bed, 2 Single beds Childrens size: FF300 (2 people) FF480 (4 people)

Extra bed in room: 100FF
Reduction: 01.09–30.06 and 4 nights

Capacity: 10 people

Françoise SENAN

«Le Chalet du Treuil»
53/55, rue de la
Fée au Bois
17450 FOURAS

tel: (0) 5 46 84 28 80
fax: (0) 5 46 84 28 80

Private house

27 km - S - LA ROCHELLE
FOURAS: Hosts will collect from station
Rail station 20km
Nearest airport 20km
Directions:- From La Rochelle, take the N137 and head towards Fouras. On entering the town, take the Ile d'Aix and La Fumée exit off the 1st roundabout. At the 2nd roundabout, take the 'Le Châlet du Treuil and Le Cimetière' Exit. Go straight on for 400 metres. Number 53-55.

Dominique FERMIGIER

«La Dune»
Allée des Merles
17132 MESCHERS

tel: (0) 5 46 02 65 00

private house

7 km - S - ROYAN
MESCHERS:
Rail station 10km
Car essential

Poitou-Charentes

ROYAN

PRICE STRUCTURE

2 Bedrooms and 1 suite

(2) bathroom with shower, double bed.
Suite: bathroom with shower, double bed, 4 single beds (childrens size): FF500 (2 people) FF2000 (10 people)

Extra bed in room: 120FF

Capacity: 10 people

17.15 ROYAN

A private sand dune leads to the beach from this Finnish style chalet. Admire the sunset and the panoramic view from the terrace overlooking the sea. A high standard of comfort and tasteful decor. The tranquility of this centuries-old maritime pine forest is best enjoyed outside the tourist season. A rare find. Weekly bookings only from 01.07–28.08

PROPERTY

✱✱✱

private parking, extensive grounds, TV lounge, telephone, kitchen available, babies free, cot supplied, swimming pool, hiking, cycling, fishing, sea or lake watersports, gliding 10km, golf course 15km

Directions:- From Royan, take the D25 along the coast towards St. Georges de Didonne and Mescher. 4km from St. Georges de Didonne, just after Suzac beach and the Haute Vienne Holiday Village, turn right into a small lane called 'Allée des Merles'. Continue down, and 'La Dune' is on the right (wooden sign, and high gate).

17.17 ROYAN

This is a new house in a quiet location, and every bedroom has its own balcony. This is La Seudre, bordered by salt marshes and oyster farms. Your hosts will recommend the best places to go for seafood (good prices and quality). The beaches are 15 km away.

PROPERTY

✱✱

private parking, garden, hosts have pets, no pets, cycling, hunting, interesting flora, mushroom picking, fishing 1km, sea or lake watersports 1km, birdwatching 2km, hiking 6km, river watersports 12km

PRICE STRUCTURE

2 Bedrooms

1 & 2: bathroom with shower, washbasin, Double bed: FF200

Extra bed in room: 70FF
Reduction: 8 nights

Capacity: 4 people

Claudie ALLAIN

4, rue de Leuze - St Nadeau
17600 ST SORNIN

tel: (0) 5 46 85 24 17

Private house

20 km - N - ROYAN
ST NADEAU: Rail station 12km
Nearest airport 65km
Car essential
Directions:- From Royan, take the D733 towards Rochefort, (or Exit 35 for Saintes from the A10, towards Ile d'Oléron and Marennes). St. Nadeau is situated 1km after the Cadeuil cross-roads. Once in the village, follow the signs for 'Entreprise Maçonnerie MJM' on the left. The house is just next to it.

Bruno HARMAND

«Maison des Bucheries»
17120 MEURSAC

tel: (0) 5 46 91 69 68
fax: (0) 5 46 91 69 68
lesbucheries@minitel.net

Residence of character

20 km - E - ROYAN
MEURSAC: Hosts will collect from station
Rail station 15km
Car essential

17.18 ROYAN

Bruno sees himself as a "gentleman peasant"! He welcomes you to his typical Charente house. The bedrooms, which overlook vineyards, are cosy and welcoming and decorated with good taste. On sale: Cognac, crafts. Fleur de Soleil member.

PRICE STRUCTURE

2 Bedrooms and 1 suite

Bonheur: bathroom with shower, 2 single beds, Single bed: FF250 (2 people) FF320 (3 people)

Paul + Virginie: bathroom with shower, double bed, 2 single beds: FF250 (2 people) FF400 (4 people)

Bergère: bathroom with shower, Double bed: FF250

Extra bed in room: 70FF

Reduction: children

Capacity: 9 people

PROPERTY

✱✱✱

off street parking, extensive grounds, lounge, hosts have pets, no pets, dinner available, extensive grounds, babies free, cot supplied, hiking, cycling, fishing 1km, mushroom picking 3km, birdwatching 5km, interesting flora 10km, sea or lake watersports 12km, golf course 20km

Basic English spoken

Directions:- At Royan take the N50 towards Saintes. After Saujon, take the D136 on the right,towards Meursac. There is a sign to "chambre d'hotes" on the right before Meursac. (If coming from Saintes, go to Pisany, then to Meursac and at Meursac head towards Saujon on the D136.).

Jack & Margaret
HOWARTH

«Rochebeaucourt»
6, Rue Rose
17400 ST JEAN D'ANGE-LY

tel: (0) 5 46 32 03 00
fax: (0) 5 46 32 03 00

Residence of character

ST JEAN D'ANGÉLY
Rail station 1km
Nearest airport
60km

17.05 ST JEAN D'ANGELY

Although in the centre of the town, the home of this English couple is a haven of peace ... totally quiet with a private interior courtyard. In the garden there are yew trees at least 250 years old. Easy to find, yet only 10 minutes from the autoroute A10. Excellent restaurants within a leisurely stroll.

PROPERTY

✱✱✱

private parking, garden, no pets, babies free, cot supplied, no smoking, closed 01/11-31/03, fishing 2km, sea or lake watersports 2km, river watersports 2km, golf course 20km, birdwatching 50km

Fluent English spoken

PRICE STRUCTURE

2 Bedrooms

Bordeaux/Cherry: Bathroom, 2 Double beds: FF480 (2 people) FF600 (4 people)

Pine: Bathroom, Double bed, 2 single beds: FF480 (2 people) FF600 (4 people)

Extra bed in room: 100FF
Reduction: 01.04–31.05 and 3 nights

Capacity: 8 people

Directions:- Exit 34 from the A10. Follow signs to Cognac-Saintes for 3km. At the second traffic lights (intersection with the N150), turn right towards the Centre-Ville. Continue for 200m to la Rue Rose.

Poitou-Charentes

ST JEAN D'ANGELY

John & Jenny ELMES

«Le Moulin de la Quine»
17350 ST SAVINIEN

tel: (0) 5 46 90 19 31
fax: (0) 5 46 90 28 37

Residence of character

15 km - S W - ST JEAN D'ANGELY
ST SAVINIEN: Hosts will collect from station
Rail station 3km
Nearest airport 50km
Car essential

17.06 ST JEAN D'ANGELY

Jenny and John, a friendly English couple, have created a really cosy atmosphere where you feel good. The bedroom leads on to an attractive and beautifully landscaped garden. St Savinien is a very beautiful village, which should not be missed. One spare room also available.

PRICE STRUCTURE

1 Bedroom

Parc: Shower room, bath-tub, Double bed, Single bed: FF280 (2 people) FF330 (3 people)

Extra bed in room: 50FF
Reduction: 2 nights

Capacity: 3 people

PROPERTY

✱✱✱

off street parking, extensive grounds, TV lounge, hosts have pets, no pets, dinner available, wheelchair access, no smoking, hiking, cycling, fishing 3km, golf course 25km, sea or lake, watersports 35km

Fluent English spoken

Directions:- Take Exit N34 from the A10. Head towards St Jean d'Angély, and then turn right on to the D18 as far as St Savinien. At the traffic lights, turn right and then under the railway bridge, left on to the D124 towards Bords. At Pontreau, there is a track on the left (by the derelict barn on the corner).

Frédérique THILL-TOUSSAINT

«Le Clos du Plantis»
1 rue du Pont -
Le Goulet
17160 SONNAC

tel: (0) 5 46 25 07 91
fax: (0) 5 46 25 07 91

Residence of character

17.12 ST JEAN D'ANGELY

This Charentaise house is 18km North of Cognac, and you will find a warm welcome of top quality. The house is quietly situated, and the bedrooms are well equipped. Pleasant garden. You are in the heart of the Roman Saintonge region near to Jarnac.

18 km - S E - ST JEAN D'ANGELY
LE GOULET: Rail station 18km
Nearest airport 120km
Car essential

PROPERTY

***

off street parking, extensive grounds, lounge, no pets, telephone, dinner available, packed lunch, babies free, cot supplied, hunting, sea or lake watersports, hiking 2km, cycling 2km, fishing 2km

Fluent English spoken

PRICE STRUCTURE

5 Bedrooms

Les Fins Bois: Bathroom, Double bed, 2 single beds: FF260 (2 people) FF480 (4 people)

Les Borderies: Bathroom, 2 Double beds, Single bed: FF260 (2 people) FF600 (5 people)

L'Océane: bathroom with shower, Double bed: FF240

Extra bed in room: 80FF

Capacity: 11 people

Directions:- On the A10 Exit St Jean d'Angély. Go to St Jean d'Angély and take the D939 towards Angoulème. After Matha turn right on to the D121 towards Cognac. Continue for 2km and Le Goulet is on the left.

Isabelle MOREAU

«Roches Blanches»
79140 LE PIN

tel: (0) 5 49 81 03 31
fax: (0) 5 49 81 03 31

Residence of character

13 km - N W -
BRESSUIRE
LE PIN: Rail station
30km
Nearest airport
95km
Car essential

79.07 BRESSUIRE

In this 19th century building, Isabelle has created an attractive new studio. Ideal for a family. The extensive grounds contain century old trees and a lake for fishing. In the summer do not miss the 'Son et Lumière' at Le Puy du Fou.

PRICE STRUCTURE

1 Bedrooms

Lounge, Kitchen, bathroom with shower, Double bed, 2 Single bed: FF250 (2 people) FF400 (4 people)

Capacity: 4 people

PROPERTY

off street parking, extensive grounds, hosts have pets, no pets, telephone, kitchen available, babies free, cot supplied, hiking, fishing, interesting flora, mushroom picking, cycling 6km, river watersports 15km, golf course 30km, sea or lake watersports 30km

Adequate English spoken

Directions:- At Bressuire, N149 towards Cholet. Before Le Peux left on to the D33 towards Le Pin. It is on the left 1km before Le Pin. There is an avenue and signs

79.02 NIORT

This house, typical of Poitou, has been well restored and here you will find a friendly welcome in the heart of the marshlands. In this nature park, the flora and the fauna are protected and you can set off to explore the area by boat from the grounds, or enjoy the indoor swimming pool. A good address.

PROPERTY

✱✱✱

off street parking, garden, TV lounge, telephone, kitchen available, babies free, cot supplied, wheelchair access, swimming pool, hiking, cycling, fishing, hunting, interesting flora, river watersports

Adequate English spoken

PRICE STRUCTURE

4 Bedrooms and 1 suite

Directoire: wheelchair access, bathroom with shower, 2 single beds: FF300

Louis Philippe 1: Bathroom with wc, Double bed, Single bed: FF300

Suite Louis Philippe 2: bathroom with shower, 2 single beds, double bed: FF300 (2 people) FF500 (4 people)

Louis XV: bathroom, wc, Double bed, Single bed: FF300 (2 people) FF400 (4 people)

Extra bed in room: 70/100FF
Reduction: 01.10–31.03 and 3 nights and children

Capacity: 12 people

Elisabeth PLAT

«Chambres d'hotes du Canal»
10, Rue de l'Ouche
79210 ARCAIS

tel: (0) 5 49 35 42 59
fax: (0) 5 49 35 01 34

Private house

20 km - W - NIORT
ARCAIS: Rail station 20km
Car essential
Directions:- At Niort, take the N11 towards Rochefort for 1km. Turn right on to the D3 for 16km. In St Hilaire la Palud, turn right on to the D101 towards Arçais. In the centre of the village, the house is close to the church and the tourist office (20m further down-signposted B&B France).

86.02 PARTHENAY

This 19th century château in the heart of Poitou, is in 25 acres of grounds, surrounded by venerable trees. A warm and lively atmosphere reigns. You may start by planning just an overnight stop, but you will not resist the temptation to stay longer in order to visit the Sauvignon wine cellars.

Laurence SARAZIN

«Château de Tréguel»
Route de Nantes
86190 CHALANDRAY

tel: (0) 5 49 60 18 95
fax: (0) 5 49 60 18 95

Château

PROPERTY

✱✱✱

off street parking, extensive grounds, TV lounge, hosts have pets, dinner available, no smoking, 2 nights minimum stay 15/11-15/03, hiking, cycling, fishing, mushroom picking, birdwatching, sea or lake watersports 4km, golf course 15km

Adequate English spoken

PRICE STRUCTURE

4 Bedrooms and 2 suites

Suite Comtesse & Suite Honneur: Television, Bathroom, 2 Double beds: FF400 (2 people) FF600 (4 people)

Comte & Pavillon: Television, Bathroom, Double bed: FF280

Jumelles 1 & 2: Television, Bathroom, Double bed: FF300

Extra bed in room: 100FF
Reduction: 3 nights

Capacity: 14 people

20 km - E - PARTHENAY
CHALANDRAY: Hosts will collect from station
Rail station 30km
Nearest airport 40km
Directions:- At Parthenay, take the N149 towards Poitiers. 500m before Chalandray, turn right into the lane. Continue for 300m. (Or, Exit 'Poitiers' from the A10, and go on to the N149 towards Parthenay/Nantes).

79.04 POITIERS

The bedroom here is large (35m^2) with rustic furniture. Situated between Futuroscope and the Marais Poitevin this old vicarage is restored in traditional style, in an enormous garden. The ideal time to visit is during the gentle months of autumn, when you will also enjoy Françoise's cooking. Gérard is a mine of information on the 200 Roman churches in the neighbourhood.

Gérard & Françoise
FREMAUX

«La Cure» AVON
79800 LA MOTHE ST
HERAY

tel: (0) 5 49 76 39 92

Private house

PROPERTY

✱✱

Private parking, Garden, TV lounge, No pets, Telephone, Dinner available, Babies free, cot supplied, Closed 1/12-1/03, Hiking, cycling, Fishing 5km, Interesting flora 10km, River watersports 10km, Golf course 20km

Basic English spoken

35 km - S W - POITIERS
AVON: Rail station 6km
Nearest airport 35km
Car essential
Directions:- At Poitiers, take the N11 then the D950 towards St Jean d'Angély. 10km after Lusignan, turn right towards Tumulus de Bougon for about 3 or 4km. At the corner of a large warehouse turn right and continue for 600m.

PRICE STRUCTURE

1 Bedrooms

Lounge, Television, (corridor)Bathroom, Shower room, 3 Single beds: FF230 (2 people) FF300 (3 people)

Extra bed in room: 50/70FF
Reduction: 4 nights and children

Capacity: 3 people

Eric LE GALLAIS

«Château de Labarom»
86380 CHENECHÉ

tel: (0) 5 49 51 24 22
fax: (0) 5 49 51 47 38

Château

20 km - N -
POITIERS
CHENECHE:
Nearest airport
20km
Car essential

PRICE STRUCTURE

5 Bedrooms

leue: bathroom with shower, 2 Single beds FF370

Tour + Piscine: bathroom, twin beds, 2 single beds: FF380 (2 people) FF580 (4 people)

ɔvary + Romantique: lounge, ɔathroom, double bed, 2 single beds: FF390 (2 people) FF590 (4 people)

Extra bed in room: 100FF

Reduction: 3 nights

Capacity: 10 people

86.04 POITIERS

Built on a 180 hectare estate, you will find peace and a closeness to nature at this wonderful Château de Labarom. The 17th century gallery and its period decorations are superb and the listed dovecote is quite outstanding. On sale: Hand–painted bone china.

PROPERTY

✱✱✱✱

private parking, extensive grounds, lounge, hosts have pets, no pets, babies free, cot supplied, swimming pool, closed 15/11-11/04, mushroom picking, fishing 4km, golf course 15km, sea or lake watersports 15km

Adequate English spoken

Directions:- A10, Exit Futuroscope. Go towards Neuville. Right on to D757 towards Vendeuvre. As you enter the village, left towards Chéneché. Cross the village, continue for 1km. Right into the lane, at the stone cross.

86.07 POITIERS

Jean-Claude CORBIN

«Château de Cibioux»
86250 SURIN

tel: (0) 5 49 87 04 89
fax: (0) 5 49 87 46 30

Château

The suite in Jean Claude's château is reached via a beautiful 16th century loggia, where you will take breakfast. You will be impressed by the good taste, simple authenticity and the discrete way in which modern comforts have been built into this wonderful place.

PROPERTY

✱✱✱✱

private parking, extensive grounds, TV lounge, hosts have pets, telephone, dinner available, hiking, cycling, fishing 10km, golf course 30km

Basic English spoken

PRICE STRUCTURE

1 Suite

Television, Telephone, Bathroom, Double bed, Single bed: FF550 (2 people) FF650 (3 people)

Reduction: 3 nights

Capacity: 3 people

60 km - S - POITIERS
SURIN: Hosts will collect from station
Rail station 15km
Nearest airport 50km
Directions:- At Poitiers, take the D741 towards Gencay. Continue on to the D1 towards Civray where you take the D35 towards Surin. In the village, follow the signs.

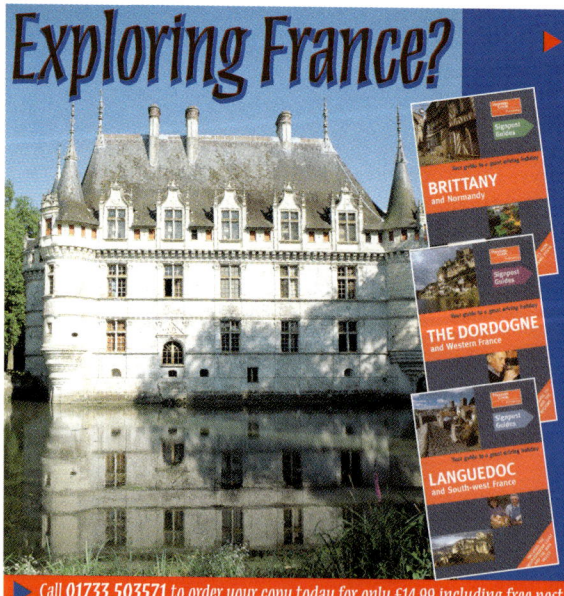

Richard & Deby EARLS

«La Boulinière»
6290 LA TRIMOUILLE

tel: (0) 5 49 91 55 88
fax: (0) 5 49 91 72 82

Residence of character

50 km - S E -
POITIERS
LA TRIMOUILLE:
Car essential

PRICE STRUCTURE

5 Bedrooms

(3) Bathroom, Double bed: FF420

(2) bathroom with shower, 2 single beds: FF420

Extra bed in room: 60FF
Reduction: 6 nights and groups and children

Capacity: 10 people

86.09 POITIERS

Richard and Deby, a friendly young English couple with 3 children, welcome you to their impressive, detached house with charming, spacious rooms. The wooded grounds are magnificent. Very convenient for visiting Futuroscope.

PROPERTY

✱✱✱

off street parking, extensive grounds, TV lounge, hosts have pets, no pets, dinner available, packed lunch, babies free, cot supplied, swimming pool, hiking, cycling, fishing, mushroom picking, birdwatching, river watersports 10km, gliding 22km, sea or lake watersports 24km, golf course 52km

English spoken

Directions:- At Poitiers, take the N147 towards Limoges. At Lussac les Châteaux, take the D727 towards Montmorillon. Continue towards La Trimouille for 10km. La Boulinière is on the right.

Denyse FOUCAULT

10 rue du Gué Rochelir
86190 VOUILLE

tel: (0) 5 49 54 10 29
fax: (0) 5 49 54 10 29

Residence of character

18 km - N W - POITIERS
VOUILLE: Nearest airport 15km
Car essential

86.10 POITIERS

Madame Foucault is a charming lady. She has just finished reorganising this new home close to Futuroscope, in order to make her guests more comfortable. She loves medieval cookery and plants and their uses. Be sure to visits the beautiful forest of Vouillé 5km away. Fleur de Soleil member.

PROPERTY

✱✱✱

off street parking, garden, TV lounge, hosts have pets, no smoking, swimming pool, closed 15/11-15/04, horse riding, hiking, cycling, fishing, mushroom picking, sea or lake watersports 8km, golf course 30km

Directions:- In Poitiers, take the N149 towards Parthenay as far as Vouillé. The house is close to the town.

PRICE STRUCTURE

1 Bedrooms and 2 suites

Marie-Antoinette: bathroom with shower, double bed: FF360

Petit Prince: bathroom with shower, bath, 2 single beds: FF300

Maisons dans le jardin:
1-Bagatelle: Kitchen, bathroom with shower, Double bed: FF280

2-Le Grand Mazet: Kitchen, bathroom with shower, 2 Double beds: FF300 (2 people) FF480 (4 people)

Extra bed in room: 80/120FF
Reduction: 2 nights

Capacity: 10 people

Alain & Claude GAIL

«Château de Masseuil»
86190 QUINÇAY

tel: (0) 5 49 60 42 15
fax: (0) 5 49 60 70 15

Château

10 km - W -
POITIERS
QUINCAY:
Hosts will collect from station
Rail station 12km
Nearest airport 10km
Car essential

PRICE STRUCTURE

2 Bedrooms and 1 suite

Empire: Lounge, Television, Kitchen, Shower room, Double bed: FF350

Louis XV: Lounge, Television, Kitchen, Shower room, Double bed: FF350

Enfants: Lounge, Television, Kitchen, 2 Single beds Childrens size: FF150

Louis XVI: Shower room, 2 single beds: FF350

Tour: washbasin, Single bed: FF150

Reduction: 3 nights

Capacity: 9 people

86.15 POITIERS

Alain and Claude will receive you in their magnificent 15th century château. Their kindness and warmth will ensure that you have an unforgettable stay with this family.

PROPERTY

****

private parking, extensive grounds, TV lounge, hosts have pets, kitchen available, no smoking, closed 1/12-1/02, hiking, cycling, fishing, river watersports, mushroom, picking 4km, sea or lake watersports 6km, golf course 15km

English spoken

Directions:- On the A10 Exit Poitiers-Nord. Follow signs to Nantes for 12km. At the bottom of the small descent before Vouillé, turn left. Masseuil is 1.5km further on.

Georges REBILLARD

«Château de la Guillonnière»
86410 DIENNÉ

tel: (0) 5 49 42 05 46
fax: (0) 5 49 42 48 34
chateaudelaguillonniere@wanadoo.fr

Château

Poitou-Charentes

86.16 POITIERS

There is a refined and friendly welcome in this superb château. Just as George Sand did, you will appreciate its peaceful atmosphere. The comfortable bedrooms and the extensive grounds are beautiful. Only 20 minutes from Futuroscope. Many magnificent Roman abbeys to visit nearby.

POITIERS

PROPERTY

✱✱✱✱

off street parking, extensive grounds, TV lounge, hosts have pets, no pets, telephone, dinner available, hiking, hunting, interesting flora, mushroom picking, birdwatching, cycling 10km, golf course 10km, fishing 10km, sea or lake watersports 15km

Fluent English spoken

15 km - S E - POITIERS
DIENNE: Rail station 15km
Nearest airport 20km
Car essential

PRICE STRUCTURE

4 Bedrooms and 1 suite

Napoléon III & George Sand: Bathroom, Double bed: FF450

Les Bucoliques: bathroom with shower, Double bed: FF350

Les Moutons: Bathroom, 3 Single bed: FF450 (1 person) FF500 (3 people)

Diane de Poitiers: Bathroom, Double bed, single bed: FF550 (2 people) FF620 (3 people)

Capacity: 12 people

Directions:- At Poitiers, take the N147 towards Limoges. Turn right on to the D2 towards Gençay. The château is between Fleuré and Vernon.

Annick & Jean-Noël
CURNIS

«Manoir de Beaumont»
2 rue des Portes Rouges
86490 BEAUMONT

tel: (0) 5 49 85 05 29
fax: (0) 5 49 85 05 29
jncurnis@adl.com

Manor House

15 km - N E - POITIERS
BEAUMONT: Rail station 15km
Nearest airport 15km
Car essential

86.20 POITIERS

You will be charmed by this 15th century hunting lodge on the Poitou wine trail (Henry IV had an affair with his cousin here!). It has now been totally refurbished, and Jean-Noël is adept at combining traditional features with modern comfort, a demonstration of all that is best in the area. You will be torn between the châteaux or Futuroscope! Fleur de soleil member.

PRICE STRUCTURE

3 Bedrooms and 1 suite

1900 & Régence: bathroom with shower, Double bed: FF350

Suite Familiale Directoire: bathroom, shower, telephone, double bed, 3 single beds: FF400 (2 people) FF700 (5 people)

Louis XVI: bathroom with shower, Double bed: FF350

Reduction: 3 nights

Capacity: 11 people

PROPERTY

***

private parking, extensive grounds, TV lounge, hosts have pets, no pets, telephone, babies free, cot supplied, mushroom picking, hiking 5km, cycling 5km, golf course 5km, fishing 5km, birdwatching 5km, sea or lake watersports 5km, interesting flora 8km

Directions:- From the A10 (between Poitiers and Châtellerault), take Exit 27. Head towards Poitiers on the N10. In the place called "La Tricherie", head towards Beaumont. When you arrive in the town centre, take the D82 in the direction of Marigny Brizay. You are in the 'Rue des Portes Rouges.' The manor is number 12.

Monique & Michel
TABAU

«Château de la Touche»
86800 SAVIGNY
L'EVESCAULT

tel: (0) 5 49 01 10 38
fax: (0) 5 49 56 47 82

Château

15 km - E -
POITIERS
SAVIGNY
L'EVESCAULT:
hosts can collect
from station,
railway station 15km
airport 20km
car essential

86.21 POITIERS

Your hosts are from the Midi and have brought warmth and sunshine into this large château. Spacious rooms, especially "L'Algarve" which is richly endowed with a harpsichord and a large modern bathroom. Mr Tabau is the president of a regional cultural association. Fleur de soleil member. On sale: jams.

PRICE STRUCTURE

3 Bedrooms

India: bathroom with wc, twin beds: FF480

Aurore: bathroom with wc, double bed: FF480

Algarve: bridal room, bathroom with wc, shower room with wc, double bed: FF680

Extra bed: 90FF
Reduction: 4 nights

Capacity: 6 people

PROPERTY

****

private parking, extensive grounds, tv lounge, hosts have pets, telephone, dinner available, babies welcome, free cot, hiking, fishing 1km, golf course 5km

Fluent English spoken

– From Poitiers, head in the direction of Limoges on the N147 (Exit number 29 from the A10 then towards Limoges). After 5km, Savigny l'Evescault is on the left. In the village, follow the signs for "Château de la Touche."

VAUCAMP

«Château de Vaumoret»
rue du Brueil Mingot
86000 POITIERS

tel: (0) 5 49 61 32 11
fax: (0) 5 49 01 04 54

Château

POITIERS
railway station 8km
airport 8km
car essential

86.22 POITIERS

This small, listed 17th century château has been perfectly restored with great style. The bedrooms are charming. This is a calm place, in verdant surroundings. You are 10 minutes from Futuroscope and 8 minutes from the centre of Poitiers. They will lend you bikes, free of charge.

PROPERTY

***

off street parking, extensive grounds, tv lounge, hosts have pets, kitchen, wheelchair access, hiking, cycling, fishing 5km, hunting 5km, interesting flora 5km, sea or lake watersports 6km, golf course 9km

Fluent English spoken

— From the A10, Exit Poitiers-Nord (N29). Head towards Limoges on the eastern bypass. After 5km, left towards Montamise on the D3. After 3km, at the cross-roads take the D18 on the right towards Sèvres. The entrance of Vaumoret is 2.5km further on, on the right.

PRICE STRUCTURE

3 Bedrooms

Four: television, bathroom with wc, double bed, 2 single beds: FF430 (2 people) FF590 (4 people)

Jaune: bathroom with wc, twin beds: FF350

Rose: bathroom with wc, twin beds: FF380

Extra bed: 90FF
Reduction: 1/11–20/12 and 2/01–15/02 and 7 nights

Capacity: 2 people

SWITZERLAND
ITALY
MEDITERRANEAN SEA
RHÔNE-ALPES
PROVENCE-ALPES-CÔTE D'AZUR
LANGUEDOC-ROUSSILLON
Bourg
Annecy
Chamonix
Aix-les-Bains
Albertville
Chambéry
Vienne
St.-Etienne
St. Jean
Grenoble
Briançon
Valence
Privas
Gap
Digne
Carpentras
Avignon
Nimes
Arles
Grasse
Nice
Draguignan
Aix-en-Provence
MARSEILLE
Toulon
MON
01
74
73
42
38
43
07
26
05
04
06
84
30
13
83

Michèle & Bernard
SANTI

«Le Moulin du Carlet»
Route de Forcalquier
04300 NIOZELLES

tel: (0) 4 92 75 28 94
fax: (0) 4 92 75 28 94

Private home

20 km - N - MANOSQUE
PARIS 1e: Châtelet-NIOZELLES: railway station 6km
airport 100km
car essential

04.07 MANOSQUE

You will find Bernard and Michelle between Le Lubéron and La Montagne de Lure. Their 18th century water mill is straight out of a tourist brochure, with a small river, view over the lavender fields and many pleasant walks. You will not be disappointed. There are also many arts and crafts workshops around here.

PROPERTY

✱✱✱

off street parking, garden, pets not accepted, babies welcome, free cot, no smoking, swimming pool, cycling, fishing, bird-watching 7km, hiking 10km, interesting flora 10km, sea or lake watersports 15km, gliding 15km, golf course 25km, mushroom picking 25km

— On the A7, Exit Avignon-Sud, head for Apt - Sisteron. On the A51, Exit La Brillane, head towards Forcalquier. Niozelles is on the N100, between La Brillane and Forcalquier. The mill is 800 m from the village, and 4 km from Forcalquier.

PRICE STRUCTURE

2 Bedrooms

Lys Orangé: shower room with wc, double bed, FF280

Agapanthe: bathroom with wc, double bed: FF320

Capacity: 4 people

Jean-Pierre BAGARRE

«Le Bosquet»
Quartier le Bosquet
83630 AIGUINES

tel: (0) 4 94 70 21 02
fax: (0) 4 94 70 22 09

Private home

10 km - S - MOUSTIERS STE MARIE
AIGUINES:
airport 100km
car essential
— At Moustiers, take the D952 towards Castellanne. Turn right on to the D957 towards Aups and then left on to the D19 towards Aiguines.

83.18 MOUSTIERS STE MARIE

A quiet authentic village very close to the lake of Ste Croix and the amazing Gorges du Verdon. Admirez, depuis la piscine ou les terrasses, the view over the lake. Your hosts run a restaurant in the village. On sale: Truffles, honey, home-made orange wine and jam.

PROPERTY

✱✱

private parking, garden, tv lounge, hosts have pets, dinner available, packed lunch, wheelchair access, swimming pool, closed: 15/11-1/04, hiking, cycling, hunting, fishing 4km, mushroom picking 4km, sea or lake watersports 4km, river watersports 4km

Basic English spoken

PRICE STRUCTURE

6 Bedrooms

(4 rooms) television, shower room with wc, double bed: FF275

(2 rooms) television, shower room with wc, double bed, single bed: FF350 (2 people) FF425 (3 people)

Extra bed: 50FF
Reduction: 1/10–30/03 and groups and children

Capacity: 14 people

Mike, Patricia & Claude
FRANTZ & PASQUINI

«Vitaverde»
Le Claus 04230 CRUIS

tel: (0) 4 92 77 00 89
fax: (0) 4 92 77 02 33
vitaverde@aol.com

Private home

20 km - S -
SISTERON
CRUIS: hosts can collect from station, railway station 22km
airport 110km

04.05 SISTERON

Here in the Alpes de Haute Provence you will find Patricia, Mike and Claude in their 17th century mas in peaceful surroundings. They are young and friendly, into Green Tourism, and will soon teach you to love this magnificent area. On sale: organic fruit and vegetables.

5 self-catering apartments, rented weekly. 50% discount outside the French school holidays.

PROPERTY

***

off street parking, extensive grounds, lounge, hosts have pets, pets not accepted, telephone, dinner available, babies welcome, free cot, no smoking, riding, hiking, cycling, interesting flora, mushroom picking, winter sports 20km, gliding 20km, golf course 40km, river watersports 75km

Fluent English spoken

— From the A51, take the Exit for Peyruis. Go on to the D951 towards St Etienne les Orgues and Cruis.

PRICE STRUCTURE

2 Bedrooms

Iris: shower room with wc, double bed: FF310

Coquelicot: kitchen, shower room with wc, double bed: FF355

Extra bed: 80FF
Reduction: 08/11–03/04 and 3 nights and groups

Capacity: 2 people

Françoise & René
FLECHE

Route des Granges
10, chemin de Valbelle
04200 PEIPIN

tel: (0) 4 92 62 47 16
fax: (0) 4 92 62 47 16
Rene.Fleche2@wanadoo.

Private home

6 km - S - SISTERON
PEIPIN:
railway station 7km
airport 115km
car essential
— A51, Exit Aubignosc. At Peipin, follow the signs "chambres d'hotes". At the second sign, turn right to take the Route des Granges. Turn right again on to the Chemin de Valbelle and continue to No.10. Take the private lane on the right. The gate is after the 2nd house.

04.08 SISTERON

Situated a stone's throw away from the village, Françoise and René offer peace and quiet. There is a panoramic view of the lower slopes of the Alps. Try the home-made jams and cakes, and you will soon share your hosts' love of this region. René enjoys hiking, and can tell you the best paths and tracks to take.

PROPERTY

✸✸

private parking, garden, pets not accepted, telephone, no smoking, closed: 01/09-01/05, hiking, cycling, fishing 2km, interesting flora 7km, birdwatching 7km, sea or lake water-sports 7km, gliding 7km, golf course 30km

Basic English spoken

PRICE STRUCTURE

2 Bedrooms

Coquelicots: lounge, telephone, shower room with wc, double bed: FF250

Genêts: telephone, shower room with wc, 2 single beds: FF230

Reduction: 3 nights

Capacity: 4 people

Pascaline LAVOIX

Les Sagnières
04200 SIGOYER

tel: (0) 4 92 62 15 74
fax: (0) 4 92 62 15 74
E-mail:
pasclav@hotmail.com

Private home

12km - N -
SISTERON
SIGOYER
car essential

04.09 SISTERON

This traditional 19th century sheep shelter, in Haute Provence, has now been converted into a haven of peace and quiet. Listen to the sound of silence. The view over the Alps and the Durance Valley is magnificent. Do not miss the sunset from the terrace. Pascaline can provide plenty of advice on walks and places of interest in this wild and enchanting region. Fleur de Soleil member.

PROPERTY

✹✹✹

off street parking, garden, pets not accepted, dinner available, swimming pool, hiking, fishing 12km, sea or lake watersports 12km

English spoken

PRICE STRUCTURE

3 Bedrooms

Pervenche: shower room with wc, bathroom, double bed, single bed: FF340 (2 people) FF360 (3 people)

Rose Trémière: shower room with wc, bathroom, double bed, single bed: FF350 (2 people) FF360 (3 people)

Miel: shower room with wc, bathroom, double bed: FF320

Capacity: 8 people

— North of Sisteron, on the N85 towards Gap, at the second roundabout take the D4, towards Theze. Go as far as the turn to Sigoyer and the D654, and turn right. Les Sagnières is 1km further on, on the left.

Claire & Isabelle
PASCALLET & GAIDON

«La Joie de Vivre»
Hameau de Salé 05100
NEVACHE

tel: (0) 4 92 21 30 96
fax: (0) 4 92 20 06 41

Private home

05.01 BRIANCON

A warm, traditional mountain house, harmoniously constructed from stone and wood. Ideal for skiing or, if you come in the autumn, for collecting mushrooms which your hostess will prepare for you the same evening. They will introduce you to the gastronomic specialities of the Alps. This valley, at altitude 1,600m has the top environmental grading for wild flowers. There are also llamas that love being taken for walks. On sale: regional produce. Half Board: 330-375 FF per person.

PROPERTY

✱✱✱

off street parking, garden, tv lounge, hosts have pets, telephone, dinner available, packed lunch, no smoking, hiking, cycling, fishing, interesting flora, mushroom picking, sea or lake watersports, winter sports,

Fluent English spoken

18 km - N - BRIANCON
NEVACHE: hosts can collect from station, railway station 18km airport 110km
— At Briançon, take the N94 towards Montgenèvre. Turn left on to the D994G towards Névache.

PRICE STRUCTURE

5 Bedrooms

Clarée: television, bathroom with wc, double bed, 2 single beds,

7° ciel: television, bathroom with wc, double bed, 2 single beds,

Thabor + Mezzanine: television, bathroom with wc, double bed, 4 single beds,

Beraude + Mezzanine: television, bathroom with wc, double bed, 4 single beds,

Nevasca: bathroom with wc, double bed, 2 single beds,

Extra bed: 110FF
Reduction: groups and children

Capacity: 2 people

Jacqueline LABORIE

«Longue Haleine»
Puy St André village
05100 BRIANÇON

tel: (0) 4 92 21 30 22
fax: (0) 4 92 21 30 22
sudalp@club-internet.fr

Private home

4 km - S W - BRIANCON
PUY ST ANDRE:
railway station 4km
car essential

05.03 BRIANCON

A friendly couple in this little village which overlooks Briançon. The house is quietly situated with a magnificent, uninterrupted view. The ski resort claims the record for the most hours of sunshine in France! As for the walks...brilliant.

Apartment: no breakfast

PROPERTY

✱✱✱

garden, pets not accepted, telephone, no smoking, closed: 08/04-08/06 & 10/09-28/12, hiking, cycling, fishing 4km, sea or lake watersports 4km, river watersports 4km, winter sports 4km, interesting flora 10km, gliding 40km

English spoken

— As you enter Briançon on the road towards Gap, at the traffic lights take the D35 towards Puy St André. As you enter the village it is the third house on the left, down a slope.

PRICE STRUCTURE

1 Bedroom and 1 Suite and 1 Apartment

Jaune: along corridor shower room with wc, washbasin, double bed: FF330

Rose/Bleue: along corridor shower room with wc, washbasin, twin beds, 2 single beds: FF330 (2 people) FF570 (4 people)

Apartment: kitchen, bathroom with wc, double bed, single bed: FF370 (2 people) FF510 (3 people)

Extra bed: 100FF
Reduction: 9/06–30/06 and 28/08–08/09 and 2 nights

Capacity: 9 people

05.02 GAP

Donald & Agnès CLARK

«La Combe Fleurie»
Route de Chaillol
05500 ST BONNET EN CHAMPSAUR

tel: (0) 4 92 50 53 97
fax: (0) 4 92 50 18 28

Private home

This area is worth a visit at any time of the year. Surrounded by ski resorts, wonderful countryside and mountains, and a good choice of sports or visits to the local markets. You are at the gateway of the national park Les Ecrins.

PROPERTY

✱✱✱

off street parking, garden, tv lounge, telephone, dinner available, packed lunch, babies welcome, free cot, hiking, cycling, fishing, river watersports, winter sports, gliding

Fluent English spoken

PRICE STRUCTURE

6 Bedrooms

Mazurka: shower room with wc, double bed: FF250

Bourrée & Badoise & Troïka: shower room with wc, double bed, 2 single beds: FF250 (2 people) FF400 (4 people)

Ronde: bathroom with wc, double bed, single bed: FF250 (2 people) FF325 (4 people)

Rigodon: shower room with wc, double bed, 5 single beds: FF250 (2 people) FF590 (7 people)

Extra bed: 50FF
Reduction: groups and children

Capacity: 24 people

15 km - N - GAP
ST BONNET: hosts can collect from station, airport 90km
— In Gap, take the N85 towards Grenoble. Turn right to Bonnet. The house is just after the village.

06.05 CANNES

Ariane CHARLIER

623, chemin Argelas
06250 MOUGINS

tel: (0) 4 93 46 55 84

Private home

A Provencal house in verdant surroundings only 10 min. from Cannes. Very quiet, with a large garden on the edge of the forest. Spacious pleasant rooms, ideal for long stays. Ariane also teaches French and Italian. On sale: wine, home-made jam, honey, hand-painted crafts.

PROPERTY

✱✱✱

private parking, garden, tv lounge, packed lunch, babies welcome, free cot, no smoking, swimming pool, hiking, interesting flora, mushroom picking, golf course 2km, fishing 8km, sea or lake watersports 8km, river watersports 13km, gliding 50km

Basic English spoken

PRICE STRUCTURE

2 Bedrooms

First room: television, kitchen, shower room with wc, double bed, cot: FF350

Second room: shower room with wc, double bed, cot: FF350

Reduction: 01/09–30/05 and 2 nights

Capacity: 4 people

4 km - N - CANNES
MOUGINS: hosts can collect from station, railway station 6km
airport 20km
car essential
— On the A8, Exit 42 'Cannes-Mougins'. Go down towards Cannes. At the 3rd set of traffic lights, there is a car park on the left with a phone box. Phone your hosts who will come and pick you up.

Patrick GUEGUEN

«Marina Cottage»
Villa N°28-246 Bd des Ecureuils
06210 MANDELIEU

tel: (0) 4 93 93 59 70
fax: (0) 4 93 49 90 12

Private home

5 km - W - CANNES MANDELIEU: hosts can collect from station, railway station 5km airport 40km

PRICE STRUCTURE

2 Bedrooms

First room: television, telephone, shower room with wc, bathroom, twin beds: FF300

Second room: double bed: FF300

Capacity: 4 people

06.08 CANNES

This American-style house on a river is part of a residence run for your comfort and safety. You reach the sea via the marina, and they also organise tennis and diving... and there is a swimming pool.

PROPERTY

off street parking, tv lounge, hosts have pets, dinner available, swimming pool, tennis, hiking, cycling, golf course, fishing, sea or lake watersports, interesting flora 5km, hunting 10km, mushroom picking 10km, gliding 30km, winter sports 50km

Basic English spoken

— On the A8 take Exit 40 to Mandelieu-La Napoule. Turn right and right again towards 'Location Orion' in the Avenue de la Siagne.

Michel & Monique
GINISTY

«Les Terrasses B5»
433 rue Janvier Passéro
06210 MANDELIEU

tel: (0) 4 93 49 02 91
fax: (0) 4 93 49 02 91

Flat

5 km - W - CANNES
MANDELIEU:
railway station 3km
airport 35km
car essential

06.20 CANNES

This lovely couple will welcome you to their large garden with terrace and lawn. There are two rooms for your use (the largest is 23 sq. metres with a large bathroom). Generous breakfast. You will also have the use of the communal swimming pool for the building and boat trips can be arranged..

PROPERTY

✱✱

off street parking, tv lounge, hosts have pets, pets not accepted, dinner available, babies welcome, free cot, wheelchair access, swimming pool, cycling, golf course 2km, fishing 3km, sea or lake watersports 3km

Basic English spoken

— A8, Exit 40 Mandelieu. Continue in the direction of Cannes-Grasse & Capitou. Take the road Janvier Passeo opposite the "Total" garage as far as No. 433, then turn left and take the road leading up to the building "Les Terrasses".

PRICE STRUCTURE

2 Bedrooms

Rose: television, bathroom with wc, double bed: FF320

Champagne: television, along corridor bathroom with wc, double bed: FF300

Extra bed: 100FF
Reduction: groups and children

Capacity: 4 people

Dominique SÉE

«La Rivolte»
Chemin des Lierres
06130 GRASSE

tel: (0) 4 93 36 81 58
fax: (0) 4 93 36 87 29
larivolte@aol.com
www.larivolte.com

Residence of character

17 km - N - CANNES
GRASSE: hosts can collect from station, railway station 17km airport 35km

PRICE STRUCTURE

7 Bedrooms

Jasmin: bathroom with wc, double bed: FF700

Rose: shower room with wc, double bed: FF550

Camélia & Mimosa & Violette: bathroom with wc, twin beds: FF500

Lavande: along corridor shower room with wc, twin beds: FF350

Lilas: 4 single beds (childrens size): FF250 (1 person) FF450 (4 people)

Extra bed: 100FF

Reduction: 1/10–1/05 and 3 nights

Capacity: 16 people

06.09 CANNES

This large 1830's building is in extensive terraced grounds in perfume country. All bedrooms have a magnificent view over the valley. Everything is geared to keeping the typical style of a traditional, large Provençal family home. They run courses on various themes. Reductions out-of-season.

PROPERTY

❋❋❋

off street parking, extensive grounds, tv lounge, pets not accepted, telephone, babies welcome, free cot, swimming pool, hiking 3km, cycling 3km, golf course 5km, hunting 10km, mushroom picking 10km, fishing 15km, sea or lake watersports 16km, river watersports 20km, gliding 30km, interesting flora 35km

Fluent English spoken

— Go to Grasse on the N85. At the station go towards Nice via 'Au Thiers'. There, after 300m, first left, then immediately turn right. Then 150m to the entrance gate and continue up the hill.

Stella ERBIBO
CHAUVET

«Stella's»
5, Av Paul Arène
06600 ANTIBES

tel: (0) 4 93 34 12 14

Private home

10 km - N E -
CANNES
ANTIBES:
airport 17km

06.11 CANNES

When you enter this former laundry, now transformed into a large house, you will find a charming interior garden, peace and quiet and spacious rooms with high ceilings. Stella has created a wonderful, traditional Provençale atmosphere in her home finished in authentic lime-wash and ochre. On sale: home-made marmalade. 01/11–01/03: advance bookings only.

PROPERTY

✱✱✱

garden, tv lounge, pets not accepted, 12 years old minimum, no smoking, fishing, sea or lake watersports

Adequate English spoken

— In Antibes, head for the port. After the roundabout continue along Avenue de Verdun and it is the second on the right.

PRICE STRUCTURE

2 Bedrooms

Second room: shower room with wc, shower room with wc, twin beds: FF350

Sous Pente: shower room with wc, 6 single beds: FF420 (2 people) FF750 (6 people)

Extra bed: 90FF
Reduction: 1/11–01/03

Capacity: 8 people

nine & Gérard RONCÉ

«Mas du Murier»
1407, Route de Grasse
06220 VALLAURIS
GOLFE JUAN

tel: (0) 4 93 64 52 32
fax: (0) 4 93 64 23 77

Residence of character

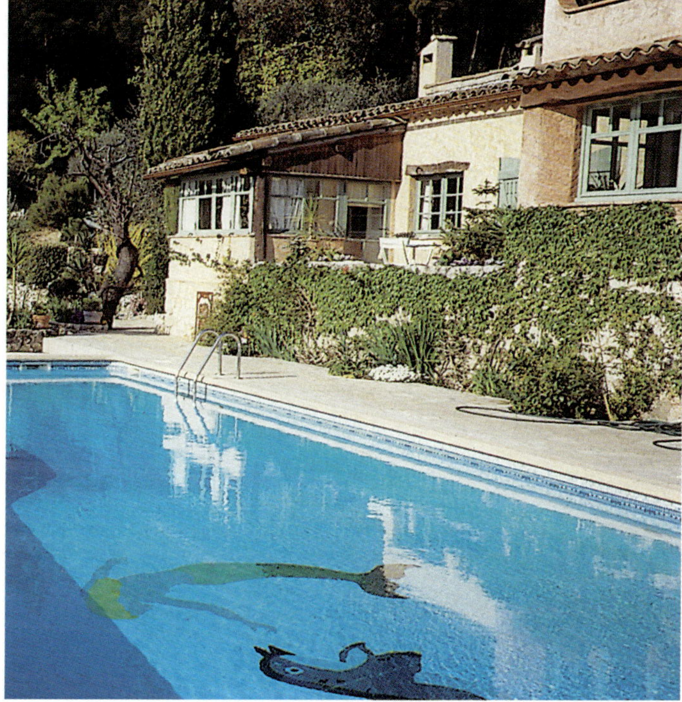

5 km - E - CANNES
VALLAURIS: hosts can collect from station, railway station 3km
airport 25km
car essential

PRICE STRUCTURE

2 Bedrooms

First room: lounge, television, telephone, bathroom with wc, twin beds: FF420

Second room: lounge, television, telephone, bathroom with wc, double bed, single bed: FF450 (2 people) FF550 (3 people)

Extra bed: 100FF

Reduction:15/10–31/03 and 4 nights

Capacity: 5 people

06.12 CANNES

A superb house in the forest. Your hosts are absolutely charming. The grounds are very well looked after and the interior decor is a great success. This is a little paradise only 4km from the sea.

PROPERTY

✱✱✱

private parking, extensive grounds, tv lounge, hosts have pets, telephone, babies welcome, free cot, wheelchair access, swimming pool, hiking, cycling, mushroom picking, fishing 3km, sea or lake watersports 4km, golf course 5km, interesting flora 30km, river watersports 30km

Basic English spoken

— In Cannes take the N7 towards Golfe Juan, then Vallauris. At Vallauris take the road for Grasse.

Christiane & Alain RINGENBACH

«Le Cheneau»
205, Route d'Antibes - D103
06560 VALBONNE

tel: (0) 4 93 12 13 94
fax: (0) 4 93 12 91 85
ringbach@club-internet.fr

Private home

10 km - N - CANNES
VALBONNE: railway station 10km
airport 16km
car essential

06.14 CANNES

Mona's place is warm and lively. A charming and pretty bedroom is furnished so as to give you maximum privacy. In a very quiet street in the centre of Paris. An excellent address. Advance booking only

PROPERTY

✱✱✱

private parking, extensive grounds, lounge, hosts have pets, pets not accepted, telephone, babies welcome, free cot, no smoking, hiking, golf course, interesting flora, cycling 5km, mushroom picking 10km, sea or lake watersports 12km, fishing 20km, river watersports 20km, gliding 40km, winter sports 60km

Degree of fluency in English: adequate

— Take the Exit for Antibes on the A8 towards Antibes/Grasse/Mougins then Sophia-Antipolis. At the Bouillides cross-roads head towards Valbonne (D103) for 3km. 100m after the restaurant called 'Le Bois Doré' and just before the bus stop, go up a small lane. It is the last house at the top, on the left, number 205.

PRICE STRUCTURE

3 Bedrooms

Noisette: shower room with wc, bathroom, twin beds: FF430

Azur & Violine: shower room with wc, bathroom, double bed: FF350

Extra bed: 120FF

Capacity: 6 people

Eve & Henri DARAN

«L'Eglantier»
14, rue Campestra
06400 CANNES

tel: (0) 4 93 68 22 43
fax: (0) 4 93 38 28 53

Residence of character

CANNES
airport 35km

PRICE STRUCTURE

4 Bedrooms

N°1 Rez-de-Jardin: telephone, bathroom with wc, twin beds: FF620

Verte Rez-de-Jardin: telephone, bathroom with wc, double bed: FF620

N°3: telephone, bathroom with wc, twin beds: FF620

N°4: telephone, bathroom, twin beds: FF480

Extra bed: 140FF

Capacity: 8 people

06.17 CANNES

Your hostess loves meeting people, and will give you a warm welcome to her beautiful, spacious Midi-style house, which dates from 1920. You have everything you need, the place is spotless and decorated with excellent taste. Enormous breakfasts are served all morning in the large dining room You are 10 mins. walk from La Croisette.

PROPERTY

✱✱✱

off street parking, garden, tv lounge, hosts have pets, telephone, no smoking, sea or lake watersports, golf course 3km

Adequate English spoken

— In the centre of Cannes, take the Boulevard Carnot and then the Rue R. Viglieno on the right. Go right to the end which leads into the Rue Campestra.

Josette & Philippe
BERNARD

«Le Mas des Arts»
219, Av de Peygros
06530 PEYMEINADE

tel: (0) 4 93 09 95 19
fax: (0) 4 93 09 95 19

Private home

20 km - N W -
CANNES
PEYMEINADE:
railway station 20km
airport 40km
car essential

06.21 CANNES

Philippe and Josette, a painter, will give you a warm welcome to their Provençal house, with a wonderful swimming pool and a panoramic view over the hills. Everything is neat and rtidy, and the breakfast generous. Josette's charm, the kindness of their daughter and Philippe's warmth easily earn them 3 "suns".

PROPERTY

✱✱✱

private parking, extensive grounds, tv lounge, pets not accepted, wheelchair access, swimming pool, fishing 10km, hunting, 10km, mushroom picking 10km, sea or lake watersports 10km, golf course 12km, gliding 15km, winter sports 50km

Fluent English spoken

— Go to Grasse on the N85 and take the D2562 towards Draguignan. Go through Peymeinade, and 1km after the village as you reach Jaïsous, follow the signs "Rivierazur" on your left for 2km.

PRICE STRUCTURE

1 Bedroom and 1 Suite

First room: along corridor shower room with wc, double bed: FF320

Suite: bathroom with wc, double bed, twin beds: FF350 (2 people) FF630 (4 people)

Capacity: 6 people

Christine CAMIA

«Villa Lou Mazet»
7, chemin du Parc
Saramartel
06160 CAP D'ANTIBES

tel: (0) 4 93 61 38 84
fax: (0) 4 93 61 38 84

Private home

10 km - E - CANNES
JUAN LES PINS:
railway station 2km
airport 15km

PRICE STRUCTURE

1 Bedroom

Television, kitchen, bathroom with wc, twin beds: FF350

Extra bed: 100FF

Capacity: 2 people

06.22 CANNES

Well-equipped and clean studio-apartment with a kitchenette, separate from the house. An ideal place to spend a few days, as it is only a few minutes from the old town of Antibes. Near the centre of Juan les Pins and the beach. Relax and enjoy the garden.

PROPERTY

✱✱

riding, cycling 1km, sea or lake watersports 1km, golf course 10km, interesting flora 15km, winter sports 80km

— A8, Exit Antibes. From the town centre, go towards Juan les Pins - Cap d'Antibes. Take the Boulevard du Cap, then right into the chemin du Crouton. Take the first turning on the left (Rue du Parc Saramartel).

Michel LEVAUX

«Villa No 10 »
Domaine du Piol
06650 OPIO

tel: (0) 4 93 77 71 71
fax: (0) 4 93 77 71 71

Private home

17 km - N - CANNES
OPIO: railway station 12km
airport 25km
car essential

06.24 CANNES

This bastide-style house is opposite the golf club, "La Grande Bastide". In a quiet and relaxing spot, the house has all modern facilites and is near tennis courts and two riding centres. There are excellent walks among the olive groves and you are only 20 minutes from the Cote d'Azur. Ten golf courses and two airports within 15km. For music lovers, there is the Antibes Jazz Festival and the Classical Music Festival at Monaco. Fleur de Soleil member.

PRICE STRUCTURE

2 Bedrooms

(2 rooms) shower room with wc, double bed: FF350

Reduction: 1/10–31/05

Capacity: 4 people

PROPERTY

✱✱✱

off street parking, pets not accepted, golf course

English spoken

— From the A8, head towards Grasse and then take Valbonne Centre (either the first or the second Exit). After Valbonne, head towards Opio. After the green-houses on the left, (Chemin du Piol) the Domaine du Piol is situated 40m on the left. It is Villa No.10, with the entrance on the left.

Paul GAZZANO

151, route de Castellar
06500 MENTON

tel: (0) 4 93 57 39 73

Residence of character

06.02 MENTON

South-facing villa in the hills above Menton. This is the Cote D'Azur as you always dreamed about it. Paul is Italian and his wife English and their home exudes warmth and kindness. Madame is a wonderful cook. 9 km from Monaco.

PROPERTY

✱✱✱

lounge, hosts have pets, dinner available, babies welcome, free cot, hiking, cycling, sea or lake watersports,

Fluent English spoken

MENTON
hosts can collect from station, railway station 2km
airport 30km
— In Menton, follow the signs to 'Hotel de Ville'. Pass in front of l'Hotel de Ville and the fire station then take the road to Castellar (be careful to take the road called 'Route de Castellar' and NOT the road to the 'Ciappes de Castellar').

PRICE STRUCTURE

4 Bedrooms

(4 rooms) bathroom with wc, double bed: FF320

Capacity: 8 people

06.06 NICE

A charming couple who love good food. Their bastide is in the centre of this old village, and is very pleasant and spotlessly clean. You will love the unobstructed view and the large garden full of wild flowers.

Alain & Michèle
MARTIN

13, Montée de la
Citadelle
06610 LA GAUDE

tel: (0) 4 93 24 71 01
fax: (0) 4 93 24 71 01
martinalain@minitel.net

Private home

PROPERTY

✱✱✱

private parking, garden, pets not accepted, telephone, dinner available, babies welcome, free cot, hiking, sea or lake watersports 10km, golf course 15km

Fluent English spoken

15 km - W - NICE
LA GAUDE:
airport 12km
car essential
— In Nice, go towards Cannes. At Cagnes sur Mer, turn right towards La Gaude and St Jeannet (8km from Cagnes on the D18). Before the village, after the sign "La Gaude", left at the "Place du Marronnier", then left into the 'Rue du Marronnier'. The hill up to the citadelle is very steep (only suitable for small cars).

PRICE STRUCTURE

2 Bedrooms

First room:-Duplex: lounge, bathroom with wc, 2 twin beds: FF300 (2 people) FF500 (4 people)

Second room: shower room with wc, twin beds: FF250

Reduction: 4 nights

Capacity: 6 people

Karim TAMZALI

10, rue Barla
06300 NICE

tel: (0) 4 93 55 88 55
fax: (0) 4 93 55 88 22

Flat

NICE
airport 5km

PRICE STRUCTURE

2 Bedrooms

television, double bed, single bed: FF300 (2 people) FF400 (3 people)

television, double bed: FF300

Capacity: 5 people

06.07 NICE

This young couple welcome you to their home in a very busy shopping street, behind the port in the heart of Nice, only 10 minutes walk from the Place Massena. The rooms are spacious and on the 2nd floor (there is a lift) of this substantial apartment building.

PROPERTY

✱✱

tv lounge, pets not accepted, telephone, babies welcome, free cot, no smoking, sea or lake watersports,

Adequate English spoken

— On the Promenade des Anglais, turn left at the war memorial. Go to the Place Garibaldi and phone your hosts. It is then a 2 minute walk (the street goes from l'Acropolis as far as the Moyenne Corniche).

06.10 NICE

This Provençale house is 2km from St Paul de Vence. You will find Béatrice quite charming, and the delightful rooms are tastefully furnished. There is also a "bar corner" and picnics are available. Good value for money at this excellent location.

Advance bookings only

PROPERTY

✱✱✱✱

private parking, garden, lounge, hosts have pets, pets not accepted, swimming pool, hiking 3km, fishing 12km, sea or lake watersports 12km, golf course 15km, interesting flora 15km, birdwatching 30km, winter sports 45km, gliding 45km, river watersports 60km

English spoken

PRICE STRUCTURE

3 Bedrooms

Les Olives: bathroom with wc, twin beds, single bed: FF400 (2 people) FF460 (3 people)

Les Blés & Les Pivoines: shower room with wc, double bed:, FF350

Extra bed: 60FF

Béatrice RONIN PILLET

«Le Clos de St Paul»
71, chemin de la Rouguière
06480 LA COLLE SUR LOUP

tel: (0) 4 93 32 56 81
fax: (0) 4 93 32 56 81

Private home

17 km - W - NICE
LA COLLE SUR LOUP:
airport 10km
car essential
— In Nice, go towards Cannes. At Cagnes sur Mer, right towards St Paul de Vence. At La Colle sur Loup, pass the church and the roundabout. At the traffic lights, go towards La Rouguière,continue straight on. The house is on the right in the 2nd valley, after the hamlet of old houses.

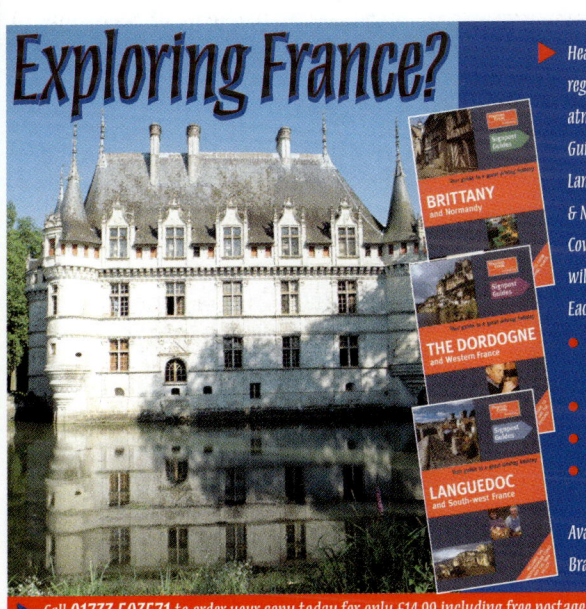

Pia MALET KANITZ

«Villa Panerâ»
8, Av Panera
06100 NICE

tel: (0) 4 92 09 93 20
fax: (0) 4 92 09 93 20

Private home

NICE
hosts can collect from station,
railway station 5km
airport 10km
car essential

PRICE STRUCTURE

1 Suite

kitchen, shower room with wc, double bed, single bed: FF350 (2 people) FF540 (3 people)

Extra bed: 100FF

Reduction: 3 nights

Capacity: 3 people

06.15 NICE

This small house is set high up in a peaceful location in Nice at the foot of the Mont Chauve. Needless to say, there are many wonderful walks close by. The small rooms are elegantly decorated with old furniture. Pia, an artist, provides a warm welcome to her lovely home.

PROPERTY

off street parking, garden, lounge, hosts have pets, telephone, 2 years old minimum age, 2 nights minimum stay, hiking 1km, cycling 2km, sea or lake watersports 2km, river watersports 2km, fishing 5km, mushroom picking 5km, hunting 15km, golf course 20km, interesting flora 20km

Adequate English spoken

— On the A8 towards Gênes (Genoa) take Exit number 54 Nice-Nord. Follow signs towards Gairaut, taking the Aspremont/Le Vens road. After 800m turn left on to the N75 and it is the second house on the right.

Michelle & Guy BENOIT

«L'Olivier Peintre»
136, rue Saint Claude
06640 ST JEANNET

tel: (0) 4 93 24 78 91/76 30
fax: (0) 4 93 24 78 77

Private home

20 km - N W - NICE
ST JEANNET:
railway station 30km
airport 20km
car essential

06.18 NICE

This house, in the old village of St Jeannet, has a pleasant garden and a swimming pool. Add to this a wonderful view and peace and quiet. The inside has great charm, and the decor in Room 1 is particularly attractive and the price well justified. Your hostess is very pleasant, and will be delighted to talk about art, in which she is an expert. It is possible to rent the whole floor as an apartment.

PROPERTY

✱✱

off street parking, garden, tv lounge, hosts have pets, pets not accepted, telephone, dinner available, kitchen, babies welcome, free cot, swimming pool, mushroom picking 5km, golf course 20km, sea or lake watersports 20km, interesting flora 50km, winter sports 80km

Fluent English spoken

— On the A8 towards Nice, Exit St Laurent du Var. Head towards La Gaude/St Jeannet (D18) as far as St Jeannet. In the village, take the main street, then continue to La Place Ste-Barbe and go up the Rue St Claude as far as No. 136.

PRICE STRUCTURE

5 Bedrooms

First room: lounge, television, telephone, shower room with wc, double bed: FF600

Second room: television, bathroom with wc, double bed: FF450

Etage-Appartement: double bed: FF350–500

(2 rooms) double bed: FF350

Capacity: 10 people

Monique & Pierre ALLIEZ

89 Bd Louis Roux
06700 ST LAURENT DU VAR

tel: (0) 4 93 31 74 35
fax: (0) 4 93 31 74 35
E-mail: alliez@club-internet.fr

Private home

5 km - W - NICE
ST LAURENT DU VAR:
railway station 6km
airport 2km
car essential

PRICE STRUCTURE

1 Suite

shower room with wc, bathroom, double bed, 2 single beds: FF350 (2 people)
FF550 (4 people)

Reduction: 3 nights

Capacity: 4 people

06.23 NICE

This Provençal villa is in a quiet location, at the centre of St. Laurent, 10 minutes from the centre of Nice and 5 minutes from the airport and beaches. There are supermarkets, a yacht harbour and restaurants nearby. This is the ideal base from which to visit the Cote d'Azur, St. Tropez, Menton, Monaco, Nice, Antibes, Cannes, Esterel, Fréjus and the hinterland, including St. Paul de Vence. Windsurfing available. A warm welcome awaits, plus many tips on what to see. Fleur de Soleil member.

PROPERTY

***

private parking, garden, pets not accepted, no smoking, closed: 22/12-03/01, fishing, sea or lake watersports

English spoken

— From Nice, on the A8, Exit 49 St. Laurent du Var. Follow the River Var and, at the third roundabout, follow "Centre-Ville - Toutes Directions" and at the traffic lights turn right. The house is No.49, immediately on the left, after the Post Office.

Laurence & René
KOLLWELTER CALMES

«Le Maisnil» Les Faïsses
du Cros
13510 EGUILLES

tel: (0) 4 42 92 64 37
fax: (0) 4 42 92 38 52
E.mail: kollwelter.
maisnil@wanadoo.fr

Private home

8 km - N W - AIX EN PROVENCE
EGUILLES: railway station 8km
airport 20km
car essential

13.30 AIX EN PROVENCE

"Le Maisnil" is a superb house in the village of Eguilles, 8km west of Aix-en-Provence. It is built, on terraces, from local stone, and its quiet and sunny location also includes a beautiful view down over the valley, thick with vines. You are only 1 hour from Marseille, Arles, Avignon, Le Luberon, Ste. Victoire, Cassis and the beaches. Fleur de Soleil member.

PROPERTY

***

off street parking, garden, lounge, babies welcome, free cot, swimming pool,

English spoken

— At Aix, take the CD10 direct to Berre. After 6km, turn on the right towards Eguilles. At the roundabout, go straight on along the Chemin de la Croix, then take the road on the left and it is the third house on the left.

PRICE STRUCTURE

3 Bedrooms

First room: shower room with wc, double bed: FF450

(2 rooms) bathroom with wc, double bed: FF450

Extra bed: 100FF

Capacity: 6 people

Quentin GENICOT

«La Cipionne»
84150 PUYVERT

tel: (0) 4 90 08 40 58

Private home

40 km - N W - AIX EN PROVENCE
PUYVERT: railway station 40km
car essential

PRICE STRUCTURE

3 Bedrooms

(3 rooms) shower room with wc, double bed: FF340

Capacity: 6 people

84.49 AIX EN PROVENCE

This old farmhouse, with its courtyard, is in the heart of the country, with an uninterrupted view over the south of the Luberon. Fleur de Soleil member.

PROPERTY

✱✱✱

off street parking, garden, pets not accepted, swimming pool, closed 16/10-31/03

English spoken

— Contact your host for detailed directions.

Pascale SOLARI

400, chemin St Simon
13540 PUYRICARD

tel: (0) 4 42 92 08 92
fax: (0) 4 42 92 06 85

Private home

10 km - N - AIX EN PROVENCE
PUYRICARD:
railway station 10km
airport 30km
car essential

13.05 AIX EN PROVENCE

Pascale loves meeting people. Her house is in the country surrounded by woods and close to Aix. This is the heart of Provence, cool pine forests and the beautiful town of Aix, famous for its International Music and Dance Festivals.

PROPERTY

✱✱

off street parking, extensive grounds, tv lounge, hosts have pets, babies welcome, free cot, swimming pool, hiking, interesting flora, cycling 10km, golf course 15km, sea or lake watersports 40km

Basic English spoken

— At Aix on the A8, head for Sisteron and join the D14 towards Puyricard. Continue on D14 towards Puy Ste Réparade. 1.8km after the 'Village du Soleil', turn right into the Chemin St Simon, then the house is on the right.

PRICE STRUCTURE

2 Bedrooms

Rez de Chaussée-Abricot: television, bathroom, double bed: FF240

Etage-Bleue: television, shower room with wc, washbasin, twin beds, cot: FF260

Extra bed: 50FF

Capacity: 4 people

Elyane & Joseph
LEONARDI

«Chicalon»
2715, chemin de la
Guiramande
13090 AIX EN
PROVENCE

tel: (0) 4 42 58 06 54
fax: (0) 4 42 58 06 54

Private home

AIX EN PROVENCE
hosts can collect from station,
railway station 5km
airport 20km
car essential

13.18 AIX EN PROVENCE

Only ten minutes from Aix-en-Provence, Elyane and Joseph's villa, nestling between the hills, offers a really warm welcome. If you enjoy food, they will be delighted to serve you their delicious regional and Italian dishes. There is a "Grande Randonnée" route nearby. Weekly lets also possible

PRICE STRUCTURE

1 Apartment

Studio Tara: lounge, television, kitchen, shower room with wc, washbasin, twin beds, single bed: FF290 (2 people) FF360 (3 people)

Reduction:01/09–31/05 and 3 nights and children

Capacity: 2 people

PROPERTY

✱✱

off street parking, extensive grounds, hosts have pets, telephone, dinner available, packed lunch, babies welcome, free cot, swimming pool, hiking, cycling, hunting, interesting flora 5km, golf course 7km, fishing 20km, sea or lake watersports 20km

Fluent English spoken

— At Aix-en-Provence, take the Pont-de-l'Arc Exit, then follow signs to Creps and then continue along the Chemin de la Guiramande, as far as number 2715. The house is straight on, at the end of this lane.

Michel DELENNE

«Villa l'Emeraude»
8, chemin Orange
13100 AIX EN
PROVENCE

tel: (0) 4 42 27 09 61
fax: (0) 4 42 27 09 61

Private home

AIX EN PROVENCE
railway station 1km
airport 25km

13.25 AIX EN PROVENCE

This is the top floor of a Thirties villa, quite independent and restored with a terrace overlooking the garden with swimming pool (covered out of season). You are in the centre of the town yet in an oasis of perfect quiet, cool silence and charm. Follow in the footsteps of Cézanne. Fleur de Soleil member.

PROPERTY

***

private parking, garden, tv lounge, pets not accepted, kitchen, babies welcome, free cot, no smoking, swimming pool, closed: 1/11-1/04, 2 nights minimum stay, cycling, fishing, mushroom picking, birdwatching, hunting 4km, interesting flora 6km, golf course 7km, sea or lake watersports 35km, river watersports 50km

Adequate English spoken

— At Aix, on the Paris-Nice autoroute, Exit Aix-Val St André. Turn left at the first roundabout and right at the second roundabout (Casino supermarket). Then turn right at the third roundabout. Take the 1st street on the left then turn right into the 'chemin d'Orange'. No. 8 is at the end of the cul-de-sac.

PRICE STRUCTURE

1 Suite

1930: lounge, television, telephone, kitchen, bathroom with wc, double bed, twin beds: FF600 (2 people) FF950 (4 people)

Extra bed: 100FF
Reduction: 1/10–31/05 and 7 nights

Capacity: 2 people

Miriam & Hervé
BOUVANT

«Domaine du Frère»
495, rue Ampère - Les Milles
13852 AIX EN PROVENCE

tel: (0) 4 42 24 24 62
fax: (0) 4 42 24 37 89
E.mail:
bouvant@easynet.fr

Private home

6 km - S - AIX EN PROVENCE
railway station 6km
airport 15km
car essential

PRICE STRUCTURE

2 Bedrooms

First room; bathroom with wc, double bed, 2 single beds: FF350 (2 people) FF590 (4 people)

Second room: shower room with wc, double bed: FF300

Extra bed: 120FF

Capacity: 6 people

13.28 AIX EN PROVENCE

This 18th century bastide was previously the residence of an upper class Aix family. All its former glory is preserved in a modern environment, in grounds surrounded by ancient trees. The welcome is warm from this Franco-Dutch family. Although in the heart of Provence, it is possible to get to all the famous places of interest in less than an hour, and your hosts will be delighted to advise you. Miriam's cooking is legendary. Fleur de Soleil member.

PROPERTY

***

off street parking, extensive grounds, pets not accepted, dinner available, swimming pool, tennis, closed: 16/10-31/03, sea or lake watersports 15km

Fluent English spoken

— On the A51, Aix-Marseille autoroute, take the third Exit to Bouc-Bel-Air, and immediately turn right on to the D59. The Domaine du Frère is 3.4km along this road.

Jacqueline LAMBERT

«Mas Sainte Anne»
3, rue d'Auriol
13790 PEYNIER

tel: (0) 4 42 53 05 32
fax: (0) 4 42 53 04 28

Private home

18 km - S E - AIX EN PROVENCE
PEYNIER: railway station 18km
airport 20km
car essential

13.31 AIX EN PROVENCE

This 18th century Provençal mas could be part of a Cézanne landscape. An exceptional location in grounds with a swimming pool, yet quiet. 18km from Aix-en-Provence, 30 minutes from the sea (Cassis or La Ciotat), and a good base for many excursions. Fleur de Soleil member.

PROPERTY

✱✱✱

off street parking, extensive grounds, swimming pool, closed: 01/08-15/08, hiking, golf course 4km

English spoken

PRICE STRUCTURE

3 Bedrooms

First room: shower room with wc, bathroom, double bed: FF400

(2 rooms) shower room with wc, double bed: FF360

Extra bed: 120FF

Capacity: 6 people

— On the A8 towards Nice, take Exit 32, Trets. Head towards Fuveau, then take the D6 towards Trets. 4km before Trets, take the D57 on the right towards Peynier. The Rue d'Auriol adjoins the Post Office, before the "Pharmacie".

Christine LAVENIR

Pont des Trois Sautets -
La Madona Bianca
13590 MEYREUIL

tel: (0) 4 42 27 41 37

Private home

2 km - W - AIX EN PROVENCE
MEYREUIL: railway station 2km
airport 20km
car essential

13.32 AIX EN PROVENCE

This house is in verdant surroundings, surrounded by the forest of Montaiguet and the vineyards of Château Simone. Nearby is the Pont de Trois Sautets, immortalised by Cézanne. Only three minutes from the town centre. Fleur de Soleil member.

PRICE STRUCTURE

2 Bedrooms

First room: shower room with wc, bathroom, double bed: FF300

Second room: bathroom with wc, double bed: FF300

Extra bed: 80/100FF

Capacity: 4 people

PROPERTY

off street parking, garden, pets not accepted, swimming pool, fishing, sea or lake watersports 20km

— On the Autoroute A8, Exit Aix Est, on to the N7 towards Nice. Turn right at the lights, towards Meyreuil and it is 500m after the Pont de Trois Sautets.

Roger & Simone
MERLIN

«Le Mas des Colverts»
Route d'Arles
13460 LES STES MARIES
DE LA MER

tel: (0) 4 90 97 83 73
fax: (0) 4 90 97 74 28

Residence of character

35 km - S W - ARLES
LES STES MARIES
DE LA MER:railway
station 35km
airport 30km

13.02 ARLES

The Provençal "mas" is situated at the end of a peninsular surrounded by lakes. Your hosts will introduce you to the heart of the Camargue, one of the favourite spots for migrant birds and pink flamingos. The view is unique.

PROPERTY

✱✱✱

off street parking, garden, lounge, packed lunch, babies welcome, free cot, 7 nights minimum stay 01/07-31/08, hiking, fishing, birdwatching, sea or lake watersports

Fluent English spoken

— In Arles, take the D570 towards Stes Maries de la Mer. As you enter Ste Marie, after the hotel Boumian, turn left on to the bridge, before the entrance to the Auberge Cavalière.

PRICE STRUCTURE

3 Apartments

(2 rooms) studios kitchen, shower room with wc, double bed, single bed: FF290 (2 people) FF325 (3 people)

Flamants: lounge, television, kitchen, shower room with wc, double bed, 2 single beds: FF500 (2 people) FF550 (4 people)

Reduction: 31/08–30/06 and 7 nights

Capacity: 10 people

Daniel BARD

«Mas des Flammes»
Chemin de Batelle
13200 ARLES

tel: (0) 4 90 96 13 45

Private home

ARLES
hosts can collect from station, railway station 4km airport 20km
car essential

PRICE STRUCTURE

2 Bedrooms and 1 Apartment

(2 rooms) shower room with wc, washbasin, double bed, single bed: FF300 (2 people) FF350 (3 people)

Studio: lounge, kitchen, shower room with wc, washbasin, double bed, single bed: FF300 (2 people) FF350 (3 people)

Extra bed: 60FF
Reduction: 3 nights

Capacity: 9 people

13.21 ARLES

This mas is nestling amongst the fields in the heart of the countryside, on the edge of Arles, and encourages you to relax. They hire out cycles, and this is the ideal way to visit La Camargue, La Crau and Les Alpilles. In Arles, there are many beautiful Roman remains and the influence of Van Gogh is everywhere. Small dog supplement: 60FF

PROPERTY

off street parking, garden, hosts have pets, dinner available, kitchen, babies welcome, free cot, wheelchair access, hiking, cycling, golf course, river watersports 5km, birdwatching 15km, gliding 15km, interesting flora 25km, fishing 30km, hunting 30km, sea or lake watersports 30km

Basic English spoken

— At Arles, head towards the hospital and then follow the signs to the Mas de Flammes.

Monique BRUNO

«Mas DOM PATER»
Chemin du Prud'homme
13210 ST RÉMY DE PROVENCE

tel: (0) 4 90 92 01 39
fax: (0) 4 90 92 09 33
mobruno@club-internet.fr

Residence of character

9 km - N - BAUX DE PROVENCE
ST REMY DE PROVENCE: railway station 19km
airport 20km
car essential

13.06 BAUX DE PROVENCE

This restored 17th century mas is typically Provençal. The welcome is warm. Enjoy the swimming pool, the pool-house and the shade after a hard day's sightseeing. Heavenly peace and quiet.

PROPERTY

✱✱✱

private parking, extensive grounds, tv lounge, hosts have pets, telephone, kitchen, packed lunch, wheelchair access, swimming pool, closed: 1/07-31/08, 2 nights minimum stay, fishing, hiking 3km, cycling 4km, gliding 7km, golf course 8km, interesting flora 30km, birdwatching 45km, sea or lake watersports 45km

English spoken

— From Les Baux, take the D5 towards St. Rémy and Avignon. (From the A7 take the Cavaillon Exit. and the D99 towards Nîmes.). At St Rémy, follow signs to Avignon for 2km. The lane is on the left, before the bus stop. Continue for 600m, and it is at the end of the lane on the left. Look for the stone sign "Mas Dom Pater".

PRICE STRUCTURE

5 Bedrooms

Fourth - Etage: bathroom with wc, twin beds: FF500

First Rez de chaussée: television, kitchen, shower room with wc, twin beds: FF500

Second Rez de chaussée: television, shower room with wc, twin beds: FF500

Third - Etage: shower room with wc, double bed: FF500

Fifth - Etage: shower room with wc, double bed: FF500

Extra bed: 75FF
Reduction: 1/11–30/12 and 1/03–15/04

Capacity: 10 people

Richard Humbert FEIGE

«Mas Clair de Lune»
Av Théodore Aubanel -
Plateau de la Crau
13210 ST RÉMY DE
PROVENCE

tel: (0) 4 90 92 63 17/02
63

Private home

9 km - N - BAUX DE PROVENCE
ST REMY DE PROVENCE: railway station 19km
airport 20km
car essential
— From Les Baux, take the D5 towards St. Rémy and Avignon. From the A7 take the Cavaillon Exit. Take the D99 until you reach St. Rémy de Provence. As you enter St Rémy, before you cross the canal, turn right then left. Go to the college (CES) towards the right. The mas is at the end on the right, facing the country trail.

13.07 BAUX DE PROVENCE

Complete calm and a very warm welcome awaits you here, under the pine trees with an unobstructed view of Les Alpilles on one side, and the Mont Ventoux on the other. The rooms and the studios are very bright and attractive. Here you will feel great ... la vie est belle!

PROPERTY

✱✱✱

off street parking, extensive grounds, hosts have pets, swimming pool, fishing, hiking 3km, cycling 4km, gliding 7km, golf course 8km, interesting flora 30km, birdwatching 45km, sea or lake watersports 45km

English spoken

PRICE STRUCTURE

2 Bedrooms and 3 Apartments

First room: television, shower room with wc, lounge, twin beds: FF350

Second room: television, shower room with wc, twin beds: FF350

(3 rooms) television, kitchen, shower room with wc, twin beds: FF350

Extra bed: 100FF

Capacity: 10 people

Anne-Marie BOUCHEZ

«Mas de la Muette»
Chemin du Mas d'Astre
13520 MAUSSANE LES ALPILLES

tel: (0) 4 90 54 36 46
fax: (0) 4 90 54 36 46

Private home

3 km - S - BAUX DE PROVENCE
MAUSSANE LES ALPILLES: railway station 15km
airport 30km
car essential

13.13 BAUX DE PROVENCE

Anne-Marie's country house is at the foot of Les Alpilles, 8km from St Rémy de Provence and its famous Provençal market. There is also Alphonse Daudet's Moulin (Fontvieille) and les Baux de Provence to visit.

PROPERTY

✱✱✱

private parking, garden, hosts have pets, hiking 1km, cycling 1km, golf course 1km, fishing 3km, interesting flora 3km, mushroom picking 3km, gliding 8km, river watersports 15km, birdwatching 20km, sea or lake watersports 50km

English spoken

— At Arles head in the direction of les Baux de Provence and follow the D17 as far as Maussane. Cross Maussane and then take the D27 on the right towards St Martin de Crau. At the bull-ring (Avenue Frédéric Mistral) turn right and then keep left.

PRICE STRUCTURE

2 Bedrooms

First room: shower room with wc, double bed: FF300

Second room: along corridor shower room with wc, twin beds: FF280

Extra bed: 85FF

Capacity: 4 people

Yvon Marcel LUTZ

«Le Mas du Petit Puits»
Chemin Mario Prassinos
13810 EYGALIERES

tel: (0) 4 90 95 91 18
fax: (0) 4 90 90 64 43

Residence of character

15 km - E - BAUX DE PROVENCE EYGALIERES: railway station 15km, airport 20km car essential

13.22 BAUX DE PROVENCE

This beautiful mas, furnished in 17th and 18th century style, is a short distance from Eygalières, a famously enchanting Provençal village. There is an uninterrupted view of Les Alpilles. They use old local recipes for their menus. Les Baux de Provence is 15 minutes away. On sale: wine, olive oil.

PRICE STRUCTURE

4 Bedrooms

N°2: television, bathroom with wc, twin beds: FF530

N°3: television, bathroom with wc, double bed:FF590

N°4: along corridor shower room with wc, double bed: FF430

N°5: television, bathroom with wc, double bed: FF630

Extra bed: 100FF

Reduction:16/09–15/06

Capacity: 8 people

PROPERTY

✱✱✱

private parking, garden, tv lounge, hosts have pets, telephone, dinner available, babies welcome, free cot, swimming pool, cycling, interesting flora, birdwatching, hiking 1km, fishing 5km, hunting 5km, mushroom picking 5km, golf course 10km, sea or lake watersports 40km

Adequate English spoken

— From the A7, take the Cavaillon Exit. Head towards St. Rémy de Provence. After 12km, turn left towards Eygalières. Go as far as the church and then head towards "Mas de la Brune" for 300m and turn left. After 100m turn left again.

Marie & François
VEILLEUX

«Mas de Beaupré»
24+787 route de St Rémy
13103 ST ETIENNE DU GRES

tel: (0) 4 90 49 02 18
fax: (0) 4 90 49 02 18
mas-de-beaupre@wanadoo.fr

Residence of character

10 km - N W - BAUX DE PROVENCE
ST ETIENNE DU GRES: railway station 8km
airport 20km
car essential

13.23 BAUX DE PROVENCE

At the foot of the Alpilles, this old mas, which has been restored, provides an unbeatable and charming stay. Chez Marie, everything is organised and simply runs smoothly. When you add to this a superb position and high standards of comfort (air-conditioned bedrooms), what more could one ask?

PROPERTY

✱✱✱✱

private parking, extensive grounds, lounge, hosts have pets, pets not accepted, babies welcome, free cot, swimming pool, hiking, cycling, interesting flora, hunting 1km, mushroom picking 1km, golf course 6km, gliding 12km, fishing 50km, birdwatching 50km, sea or lake watersports 50km

Adequate English spoken

PRICE STRUCTURE

2 Bedrooms

First room: bathroom with wc, twin beds, single bed (childrens size): FF450

Second room: bathroom with wc, twin beds, cot: FF450

Extra bed: 50FF

Capacity: 5 people

— Go to St Rémy and then take the D99 towards Tarascon-Nîmes (from the A7, Exit Cavaillon). The house is 500m before St Etienne du Grés on the left (sign "24+787").

Carolyn WOOD

«Aux Deux Soeurs»
Le Vieux chemin d'Arles
13103 ST ETIENNE DU GRES

tel: (0) 4 90 49 10 18
fax: (0) 4 90 49 10 30
ads.wood.gites@infonie.fr

Private home

15 km - N W - BAUX DE PROVENCE
ST ETIENNE DU GRES:
railway station,6km
airport 40km
— At St. Rémy, take the D99 towards Tarascon-Nîmes, then the D27 towards les Baux de Provence. Then turn right towards St. Etienne du Grès. After 3km, turn left and follow the signs to "Deux Soeurs" (On the A7, Exit Cavaillon and then take the D99 towards Nîmes).

13.26 CASSIS

This beautiful 19th century Proven al bastide and its outbuildings, nestle in a valley at the heart of Les Alpilles. You are near St. Rémy de Provence and St. Etienne du Grès. Enjoy the shade of the trees and the swimming pool. A beautiful spot...

PROPERTY

****

off street parking, extensive grounds, lounge, hosts have pets, telephone, dinner available, packed lunch, babies welcome, free cot, swimming pool, hiking, cycling, hunting, fishing 3km, golf course 6km, gliding 12km, interesting flora 30km, bird-watching 30km, sea or lake watersports 50km

Fluent English spoken

PRICE STRUCTURE

2 Bedrooms and 1 Apartment

Nénuphar: television, telephone, bathroom with wc, double bed, single bed (childrens size): FF600 (2 people) FF600 (3 people)

Hiboux: television, telephone, bathroom with wc, twin beds: FF500

Grenier 100m²: lounge, television, telephone, kitchen, bathroom with wc, double bed, 2 single bed: FF700 (2 people) FF850 (4 people)

Reduction: 8 nights

Capacity: 9 people

Maud & Gabriel
APICELLA

«La Bastidaine»
6bis, Av des Albizzi
13260 CASSIS

tel: (0) 4 42 98 83 09
fax: (0) 4 42 03 47 17

Private home

CASSIS
hosts can collect from station,
railway station 1km
airport 40km
car essential

13.24 MARSEILLE

This old wine groweris bastide is spacious, and the beige-rose colour of the walls sets the tone of a place where you will feel at home. It is easy to find, yet quietly situated amongst the pines. Be sure to visit the famous Calanques de Cassis, where there is also a top sub-aqua centre. Fleur de Soleil member. On sale: Home-made jam.

PROPERTY

✱✱✱

private parking, garden, hosts have pets, dinner available, no smoking, hiking, cycling, sea or lake watersports, fishing 1km, golf course 15km

Adequate English spoken

PRICE STRUCTURE

4 Bedrooms

First room: shower room with wc, double bed, twin beds: FF420 (2 people) FF620 (4 people)

Second and third rooms: shower room with wc, wash-basin, double bed: FF380

Fourth room: shower room with wc, washbasin, double bed: FF420

Extra bed: 100FF
Reduction: 15/11–15/03 and 7 nights and groups

Capacity: 10 people

— From the A50, Exit Cassis. High up above the town, at the traffic lights, head towards the station and Roquefort la Bedoule. When you are in the Avenue des Abizzi, it is 300m further on, on the right.

Catherine ARNOULT

13, Promenade Georges
Pompidou
13008 MARSEILLE

tel: (0) 4 91 71 14 85
fax: (0) 4 91 71 14 85

Private home

MARSEILLE
airport 25km

PRICE STRUCTURE

1 Bedroom

shower room with wc, double bed, FF420

Capacity: 2 people

13.27 MARSEILLE

A 19th century house with a garden, close to the sea, with a view of the beach and the sailing boats. There is easy parking and a bus from outside the front door goes to the sports stadium or the old port, via the Corniche. There are many restaurants in the area and, although at the heart of Marseille, it easy to reach the south (Calanques de Cassis) and the north (Aix-en-Provence). Fleur de Soleil member.

PROPERTY

garden, pets not accepted, sea or lake watersports

English spoken

— In Marseille, at the end of the Prado beach, near to the Hotel Concorde Palm Beach.

Martine & Jean-Yves
DUSSART

198, Avenue de la
Panouse
13009 MARSEILLE

tel: (0) 4 91 41 01 74
fax: (0) 4 91 41 01 74

Château

MARSEILLE
airport 30km

13.29 MARSEILLE

The Château de la Panouse, which overlooks the city of Marseille, is a haven of tranquility between the sea and the mountains. Built in the 19th century by a Marseille ship owner, the property covers over 14,000m² and is a good starting point for hiking trips into the Massif des Calanques. Fleur de Soleil member.

PROPERTY

✱✱✱

off street parking, extensive grounds, lounge, dinner available, swimming pool, hiking, sea or lake watersports

English spoken

PRICE STRUCTURE

2 Bedrooms

First room: bathroom with wc, double bed: FF300

Second room: bathroom with wc, double bed: FF350

Extra bed: 100FF

Capacity: 4 people

— South-east of Marseille, near to the road to Cassis. Contact your host for more detailed information.

Annick NIEL

«Villa Fanny»
33, chemin des Cabanes
13500 ST JULIEN MARTIGUES

tel: (0) 4 42 07 36 06
fax: (0) 4 42 40 38 03

Private home

23 km - W - MARSEILLE
ST JULIEN MARTIGUES:
railway station 8km
airport 15km
car essential

PRICE STRUCTURE

2 Bedrooms

Nicky: shower room with wc, bathroom, double bed, FF280

Kathy: shower room with wc, bathroom, double bed: single bed: FF280 (2 people) FF430 (3 people)

Capacity: 5 people

13.33 SALON DE PROVENCE

This pleasant villa in the Martigues countryside, surrounded by vineyards, has a typical Mediterranean garden It is 5 minutes from the coast, beaches and the Venise Provençale. A good base for visiting Marseille, les Calanques, La Camargue, Les Alpilles and Aix-en-Provence. There is riding, water sports and tennis nearby and the welcome is warm and friendly. Fleur de Soleil member.

PROPERTY

✱✱✱

off street parking, garden, dinner available, swimming pool, hiking, fishing 5km, sea or lake watersports 5km

English spoken

— Fom Marseille, Aix-en-Provence or Arles, head in the direction of Cote Bleue, Carry le Rouet. Exit at Saussey/St. Julien.

13.10 SALON DE PROVENCE

Michael John FROST

«Mas de la Rabassière»
Route de Cornillon
13250 ST CHAMAS

tel: (0) 4 90 50 70 40
fax: (0) 4 90 50 70 40

Private home

Totally peaceful, this is pure Provence. A view over the Etang de Berre and the sea, and a sailing boat at your disposal... Michael is English and here you will find comfort, helpfulness, a sense of humour, warmth and kindness. His Provençal cooking and home-made croissants are pretty good too!

PROPERTY

✱✱✱

private parking, extensive grounds, tv lounge, pets not accepted, telephone, dinner available, babies welcome, free cot, wheelchair access, no smoking, swimming pool, tennis, hiking, cycling, mushroom picking 1km, fishing 2km, sea or lake watersports 2km, golf course 5km, birdwatching 30km

Fluent English spoken

15 km - S - SALON DE PROVENCE
ST CHAMAS: hosts can collect from station, railway station 5km
airport 25km
— From the A7 towards Marseille, Exit Rognac and take the N113 towards Salon. At La Fare, turn left on to the D10 towards Miramas. At the traffic lights after the Roman bridge, turn right on to the D70 towards Cornillon for 2.7km. Turn left and continue for 200m. The house is on the left (2nd gate).

PRICE STRUCTURE

2 Bedrooms

First room: telephone, bathroom with wc, double bed, single bed: FF700

Second room: telephone, along corridor bathroom with wc, double bed, single bed: FF700

Capacity: 6 people

Roselyne & Giordano
FOGLIA

«Le Gallatras»
Route de Caireval
13410 LAMBESC

tel: (0) 4 42 92 75 70
fax: (0) 4 42 92 75 92

Residence of character

15 km - E - SALON DE PROVENCE LAMBESC: hosts can collect from station, railway station 20km airport 40km car essential

13.15 SALON DE PROVENCE

PRICE STRUCTURE

2 Bedrooms

bathroom with wc, double bed: FF400

bathroom with wc, double bed: FF380

Capacity: 4 people

The house is located between Salon and the lovely town of Aix where life is as good as it gets. The lovely countryside of Aix is awash with vineyards and oaks...and your friendly hostess, Roselyne, will serve you an excellent breakfast in her tastefully decorated and elegant home. You will definitely return here.

PROPERTY

✱✱✱

off street parking, extensive grounds, hosts have pets, pets not accepted, babies welcome, free cot, swimming pool, hiking, cycling, mushroom picking, golf course 8km, sea or lake watersports 40km

— Lambesc is situated on the N7 (from the A7 take the Exit towards Salon). Go in the direction of Lambesc-Centre. At the Post Office (La Poste), head towards Caireval for 1.5km and the house is on the left.

Mireille & Robert
JAUFFRET

55, rue de la Liberté
13980 ALLEINS

tel: (0) 4 90 59 36 87
fax: (0) 4 90 57 39 13

Private home

20 km - N - SALON DE PROVENCE
ALLEINS: railway station 14km
airport 30km
car essential

13.19 SALON DE PROVENCE

If you stay with Mireille and Robert at the heart of this quiet little village, between the Alpilles and the Lubéron, you will benefit from their expert advice on excursions and your choice of which festival to book. In their cute, little house you may be lucky to have breakfast served on the terrace (home-made patisseries and jam). You are near to Aix-en-Provence, Avignon and Arles. Fleur de soleil member.

PROPERTY

✱✱

private parking, lounge, no pets, babies welcome, free cot, cycling, golf course 2km, hiking 5km

— From the A7, Exit 26 Sénas and then take the N7 towards Aix-en-Provence. Turn right towards Alleins. In the village, park on the "Place de la Mairie" and walk down the "Impasse Lavoisier" on the left of the tower.

PRICE STRUCTURE

1 Suite

lounge, shower room with wc, twin beds: FF260

telephone, single bed: FF220

Extra bed: 100FF

Capacity: 3 people

Belle Viste

650, chemin de Maran
83330 LE BEAUSSET

tel: (0) 4 94 98 62 11
fax: (0) 4 94 98 62 11

Residence of character

7 km - N E - BANDOL
LE BEAUSSET: hosts can collect from station, railway station 7km
airport 40km
car essential

PRICE STRUCTURE

2 Bedrooms and 1 Suite

First room: shower room with wc, double bed: FF350

Second room: shower room with wc, twin beds: FF350

Suite: shower room with wc, double bed: 2 single beds (childrens size): FF350 (2 people) FF600 (4 people)

Extra bed: 100FF

Capacity: 8 people

83.21 BANDOL

You will be overwhelmed by the taste and originality of this place, with its large swimming pool and magnificent views. Each bedroom opens on to the terrace. The sea, Châteauvallon and Le Castellet are just a few places well-worth a visit.

PROPERTY

✱✱✱

private parking, garden, tv, hosts have pets, no pets, telephone, swimming pool, hiking 1km, cycling 1km, golf course 6km, fishing 7km, sea or lake watersports 7km

English spoken

— On the A50 Marseille-Toulon, exit number 11 for Le Castellet. Follow signs for Le Beausset and take the N8 towards Toulon. At the second roundabout turn right and it is the road after the Shell petrol station.

Patricia BREBION

«Lou Bastidoun»
390, chemin du Canadeau
La Migoua 83330 LE BEAUSSET

tel: (0) 4 94 90 26 12
fax: (0) 4 94 98 71 54
e-mail: bastidoun@aol.com
http//www.members.aol.com/bastidoun

Residence of character

13 km - N E - BANDOL
LE BEAUSSET:
railway station 13km
airport 40km
car essential

83.25 BANDOL

This bastide is out in the wilds, on a hill. Ideal if you are looking for a quiet place with character. The bedrooms are brand new, and very well decorated and have a separate entrance. Make use of the swimming pool, and enjoy the very warm welcome from your hostess.

PROPERTY

****

off street parking, extensive grounds, tv lounge, hosts have pets, no smoking, swimming pool, cycling 4km, hiking 5km, gliding 7km, golf course 10km, fishing 10km

Basic English spoken

—— On the A50, Exit La Cadière, Le Castellet. Head towards Le Beausset. At the first roundabout, turn right towards Beausset Vieux - Le Rouve. 3km further on, in the hamlet of La Migoua, take the Chemin du Canadeau on the right.

PRICE STRUCTURE

2 Bedrooms

Marine: television, shower room with wc, washbasin, double bed, single bed: FF380 (2 people) FF580 (3 people)

Anglaise: television, shower room with wc, washbasin, double bed: FF380

Extra bed: 100FF
Reduction: 3 nights

Capacity: 5 people

Pierre & Jean ROGER & RIEDINGER

«Chez Pierre»
9, rue Montenard
83890 BESSE SUR ISSOLE

tel: (0) 4 94 69 79 84

Private home

15 km - S E - BRIGNOLES
BESSE SUR ISSOLE: railway station 35km
airport 35km
car essential

PRICE STRUCTURE

2 Bedrooms

Jaune: shower room with wc, double bed: FF330

Fleurs: bathroom with wc, twin beds: FF330

Extra bed: 100FF

Reduction: 01/04–31/05 and 2 nights

Capacity: 4 people

83.26 BRIGNOLES

Pierre has decorated this house, on three floors, with great taste and charm Everything is designed for your well-being. The atmosphere is friendly, yet the location is quiet, in the heart of this 17th century listed village. The ideal spot from which to explore Provence and enjoy its festivals.

PROPERTY

✱✱✱

private parking, garden, tv lounge, hosts have pets, no pets, telephone, 12 years of age minimum age, closed: 01/11-31/03, hiking, fishing, sea or lake watersports, mushroom picking 1km, hunting 2km, golf course 15km

Adequate English spoken

— On the A8, Exit Brignoles. Take the M7 towards Le Luc. After 13 km turn right to Besse sur Issole. When in the village, go as far as the fountain and the statue, and then take Rue Montenard.

Michael & Laurence ALTMAN

«Mas de l'Hermitage»
St Pons 83830
FIGANIERES

tel: (0) 4 94 67 94 94
fax: (0) 4 94 67 83 88

Private home

10 km - N - DRAGUIGNAN
FIGANIERES: hosts can collect from station, railway station 20km
airport 95km
car essential

83.23 DRAGUIGNAN

Take in the lovely open views of the area, with its park, woods and play area for children as you enjoy breakfast on the terrace. Laurence and Michael made the right decision in leaving Britain, and have created the ideal environment in which to relax...with Laurence attending to all the little extras that will make your stay so memorable. Fleur de Soleil member.

PROPERTY

✱✱✱

off street parking, extensive grounds, hosts have pets, no pets, telephone, dinner available, kitchen, babies welcome, free cot, wheelchair access, swimming pool, hiking, cycling, hunting, interesting flora, mushroom picking, birdwatching, golf course 12km, sea or lake watersports 28km, gliding 30km, river watersports 38km

Fluent English spoken

— On the A8 exit number 36 Le Muy, and head towards Draguignan. At the second roundabout take the D54 towards Figanières for 17km. Carry straight on at the junction with the road to Fayence, and the house is 150m on the left (sign).

PRICE STRUCTURE

3 Bedrooms and 4 Apartments

Menthe: lounge, kitchen, bathroom with wc, twin beds: FF350

Olive: kitchen, shower room with wc, double bed: FF350

Bergamote: lounge, kitchen, shower room with wc, twin beds, 2 single beds (childrens size): FF350 (2 people) FF550 (4 people)

Thym: lounge, bathroom with wc, double bed: FF350

Anis: lounge, shower room with wc, twin beds: FF350

Safran: lounge, kitchen, shower room with wc, twin beds: FF350

Santoline: lounge, kitchen, shower room with wc, double bed: FF350

Extra bed: 130FF
Reduction: 01/10–01/04 and 7 nights

Capacity: 16 people

Gilles & Sylvie BARREME

1, Chemin de Braou
83670 TAVERNES

tel: (0) 4 94 72 31 04
fax: (0) 4 94 72 31 04

Farm

83.15 ST MAXIMIM LA STE BAUME

You will certainly thank your hosts for taking you to the olive-oil press and the wine cooperative. Olive-oil, wine and pottery are typical of the Midi and well worth bringing back. On sale: Olive-oil, wine.

PROPERTY

✱✱

off street parking, garden, tv lounge, dinner available, packed lunch, babies welcome, free cot, swimming pool, cycling, sea or lake water-sports 16km

Adequate English spoken

20km- N E- ST MAXIMIM LA STE BAUME TAVERNES:
railway station 35km
airport 70km
car essential
— On the A8 Aix/Nice, take the exit to St Maximin where you take the D560 towards Tavernes and Riez. The house is at the crossroads with the D554 towards Ginasservis (signposted).

PRICE STRUCTURE

2 Bedrooms

First room: Rez de Chaussée: television, shower room with wc, double bed: FF280

Second room: Rez de Chaussée: television, kitchen, shower room with wc, twin beds: FF280

Extra bed: 80FF Reduction: 1/03–30/06 and 1/09–30/11 and 10 nights and groups and children

Capacity: 2 people

83.20 ST RAPHAEL

This charming English lady knows only too well how to give her guests a great welcome. She has discovered a wonderful place in Provence that is the envy of all those who wish they had discovered it first. This magnificent village is full of character. You will feel at home here...

Jennifer PRESTON

Les Bas Baudissets
83440 ST PAUL EN FORET

tel: (0) 4 94 76 37 58
fax: (0) 4 94 76 32 82

Private home

PROPERTY

✱✱✱

off street parking, garden, tv lounge, hosts have pets, no pets, dinner available, 6 years of age minimum, swimming pool, closed: 31/10-31/03, hiking, cycling, interesting flora 3km, fishing 4km, mushroom picking 5km, birdwatching 5km, gliding 5km, sea or lake watersports 15km, golf course 20km

Fluent English spoken

20 km - N - ST RAPHAEL
ST PAUL EN FORET:
railway station 20km
airport 70km
car essential
— On the A8 exit Les Adrets. Take the D37 to join up with the D562 (Grasse-Draguignan). Turn left towards Draguignan. At the "Lou Pascouren" auberge on the D4, turn left towards Fréjus. In St Paul, stay on this road and phone so that your host can come and fetch you.

PRICE STRUCTURE

2 Bedrooms

First room: television, bathroom with wc, twin beds: FF500

Second room: single bed: FF200

Extra bed: 80FF
Reduction: 01/04–30/06 and 01/09–31/10

Capacity: 3 people

Ursula ROQUES

«Le Mas Rouge»
83120 PLAN DE LA
TOUR

tel: (0) 4 94 43 75 88
fax: -(0) 1 42 65 93 53

Private home

10 km - N W - STE MAXIME
PLAN DE LA TOUR:
railway station 34km
airport 110km
car essential
— In Ste Maxime, take the D25 towards Le Muy and the A8. Turn left on to the D74 towards Plan de la Tour. There, turn right on to the D44 towards Le Muy. After Vallaury, continue for 1km. The house is on the right, down below the road.

83.07 STE MAXIME

Not easy to find, but once you get there you will enchanted by Ursula. Here you are near to St. Tropez but you will benefit from the quiet of the hinterland of the Var, amongst the vines and in the heart of the 'Massif des Maures'.

PROPERTY

✱✱✱

off street parking, garden, tv lounge, hosts have pets, no pets, babies welcome, free cot, swimming pool, closed: 1/10-31/05, hiking, golf course 10km, sea or lake watersports 10km

Adequate English spoken

PRICE STRUCTURE

3 Bedrooms

First & second rooms: shower room with wc, double bed: FF260

Third room: kitchen, shower room with wc, double bed: FF380

Extra bed: 50FF
Reduction: 1/09–1/07

Capacity: 6 people

Dominique & Pierre MENARD

«L'Aumonerie»
620, avenue du Font Brun
83320 CARQUEIRANNE

tel: (0) 4 94 58 53 56

Private home

15 km - W - TOULON
CARQUEIRANNE: railway station 15km
airport 6km

83.10 TOULON

This old house has been completely restored and is beautifully calm and relaxing. You are at the water's edge, on a private beach, with trees and a lawn. Breakfast is served on the terrace overlooking the sea. Hyères is only 5km away, from where the boat leaves for Les Isles d'Or. The Foret des Maures and its picturesque villages are very close. Fleur de Soleil member.

PROPERTY

✱✱✱

off street parking, extensive grounds, no pets, sea or lake watersports,

English spoken

— From Toulon, take the autoroute towards Nice, Exit 2 to Le Pradet. At Carqueiranne, go straight on at three roundabouts, then take the second road on the right.

PRICE STRUCTURE

3 Bedrooms and 1 Apartment

First room: bathroom with wc, double bed: FF480

Second room: shower room with wc, double bed: FF480

Third room: shower room with wc, twin beds: FF380

Studio: kitchen, shower room with wc, double bed: FF550

Extra bed: 150FF
Reduction: 01/09–30/04

Capacity: 8 people

Brigitte & Roger
BERCEOT

«Les Capriers»
chemin de la Canolle
83200 TOULON

tel: (0) 4 94 09 05 37
fax: (0) 4 94 92 13 60

Private home

TOULON
railway station 3km
airport 25km
car essential

PRICE STRUCTURE

1 Bedroom and 1 Suite and 1 Apartment

First room: kitchen, shower room with wc, bathroom, double bed, single bed: FF280 (2 people) FF380 (3 people)

Second room: shower room with wc, bathroom, double bed: FF230

double bed: FF200

Extra bed: 100FF

Capacity: 7 people

83.28 TOULON

This is a small, detached house, in the exotic grounds of the older main house. There is a swimming pool and you are also close to the Cote d'Azur and St. Tropez, Aix-en-Provence and Avignon. This is a good base for many excursions, such as the Iles d'Hyères, Calanques and the Gorges du Verdon. Fleur de Soleil member.

PROPERTY

***

off street parking, garden, no pets, dinner available, no smoking, swimming pool, hiking

English spoken

— Contact your host for detailed directions.

Amélie & Robert DIDIER

21, chemin des
Marguerites
La Fossette
83980 LE LAVANDOU

tel: (0) 4 94 71 07 82
fax: (0) 4 94 71 07 82

Private home

40 km - E -
TOULON
LE LAVANDOU:
railway station 40km
airport 20km
car essential

83.29 TOULON

This villa, in a quiet, wooded garden, has a wonderful view over the sea and Les Isles du Levant- Port Cros. You are 3km from the town centre and 400m from a sandy beach, where sea fishing, sailing and diving can be enjoyed. Aix-en-Provence, Cannes, St. Tropez, typical Provençal villages and the Gorges du Verdon are nearby. From Le Lavandou, take a boat to Les Iles Porquerolles and Port Cros. Fleur du Soleil member.

PRICE STRUCTURE

1 Suite

bathroom with wc, 2 double beds: FF360 (2 people) FF580 (4 people)

Capacity: 4 people

PROPERTY

✱✱✱

off street parking, garden, no pets, fishing, sea or lake water-sports,

English spoken

— When you are near, ring your hosts and they will come and pick you up from the Tourist Office.

Aline VERDON

«Villa Manou»
58, chemin de la Baume
83200 TOULON

tel: (0) 4 94 09 34 02

Private home

TOULON
railway station 1km
airport 20km
car essential

PRICE STRUCTURE

1 Suite

shower room with wc, double bed: FF360

+ bathroom with wc, double bed: FF320

Extra bed: 100FF

Capacity: 4 people

83.30 TOULON

This Provençal house has a 2000m² garden with a swimming pool. It is beautifully quiet, and has two bedrooms (one en-suite), a lounge with your own separate entrance. It is near to the beaches, golf and tennis. Fleur de Soleil member.

PROPERTY

✱✱✱

off street parking, garden, lounge, dinner available, no smoking, swimming pool, golf course

English spoken

— Head towards Toulon Ouest, Exit 15.

Pierre MARIETTE

«La Mostre Soleira»
19, rue de la Republique
84480 BONNIEUX

tel: (0) 4 90 75 81 02

Private home

10 km - SE - APT
BONNIEUX: airport 40 km
car essential

84.23 APT

A well equipped village house, in a wonderful listed village in the Luboron. It is on the promontory 'Le Mont St Michel de Provence', and so affords a magnificent view of the Luboron mountain. This is Peter Mayle country.

PROPERTY

✱✱✱

hosts have pets, kitchen, babies welcome, cots free, hiking cycling, fishing, interesting flora, mushroom picking, sea or lake watersports, river watersports, golf course, winter sports

English spoken

PRICE STRUCTURE

5 Bedrooms

4 & 7: bathroom with wc, twin beds: FF230

6 & 9: bathroom with wc, double bed: FF230

8: bathroom with wc, single bed: FF200

Free extra bed
Reduction: 8 nights

Capacity: 9 people

— At Apt, take the N100 towards Avignon then turn left towards Bonnieux.

13.11 AVIGNON

A lovely, quiet village house, with an interior courtyard. Alyne is a mine of information on the various walks, activities and interesting places to visit in the region. She is a real "méridionale", who loves her country.

PROPERTY

✱✱

private parking, lounge, hosts have pets, no pets, babies welcome, free cot, wheelchair access, no smoking, cycling, fishing, hiking 5km, golf course 10km, interesting flora 40km, birdwatching 40km, sea or lake watersports 40km

English spoken

PRICE STRUCTURE

1 Suite

Lounge, kitchen, bathroom with wc, 2 double beds, single bed: FF300 (2 people) FF540 (5 people)

Extra bed: 80FF

Reduction: 3 nights

Capacity: 5 people

Gilbert & Alyne JOUVE

19 bis Avenue Dr Perrier
13160 CHATEAURE-
NARD

tel: (0) 4 90 94 63 23

Private home

9 km - S - AVIGNON
CHATEAURENARD:
railway station 9km
airport 9km
car essential
— From the A7, take the Exit Avignon-Sud. Then via the N7, take the D28 towards Tarascon as far as Châteaurenard.

André & Annie MALEK

«Le Rocher Pointu»
30390 ARAMON

tel: (0) 4 66 57 41 87
fax: (0) 4 66 57 01 77
amk@imaginet.fr
www.imaginet.fr/~amk

Private home

12 km - S W - AVIGNON
ARAMON: hosts can collect from station, railway station 12km
airport 12km
car essential

PRICE STRUCTURE

4 Bedrooms and 2 Apartments

Noix de Coco: shower room with wc, double bed: FF390

Bleue: shower room with wc, twin beds: FF390

Clair de Lune: shower room with wc, double bed, single bed: FF445 (2 people) FF545 (3 people)

Ecurie: bathroom with wc, double bed: FF445

Studios 1: kitchen, shower room with wc, double bed: FF555

Studios 2: kitchen, shower room with wc, twin beds: FF555

Capacity: 13 people

30.11 AVIGNON

Provençal mas in green countryside, surrounded by 7 hectares of 'garrigue'. Both the bedrooms and the public rooms are warm and comfortable. Substantial breakfasts served on the terrace. Guests are welcome to use the swimming pool and barbecue.

PROPERTY

✱✱✱

off street parking, extensive grounds, tv lounge, hosts have pets, no pets, telephone, kitchen, babies welcome, free cot, swimming pool, closed: 1/11-28/02, hiking, fishing 3km, sea or lake watersports 15km, river watersports 15km

Adequate English spoken

— In Avignon, take the 'Pont de l'Europe' towards Nîmes. Just after the bridge, take the D2 along the Rhone towards Aramon. Before the next bridge, turn right on to the D126 towards the N100, and continue for 2.3km. Then turn left.

84.03 AVIGNON

We fell in love with Caroline, whose welcome proves how warm the welcome from the Midi people can be. You will be surrounded by ponies, sheep and angora goats. 10 mins from Avignon. On sale: Honey, eggs, poultry, jam.

PROPERTY

****

off street parking, extensive grounds, tv lounge, hosts have pets, telephone, dinner available,

Fluent English spoken

PRICE STRUCTURE

2 Bedrooms and 1 Suite

Colline & Coté Jardin & Village: television, shower room with wc, twin beds: FF285

Ventoux: television, shower room with wc, 4 single beds: FF240 (2 people) FF480 (4 people)

Lubéron: television, shower room with wc, double bed, 2 single beds: FF240 (2 people) FF480 (4 people)

Capacity: 14 people

Caroline & Vincent
SOULAT CORNILLE

«Les Vertes Rives»
Chemin des Magues
84470 CHATEAUNEUF
DE GADAGNE

tel: (0) 4 90 22 37 10
fax: (0) 4 90 22 03 31
http://www.pageszoom.tm.fr

Farm

10 km - E - AVIGNON
CHATEAUNEUF DE GADAGNE: hosts can collect from station
railway station 15km
airport 7km
— At Avignon, take the N100 towards Morières, Isle sur Sorgue and Apt. At Châteauneuf de Gadagne, turn right on to the D6 towards Caumont for 300m. Turn left and continue for 800m. The property is on the right.

Elisabeth & Philippe LAMBERT

«Le Clos des Saumanes»
519, chemin de la Garrigue
84470 CHATEAUNEUF DE GADAGNE

tel: (0) 4 90 22 30 86
fax: (0) 4 90 22 30 68
closaumane@aol.com

Residence of character

10 km - E - AVIGNON
CHATEAUNEUF DE GADAGNE:
railway station 9km
airport 5km
car essential

PRICE STRUCTURE

4 Bedrooms

La Vigne: bathroom with wc, double bed, 2 single bed: FF450 (2 people) FF650 (4 people)

Plein Sud & La Cigale & La Pinède: bathroom with wc, double bed: FF400

Capacity: 10 people

84.41 AVIGNON

Here, you will find a warm family welcome in this 18th century bastide amongst the vines and pine trees. A quiet, cool place. Elizabeth, from her extensive knowledge of the area, will be only too pleased to advise on excursions in the area, and you are only 9 km from Avignon, known for its famous arts festival. Fleur de Soleil member.

PROPERTY

✱✱✱

off street parking, extensive grounds, lounge, hosts have pets, telephone, babies welcome, free cot, hiking, cycling, golf course 5km, fishing 10km, river watersports 15km, mushroom picking 20km, interesting flora 25km, winter sports 35km

Fluent English spoken

— At Avignon, take the N100 towards L'Isle sur la Sorgue. At Châteauneuf de Gadagne, turn left on to the D6 towards Jonquerettes and St Saturnin les Avignon. At Jonquerettes, turn left on to the D97 as far as the Clos des Saumanes.

François & Monique GRECK

«Mas du Grand Jonquier»
RD22
84800 LAGNES

tel: (0) 4 90 20 90 13
fax: (0) 4 90 20 91 18

Residence of character

25 km - E - AVIGNON
LAGNES: railway station 25km
airport 18km
car essential

84.04 AVIGNON

Situated between the Vaucluse and the Lubéron mountains, this house has a swimming pool and a solarium in its 5 acre orchard. Only 20 mins from Avignon, and 10 mins from Gordes, it offers an excellent combination of 'farniente', sport, tourism and wonderful evenings arounds Monique's excellent table.

PROPERTY

✱✱✱✱

off street parking, extensive grounds, lounge, hosts have pets, no pets, telephone, dinner available, swimming pool, hiking, cycling, interesting flora 1km, golf course 5km, gliding 20km

Adequate English spoken

— On the A7, take the exit 'Avignon-Sud'. Go towards Apt, Sisteron, Digne. At Petit Palais, continue straight on for 1,8km. The property is on the left. (18km from the autoroute).

PRICE STRUCTURE

6 Bedrooms

Basilic & Olivier: television, telephone, shower room with wc, double bed: FF480

Thym & Romarin: television, telephone, shower room with wc, twin beds: FF480

Amandier: television, telephone, shower room with wc, double bed, 2 single bed: FF480 (2 people) FF680 (4 people)

Figuier: television, telephone, shower room with wc, 3 single beds, FF480 (2 people) FF580 (4 people)

Extra bed: 100FF

Capacity: 15 people

Robert & Elisabeth NEGREL

«La Pastorale»
Route de Fontaine de Vaucluse
84800 LAGNES

tel: (0) 4 90 20 25 18
fax: (0) 4 90 20 21 86

Residence of character

25 km - E - AVIGNON
LAGNES: railway station 25km
airport 15km
car essential

PRICE STRUCTURE

4 Bedrooms

Bleue: shower room with wc, twin beds, single bed: FF330(2 people) FF410 (3 people)

Rose: bathroom with wc, twin beds: FF330

Verte: shower room with wc, double bed, 3 single bed: FF330 (2 people) FF570 (5 people)

Brique: bathroom with wc, twin beds, 2 single bed: FF330 (2 people) FF490 (4 people)

Extra bed: 80FF

Capacity: 14 people

84.05 AVIGNON

You will be in heaven, sitting in the shade of a 300 year old plane tree in this green and tranquil haven. An ideal base and an excellent area for antiques. L'Isle-sur-Sorgue, Fontaine de Vaucluse and Gordes are only 5 minutes away. On sale: Antiques.

PROPERTY

✱✱✱

private parking, extensive grounds, lounge, hosts have pets, kitchen, hiking, cycling, interesting flora 1km, golf course 5km, gliding 20km

Fluent English spoken

— From the A7, take exit 'Avignon-Sud'. Go towards Apt. At Petit Palais, go towards Fontaine de Vaucluse. The house is on the D24, on the small portion between the N100 and the D99. ('La Pastorale' sign and antique shop).

Fabienne & Hervé ALBA

«Le Grand Jas»
Rue du Bariot
84800 LAGNES

tel: (0) 4 90 20 25 12
fax: (0) 4 90 20 29 17
grandjas84@aol.com

Residence of character

25 km - E -
AVIGNON
LAGNES: railway station 30km
airport 60km
car essential

84.42 AVIGNON

Fabienne and Hervé live in a mas full of character, very well placed at the foot of the Monts de Vaucluse. Many walking and hiking routes start from here, so it is a good way to get to know this magnificent area. Fleur de Soleil member. Out of season there is up to 20% discount.

PROPERTY

✱✱✱

private parking, garden, tv lounge, hosts have pets, no pets, babies welcome, free cot, no smoking, swimming pool, hiking, cycling, interesting flora 1km, golf course 5km, sea or lake watersports 5km, fishing 6km, gliding 20km

Fluent English spoken

PRICE STRUCTURE

4 Bedrooms

Syrah: shower room with wc, twin beds, single bed: FF420 (2 people) FF480 (3 people)

Picholine & L'ocrette: shower room with wc, double bed: FF420

Pastillère: shower room with wc, double bed, single bed: FF420 (2 people) FF480 (3 people)

Extra bed: 60FF
Reduction: 16/09–31/05

Capacity: 10 people

— From Avignon, take the N100 towards Apt. At L'Isle sur Sorgue, continue on the N100 and then turn left on to the D99 as far as Lagnes. Go up into the village, and it is the last house on the left just as you are leaving the village.

Jean-Marie SECCHI

«Château Domaine des Costières»
1634 Route de Carprentras D.938
84800 L'ISLE sur SORGUE

tel: (0) 4 90 38 39 19
fax: (0) 4 90 38 39 19

Residence of character

25 km - E - AVIGNON
ISLE SUR LA SORGUE: hosts can collect from station, railway station 3km airport 20km

84.06 AVIGNON

17th century mas, surrounded by an enormous estate. L'Isle-sur-Sorgue is famous for its antiques. Fontaine de Vaucluse is very close. An excellent base for exploring this wonderful area. A good address, known for its food.

PRICE STRUCTURE

6 Bedrooms

First room: shower room with wc, washbasin, double bed: FF400

Second room: shower room with wc, washbasin, double bed: FF350

Third, fourth and fifth rooms: shower room with wc, double bed: FF350

Sixth room: shower room with wc, twin beds: FF350

Extra bed: 100FF

Capacity: 12 people

PROPERTY

✱✱✱

private parking, extensive grounds, tv lounge, hosts have pets, dinner available, babies welcome, free cot, no smoking, hiking, golf course 1km

Fluent English spoken

— In Avignon, take the N100 towards Morières, Isle sur Sorgue and Apt. The property is 1km from Isle sur Sorgue, on the D938 towards Carpentras (signposted).

Pierette & Régis
SOUBRAT

«Mas de la Coudoulière»
1854, Route de
Carpentras
84800 L'ISLE SUR LA
SORGUE

tel: (0) 4 90 38 16 35
fax: (0) 4 90 38 16 89
www.isle-sur-sorgue-en-provence.com/mas-coudou/

Private home

25 km - E -
AVIGNON
ISLE SUR LA
SORGUE: hosts can
collect from station
railway station 20km
airport 20km
car essential

84.38 AVIGNON

The welcome is very warm and you will be charmed by this 18th century Mas and want to stay much longer here, surrounded by the scents of the Mediterranean. The bedrooms are spacious and decorated with excellent taste, making you look forward to bedtime. 2 self-catering apartments, rented weekly.

PROPERTY

✱✱✱

off street parking, garden, tv lounge, hosts have pets, telephone, dinner available, babies welcome, free cot, swimming pool, cycling 1km, fishing 1km, river watersports 2km, hiking 3km, hunting 3km, mushroom picking 3km, golf course 7km, interesting flora 10km, birdwatching 10km

Basic English spoken

— At Avignon take the N100 towards Morières as far as l'Isle sur Sorgue. Then take the D938 towards Carpentras for 1km. After the roundabout turn right 200m after les Pépinières du Chêne Vert and follow the signs to the Mas.2 self-catering apartments, rented weekly.

PRICE STRUCTURE

4 Bedrooms and 1 Suite

Olivier: shower room with wc, double bed: FF385

Figuier: shower room with wc, double bed: FF385

Mûrier: shower room with wc, twin beds: FF385

Cade & Amandier: bathroom with wc, double bed: FF445

Acacia: bathroom with wc, twin beds: FF445

Extra bed: 100FF
Reduction: 01/10–30/05

Capacity: 12 people

Etienne JAMET

«Ferme Jamet» Chemin de Rhodes
Ile de la Barthelasse
84000 AVIGNON

tel: (0) 4 90 86 88 35
fax: (0) 4 90 86 17 72
www.avignon-et-provence.com/ferme-jamet/

Residence of character

AVIGNON ILE DE LA BARTHELASSE: railway station 6km airport 80km

84.31 AVIGNON

An old mas, surrounded by plane trees, on an isle in the middle of the Rhone. This is how you expect Provence to be. Avignon is not to be missed: sight-seeing, culture, history, architecture ... Plan on staying several days here.

Price structure

6 Bedrooms and 6 Apartments

Matisse: telephone, bathroom with wc, 2 single beds: FF790

Marquet: telephone, bathroom with wc, twin beds: FF650

Dufy: telephone, shower room with wc, double bed: FF650

Derain: telephone, shower room with wc, double bed: FF590

Cézanne: telephone, kitchen, bathroom with wc, double bed, single bed: FF700 (2 people) FF800 (3 people)

Manguin & Renoir & Monet: telephone, kitchen, shower room with wc, double bed: FF750

(2 rooms): lounge, telephone, kitchen, bathroom with wc, double bed, 2 single beds: FF700 (2 people) FF900 (4 people)

(1 room): lounge, telephone, kitchen, shower room with wc, double bed, 2 single beds: FF800 (2 people) FF1200 (4 people)

Degas: telephone, along corridor shower room with wc, 2 single beds: FF520

Extra bed: 100FF
Reduction: 1/10–30/06

Capacity: 31 people

PROPERTY

✱✱✱

off street parking, extensive grounds, tv lounge, hosts have pets, no pets, telephone, swimming pool, tennis court, closed: 1/11-1/04, cycling, fishing 2km, sea or lake watersports 2km, golf course 15km, river watersports 30km

Fluent English spoken

— From the A7, exit Avignon Nord. Follow Avignon-Centre and the banks of the Rhone. Take the 1st bridge (Daladier) towards Villeneuve lez Avignon. From the bridge, turn right towards La Barthelasse. Follow the signs to Ferme JAMET'.

Isabelle de
MAINTENANT

«Domaine La Nesquière»
5419, Route d'Althen
84210 PERNES LES
FONTAINES

tel: (0) 4 90 62 00 16
fax: (0) 4 90 62 02 10

Farm

25km - E -
AVIGNON
PERNES LES
FONTAINES:
railway station 15km
airport 15km
car essential

84.44 AVIGNON

This is a large mas, surrounded by agricultural land, beside a river shaded by tall trees. Isabelle will be delighted if you try some of her excellent local produce, and take her advice on where to visit. There are antiques at the Isle sur Sorgue and numerous festivals in the summer. Overnight "gîte" also available.

PROPERTY

✱✱✱

private parking, extensive grounds, tv lounge, hosts have pets, telephone, dinner available, closed: 15/11-15/02, hiking, cycling, fishing 10km, river watersports 10km, golf course 15km

Fluent English spoken

— Take the Exit for Avignon Nord from the A7 then head towards Carpentras on the D942. Take the exit on the left "Les Valayans, Le Thor". Continue for 1km then left on the D38 towards Pernes les Fontaines.After 4km, the "Chemin de La Nesquière" is on the right.

Price structure

2 Bedrooms and 2 Suites

Antonine: lounge, television, telephone, shower room with wc, double bed, 2 single beds: FF350 (2 people) FF550 (4 people)

Edme: lounge, television, shower room with wc, double bed, 2 single beds: FF350 (2 people) FF550 (4 people)

Granny: television, telephone, shower room with wc, double bed: FF295

Adélaïde: television, telephone, bathroom with wc, twin beds: FF350

Gîte Sejour 1: lounge, telephone, kitchen:
telephone, shower room with wc, double bed, 2 single beds: FF290 (2 people) FF435 (4 people)
(2) telephone, along corridor shower room with wc, twin beds: FF290
telephone, shower room with wc, double bed: FF290

Gîte Sejour 2: lounge, telephone, kitchen:
telephone, along corridor shower room with wc, double bed: FF240
telephone, double bed: FF240
(2) telephone, twin beds: FF240

Extra bed: 50/80FF

Capacity: 30 people

Andrée & Charles
BARAIL

«Mas du Clos de
l'Escarrat»
84150 JONQUIERES

tel: (0) 4 90 70 39 19
fax: (0) 4 90 70 39 19
E-mail: barail@club-internet.fr

Private home

20 km - S W - AVIGNON
JONQUIERES:
railway station 20km
airport 80km
car essential

PRICE STRUCTURE

2 Bedrooms and 1 Suite and 2 Apartments

Ventoux & Montmirail: television, kitchen, shower room with wc, double bed: FF380

Ouvèze: shower room with wc, double bed: FF480

Extra bed: 140FF

Capacity: 6 people

84.48 AVIGNON

Le Mas du Clos de l'Escarrat is an old Provençal farmhouse, in the middle of the fields facing the Mont Ventoux, which has been restored to high standards of comfort, whilst maintaining all the charm of its old stone walls. There are two separate studios with their own balcony. Two bedrooms overlook the garden and have TV and a small kitchen. Here, you are at the heart of the Cotes du Rhone vineyards, in a region which is also rich in cultural festivals, antiques and historic and archeological sights. There is a large choice of walks, sightseeing visits or cycling routes, as well as the famous Route des Vins. Fleur de Soleil member.

PROPERTY

✱✱✱

off street parking, garden, no pets, hiking, cycling

English spoken

— Contact your host for detailed directions.

Monique JULLIEN

«La Bastide»
Rue Marguerite Tauriac
84310 MORIERES LES AVIGNON

tel: (0) 4 90 33 49 96
fax: (0) 4 90 33 49 96

Private home

4 km - E - AVIGNON
MORIERES LES AVIGNON: railway station 5km
airport 10km
car essential

84.50 AVIGNON

"La Bastide", a 200 year old mas, has been restored with great taste. You are near to Avignon, the Exhibition Centre and two golf courses. Fleur de Soleil member.

PROPERTY

***

off street parking, garden, no pets, babies welcome, free cot, no smoking, closed: 02/12-19/01, golf course

English spoken

PRICE STRUCTURE

4 Bedrooms

First room: shower room with wc, bathroom, double bed, single bed: FF300 (2 people) FF350 (3 people)

Second room: shower room with wc, double bed, single bed: FF300 (2 people) FF350 (3 people)

(2 rooms) shower room with wc, double bed: FF300

Capacity: 10 people

— From the A7, take Exit Avignon Sud, towards Avignon. Turn right towards the Parc Expositions, the go straight to Morières.

Ludovic & Eliane
CORNILLON

«Domaine St Luc»
26790 LA BAUME DE
TRANSIT

tel: (0) 4 75 98 11 51
fax: (0) 4 75 98 19 22

Farm

14 km - N E -
BOLLENE
LA BAUME DE
TRANSIT: railway
station 25km
airport, 150km
car essential

PRICE STRUCTURE

6 Bedrooms

First, third and fourth rooms: bathroom with wc, double bed: FF390

Second room: bathroom with wc, twin beds: FF390

Fifth room: bathroom with wc, double bed, single bed: FF390 (2 people) FF450 (3 people)

Sixth room: bridal room, bathroom with wc, double bed: FF590

Reduction: groups

Capacity: 13 people

26.27 BOLLENE

Ludovic has restored this 18th century mas with excellent taste. His warm, enthusiastic welcome and his love of wine is only surpassed by his passion for truffles, which you can try for yourself in some of the dishes of Eliane's excellent regional cooking. On sale: Their own wine.

PROPERTY

***

off street parking, garden, tv lounge, hosts have pets, dinner available, swimming pool, hiking 1km, fishing 1km, mushroom picking 1km, golf course 10km

Adequate English spoken

— From the A7 Exit Bollène. Then take the D994 as far as Suze la Rousse and left towards St Paul Trois Châteaux. The grounds are on the left on the D117 after 5.5km.

Bernard VANSTEEN-BERGHE

«Les Terrasses»
Chemin de la Tour
26230 CHAMARET

tel: (0) 4 75 46 93 57
fax: (0) 4 75 46 93 57

Residence of character

Châtelet- Hotel de Ville- Marais- 1e - PARIS
CHAMARET: railway station 30km
airport 150km
car essential

26.31 BOLLENE

This beautiful, terraced stone house is built into the walls of the medieval village, at the foot of a 12th century tower. There is a superb view over the lavender and the truffle woods. Grignan and its château are just minutes away. This part of Provence is well worth getting to know and Bernard can provide local information so that you do not miss out on anything. Fleur de Soleil member.

PROPERTY

✱✱✱

off street parking, garden, tv lounge, riding, hiking, cycling, fishing, hunting, interesting flora, mushroom picking, golf course 5km, gliding 25km, river watersports 30km

Adequate English spoken

— Take the Bollène Exit from the A7. Head towards St Paul Trois Châteaux on the D458. Continue on the D59 and then go on the D71 as far as Chamaret. Les Terrasses can be found at the top of the village, beneath the tower.

PRICE STRUCTURE

2 Bedrooms and 1 Suite

Bleue: telephone, shower room with wc, double bed: FF320

Jaune: bathroom with wc, double bed, single bed: FF320 (2 people) FF380 (3 people)

Suite: lounge, bathroom with wc, 2 double beds: FF390 (2 people) FF510 (4 people)

Extra bed: 60FF

Capacity: 9 people

Pierre-Jean & Suzanne CHAMBON

«Le Mas Chamffras»
Chemin de Carsan-
Quartier Vallien
30130 ST ALEXANDRE

tel: (0) 4 66 39 39 07
fax: (0) 4 66 39 39 07

Private home

15 km - S W - BOLLENE
ST ALEXANDRE: hosts can collect from station, railway station 35km airport 35km car essential

30.12 BOLLENE

A friendly couple in this Provençal mas, surrounded by pine trees. Nudism is allowed, but only around the swimming pool. You must then get dressed to visit les Gorges de l'Ardèche, the Pont du Gard and Vaison la Romaine. There are also local festivals.

PRICE STRUCTURE

2 Bedrooms

television, shower room with wc, double bed: FF330

television, bathroom with wc, double bed: FF330

Extra bed: 120FF
Reduction: 01/10–31/05

Capacity: 4 people

PROPERTY

✱✱✱

off street parking, extensive grounds, hosts have pets, no pets, dinner available, babies welcome, free cot, swimming pool, hiking, cycling, fishing, mushroom picking, river watersports 10km

Adequate English spoken

— From the Exit 'Bollène' on the A7, take the D994 towards Pont St Esprit. Take the N86 towards Bagnols sur Cèze. Turn right towards Carsan - St Alexandre and follow the signs.

30.18 BOLLENE

An old silkworm farm, renovated with great character. Here you can relax or take a dip in the pool. Visit Pont St Esprit and explore the Forêt de Valbonne. If you like canoeing, you will know that the Gorges de l'Ardèche are fantastic. 5 self-catering apartments.

Bernard PELLOUX

«Mas Canet»
Chemin de Gavanon
30130 ST PAULET DE CAISSON

tel: (0) 4 66 39 25 96
fax: (0) 4 66 39 25 82

Residence of character

PROPERTY

✱✱✱

off street parking, extensive grounds, lounge, hosts have pets, swimming pool, hiking, cycling, interesting flora, mushroom picking, fishing 9km, river watersports 9km, golf course 40km

Basic English spoken

15 km - W - BOLLENE
ST PAULET DE CAISSON:
railway station 50km
airport 70km
car essential
— From the A7, take the Exit for Bollène. Head for Pont St Esprit, then D23 in the direction of La Chartreuse de Valbonne for 7km.

PRICE STRUCTURE

6 Bedrooms

(3 rooms) shower room with wc, double bed: FF306

(3 rooms) bathroom with wc, double bed: FF316

Extra bed: 75FF
Reduction: 30/09–01/06

Capacity: 12 people

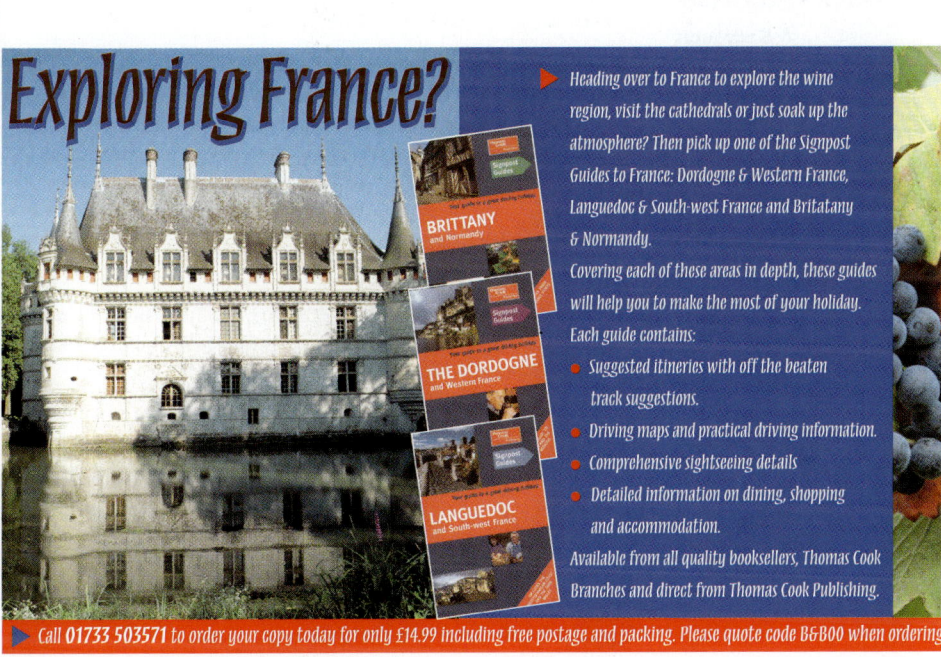

Pierre & Monique
CARDINAEL

«Mas Zazézou»
Quartier Malatras
84840 LAMOTTE DU
RHÔNE

tel: (0) 4 90 40 45 16
fax: (0) 4 90 40 45 16

Private home

5 km - S W -
BOLLENE
LAMOTTE DU
RHONE: hosts can
collect from station,
railway station 5km
airport 60km

PRICE STRUCTURE

3 Bedrooms

Sud & Pilote & Océane:
shower room with wc,
double bed: FF280

Extra bed: 80FF

Capacity: 6 people

84.33 BOLLENE

Monique is from Brussels. Her isolated country house is shaded by a 200 year old weeping willow. The spacious dining room is furnished with good taste. You will enjoy barbecues beside the swimming pool, or try your hand at painting or pottery.

PROPERTY

***

off street parking, garden, tv lounge, hosts have pets, dinner available, swimming pool, fishing, cycling 3km, hiking 10km, river watersports 15km, golf course 25km

Fluent English spoken

— From the A7, take the Bollène Exit. Then take the D994 towards Pont St Esprit. After Lamotte du Rhone, at the last roundabout, turn right and follow the signs.

Dominik & Gilles
FIGUIERE de BRES

«Mas des Pradines»
Route de St Ariès
84500 BOLLENE

tel: (0) 4 90 30 23 61
fax: (0) 4 90 30 97 62
E.mail:
Gilles.Rougier@wanadoo.fr

Private home

6 km - S - BOLLENE
ST ARIES: railway station 30km
airport 130km
car essential

84.52 BOLLENE

Dominik and Gilles welcome you to their rare, square-shaped 18th century mas, with interior courtyard, set amongst the vines. They combine charm with a high level of comfort and a very pleasant lifestyle. The bedrooms are tastefully decorated and there is a nice peaceful garden, with olive trees and lavender. Take breakfast under the arbour or beside the pool. You are in the heart of the Vaucluse, on the wine route, and Avignon, Orange, Vaison- la- Romaine, Uzès, Grignan, l'Ardèche, Mont Ventoux and the Dentelles de Montmirail are only 30 minutes drive. There is also a tennis court 5 minutes away and wine cellars in the vicinity. Fleur de Soleil member.

PRICE STRUCTURE

2 Bedrooms and 1 Suite

(2 rooms) bathroom with wc, double bed: FF490

Suite: shower room with wc, 2 twin beds: FF490 (1 person) FF630 (2 people)

Capacity: 8 people

PROPERTY

✱✱✱

off street parking, garden, no pets, dinner available, swimming pool

Adequate English spoken

— In Bollene, take the D26 towards Mondragon. At the sports stadium, turn left towards St. Ariès and continue for 1.3km. In St. Ariés, continue straight on down and then go up a steep hill with bends for 1.5km. On reaching the top, facing the wells, turn right and continue for 800m. The mas is 50m further on, on the right.

84.13 CARPENTRAS

Gérard RUEL

«Maison Provençale»
Le Village
84210 VENASQUE

tel: (0) 4 90 66 02 84
fax: (0) 4 90 66 61 32

Private home

This old village house has been restored and its stone façade is very beautiful. From the terrace there is a superb, panoramic view and the whole place has a very warm, welcoming atmosphere. Near to Gordes and the 'Abbaye de Sénanque'.

PROPERTY

off street parking, tv lounge, hosts have pets, kitchen, babies welcome, free cot, closed: 31/12-1/02, hiking, golf course

Basic English spoken

10 km - S E - CARPENTRAS
VENASQUE: airport 30km
car essential
— At Carpentras, take the D4 towards Vénasque. The house, with light grey shutters is opposite the Post Office.

PRICE STRUCTURE

4 Bedrooms and 1 Apartment

Emma: shower room with wc, double bed, single bed: FF230 (2 people) FF280 (4 people)

Chloé: bathroom with wc, double bed, single bed: FF230 (2 people) FF280 (4 people)

Agathe & Gigi: shower room with wc, double bed: FF230

Maya: kitchen, shower room with wc, double bed, single bed: FF250 (2 people) FF300 (3 people)

Capacity: 13 people

84.40 CARPENTRAS

Pierre & Françoise GERBAUD

«Clos St Louis»
Route du Mont Ventoux
84410 BEDOIN

tel: (0) 4 90 65 60 62
fax: (0) 4 90 65 60 62

Private home

You will find absolute peace in this mas, 800 m from the village. It has a swimming pool and a superb chestnut tree in the shade of which you will take your breakfast with a view over the Mont Ventoux. Add to this, Françoise and Pierre with their smile and warm welcome... a picture typical of Provence.

PROPERTY

✱✱

private parking, garden, tv lounge, hosts have pets, dinner available, babies welcome, free cot, swimming pool, hiking, cycling, hunting, interesting flora, mushroom picking, birdwatching, winter sports 10km, fishing 15km, gliding 15km, river watersports 45km

PRICE STRUCTURE

2 Bedrooms

2 double beds: FF250 (2 people) FF500 (4 people)

Capacity: 4 people

15 km - N E - CARPENTRAS
BEDOIN: railway station 40km
airport 120km
car essential
— At Carpentras, take the D974 towards Bedoin and the Mont Ventoux.

Marianne MYIN

«Siloé»
Le Canadel
84570 MORMOIRON

tel: (0) 4 90 61 87 67
fax: (0) 4 90 61 87 55

Private home

11 km - E -
CARPENTRAS
MORMOIRON:
railway station 30km
airport 30km
car essential

PRICE STRUCTURE

3 Bedrooms

First & second rooms: shower room with wc, double bed: FF290

Third room: shower room with wc, twin beds, single bed: FF290 (2 people) FF350 (3 people)

Reduction: 1/09–30/06

Capacity: 7 people

84.47 CARPENTRAS

If you choose Marianne and Jacques' place, you will get a warm welcome, peace and quiet, wonderful countryside and a view over the Mont Ventoux, as well as use of the swimming pool. A great place to unwind and recharge your batteries. They organise weekly "Conversation Française" packages, which include excursions throughout Provence. An excellent way to improve your French and to get to know this area.

PROPERTY

❋❋❋

off street parking, extensive grounds, tv lounge, hosts have pets, no pets, telephone, dinner available, packed lunch, wheelchair access, swimming pool, closed: 15/12-15/01, hiking, cycling, fishing, hunting, mushroom picking, sea or lake watersports, interesting flora 15km, birdwatching 15km, golf course 20km, river watersports 20km

Adequate English spoken

— At Carpentras, take the D942 towards Mormoiron and Sault. When you reach Mormoiron, continue towards Sault for 300m. Turn right at the sign "Domaine des Anges" and go towards Le Canadel for 2km. At fire hydrant 21, there is a sign to "Siloé" on the right.

84.19 VAISON LA ROMAINE

A beautiful Provençal farm with links with the Knights Templar, known as the 'Château de la Baude'. Previously fortified, and painstakingly restored by Gérard, it now offers high standards of comfort in its six bedrooms. A fantastic address in Provence. Dinner on the terrace is not to be missed.

PROPERTY

✱✱✱✱

off street parking, extensive grounds, tv lounge, hosts have pets, telephone, dinner available, packed lunch, babies welcome, free cot, swimming pool, tennis court, closed: 20/12-26/12, 6 nights minimum stay 1/07-31/08, fishing 1km, hiking 2km

English spoken

PRICE STRUCTURE

4 Bedrooms and 2 Suites

Duplex Lavandin & Duplex Citronnelle: shower room with wc, 2 twin beds: FF880

Tilleul & Oliviers: shower room with wc, 3 single beds: FF580 (2 people) FF680 (3 people)

Romarin: shower room with wc, bathroom, twin beds: FF580

Verveine: shower room with wc, twin beds: FF580

Extra bed: 100FF
Reduction: children

Capacity: 16 people

Gérard & Chantal MONIN

«Le Château de la Baude»
84110 VILLEDIEU

tel: (0) 4 90 28 95 18
fax: (0) 4 90 28 91 05

Residence of character

6 km - N W - VAISON LA ROMAINE
VILLEDIEU:
airport 55km
car essential
— At Vaison, take the D51 towards Villedieu.

Charles & Renaud
HAGGAI-TERRISSE

«La Calade»
Rue Calade
84110 ST ROMAIN EN
VIENNOIS

tel: (0) 4 90 46 51 79
fax: (0) 4 90 46 51 82

Private home

2 km - N E -
VAISON LA
ROMAINE
ST ROMAIN EN
VIENNOIS:hosts can
collect from station
railway station 40km
airport 40km
car essential

PRICE STRUCTURE

4 Bedrooms

(1 room) bathroom with wc, double bed: FF400

(3 rooms) shower room with wc, twin beds: FF400

Capacity: 8 people

84.46 VAISON LA ROMAINE

This village house, very quiet, has an interior courtyard with a terrace on the roof, with an excellent view of the surrounding mountains. Renaud and Charles will welcome you with the same delight and enthusiasm that they have put into restoring this house. The area around Vaison is also well worth a detour. Fleur de soleil member.

PROPERTY

✱✱✱

lounge, no pets, kitchen, closed: 30/10-1/03, 2 nights minimum stay, hiking, cycling, sea or lake watersports 10km, golf course 40km

Fluent English spoken

— On the A7, Exit Bollène, towards Nyons and then Vaison la Romaine. At Vaison, go towards Nyons on the D71 for St Romain.

Florence & Manuel
LEPEZ

«La Ponsarde»
Bellevue
84600 GRILLON

tel: (0) 4 90 35 63 47
fax: (0) 4 90 35 63 47
E-mail :
ivernenco@wanadoo.fr

Private home

5 km - W - VALREAS
GRILLON: railway
station 25km
car essential

84.51 VALREAS

Florence and Manuel welcome you to "L'Ivernenco", which is a restored old silk factory, near to the château at Grignan. The bedrooms are spacious and the period living room overlooks 14 hectare of grounds, with a wonderful view over the countryside, famous for truffles, vineyards and lavender. There is plenty of hiking, cycling, riding and golf to be enjoyed in this area. Fleur de Soleil member.

PROPERTY

✱✱✱

off street parking, extensive grounds, dinner available, swimming pool, hiking, cycling, golf course

English spoken

— On the A7, Exit Montélimar Sud and head towards Valréas, Nyons. The house is 4km after Grignan.

PRICE STRUCTURE

1 Bedroom and 2 Suites

Olivier: shower room with wc, double bed: FF350

Tournesol/Lilas: shower room with wc, double bed, 2 single beds: FF350 (2 people) FF600

Lavande: shower room with wc, bathroom, 2 double beds: FF350 (2 people) FF500 (4 people)

Extra bed: 60/80FF

Capacity: 10 people

BOURGOGNE
FRANCHE-COMTE
SWITZERLAND
RHÔNE-ALPES
AUVERGNE
ITALY
PROVENCE-ALPES-CÔT D'AZUR
LANGUEDOC-ROUSSILLON
MEDITERRANEAN SEA
89
21
70
90
25
39
71
03
69
01
74
42
63
73
38
43
07
26
05
48
84
30
04
06
13
34
83
DIJON
Vesoul
Belfort
BESANÇON
Dole
Beaune
Autun
Pontarlier
Chalon-sur-Saône
Lons
Moulins
Macon
Bourg
Vichy
Roanne
Annecy
Chamonix
Thiers
LYON
CLERMONT-FERRAND
Aix-les-Bains
Albertville
Chambéry
Vienne
St.-Etienne
St. Jean
Grenoble
le Puy
Valence
Briançon
Privas
Gap
Mende
Alès
Digne
Millau
Carpentras
Avignon
Nimes
Arles
Nice
Grasse
MONTPELLIER
Aix-en-Provence
Draguignan
Béziers
MARSEILLE
Toulon
Perpignan

Thérèse & Pierre LINOSSIER

Le bourg - Burdignes
42220 BOURG-ARGENTAL

tel: (0) 4 77 39 60 81

Farm

20 km - N W -
ANNONAY
BURDIGNES:
railway station 20km
airport 35km
car essential

42.08 ANNONAY

This ferme-auberge, on the Pilat plateau near to l'Ardèche, is a working livestock farm, and will give you a good insight into French farm life: looking after the animals, working in the fields and the village fete in August. In the season, there is good downhill and cross-country skiing in this area. On sale: Milk, cheese charcuterie, veal. Out of season, the Auberge closes on Wednesdays.

PRICE STRUCTURE

5 Bedrooms

(5 rooms) double bed: FF200

Extra bed: 84FF

Capacity: 10 people

PROPERTY

hosts have pets, dinner available, packed lunch, hiking, cycling, winter sports 5km

Adequate English spoken

— On the main N82 St. Etienne - Annonay road, at Bourg Argental, take the D29 towards Burdignes.

Danièle & Jacques
LABERE

«Auberge du Château»
Bobigneux
42220 ST SAUVEUR EN RUE

tel: (0) 4 77 39 24 33
fax: (0) 4 77 39 25 74

Château

20 km - W - ANNONAY
ST SAUVEUR EN RUE:
railway station 26km
airport 80km
car essential

42.12 ANNONAY

An auberge in the 'Parc du Pilat', kingdom of forests, green pastures and open spaces. The château dates from the 16th century. Jacques spends a lot of the time in the kitchen and he will probably tell you about Greenland where he lived for 20 years... On sale: Cheese and charcuterie. The auberge is closed on Wednesdays.

PRICE STRUCTURE

6 Bedrooms

First room: shower room with wc, washbasin, double bed, single bed: FF260 (2 people) FF310 (3 people)

Second room: shower room with wc, washbasin, twin beds: FF260

Third and fourth rooms: shower room with wc, washbasin, double bed: FF260

Fifth room: shower room with wc, washbasin, 2 double bed: FF260 (2 people) FF335 (4 people)

Sixth room: lounge, shower room with wc, washbasin, double bed: FF260

Capacity: 15 people

PROPERTY

✱✱

off street parking, extensive grounds, tv lounge, hosts have pets, telephone, dinner available, packed lunch, babies welcome, free cot, wheelchair access, closed: 01/01-28/02, hiking, cycling, fishing, hunting, interesting flora, mushroom picking, winter sports 10km, golf course 15km, river watersports 30km

Basic English spoken

— At Annonay, take the N82 towards Bourg-Argental. The auberge is on the D503 between Bourg-Argental and St Sauveur.

Véronique CHAYNE

«Domaine le Vernadel»
Le Chadenet
07600 ASPERJOC

tel: (0) 4 75 94 67 92
fax: (0) 4 75 37 55 13

Residence of character

12 km - N -
AUBENAS
LE CHADENET:
hosts can collect from station, railway station 7km
car essential

07.01 AUBENAS

This stone-built house dates from 1652 and is set amidst magnificent scenery dominated by chestnut trees. The Chayne family will be delighted to introduce you to the secrets of their region: the flora and fauna, rock climbing or caving and at the end of a hard day, their local dishes. On sale: honey, jam, chestnuts.

PROPERTY

✱✱✱

private parking, garden, tv lounge, hosts have pets, dinner available, packed lunch, babies welcome, free cot, swimming pool, 7 nights minimum stay 15/07-28/08, hiking, mushroom picking, sea or lake watersports,

Adequate English spoken

— In Aubenas, take the N102 towards Vals les Bains where you turn right on to the D578 towards Antraigues. Turn left on to the D243 then right on to the D543. Go over the bridge, then follow the signs for 3 km.

PRICE STRUCTURE

4 Bedrooms and 1 Apartment

Acacia: kitchen, shower room with wc, washbasin, double bed: FF350

Tilleul & Bruyère: shower room with wc, washbasin, double bed, single bed: FF340 (2 people) FF410 (3 people)

La Castagne & La Merle: shower room with wc, washbasin, double bed: FF340

Extra bed: 70FF
Reduction: 1/10–29/05 and children

Capacity: 12 people

Gabrielle POLETTE

Les Lauzières
07110 TAURIERS

tel: (0) 4 75 39 14 15
fax: (0) 4 75 39 14 15

Private home

18 km - S W - AUBENAS
TAURIERS: hosts can collect from station, railway station 60km car essential

PRICE STRUCTURE

4 Bedrooms

First, second and third rooms: television, shower room with wc, double bed: FF230

Fourth room: television, shower room with wc, double bed, single bed: FF230 (2 people) FF290 (3 people)

Extra bed: 60FF
Reduction: 4 nights

Capacity: 9 people

07.19 AUBENAS

The newly-furnished rooms, the generous, well-served breakfast, the peace and quiet of the grounds and the kindness and warm welcome of Mme. Polette and her son, will make you sorry to leave this place. Situated in the heart of L'Ardèche, there are numerous stone villages to visit in the area.

PROPERTY

***

private parking, extensive grounds, tv lounge, hosts have pets, no pets, kitchen, babies welcome, free cot, wheelchair access, closed: 01/11-01/04, hiking, cycling, fishing, interesting flora, sea or lake watersports 6km, river watersports 13km, winter sports 60km

Adequate English spoken

— At Aubenas, take the D104 towards Alès. After Uzer, turn right on to the D5. In Largentière, take the D305 as far as Tauriers, then Route de Joannas for 1.5km. Careful! It is the second B&B house on the left.

07.05 VALLON PONT D'ARC

Francis & Michèle
RANCHIN

Quartier les Ranchins - Pradons
07120 RUOMS

tel: (0) 4 75 93 98 33

Farm

This very beautiful, stone vineyard house has been completely restored and is 10km from the gorges of the Ardèche. There is beautiful view from the terrace over the vines and the surrounding countryside. Visit the old villages, as well as the wool museum, or let Jean take you to the wine growers co-operative. On sale: wine.

PROPERTY

off street parking, garden, tv lounge, hosts have pets, babies welcome, free cot, hiking, cycling, fishing, river watersports 2km

PRICE STRUCTURE

5 Bedrooms

Syrah & Sauvignon: shower room with wc, double bed, 2 single bed: FF240 (2 people) FF360 (4 people)

Grenache & Viognier: shower room with wc, double bed, single bed: FF240 (2 people) FF300 (3 people)

Chardonnay: shower room with wc, double bed: FF240

Capacity: 16 people

10 km - N - VALLON PONT D'ARC
PRADONS: hosts can collect from station, railway station 50km
airport 20km
— At Vallon Pont d'Arc take the D579 towards Aubenas. The farm is 2.5km after Pradons.

30.19 VALLON PONT D'ARC

Isabelle & Antoine
AGAPITOS

«Mas Escombelle»
30430 BARJAC

tel: (0) 4 66 24 54 77
fax: (0) 4 66 24 54 77

Residence of character

Charm and beauty... Isabelle and Antoine have wonderfully restored this 18th century mas at the gateway to the Ardèche. There is a beautiful internal courtyard and a high stone vaulted ceiling. The wild beauty of this region well worth a few extra days. On sale: Lavender essence and wine.

PROPERTY

✱✱✱

off street parking, garden, lounge, hosts have pets, telephone, dinner available, packed lunch, swimming pool, hiking, cycling, mushroom picking, golf course 10km, fishing 12km, river watersports 12km

Fluent English spoken

13 km - S - VALLON PONT D'ARC
BARJAC:
railway station 50km
airport 60km
car essential
— At Vallon Pont d'Arc take the D579 towards Barjac. The mas is before you enter Barjac, 300m before the Gendarmerie.

PRICE STRUCTURE

4 Bedrooms and 1 Apartment

Bateau: shower room with wc, double bed, single bed: FF300 (2 people) FF400 (3 people)

Monacale: shower room with wc, double bed, 2 single beds: FF300 (2 people) FF500 (4 people)

Piscine & Contemporaine: shower room with wc, twin beds: FF300

Extra bed: 100FF

Capacity: 11 people

Maryse MAITRE

«Lauria»
Les Gallands
26410 MENGLON

tel: (0) 4 75 21 19 45
fax: (0) 4 75 21 19 45
E-mail :
mamaitre@aol.com

Private home

14 km - S E - DIE
MENGLON: railway station 14km
car essential

26.34 DIE

This comfortable house is in a quiet hamlet, between the Vercors and the Drome Provençale and is a nice place to unwind after a day hiking or visiting the region and its countryside. Fleur de Soleil member.

PROPERTY

✱✱✱

off street parking, no pets, dinner available, no smoking, closed: 01/12-31/01, hiking, interesting flora, mushroom picking

English spoken

— D93, Crest-Die. On leaving Die, follow signs to Gap. At the Pont de Quart, turn left to Chatillon en Dois. Before Chatillon, follow signs to Luc en Diois, then Les Payats. Then, turn left towards Les Gallands. Lauria is at the end of the road.

PRICE STRUCTURE

2 Bedrooms and 1 Suite

Terrasse & Bleue: shower room with wc, double bed: FF250

Blanche/Rose: shower room with wc, 2 double beds: FF220 (2 people) FF440 (4 people)

Extra bed: 115FF
Reduction: 2 nights

Capacity: 8 people

Odette HENRI

Rue des Tilleuls
26740 ST MARCEL LES SAUZET

tel: (0) 4 75 46 13 83
fax: (0) 4 75 46 18 30

Private home

6 km - E - MONTELIMAR
ST MARCEL LES SAUZET: railway station 40km
airport 40km
car essential

Rhones-Alpes

MONTELIMAR

PRICE STRUCTURE

2 Bedrooms

(2 rooms) shower room with wc, double bed: FF300

Extra bed: 100FF

Capacity: 4 people

26.33 MONTELIMAR

Here, you will remember the warm, smiling welcome and the plentiful breakfast. This farm, with its ancient mulberry tree, also produces its own vegetables and herbs. There are interesting walks, and potters, glass-makers and wine cellars to visit. Your hostess will recommend good restaurants and interesting little shops. There is the Festival of Avignon, as well as as ancient villages and botanical gardens. For the more energetic, try canoeing on the Drome and riding. Your hostess also organises French language courses and her house is particularly practical for blind guests. Fleur de Soleil member.

PROPERTY

***

off street parking, garden, tv, dinner available, hiking, cycling, river watersports,

English spoken

— From the A6, Exit Montélimar Nord, take the N7 to La Coucourde (3km). Then, take the D74 to Sauzet for 6km and the house is on the right.

Jacques & Renée
CRAMMER

«L'Eygalière»
Quartier Coussaud
26300 ALIXAN

tel: (0) 4 75 47 11 13
fax: (0) 4 75 47 13 35
E-mail:
jcrammer@easynet.fr

Private home

8 km - S - ROMANS SUR ISERE
ALIXAN: hosts can collect from station, railway station 12km
airport 8km
car essential

26.22 ROMANS SUR ISERE

You can stay here for a day, a week or a year without getting bored. The warmest of welcomes, wonderful furnishings, a magnificent flower garden, superb swimming pool, a trout stream, fine cuisine... and the most charming of hosts. Fleur de Soleil member. 03/01–01/03 : advance booking only

PROPERTY

***

private parking, garden, tv lounge, hosts have pets, dinner available, babies welcome, free cot, swimming pool, closed: 4/11-01/03, cycling, fishing, golf course 4km, gliding 8km, hiking 12km, mushroom picking 12km

Fluent English spoken

— From the A49 Valence-Grenoble, take Exit 6 and then follow the D538 towards Crest. At Alixan, turn left on to the D101 towards Besayes, 500m from the village, turn left and continue for 100m.

PRICE STRUCTURE

3 Bedrooms

First room: bathroom with wc, double bed: FF350

Second room: shower room with wc, double bed: FF350

Third room: shower room with wc, double bed: FF350

Extra bed: 100FF
Reduction: children

Capacity: 6 people

Isabelle MAGNIN

Le Petit Chantuzet
Quartier les Ariennes
26260 ST DONAT

tel: (0) 4 75 45 02 84
fax: (0) 4 75 45 02 84

Residence of character

15 km - N - ROMANS SUR ISERE
ST DONAT: hosts can collect from station, railway station 15km
airport 100km
car essential

26.29 ROMANS SUR ISERE

A typical Provençal house on top of a hill in peaceful surroundings, amongst the apricot trees. Admire the beautiful view over the Vercors. You can relax in the garden full of flowers, swim in the nearby lake or enjoy the Bach Festival. On sale: honey, apricot juice, apricots.

PRICE STRUCTURE

2 Bedrooms

Bleue: television, along corridor shower room with wc, double bed: FF250

Rose: shower room with wc, washbasin, double bed: cot FF250

Extra bed: 100FF
Reduction: 01/11–31/03 and 3 nights and children
Capacity: 4 people

PROPERTY

✹✹

off street parking, garden, tv lounge, dinner available, babies welcome, free cot, no smoking, hiking, cycling, mushroom picking, fishing 2km, sea or lake watersports 2km, golf course 20km, interesting flora 30km, birdwatching 30km, winter sports 50km

Adequate English spoken

— Take the Tain l'Hermitage Exit from the A7 and then the D67 for Saint-Donat. From there, head in the direction of Châteauneuf-de-Galaure, then at the next roundabout, turn left to the town centre. Take the second left after the cemetery towards 'Les Ariennes'. The house is at the top of the hill.

26.30 ROMANS SUR ISERE

Close to the capital of the shoe industry and 30km from the Vercors, this couple, who are also beekeepers, will welcome you into the tranquility of their home. You will love their house, both inside and out. The bedrooms are spacious and comfortable with beautiful antique furniture. You will never want to leave... On sale: honey and other bee-hive products

Jacques & Thérèse
BLANCHY

«Le Rucher de Jabelin»
26100 ROMANS SUR
ISERE

tel: (0) 4 75 02 36 97

Residence of character

PROPERTY

✸✸✸

off street parking, extensive grounds, tv lounge, hosts have pets, babies welcome, free cot, swimming pool, hiking, cycling, hunting, birdwatching, fishing 2km, mushroom picking 5km, gliding 5km, sea or lake watersports 14km, golf course 18km, winter sports 50km

Adequate English spoken

PRICE STRUCTURE

4 Bedrooms

Empire: shower room with wc, twin beds: FF250

Vercors: bathroom with wc, double bed: FF250

Abeilles: shower room with wc, double bed: FF250

Ardèche: along corridor shower room with wc, double bed: FF250

Reduction: 4 nights

Capacity: 8 people

ROMANS SUR ISERE
railway station 3km
airport 90km
car essential
— Just before Romans, go past the hospital (Centre Hospitalier) and turn left. Follow the signs. The house is 800m further on.

Geneviève MATHON

«Le Sert»
26190 ST JEAN EN ROYANS

tel: (0) 4 75 47 70 53

Private home

20 km - E - ROMANS SUR ISERE
ST JEAN EN ROYANS:
railway station 20km
airport 50km
car essential

PRICE STRUCTURE

4 Bedrooms

First room: twin beds: FF250

Second and third rooms: double bed, single bed: FF220 (2 people) FF290 (3 people)

Fourth room: double bed: FF220

Capacity: 4 people

26.32 ROMANS SUR ISERE

Geneviève's house is in Le Vercors, the bastion of the the French Resistance, whose history is immortalised by numerous museums and monuments in this area. It is also wonderful for lovers of dramatic scenery: spectacular caves, impressive gorges, scenic roads and lots of hiking and ski routes in this National Park. The local walnuts, ravioli and goat's cheese are much prized by food lovers. Whatever you decide to do, you can always come back and rest your legs in the shade in Geneviève's garden.

PROPERTY

✱✱

private parking, garden, tv lounge, no pets, dinner available, babies welcome, free cot, no smoking, hiking, cycling, interesting flora, fishing 1km, mushroom picking 1km, birdwatching 15km, river watersports 15km, gliding 25km, golf course 30km, sea or lake watersports 50km

— On the A49 Grenoble - Valence, Exit 8 (towards St. Nazaire en Royans, then St. Jean en Royans), or Exit 9 (towards St. Romans, St. Just de Claix then St. Jean en Royans).

Lucette&Paul
CHARIGON CHAMPEL

«Domaine du Grand Lierne»
26120 CHATEAUDOUBLE

tel: (0) 4 75 59 80 71
fax: (0) 4 75 59 49 41

Private home

15 km - E - VALENCE
CHATEAUDOUBLE:
railway station 15km
airport 100km
car essential

26.11 VALENCE

This charming stone house, with its square tower in typical "dauphinoise" style, is in the Vercors foothills, in wooded grounds full of flowers. The decor is classic and classy and the house is full of antique furniture and other objects belonging to the family. Breakfast is served on a sunny terrace, and includes local fruit and home-made jam. There is fishing, tennis, a swimming pool, golf and (in the season) skiing in the Vercors National Park. There is a J.S. Bach festival in the summer and you are near to the vineyards of the Cotes du Rhone and Diois. Fleur de Soleil member.

PROPERTY

***

off street parking, extensive grounds, no pets, no smoking, hiking, golf course, fishing

English spoken

— 15km east of Valence, via the D58. Then head for Chabeuil-Peyrus - Parc du Vercors. It is the first house on the left, 1km after "Les Faucons".

PRICE STRUCTURE

4 Bedrooms

Terrasse: lounge, shower room with wc, double bed: FF320

Bleue & Blanche: shower room with wc, bathroom, double bed: FF280

Rose: shower room with wc, double bed: FF250

Extra bed: 100FF

Capacity: 8 people

Marie-Jeanne
KATCHIKIAN

«La Pineraie»
383, Chemin Bel-Air
26320 ST MARCEL LES
VALENCE

tel: (0) 4 75 58 72 25
marie.katchikian@club.fr
ancetelecom.fr

Residence of character

7 km - N E -
VALENCE
ST MARCEL LES
VALENCE:
railway station 7km
airport 15km
car essential

PRICE STRUCTURE

2 Bedrooms

Bleue: bathroom with wc, double bed: FF290

Fleurie: shower room with wc, twin beds: FF300

Reduction: 3 nights and children

Capacity: 4 people

26.13 VALENCE

Five minutes from the A49 and ten minutes from the A7, this beautiful house offers you a magnificent view of the Vercors mountains. The breakfasts are served with home-made jam and patisseries. You are on the wine trail and near to the Vercors. A great place to stay. Fleur de Soleil member.

PROPERTY

✱✱✱

private parking, extensive grounds, tv lounge, babies welcome, free cot, hiking 5km, cycling 5km, fishing 5km, golf course 15km, winter sports 40km

English spoken

— From the A7 take the Valence-Nord Exit. In the centre of Bourg les Valence, turn left at the fourth set of traffic lights towards Grenoble-Romans. In Saint Marcel les Valence, just after the town hall square, turn left then continue straight after the Stop sign. The entrance is on the left (large white wall) and the house is at the far end of the lane.

Josette DUCOIN

«Place de la Fontaine»
26120 CHATEAUDOU-BLE

tel: (0) 4 75 59 80 26
fax: (0) 4 75 59 42 86

Private home

16 km - E -
VALENCE
CHATEAUDOUBLE:
railway station 18km
airport 6km
car essential

26.28 VALENCE

Stop at Josette's place in this village house and you are on the doorstep of the beautiful Vercors. Josette is retired and loves travel, reading, music and singing. Fleur de soleil member.

PROPERTY

✱✱

private parking, no pets, kitchen, babies welcome, free cot, no smoking, hiking, cycling, fishing, mushroom picking, interesting flora 8km, gliding 10km, golf course 20km, hunting 20km, winter sports 20km, river watersports 30km

English spoken

PRICE STRUCTURE

2 Bedrooms

First room: lounge, double bed, single bed: FF210 (2 people) FF260 (3 people)

Second room: along corridor lounge, double bed: FF200

Reduction: 2 nights

Capacity: 5 people

— From the A7 take Exit Valence-Sud in the direction of Grenoble. After 5km turn right on to D68 towards Chabeuil. On entering the town turn left towards Romans and take the D68 again on the right, continuing towards Le Vercors for 5km. Châteaudouble is on the right.

Bernard & Gillian FABRE

«Le Sardonnier»
Sardonne
38114 ALLEMONT

tel: (0) 4 76 80 76 93
fax: (0) 4 76 80 76 93

Private home

10 km - N W - L'ALPE D'HUEZ
SARDONNE:
railway station 50km
airport 80km
car essential
— On the N85 from Grenoble towards Briançon, turn left on to the D526 towards Rochetaillé, le Col du Glandon, le Croix de Fer. After the dam, turn right towards Sardonne, Villard Reculas. The house is in Sardonne.

38.01 L'ALPE D'HUEZ

A mountain chalet, 1000 metres up in this typical 'Oisans' village, with a wonderful vaulted room with an open fireplace. You can go skiing or walking with Bernard, who is a ski instructor and mountain guide. Gillian is English. Sardonne is linked to the ski slopes of Alpe d'Huez.

PROPERTY

✸

off street parking, lounge, hosts have pets, no pets, dinner available, kitchen, packed lunch, babies welcome, free cot, hiking, cycling, sea or lake watersports 5km, river watersports 5km, winter sports 5km

Fluent English spoken

PRICE STRUCTURE

4 Bedrooms

Chambre: double bed: FF240

Dortoir 1: 4 single beds: FF240 (2 people) FF440 (4 people)

Dortoirs 2 & 3: 7 single beds: FF440 (2 people) FF840 (7 people)

Capacity: 20 people

38.09 BOURGOIN-JALLIEU

This small country house has been delightfully restored and is half-way up the hill in a peaceful, green environment. Sophie loves to spoil her guests and her breakfasts are delicious. An excellent address.

PROPERTY

✸✸✸

hosts have pets, pets not accepted, closed: 01.12.99–02.01.00 and 08.07.00-07.09.00

English spoken

PRICE STRUCTURE

1 Bedroom

television, bathroom with wc, double bed: FF280

Capacity: 2 people

Jacques & Sophie DE LANGHE

«La Cabillonière»
38440 STE ANNE sur GERVONDE

tel: (0) 4 74 58 38 83

Private home

15 km - S - BOURGOIN-JALLIEU
STE ANNE SUR GERVONDE:
airport 30km
car essential
— In Bourgoin, take the N85 towards Grenoble. In La Combe-Les Eparres, at the set of traffic lights, turn right on to the D56 towards Tramolé. In Les Châtaigniers, turn left towards La Cabillonière

Marie-France COULLET

«Vallon Libre»
Les Goirands
38710 ST SEBASTIEN

tel: (0) 4 76 34 93 43
fax: (0) 4 76 34 93 61

Private home

50 km - S -
GRENOBLE
ST SEBASTIEN:
railway station 20km
airport 90km
car essential

PRICE STRUCTURE

2 Bedrooms

Obiou: washbasin, twin beds: FF230

Châtel: washbasin, double bed: FF210

Reduction: 1/09–30/04 and 3 nights

Capacity: 4 people

38.03 GRENOBLE

You will be enthralled by Marie-France who is mad on photography and cooking. She has restored this farmhouse and you will enjoy the quiet and the magnificent view over the Vercors. The ecology centre, 'Terre Vivante', is nearby. Bungee jumping, hiking, riding…. Bread and pizza from the charcoal oven. 1 extra room

PROPERTY

✱✱

off street parking, garden, tv lounge, no pets, dinner available, packed lunch, babies welcome, free cot, no smoking, closed: 01/11-31/11, hiking, cycling, mushroom picking, winter sports 10km, sea or lake watersports 20km

Adequate English spoken

— At Grenoble, N85 towards Gap. 2km after La Mure, right on to the D526 towards Mens. After the 'Pont de Ponsonnas' (bungee jumping bridge), left on to the D227 towards Cordéac. At St Sébastien, after the 'Salle des fêtes' & the 'Mairie', follow the signs for 1km.

Johanna LEGER

«La Chantournelle»
6, chemin des Tilleuls
38700 CORENC

tel: (0) 4 76 88 06 25
fax: (0) 4 76 88 09 19

Private home

5 km - N -
GRENOBLE
CORENC:
railway station 8km
airport 35km
car essential

38.16 GRENOBLE

Your hosts will welcome you to their family home, built in 1745, which has been completely restored. It is on the edge of La Chartreuse, with a fantastic panoramic view over the Belledonne Plateau and Grenoble. La Chartreuse is a great favourite with hikers and nature lovers, in the summer or winter.

PROPERTY

✱✱✱

off street parking, garden, tv lounge, no pets, telephone, kitchen, babies welcome, free cot, wheelchair access, hiking, cycling 10km, fishing 10km, hunting 10km, interesting flora 10km, mushroom picking 10km, winter sports 10km, gliding 10km

Fluent English spoken

— At Grenoble, follow "les quais", the road that runs along the edge of the mountain, beside the River Isère as far as the road to Le Sappey, Col de Porte, which you will see on the left. At Corenc Village, after the white building take the first road on the left, and then the first lane on the right

PRICE STRUCTURE

6 Bedrooms and 1 Apartment

First room: television, telephone, shower room with wc, washbasin, twin beds: FF350

Second room: television, telephone, shower room with wc, twin beds: FF350

(3 rooms) television, telephone, bathroom with wc, twin beds: FF350

Sixth room: television, telephone, bathroom with wc, double bed: FF350

Studio: wheelchair access, kitchen, shower room with wc, double bed: FF350

Capacity: 14 people

38.15 VIENNE

Raymond & Andrée PASQUARELLI

«Le Rucher de Prailles»
6/8 Chemin de Prailles
38370 ST CLAIR DU RHONE

tel: (0) 4 74 87 29 15

Private home

Andrée and Raymond have a lovely house with swimming pool, surrounded by a hectare of grounds. It is an ideal location to relax, go fishing and sample the quality wines of the region. Have you tasted the wine from Condrieu? Have you heard of the 'Cote Roti'? Warmth and kindness await you in this beautifully decorated home, offering excellent quality meals. On sale: Honey, jam.

PROPERTY

✱✱✱

extensive grounds, tv lounge, dinner available, kitchen, swimming pool, fishing 2km, hiking 3km, interesting flora 3km, river watersports 5km, birdwatching 10km, sea or lake watersports 10km, gliding 20km

Basic English spoken

VIENNE
ST CLAIR DU RHONE: host can collect from station, railway station 3km airport 50km car essential — At Vienne take the D4 towards Roches de Condrieu. 3km after St Clair du Rhone follow the signs to the right. (From the A7, Exit Chanas, follow signs "Péage de Roussillon" then take the D4 towards Les Roches de Condrieu. The house is on the left before St Clair du Rhone).

PRICE STRUCTURE

5 Bedrooms

Terrasse: shower room with wc, double bed, 2 single beds (1=childrens size): FF300 (2 people) FF400 (4 people)

Coté Jardin: kitchen, shower room with wc, 3 single beds: FF300 (2 people) FF400 (3 people)

Rivière: kitchen, bathroom with wc, double bed, single bed; FF300 (2 people) FF400 (3 people)

Chambre Rose: shower room with wc, double bed: FF250

Tournesols: shower room with wc, 3 single beds: FF250 (2 people) FF350 (3 people)

Capacity: 15 people

Madeleine CHARTIER

«La Violetterie»
71740 ST MAURICE L
CHATEAUNEUF

tel: (0) 3 85 26 26 60
fax: (0) 3 85 26 26 60

Private home

30 km - N -
ROANNE
ST MAURICE LES C.:
railway station 6km
airport 100km
car essential

71.12 ROANNE

This is a traditional Brionnois farmhouse. The courtyard serves as a car park and you can sit in the wooded grounds, or enjoy a barbecue or picnic in total privacy. There is a famous restaurant nearby and excellent antique shops in the village. The river is excellent for trout fishing and there are many hiking trails, as well as the Roman Churches of the Brionnois Route. Fleur de Soleil member.

PROPERTY

***

off street parking, extensive grounds, no pets, dinner available, closed: 12/11-22/04, hiking, fishing

PRICE STRUCTURE

3 Bedrooms

First room: shower room with wc, bathroom, double bed: FF280

Second room: shower room with wc, 2 single beds: FF280

Third room: shower room with wc, 5 single beds: FF280 (2 people) FF450 (5 people)

Extra bed: 70FF

Capacity: 9 people

— From Charlieu, take the D987 to La Clayette. After going through Châteauneuf, it is the second house on the left towards La Clayette.

Jacotte & Elia

CATTEAU & VERNAY
«Chez Jacotte & Elia»
Le Plat 42330 ST GALMIER

tel: (0) 4 77 54 08 27
fax: (0) 4 77 54 18 94
ıfecouettejacotte@minitel.net

Private home

20 km - N - ST ETIENNE
ST GALMIER: host can collect from station, airport 12km
car essential

PRICE STRUCTURE

4 Bedrooms

Grande: television, shower room with wc, 2 double bed: FF350 (2 people) FF500 (4 people)

Rose: shower room with wc, twin beds: FF330

Exotique: along corridor bathroom with wc, twin beds: FF330

Turquoise: double bed: FF350

Extra bed: 100FF

Reduction: 3 nights

Capacity: 10 people

42.05 ST ETIENNE

Just 10 minutes from the A72, this beautifully restored farm is situated in a quiet area between the Monts de Forez and the Parc du Pilat. A beautiful place with a clear view, where your two hostesses will take care of everything. After a delicious meal, they will advise you on activities and museums in the area. Hard tennis court.

PROPERTY

✱✱✱

private parking, garden, tv lounge, hosts have pets, dinner available, kitchen, babies welcome, free cot, tennis court

Fluent English spoken

— At St Etienne, take the A72 towards Roanne and exit at Andrézieux, Veauche, St Galmier. Then the D12 towards Chazelles sur Lyon. At St Galmier, follow Chazelles. Opposite 'Citroën', turn right on to the small road signposted 'sous le bois'. Continue for 3.5km. It is the first farm on the left.

Roland & Marie-Pierre VIALLY

«Ferme du Nizon»
Le Nizon
42110 VALEILLE

tel: (0) 4 77 28 91 50

Farm

40 km - N - ST ETIENNE
VALEILLE: host can collect from station, railway station 7km
airport 20km
car essential

42.06 ST ETIENNE

This friendly young couple live on a typical Forez farm. You are at the peaceful heart of this region, full of lakes and thermal springs. The "Ecopole du Forez" nature reserve is only 10km away. On sale: Saucissons and eggs.

PROPERTY

**

off street parking, garden, tv lounge, hosts have pets, telephone, dinner available, kitchen, babies welcome, free cot, swimming pool, hiking, cycling, fishing 3km, birdwatching 10km

Adequate English spoken

PRICE STRUCTURE

2 Bedrooms

Chambres 1 & 2: television, washbasin, double bed, single bed: FF200 (2 people) FF250 (3 people)

Extra bed: 50FF
Reduction: 3 nights

Capacity: 6 people

— From the A72, Exit Feurs. Then take the N89 towards Feurs and the D89 towards Lyon. Then right on to the D10 towards Valeille, then (before Valeille) left towards Le Nizon.

Jean & Jacqueline
FLEITOU

«Domaine de Gorneton»
Trembas
38670 CHASSE sur
RHONE

tel: (0) 4 72 24 19 15
fax: (0) 4 72 24 19 15

Manor house

20 km - S - LYON
CHASSE SUR
RHONE: host can
collect from station,
railway station 3km
airport 20km

PRICE STRUCTURE

3 Bedrooms

Cythère: television, shower room with wc, double bed: FF480

Soleil: television, bathroom with wc, twin beds: FF480

Duplex-Lions: lounge, television, bathroom with wc, 2 double beds: FF680

Extra bed: 150FF

Capacity: 2 people

38.12 LYON

The food is good, your hosts are very nice and know how to make you feel welcome. This very beautiful property is well placed : 15min from the centre of Lyon, 5 min from Vienne and convenient for several main roads. It is also near the famous 'Cote Rotie' vineyards.

PROPERTY

✱✱✱✱

private parking, extensive grounds, tv lounge, hosts have pets, no pets, dinner available, babies welcome, free cot, swimming pool, tennis court, hiking, fishing 5km, interesting flora 5km, birdwatching 5km, gliding 5km, golf course 10km, sea or lake watersports 12km, river watersports 12km

English spoken

— At the intersection of the A7 Lyon-Marseille, the A46S eastern by-pass of Lyon and the A47 towards St Etienne. Exit Chasse and head towards the Centre Commercial, go under the railway bridge, then left and then right towards Trembas. 2km on the right.

69.02 LYON

This 18th century residence is only 40km from Lyon, but beautifully quiet. Vineyards stretch as far as the eye can see from this typical Beaujolais house. Madame Roux welcomes you with charm and kindness to her comfortable home.

Anne ROUX

«Domaine de La Javernière»
La Javernière
69910 VILLIÉ MORGON

tel: (0) 4 74 04 22 71
fax: (0) 4 74 69 14 44

Manor house

PROPERTY

****

off street parking, extensive grounds, lounge, hosts have pets, telephone, babies welcome, free cot, closed: 15/12-15/01, hiking, cycling, golf course 20km

Fluent English spoken

40 km - N W - LYON
VILLIE MORGON:
railway station 8km
airport 50km
car essential
— On the A6, take the exit Belleville. In Belleville, take the D37 towards Baujeu. In Cercié, turn right towards Morgon. The property is on the right, between Morgon and Villié Morgon.

PRICE STRUCTURE

9 Bedrooms

Patricia & Rose: shower room with wc, double bed: FF710

Valentine & Thibault: bathroom with wc, twin beds: FF710

Bleue & Jaune & Empire: bathroom with wc, double bed: FF710

Gauthier: lounge, shower, single bed: FF410

Verte: shower room with wc, twin beds: FF710

Extra bed: 210FF

Capacity: 17 people

Jeannine EXCOFFIER

«Aux Magnolias»
Le Pavillon de Flore
9,Cours Albert Thomas
69003 LYON

tel: (0) 4 72 12 10 14
fax: (0) 4 72 12 10 14
excoffierjeannine@minitel.net
www.gites.net/exco472/

Flat

LYON
railway station 1km
airport 20km

PRICE STRUCTURE

2 Bedrooms

First room: television, bathroom with wc, double bed: FF310

television, single bed: FF210

Extra bed: 100FF
Reduction: 2 nights

Capacity: 3 people

69.07 LYON

Jeannine used to be an English teacher. Her apartment, with its private garden (what bliss in a city!) is in a good area, handy for the metro, yet still very quiet. Full of flowers, the welcome is warm and friendly, and you will get on well with Jeannine, so stay as long as you like. 1 extra single room

PROPERTY

off street parking, garden, lounge, dinner available, wheelchair access,

Fluent English spoken

— On the A7 go towards Lyon Centre, presqu'île. Exit Bellecour then turn right on to the 'pont de la Gullotière'. Take the 'Grande rue de la Guillotière' then the 'Avenue des Frères Lumière'. At 'rue des Tuiliers',turn left then left again in to Cours Albert Thomas. Métro: Sans-Souci (Line D)

Jacqueline PERRODIN

54, Bd de la Croix-Rous
69001 LYON

tel: (0) 4 78 28 16 32
fax: (0) 4 78 28 16 32
E-mail: jacqueline.perrodin@wanadoo.fr

Flat

LYON
railway station,
airport 20km
car essential

69.09 LYON

On a wide avenue, this small block of flats, dating from the turn of the century, is near to the centre of Lyon (a listed UNESCO city), in the classy area of La Croix-Rousse. There are plenty of shops nearby and this area has good public transport links. The beautiful apartment is very comfortable and beautifully furnished and the bedrooms lead directly on to a quiet, private garden. Garage available. There is a golf course 3km away. Fleur de Soleil member.

PROPERTY

✱✱✱

off street parking, garden, tv lounge, babies welcome, free cot

English spoken

— By car, follow signs to Lyon Centre and then Croix-Rousse. By métro: Croix-Rousse. Bus: 13, 18, 45 and get off at Clos-Jouve.

PRICE STRUCTURE

2 Bedrooms

Anges: lounge, double bed: FF280

Fleurs: lounge, single bed: FF200

Capacity: 3 people

Alexandra & Olivier du MESNIL du BUISSON

«Château de Longsard»
4060,rte de Longsard
69400 ARNAS Solange RIVIER

tel: (0) 4 74 65 55 12
fax: (0) 4 74 65 03 17
longsard@wanadoo.fr

Château

5 km - N - VILLEFRANCHE SUR SAONE ARNAS EN BEAUJOLAIS:
railway station 6km
airport 30km
car essential

69.08 VILLEFRANCHE SUR SAONE

This large 18th century wine grower's house, with its superb garden, has views over the idyllic countryside: groves, 100 year old cedars of Lebanon and an Egyptian obelisk presented last century by one of Bonaparte's generals. The comfortable interior has been restored in good taste. On sale: Beaujolais, Chardonnay.

PRICE STRUCTURE

5 Bedrooms

Musique & Rose: bathroom with wc, double bed: FF600

l'Eau: bathroom with wc, twin beds: FF600

Suite Est: bathroom with wc, double bed: FF750

Suite Ouest: bathroom with wc, double bed: FF570–FF830

Extra bed: 80FF

Capacity: 10 people

PROPERTY

****

private parking, extensive grounds, tv lounge, hosts have pets, dinner available, babies welcome, free cot, hiking, cycling, fishing 5km, mushroom picking 8km, river watersports 8km, golf course 20km

Fluent English spoken

— At Villefranche sur Saone, take the N6 towards Macon. After 6km, turn left towards Arnas. Go through the village, and the château is 1.5km further on, on the right.

«Le Pigeonnier»

Le Château
73670 ST PIERRE D'EN
TREMONT

tel: (0) 4 79 65 89 74
fax: (0) 4 79 65 89 74

Private home

25 km - S -
CHAMBERY
ST PIERRE
D'ENTREMONT:
host can collect
from station,
railway station 25km
airport 25km
car essential

73.11 CHAMBERY

Your lively hostess has almost finished the work to her brand new home. There is a superb view of La Chartreuse and you are only a few minutes from one of the most beautiful rock formations. Wonderful walking country and also good for downhill skiing as well as gentler slopes for family skiing holidays. On sale: Honey, jam, paintings glass.

PROPERTY

✱✱

off street parking, tv lounge, hosts have pets, telephone, dinner available, kitchen, packed lunch, babies welcome, free cot, wheelchair access, no smoking, hiking, interesting flora, mushroom picking, winter sports, fishing 2km, cycling 6km, gliding 12km

Fluent English spoken

PRICE STRUCTURE

4 Bedrooms

(4 rooms) television, kitchen, shower room with wc, washbasin, double bed, 2 single bed: FF220 (2 people) FF380 (4 people)

Reduction: groups and children

Capacity: 16 people

— In Chambery, D912 towards the 'Col du Granier' and 'St Pierre'. Follow the sign 'Le Château' at the end of the village. (From Grenoble, take the D520 in Voreppe).

François LUPIN

«La Cave de la Ferme»
302, rue du Grand Pont
74270 FRANGY

tel: (0) 4 50 44 75 04
fax: (0) 4 50 44 75 04

Farm

25 km - N W - ANNECY
FRANGY: railway station 15km
airport 30km
car essential

PRICE STRUCTURE

3 Bedrooms

Souris: shower room with wc, double bed: FF260

Canards: shower room with wc, twin beds: FF260

Girafe: kitchen, shower room with wc, double bed: FF260

Extra bed: 70FF
Reduction: 5 nights

Capacity: 6 people

74.06 ANNECY

This is a rustic family inn, particularly well-known for its typical, regional dishes. Be sure to try fondue, raclette and "diots" washed down with their local wine. If you come in September, you could take part in the wine harvest, as they are producers of "Roussette de Savoie". On sale: Their own wine.

PROPERTY

✸✸

off street parking, garden, dinner available, babies welcome, free cot, hiking, fishing, cycling 15km, sea or lake watersports 15km, winter sports 30km

English spoken

— From the A40, Exit Eloise-Frangy, take the N508 towards Annecy.

Monique et Joseph
PORRET

«La Cascade»
83, Route de la Forge -
Vesonne
74210 FAVERGES

tel: (0) 4 50 44 65 48

Private home

25 km - S E -
ANNECY
VESONNE: host can collect from station, railway station 25km
car essential

74.07 ANNECY

Monique & Joseph are a likeable couple, and offer a simple and friendly welcome in their old farmhouse, 5 mins from the N508. It has been well modernised, the rooms are bright and they all have a balcony overlooking the river. You are near to the ski slopes in winter, and in the summer it is an ideal base for excursions to this area.

PROPERTY

✹✹

off street parking, garden, hosts have pets, no pets, kitchen, babies welcome, free cot, no smoking, hiking, cycling, fishing, mushroom picking, river watersports, sea or lake watersports 4km, golf course 6km, winter sports 6km

PRICE STRUCTURE

4 Bedrooms

First room: shower room with wc, double bed, single bed: FF200 (2 people) FF260 (3 people)

Second & fourth rooms: shower room with wc, double bed: FF200

Third room: shower room with wc, twin beds, single bed: FF200 (2 people) FF260 (3 people)

Extra bed: 60FF

Capacity: 10 people

— At Annecy, take the N508 towards Albertville for 26km. Turn left on to the D42 towards 'Le Col de la Forclaz'.

74.08 ANNECY

Jean-Paul DAVIET

«Auberge Ferme de la Caille»
18, Chemin de la Caille
74330 LA BALME DE SILLINGY

tel: (0) 4 50 68 85 21
fax: (0) 4 50 68 74 56

Farm

12 km - N W - ANNECY LA BALME DE SILLINGY: airport 8km car essential — From the A41, exit Annecy Sud. N508 towards Bourg en Bresse. At La Balme, D3 towards Pont de la Caille and follow the signs.

This place is organised rather like a family holiday complex. It is modern, the bedrooms are small but pleasant, all in the style of a Savoy mountain chalet, with a large rustic dining room. Les Ponts de la Caille are very impressive and should not be missed.

PROPERTY

off street parking, garden, television, hosts have pets, no pets, dinner available, babies welcome, free cot, wheelchair access, tennis court, cycling, fishing, mushroom picking 1km, hiking 2km, golf course 2km, interesting flora 8km, sea or lake watersports 10km, river watersports 20km, gliding 25km, winter sports 30km

PRICE STRUCTURE

7 Bedrooms

First room: television, telephone, bathroom with wc, double bed, 2 single beds: FF415

Second room: television, telephone, bathroom with wc, 4 single beds: FF415

Sympa: television, telephone, bathroom with wc, double bed, 3 single beds: FF415

Petites (3): television, telephone, bathroom with wc, double bed: FF305

wheelchair access, television, telephone, bathroom with wc, lounge, twin beds: FF305

Capacity: 21 people

Carole BARRUCAND-FONT

«Les Charretières»
428, route des Mongets
74320 SEVRIER

tel: (0) 4 50 52 43 30
fax: (0) 4 50 52 43 30

Private home

5 km - S - ANNECY
LES MONGETS:
host can collect from station
railway station 6km
airport 12km

74.09 ANNECY

Carole now runs her mother Nicole's pleasant house, full of flowers. The bedrooms are small and quiet. Close to Annecy, this place is a good base for visiting this region and for enjoying the lake, which is only 50 metres away. 2 self-catering apartments, rented weekly.

PROPERTY

✱✱

off street parking, extensive grounds, no pets, dinner available, kitchen, babies welcome, free cot, cycling, fishing, sea or lake watersports, hiking 1km, interesting flora 1km, mushroom picking 1km, golf course 10km, winter sports 10km

English spoken

PRICE STRUCTURE

6 Bedrooms

(6 rooms) lounge, double bed: FF260

Extra bed: 30FF
Reduction: 01/10–01/05

Capacity: 12 people

— From the A41, take the Exit Annecy-Sud and then the N508 towards Albertville. At Sevrier, turn left immediately after the 'Bowling'.

Manu & Laurence
LUCOT DOS SANTOS

«Chalet Beauregard»
182, Montée de la Mollard
74400 CHAMONIX MONT-BLANC

tel: (0) 4 50 55 86 30
fax: (0) 4 50 55 86 30
manu-laurence@chalet-beauregard.com
www.chalet-beauregard.com

Private home

CHAMONIX
airport 80km
— At Chamonix-Sud, head towards Téléphérique du Brévent. After 2 roundabouts and 1 set of traffic lights, turn left at the third roundabout, and take La Montée de Molard. It is the second chalet on the right after the Gendarmerie.

74.11 CHAMONIX

This is a typical mountain chalet in the heart of Chamonix, with four well-equipped bedrooms each with a balcony and a magnificent view over Mont Blanc and the glacier. Chamonix is a really an exceptionally pleasant little town in a wonderful setting.

PROPERTY

private parking, garden, tv lounge, no pets, telephone, 2 years old minimum, no smoking, closed: 20/10-20/12, hiking, cycling, interesting flora, mushroom picking, river watersports, winter sports, fishing 1km, golf course 2km, sea or lake watersports 10km

Fluent English spoken

PRICE STRUCTURE

5 Bedrooms and 1 Suite

L'Aiguille du Goûter: shower room with wc, twin beds: FF375

La Verte & Les Drus: shower room with wc, double bed: FF375

L'Aiguille du Midi: bathroom with wc, double bed: FF375

Le Mont Blanc: shower room with wc, double bed, 2 single beds: FF505 (2 people) FF608 (4 people)

Le Paradis: along corridor bathroom with wc, double bed, single bed: FF375 (2 people) FF505 (3 people)

Extra bed: 100FF
Reduction: 7 nights and children

Capacity: 17 people

INDEX

INDEX